Badass Feminist Politics

Badass Feminist Politics

Exploring Radical Edges of Feminist Theory, Communication, and Activism

EDITED BY SARAH JANE BLITHE AND JANELL C. BAUER

Rutgers University Press

New Brunswick, Camden, and Newark, New Jersey, and London

Library of Congress Cataloging-in-Publication Data
Names: Blithe, Sarah, editor. | Bauer, Janell C., editor.
Title: Badass feminist politics: exploring radical edges of feminist theory, communication, and activism / edited by Sarah Jane Blithe and Janell C. Bauer.
Description: New Brunswick: Rutgers University Press, 2022. | Includes bibliographical references and index.
Identifiers: LCCN 2021020310 | ISBN 9781978826588 (paperback) | ISBN 9781978826595 (hardback) | ISBN 9781978826601 (epub) | ISBN 9781978826618 (mobi) | ISBN 9781978826625 (pdf)
Subjects: LCSH: Feminist theory—Political aspects—United States. | Feminism—Political aspects—United States. | Equality—United States.
Classification: LCC HQ1191.U6 B34 2022 | DDC 305.420973—dc23
LC record available at https://lccn.loc.gov/2021020310

A British Cataloging-in-Publication record for this book is available from the British Library.

www.rutgersuniversitypress.org

Manufactured in the United States of America

For our feminist mothers, Georgia Bauer and Jane Coleman, who stood behind us and then taught us to stand up for ourselves and others.

To our children, Brooklynn, Braxton, Quinn, and Vance, may you grow into your own badass feminist selves.

In memory of Ruth Bader Ginsburg and all the women who poured themselves into paving a way for women to thrive.

Contents

Badass Feminist Politics

1

Introduction

• •

SARAH JANE BLITHE

AND JANELL C. BAUER

On September 22, 2020, the forty-fifth president of the United States signed an executive order to prohibit diversity and inclusivity training that suggests the United States is fundamentally racist and sexist and that discuss unconscious biases based on race or sex. The order expressly forbids any inclusivity training that makes people feel "discomfort, guilt, anguish, or any other form of psychological distress on account of his or her race or sex" or trainings that "claim that, consciously or unconsciously, and by virtue of his or her race or sex, members of any race are inherently racist or are inherently inclined to oppress others, or that members of a sex are inherently sexist or inclined to oppress others."[1] Further, the order prohibits trainings that teach that "meritocracy or traits such as a hard work ethic are racist or sexist, or were created by a particular race to oppress another race."[2]

Arguably, this order could prohibit university gender classes—at minimum, it severely undermines the purpose of gender courses. Meritocracy has long been identified as mythical.[3] What will a gender- or race-based course look like if professors are required to ignore differences among individuals that affect the chances of success? This order would seem to limit opportunities for scholarship grants for scholars who study the problematic nature of structural racism and sexism. In the face of such restrictive and harmful directives, feminist activism must not retreat but should instead grow stronger in its effort to achieve social justice.

President Donald Trump's executive order came on the heels of the #MeToo movement and in the midst of a renewed #BlackLivesMatter movement in which scholarly conversations about racism, white fragility, reparations, sexual assault, harassment, and more burst into the public sphere as colloquial conversation points. In the middle of what promised to be exciting progress in the pursuit of equity, the executive order represented a powerful counternarrative designed to keep structural racism and sexism firmly intact. The order draws on discourses of fear and false narratives of equality to suggest that inclusivity interventions are unnecessary and, further, harmful to the white male majority.

We are far from achieving equity in the United States. Black Americans in the United States are far more likely to be murdered by police, to be incarcerated, or to be hungry than their fellow white citizens. White women and women of color are systematically paid less, make up only 3 percent of the top echelons of organizations, and are more likely to opt out. Rampant femicide on the U.S. border and throughout Latin American has stolen the lives of thousands of Latinas and Indigenous women.[4] Families are separated at the U.S.-Mexico border, where children are held in detention camps and women are involuntarily sterilized. Police used tear gas and water cannons against protesters at the Standing Rock Sioux reservation, defending an oil pipeline.[5] DREAMers, Muslims, the LGBTQI+ community, rape survivors, sex workers, and immigrants have all been marginalized and systematically hurt in recent years by a system that continually reifies privilege and denigrates people from marginalized groups.

During this difficult time and despite such restrictions, badass feminist advocates and coconspirators persist and resist, forming dialogues that call to resist inequality in its many forms. Addressing the oppression of women of color, women with (dis)abilities, LBTQI+ individuals, and white women across cultures and contexts remains a central posit of feminist struggle and requires "a distinctly feminist politics of recognition."[6] However, as second- and third-wave debates about feminism have revealed, there is no single way to express a feminist politic. Rather, living badass feminist politics requires individual interpretation and struggle, collective discussion and disagreement, and recognizing difference among women as well as points of convergence in feminist struggle.

The badass is a symbol for fourth-wave feminists, harkening back to the strong feminist advocates who came before and blazing new paths through previously private terrain.[7] Previously reserved for dangerous, bullying, or criminal men, "badass" referred to a particular type of tough-guy masculinity that was decidedly unfeminist. Reclaimed by women, "badass" is now used to celebrate, appreciate, and collectively demand gender equality. It has "become a term of endearment—shorthand for 'empowered.'"[8] Badass feminists are vocal in their pursuit of justice, insistent on representative feminisms, and strong enough to break harmful patriarchal patterns.

We take up the term *badass feminism* thoughtfully. Certainly, as Chimamanda Ngozi Adichie claimed, "The word feminist is so heavy with baggage, negative baggage."[9] This is true despite the recent reclamation of the term. Feminism is scorned, spit out as a critique, reviled, even as it strives to make the world better. We take it up anyway and wear it as a badge of honor. We know that terms like *badass*, such as *fierce* or *fiery*, are often weaponized against those they purportedly admire—at once paying tribute to strength and pushing boundaries *and also* demonizing those who take up strength to challenge systems of inequality. Girls and women are labeled as "bad" when they stand up for themselves, when they are a little too loud, a little too unruly. This is disproportionately true for women of color, who are lauded for strength but disciplined for being "aggressive." Feminists, especially feminists of color, are accused of being overly angry, and "anger in a woman is threatening."[10] Terms that suggest women can and should take up their power are loaded. As Mikki Kendall claimed, "Being fierce has its consequences. . . . Being strong or fierce or whatever appellation is applied to the ones who get brutalized, who sue, who wind up in the ground with those she leaves behind begging the world to #SayHerName sounds great, but the labels are cold comfort if we don't do more to solve the problems that they are fighting."[11] Thus, we take up badass with the assumptions that it is not an empty term but one that purposefully evokes individual strength *and* a collective march for social justice. The authors and projects included in this book are pushing boundaries in important feminist contexts, taking up space where they have previously been pushed out, and using their voices when they have been previously silenced. For us, badass denotes those who are unapologetic in their feminism, who will not be reined in, who take up their own power in the pursuit of social justice.

Badass feminism can have vastly different definitions. For some activists, eating vegan to boycott mass meat production or not doing business with companies that exploit workers are examples of living feminist politics. For others, marching in protests, delivering public speeches, and canvassing represent a life of feminist resistance. Feminists write in a variety of forms: tweets, manifestos, poetry, blogs, or white papers about tactics to "make it" in male-dominated industries, in homophobic communities, in abusive relationships, in becoming mothers or choosing to be child-free. In this book, and in our lives, we ask what it means to live unapologetic feminist politics in the everyday choices and actions, contributions, theories, and claims that feminists make. As feminist Sara Ahmed (2017) wrote, "Living a feminist life does not mean adopting a set of ideals or norms of conduct, although it might mean asking ethical questions about how to live better in an unjust and unequal world (in a not-feminist and anti-feminist world); how to create relationships with others that are more equal; how to find ways to support those who are not supported or are less supported by social systems; how to keep coming up against histories that have become concrete, histories that have become as solid as walls."[12] Living better in an unjust world is difficult but a goal worth pursuing.

Feminist scholars have elucidated myriad ways to enact social justice. Nina M. Lozano-Reich and Dana L. Cloud argued that oppression and inequality prevent invitational rhetoric from being civil. They argue that the uncivil tongue is a more effective way to advocate for change.[13] Bernadette Calafell argued that performance carries the potential to disrupt unjust systems that cast women of color as monsters. She suggests that activists should intercede in hostile spaces.[14]

By the early 2000s, feminists argued that there is no singular feminism but rather a series of feminisms, with myriad strategies for achieving equity and multiple perspectives and foci.[15] As these forms of feminism have developed, new strategies for theory, advocacy, and practice have emerged in the continued pursuit for equity across social identity categories. Yet with these new developments, in light of an executive order and counternarrative that feminism is unnecessary, old questions persist and new questions have arisen: Do we need feminism? What does it mean to be feminist in this moment? What projects and foci deserve the attention of feminism? Are feminists advocates, theorists, or both?

Intersectionality

In this book, we take an intersectional approach to feminism.[16] Fundamentally, intersectionality is the theory that multiple forms of oppression intersect with each other in multiple and complicated ways.[17] Feminists of color have talked about interlocking oppressions for decades,[18] but intersectionality as a concept was firmly rooted in feminist theorizing when Kimberlé Crenshaw coined the term in 1989.[19] Intersectionality emerged in response to the violence that women of color experience and the oppressions women of color face that do not align with the experiences of white women. Integrating an antiracist agenda with gender politics was a major milestone in the development of feminist theory and enables feminist theorizing and advocacy to move beyond white essentialism toward a recognition of how differences between women matter.[20] Intersectional feminism is a political act that embraces the nuance of how gender oppression is experienced in the fight for gender equity for diverse women and gender experiences. Intersectionality now also refers to the theory or methodology used for studying structural, political, or representational inequalities and includes multiple axes of oppression.[21]

Early adoptions of intersectionality focused on differences of gender, race, and class. Later, feminists recognized sexuality, age, and (dis)ability as important markers of identity difference.[22] More recently, other intersections, such as gender identity, religion, nationality, physiological variance, body diversity, parental status, and military status, have been added to the growing list of ways women might be different.[23] Some critiques of intersectionality point out that recognizing all differences dilutes the discrimination experienced by race or gender, therefore reducing the theory's potential to reduce discrimination. However, feminist work has generally grown to include multiple axes of difference that "count" as intersections. Additionally, we continue to learn as a movement how to embrace complicated nuances in experience and move forward with activism that endeavors to eliminate oppression in many forms. We believe that considering multiple axes is important to recognize the everyday experiences of oppression and privilege.

Intersectionality is particularly useful in helping white feminists recognize their own privilege.[24] Essentialist narratives conflate and reflect hegemonic versions of identity and render invisible the experiences of women with nondominant identities.[25] Patricia Hill Collins argued that intersectional analyses can help individuals recognize 'the oppressor within,' particularly for those in privileged groups.[26] Of course, it can be difficult for privileged feminist scholars to recognize that the very claims they make, and the methodologies on which they rely, are entrenched in colonial legacies that are deeply biased by raced, classed, and gendered heuristics.[27] Yet intersectionality holds the promise to decenter white feminism and make space for other ways of being, thinking, and experiencing privilege.

From Intersectionality to Inclusivity

Perhaps the greatest promise of intersectionality is inclusivity. Often, feminist researchers pay only lip service to the possibilities raised through intersectional analyses, yet true attention to intersections of social identity can provide more inclusive, practical responses to inequality. For decades, feminists have fought against a long legacy of white essentialism. Intersectionality can "act as a corrective against the white solipsism, heteronormativity, elitism, and ableism of dominant power and hegemonic feminist theory by making social locations and experiences visible that are occluded in essentialist and exclusionary constructions of the category 'women.'"[28]

As the concept of intersectionality has developed, it has expanded to include other social identities beyond gender, race, and class. Including sexuality,[29] (dis)ability, body size, gender identity, geographical location, and physiologies,[30] intersectionality is one of the most nuanced ways to study power. It takes into account both individual experiences and the power-laden structures that give meaning to social identity categories.[31] Taking a broad approach to intersectionality runs the risk of diluting the arguments about race. If all social identity categories matter, is intersectionality still an effective theory to guide research about power? In this book, we assume that a broad approach to intersectionality is better for achieving inclusivity. At the same time, we center aspects of social identity that people do not opt into including race, gender, health status, sexual orientation, and body type (but excluding others such as religion and political affiliation).

For these reasons, we adopt an intersectional lens in this book. From inception, it has been important for us, as white women, to acknowledge the privilege we hold as white women, even as we think through some of the ways we experience oppression in the academy. It has also been important in this project to focus on a multitude of ways people experience oppression and how they resist structural inequalities. The chapters in this book represent a wide range of social identities and experiences that reveal, without a doubt, that experiences are largely dependent on those intersections in our identities. Finally, we adopt this framework because intersectionality can aid the study of oppression at multiple levels,[32] which aligns with the theme of this book: how to live as badass feminists in everyday life *and* in macro-transformative social movements.

Venturing Onward

We are undertaking this project because, across the globe, women have not yet achieved equality, equity, or inclusion and we still lack meaningful participation in most institutions.[33] Too many barriers remain intact; too much violence, too low wages, too much stigma, too few allies. As Petersen described, "Our society does not value, trust, or elevate women in the same way it values, trusts, or elevates men. And that doesn't even account for the way that women who are older, or not white, or fatter, or queer, or possess any other unruly quality, fit into that equation."[34] Much work remains in the pursuit of identity justice. At the same time, working toward feminist goals can seem insurmountable. It can seem exhausting. It can seem as if there is no right answer, and complex overlapping circumstances seem to negate a clear path for advocacy. And yet, we must continue.

Finding Our Feminist Voices

The complexity of finding a feminist voice and path is what sparked this project. We first conceived of this book while we strategized, then reflected on, our experiences with the academic job market. Sarah, knowing that mothers often face discrimination in hiring and promotion, especially in academia, experimented with hiding and revealing her maternal status during job interviews. She wondered, which is the most "feminist" move? Either pandering to the system, hiding her children to appear more of an "ideal type" candidate and therefore more likely to get the job, or embracing her identity and trying to prove that women can be multifaceted (mothers and academics) while potentially facing discriminatory hiring practices?

At the same time, Janell, unmarried when she went on the job market, struggled with related questions. She wondered what it would really mean to give up unearned privilege during her job search—and if she could afford to do so. Should she reveal her (then-)single, childless status, potentially giving her an advantage over other women, or resist this systemic privilege and remain ambiguous about her status, potentially subjecting her to assumed maternal discrimination? Or was it a more feminist act to do what was necessary to get a position where she could fight for gender equity from the inside? Years later, she had a job interview while pregnant, which brought her body and identity as a mother into her candidacy for a new workplace. When and how to address her plans for maternity leave required deep consideration of career demands, financial security, and where her feminist politics lay in the picture. We both ended up with tenure-track jobs, but we walked away unsure about whether our strategies enacted a feminist ethic or if they propagated harmful stereotypes about gender, motherhood, partnership, economic position, and hiring. We reflected on the privilege we held in order to make choices about where and how to reveal different aspects of ourselves and our lives during a competitive job search.

Throughout our early careers, we have collaborated on other projects that dance around a similar theme. We have engaged in collaborative sensemaking about our identities and feminisms in a variety of situations and phenomena including women's friendships, female breadwinning, academic mothering, feminist pedagogy, and our experiences on hiring committees. All of these contexts provided moments of transformation surrounded by contexts steeped in intersecting oppressions. Yet questions around what transformation looks like and how feminist/activists should proceed are not easily answered. Transformation depends on many factors, and the political climate surrounding the actions can determine what works for some and what does not work for others in the path to equity.

Once Janell posed the question, *"What does it mean to live feminist politics?"* we realized that this question had applications for a multitude of feminist conundrums in our everyday lives and in large-scale social movements. Particularly in the current political landscape, we assumed that the answer to what it means to live unapologetically feminist, or to be a badass feminist, is rhetorical in nature: there is no single answer but depends on identity intersections, organizational, cultural, and relational contexts, a multitude of feminist goals, theories, issues, and lenses. We realized that living feminist politics is a series of strategies, foci, efforts to resist oppression, and the grit to persist despite domination.

Feminist Pedagogy

Instructors taking up feminist pedagogy actively work to reduce power inequities in the classroom by shifting the emphasis from distribution/transfer of knowledge to collaborative creation of knowledge.[35] A redistribution of power makes it possible to empower students to engage more fully in their own education. Such an approach places a strong emphasis on voice and makes complex efforts to ensure all voices are heard.[36] In this way, education can be a practice of freedom, where students can critically challenge course material.[37]

Power is not a zero-sum game. Teachers can both hold their own power and also share power with students. However, to achieve shared power, teachers must be willing to make space for student voices and give up some of their control.[38] As Shewsbury explained, "Empowering pedagogy does not dissolve the authority or the power of the instructor. It does move from power as domination to power as creative energy."[39] Shifting from conceptualizing teaching as an authoritarian act to teaching as a collaborative, empowering activity can enable students to learn in deeper, more meaningful ways.

Intersectional feminist teaching can create more collaborative and inclusive classrooms if teachers relinquishing their power also take into account unconscious biases that have shaped the way they share and acquire knowledge.[40] Carlos Tejeda and Manuel Espinoza called for an anticolonial and decolonizing pedagogical praxis to subvert colonial domination and the ideological frameworks that have shaped the majority of educational structures, particularly those that determine success or failure in schooling.[41] This book heeds this call and others that demand more representation in classrooms to help develop more inclusive educational environments.

Contributions to Badass Feminist Politics

The contributors included in this book persist in their work for equality and equity, and they resist violent, racist, homophobic, transphobic, xenophobic, and sexist language and action during this tension-filled political moment.

The chapters in this collection explore issues of persistence and resistance in a variety of contexts. They emphasize voice, visibility, recognition, and narrative. The authors take up important questions and highlight how individuals are resisting oppressive structures and persisting despite obstacles. Taking up current issues and new theoretical perspectives, the authors offer novel perspectives into what it means to live as a badass feminist.

The book is broken into four parts that highlight relevant areas for study: Black Lives Matter, the material body, mediated activism, and new theories to push feminist activism forward. Each part contains a preview, which includes overarching discussion questions to help students think across the readings in the section. In addition, each reading ends with specific discussion questions and a "Try This" deep-thinking extension activity. These features will help instructors who assign the entire book or those who assign selected chapters for their class. Instructors can use the "Try This" activities or the section questions as classroom assignments, and students can use these features to guide the development of their open-ended essay topics.

In the remainder of this opening section, we include a chapter about feminist pedagogy and some ideas to adopt in an activist feminist classroom. Next, the first part, Black Lives Matter: Research and Reflections, is a collection of writings about the #BlackLivesMatter movement, digital activism, education, race-based stereotypes, and the personal experiences and stories of Blackademics.[42] In chapter 3, Angela N. Gist-Mackey, Ashley R. Hall, and Shardé M.

Davis discuss the risks of truth telling for Black-ademics. The authors offer accounts of the risk, exploitation, and consumption of truth telling. In chapter 4, Anita Mixon calls for attention to Black Indigenous activism and an end to environmental racism. She specifically attends to activism by the Gullah/ Geechee Nation as a particular example of #BlackLivesMatter. Andrea Ewing outlines the ways in which Black women are tired from the constant pressures of race-based activism in chapter 5. Her words are poetic yet poignant as she lists invisible labor. In chapter 6, Shardé Davis shares her experiences with digital activism and the viral movement she started, #BlackintheIvory. Sharing personal Facebook posts, Davis illuminates the difficulties and risks of activism. Prisca S. Ngondo shares her experiences with fear, despair, and exhaustion in chapter 7 and creates a compelling call for allies to lighten the load. As she describes her experiences with the #BlackLivesMatter movement, she builds to a list of ideas for coconspirator support.

Cerise L. Glenn questions why #BlackLivesMatter seems to overlook Black women in chapter 8. She argues that Black women are continually pushed to the margins of race-based advocacy. In chapter 9, Melanie Duckworth and Kelly J. Cross propose a holistic approach to transform institutions of higher education to become actively antiracist. The authors present a model to implement culturally responsive pedagogy. Idrissa Snider problematizes the whitewashed educational curriculum in chapter 10. Ultimately, she argues that African American history should be taught beginning in elementary school. In chapter 11, Rebecca Mercado Jones and Jayna Marie Jones discuss the racial implications of intimate partner violence. Their stories are raw and present an important case for considering the intersections of gender, race, and violence. Siobhan Smith-Jones and Johnny L. Jones examine organizational statements that support #BlackLives-Matter in chapter 12. They ultimately assert that they do not acknowledge random endorsements of Black Lives Matter because most of the organizations making statements are unaware of, or unwilling to address, structural racism. In chapter 13, Savaughn Williams shares her story about the ways in which her body was systematically disciplined and violated. She illuminates the pressures and stereotypes assigned to Black girls' sexualities. In chapter 14, Robin M. Boylorn reflects on the trauma experienced through the murders of Black people. She draws particular attention to the families of victims, those left alone and grieving after murder. In chapter 15, Tina M. Harris identifies differences between performative support and true allies and coconspirators. She argues that allyship is an important tool to begin to dismantle racism.

The second part includes chapters about the material body. Cassidy D. Ellis and Sarah Gonzalez Noveiri deliver a powerful co-constructed critical autoethnography to illustrate how theory exists on and within the bodies of fat women in chapter 16. They weave their personal narratives with a rhetorical analysis of Amy Schumer's *I Feel Pretty* and point to a disconnection between "body positivity" and performances of fatness as presented in the film. They look at nonnormative bodies through the lens of trauma and shame and explore how fat bodies are disembodied.

In chapter 17, Ruth J. Beerman and Michael S. Martin studied selfies from the #GetYourBellyOut social media campaign that brings awareness to people living with ostomy bags. They weave narratives of personal experience with literature about visibility politics and explore what it means to live in a stigmatized body. The vignettes are raw and real, shedding light on the experiences of a population of people who are rarely studied and who grapple with the material effects of the ways in which their bodies clash with societal expectations every day.

Lydia Huerta Moreno explores the intersections of being Latinx, queer, and a first-time tenure-track faculty member through the experience of a Title IX investigation at a small rural southwest school in chapter 18. Drawing from the writing practice of an autoethnographic "layered account," she integrates introspection, theoretical thinking, emotional experience, and statistics to evaluate moments of tension. By examining intersections of her identity, she is able to unveil the internalized sexism in the strategies of survival she practiced in the face of sexual harassment by Chicano- and Latino-identifying men and through institutional violence. She uses this autoethnographic account to dismantle the painful and complicated intersections of her internalized sexism as part of her feminist praxis.

Chapters 19 through 21 explore what it means to live feminist politics in mediated environments and through social media. In chapter 19, Ana Gomes Parga illustrates how memes of the telenovela character Mónica Robles can be used to control and police womanhood while also empowering women. She identifies how Robles is a role model with positive and negative features. The wild success of the show *El Señor de los Cielos*, coupled with the Mexican government's critique of narco-novela (telenovelas that center stories about cartels) makes this analysis significant as a means to understand the power of memes and as cultural insight.

Maureen Ebben and Cheris Kramarae explore how artificial intelligence (AI) and algorithms produce and circulate meanings in gendered ways in chapter 20. They initiate a thoughtful discussion about some of the most pressing issues of AI for feminist communication scholars and seek to promote increased awareness, inclusive dialogue, resistance, and a more feminist and inclusive culture in AI.

In chapter 21, Kathleen Rushforth recounts the silencing of Elizabeth Warren during the 2017 nomination hearing for Jefferson Sessions for U.S. attorney general. She analyzes the framing of the event and how Warren's message found voice through the #LetLizSpeak campaign. Reactions to the event emerged as themes and revealed that people reacted to the silencing not only as sexist but also as a breach of procedure. However, in the retelling and retweeting of the event, Warren's message reached a much broader audience than it would have in the hearing alone. Ultimately, Rushforth makes the case that hashtag activism can make space for individuals who have been silenced to speak and act as collective agents.

In the final part, chapters 22 through 24 take up innovative ways to theorize feminism, pushing feminist organizing and activism in new directions. James McDonald and Sara DeTurk argue that attending to closeting processes can facilitate socially just organizing across multiple lines of difference in chapter 22. They advocate for not only space for visibility but also a protected space to strategically maintain invisibility. By paying attention to closeting processes, social justice advocates can create alliances that do not rely on essentialized categories.

In chapter 23, Danette M. Pugh-Patton and Antonio L. Spikes extend *ratchet feminism*. They argue that the burden of "ratchet" falls onto Black women and that it can be reclaimed and used to resist politics of respectability. The authors argue further that ratchet feminism, though most often applied to popular culture, has applications in politics and other areas of academic study. Playing with intersections of race and gender performances, ratchet feminism can be understood as individual and collective action against oppression.

Finally, in chapter 24, Jenna N. Hanchey argues that feminist theory in communication studies needs to take up Afrofuturism to persevere and transform. Afrofuturism is creative production and study based in Black liberation that imagines radical futures. Hanchey explores how three tenets of Afrofuturism—understanding how change is inevitable, the vitality of roots, and recognizing that liberation must be for everyone if it will be for anyone—provide a means to rethink feminist theory with Blackness and radical potentiality at the center. Afrofuturism makes impossible feminist futures possible.

Taken together, these chapters provide an array of questions and answers about what it means to live feminist politics. As scholars and activists, we have all encountered diverse and systemic silencing. Nevertheless, we persist. This book is a testament to resilience, resistance, and forward thinking about what these themes all mean for new badass feminist agendas.

Notes

1 Donald J. Trump, "Executive Order on Combating Race and Sex Stereotyping," September 22, 2020, https://www.whitehouse.gov/presidential-actions/executive -order-combating-race-sex-stereotyping/?fbclid=IwAR1GdqKeTYw26oNd5yfXUc VUW6aXdHc1ym2HXQITmRl7LWZZO6cv3FhYmbI.

2 Ibid.

3 Amy Liu, "Unraveling the Myth of Meritocracy within the Context of US Higher Education," *Higher Education* 62, no. 4 (2011): 383–397; Mark A. Godsey, "Educational Inequalities, the Myth of Meritocracy, and the Silencing of Minority Voices: The Need for Diversity on America's Law Reviews," *Harvard Blackletter Law Journal* 12 (1995): 59; Leslie S. Jones, "The Myth of Meritocracy and Delusions of Equity: Cultural Impediments to Diversity in Natural Science Programs," (1998).

(paper presented at the Annual Meeting of the American Educational Research Association, San Diego, CA, 1998, pp. 1–12); Heike Solga, "The Social Investment State and the Myth of Meritocracy," in *Combating Inequality: The Global North and South*, ed. Alexander Gallas, Hansjörg Herr, Frank Hoffer, and Christoph Scherrer (Abingdon, UK: Routledge, 2015): 199.

4 Lydia Huerta Moreno, "Hablar sobre la violencia de género en las redes sociales: El caso de Diana la Cazadora," in *Tácticas y estrategias contra la violencia de género: Antología*, ed. Patricia Ravelo Blancas, Sergio G. Sánchez Díaz, María Laura Torres-Ruiz, Susana Báez Ayala, Dennis Bixler-Márquez, Silvia Chávez-Baray, Héctor Domínguez Ruvalcaba, Georgina Martínez, Javier Melgoza, Eva Moya (Mexico City: Ciesas Fonca, 2015), 137–158.

5 Alan Taylor, "Water Cannons and Tear Gas Used against Dakota Access Pipeline Protesters," *The Atlantic*, November 27, 2019, https://www.theatlantic.com/photo /2016/11/water-cannons-and-tear-gas-used-against-dakota-access-pipeline-protesters /508370/.

6 Bruce Baum, "Feminist Politics of Recognition," *Signs: Journal of Women in Culture and Society* 29, no. 4 (2004): 1073–1102.

7 Meghan Daum, "Please Stop Calling Yourself a 'Feminist Badass,'" Quillette, November 19, 2019, https://quillette.com/2019/11/19/please-stop-calling-yourself-a -feminist-badass/.

8 Hermione Hoby, "The Problem with Being 'badass,'" *The Guardian*, December 7, 2015, https://www.theguardian.com/lifeandstyle/2015/dec/07/problem-being -badass-feminism-women-behave-like-men.

9 Chimamanda Ngozi Adichie, *We Should All Be Feminists* (New York: Vintage Books, 2012), 9.

10 Ibid.

11 Mikki Kendall, *Hood Feminism* (New York: Viking, 2020), 130, 133.

12 Sarah Ahmed, *Living a Feminist Life*, (Durham, NC: Duke University Press),1.

13 Nina M. Lozano-Reich and Dana L. Cloud, "The Uncivil Tongue: Invitational Rhetoric and the Problem of Inequality," *Western Journal of Communication* 73, no. 2 (2009): 220–226.

14 Bernadette Marie Calafell, "Monstrous Femininity: Constructions of Women of Color in the Academy," *Journal of Communication Inquiry* 36, no. 2 (2012): 111–130.

15 Kimberlé Crenshaw, "Mapping the Margins: Intersectionality, Identity Politics, and Violence Against Women of Color," *Stanford Law Review* 43 (1990): 1241.

16 Anna Carastathis, "The Concept of Intersectionality in Feminist Theory," *Philosophy Compass* 9, no. 5 (2014): 304–314; Sumi Cho, Kimberlé Williams Crenshaw, and Leslie McCall, "Toward a Field of Intersectionality Studies: Theory, Applications, and Praxis," *Signs: Journal of Women in Culture and Society* 38, no. 4 (2013): 785–810.

17 Ann Garry, "Intersectionality, Metaphors, and the Multiplicity of Gender," *Hypatia* 26, no. 4 (2011): 826–850.

18 bell hooks, *Ain't I a Woman* (Boston: South End Press, 1981).

19 Kimberlé Crenshaw, "Demarginalizing the Intersection of Race and Sex: A Black Feminist Critique of Antidiscrimination Doctrine, Feminist Theory and Antiracist Politics," *University of Chicago Legal Forum* (1989): 138–167.

20 Crenshaw, "Mapping the Margins."

21 Carastathis, "The Concept of Intersectionality."

22 Nira Yuval-Davis, "Intersectionality and Feminist Politics," *European Journal of Women's Studies* 13, no. 3 (2006): 193–209.

23 Helma Lutz, "Intersectional Analysis: A Way out of Multiple Dilemmas?" (paper presented at the International Sociological Association Conference, Brisbane, Australia, 2002).

24 Garry, "Intersectionality, Metaphors."

25 Yuval-Davis, "Intersectionality and Feminist Politics."

26 Patricia Hill Collins, "Toward a New Vision: Race, Class, and Gender as Categories of Analysis and Connection," in *Race, Gender and Class*, ed. Bart Landry (New York: Routledge, 2016), 65–75.

27 Garry, "Intersectionality, Metaphors."

28 Carastathis, "The Concept of Intersectionality."

29 Cherríe Moraga, "La Güera," in *This Bridge Called My Back: Writings by Radical Women of Color*, 4th edition, ed. Cherríe Moraga and Gloría Anzaldúa (Albany: SUNY Press), 22–29.

30 Sarah Jane Blithe and Jenna N. Hanchey, "The Discursive Emergence of Gendered Physiological Discrimination in Sex Verification Testing," *Women's Studies in Communication* 38, no. 4 (2015): 486–506.

31 Wendy Smooth, "Intersectionality from Theoretical Framework to Policy Intervention," in *Situating Intersectionality: Politics, Policy, and Power*, ed. Angelia R. Wilson (New York: Palgrave Macmillan, 2013), 11–41.

32 Patricia Hill Collins, "Some Group Matters: Intersectionality, Situated Standpoints, and Black Feminist Thought," in *A Companion to African-American Philosophy*, ed. Tommy L. Lott and John P. Pittman (Oxford: Blackwell, 2003), 205–229.

33 Anne Helen Petersen, *Too Fat, Too Slutty, Too Loud: The Rise and Reign of the Unruly Woman* (New York: Plume, 2017).

34 Ibid., xv.

35 Paulo Freire, *Pedagogy of the Oppressed, 50th Anniversary Edition* (New York: Bloomsbury Publishing Inc., 2018); Maralee Mayberry, "Reproductive and Resistant Pedagogies," in *Meeting the Challenge: Innovative Feminist Pedagogies in Action*, ed. Maralee Mayberry and Ellen Cronan Rose, (New York: Routledge, 1999), 1–22.; Sarah Jane Blithe and Brian Fidelibus, "Faculty-Undergraduate Course Curriculum Collaboration," *College Teaching* (2015): 1–10

36 bell hooks, *Teaching to Transgress* (New York: Routledge, 1994).

37 Ibid.

38 Jennifer Mary Gore, *The Struggle for Pedagogies: Critical and Feminist Discourses as Regimes of Truth* (New York: Psychology Press, 1993); Kathryn Pauly Morgan, "The Perils and Paradoxes of Feminist Pedagogy," *Resources for Feminist Research* 16, no. 3 (1987): 49–52.

39 Carolyn M. Shrewsbury, "What Is Feminist Pedagogy?," *Women's Studies Quarterly* 15, nos. 3 and 4 (1987): 6–14.

40 Freire, *Pedagogy of the Oppressed*; hooks, *Teaching to Transgress*.

41 Carlos Tejeda, Manuel Espinoza, and Kris Gutierrez, "Toward a Decolonizing Pedagogy: Social Justice Reconsidered," in *Pedagogies of Difference: Rethinking Education for Social Change*, ed. Peter Pericles Trifonas (New York: Routledge, 2003), 9–38.

42 See Gist-Mackey, Hall, and Davis in this collection.

2

Badass Activities for Threading Together Theory, Pedagogy, and Activism

• •

JANELL C. BAUER AND

SARAH JANE BLITHE

In this book, we work to consider the many facets of living a feminist life. As academics, we weave gender equality into our research, inquiry, approaches to service, and of course, pedagogy. As we teach students about gender equity, we emphasize that feminism is more than a collection of theories and historical moments but is rooted in activism and organizing to end gender oppression.

To help facilitate this bridge between feminist theory, pedagogy, and activism, we have curated class activities and projects that create opportunities for students to apply the theories and concepts they learn to everyday activism. What follows is a collection of ideas for bringing intersectional feminist activism to life in the classroom.

Summary of Activities

1 Start your own feminist blog
2 Create a social justice kit or website
3 Control what you consume by diversifying news, entertainment, and social feeds

4 Join your community through service learning
5 Partake in public performances

#1 Feminist Blogging

Feminists have used blogging to engage in digital activism that brings awareness to gender injustice, build community, develop individual and collective voices, and call for action on issues related to gender inequality that connect with diverse aspects of social identity. Students can start their own individual or collective class blogs to develop their voice and gain experience with digital activism.

Start by exploring various types of feminist blogs. Here are a few to review:

- Shout Out! JMU: A student feminist blog collective
- Crunk Feminist Collective
- Amy Poehler's Smart Girls
- *Ms.* magazine
- Feministing (now shut down but was one of the most influential for fifteen years)
- Brown Girl Magazine

Initial Steps to Get Your Blog Up and Running

Developing your own blog is something that anyone can do, even without a lot of web or social media experience. Here are a few core steps to begin the process. Students should discuss the ideas they are passionate about while also considering form and logistics.

Format. Consider if you want your blog to be associated with a class or to run more independently as a student club or organization. If you want to run as an organization, you can check out the questions below about finding a community on campus.

Organization. Once you have a core group of bloggers decide on a structure, do you want to establish leadership through student editors or function as independent contributors? How will content be reviewed for quality control? What opportunities will there be to debrief blog content and to discuss posts that are more controversial or that individual group members may be uncomfortable with?

Blog Platform. Select your blog platform. New platforms are designed to be user friendly and often have entry-level options that are free. A few options include WordPress, Wix, and Blogger. You could also involve web design students if you want to build your own site.

Title and Mission. Name your blog and write your core mission and values, then determine a posting schedule. Do you want your blog to have new posts each day or week? Make decisions that are manageable for the group you have. With a class, it can be easier to post daily; with a club made up of fewer contributors, weekly posts work better. Students can also decide if they want to publish under their own name or a pseudonym.

Commenting. Another important thing to consider up front is how you will handle comments on your blog. Do you want comments to be open or moderated? Will editors or contributors approve and respond to posts? This is a good time for everyone to prepare for how to handle trolling comments. In our experience, it is best to set it up so that comments have to be approved by either the editors or authors. Students should not feel obligated to post or respond to comments that are disrespectful or aggressive.

Content Plan. Define the scope of your blog. Do you want it to be focused on a specific audience or aspect of feminism, or do you want to focus on social justice more broadly? Once you decide, create a content ideas bank where everyone generates a list of topics they may want to write about over the semester. Give feedback and share ideas and resources.

Visibility and Social Media. One of the biggest questions is how to get people to read your blog. The most common answer is to create social media accounts where you publicize your content. Students often gravitate toward Instagram and Twitter based on their target audience and current threads for social activism. Decide if you want each blogger to create their own social media posts to publicize their blogs or if you want to identify a student as the social media manager who would be responsible for all the social content and interaction.

Additional Activities for Identifying Resources and Getting Started

1 Identify where is consciousness-raising happening on your campus.
   a What are the feminist and social justice organizations on your campus? What student groups highlight cultural diversity as a primary mission? What women's health organizations are on your campus?
2 Identify faculty and staff advisors for gender-/sexuality-related student groups. They could be allies, advisors, or advocates for your blog.
3 Seek out programming in your residence halls that support conversations about gender diversity and identity. These can be an excellent source of information and support. It can also be a place to recruit new bloggers.
4 Look on social media for social accounts that are associated with your university. What platforms do you see the most activity on and what accounts are active?
5 Discuss the role that feminist and social justice blogging play on your college campus. Are there voices that are not heard or recognized? Might blogging and digital activism create support and community or visibility for a marginalized experience?

Blogging as Feminist Activism and Consciousness Raising

One way that feminists began to build their voice and amplify visibility was through blogging. In 2009, Julie Zeilinger, sixteen, launched *The FBomb*. Her teen feminist blog filled a void for teen girls who were looking for a feminist community. She often linked to gender-progressive websites such as Jezebel and Feministing where mainstream feminist writing was growing in popularity.[1] Although critics of feminist blogging argued that it would likely lead to little substantive change, in contrast to physical organizing, it served an important function. Teen girls have demonstrated how blogging acts as an important mechanism for their participation in feminist politics and crafts a new path forward for community and feminism in the virtual space.[2] Feminist blogging opened up space for more diverse voices with a relatively low barrier to entry. It also created opportunities for consciousness raising in the new digital space.

In this book several of the authors reference ideas and theories developed on the Crunk Feminist Collective blog. Their mission statement begins, "The Crunk Feminist Collective (CFC) will create a space of support and camaraderie for hip hop generation feminists of color, queer and straight, in the academy and without, by building a rhetorical community, in which we can discuss our ideas, express our crunk feminist selves, fellowship with one another, debate and challenge one another, and support each other, as we struggle together to articulate our feminist goals, ideas, visions, and dreams in ways that are both personally and professionally beneficial."[3]

This mission aligns with the goals of many feminist bloggers seeking to build community, share ideas, validate experiences, and work toward developing more inclusive spaces. Feminist blogs reach large, public audiences, while simultaneously sparking private internal dialogue and self-reflection. Employing what Foss and Griffin term invitational rhetoric, feminist blogging can be seen as offering perspectives without demands of audience action or change.[4] Undoubtedly, when seen as a rhetorical device, consciousness-raising can be used to better understand critical perspectives that focus on personal experiences as well as social injustices. Feminist blogging is part of an intersectional approach to consciousness raising in the digital age that focuses on a wider, more diverse scope of women addressing how gender is understood and experienced in relation to other aspects of identity.

Shout Out! JMU Case Study: Creating a Student-Led Feminist Blog on Campus

In 2006, Dr. Melissa Alemán began a monthly consciousness-raising group to discuss issues related to gender climate on the James Madison University campus. Students described feeling constant pressure around alcohol culture, hookup culture, and how they should dress and look. Female faculty described feeling disposable. Both students and faculty were looking for a place to share their experiences, validate the impact of the climate, create opportunities to be heard, and make plans for influencing meaningful change on campus.

Although primarily attended by students, it was also supported and attended by faculty. Over time, faculty and students sought resources for crafting an online forum for their conversations. In 2009, they were awarded a university diversity grant to invite Jessica Valenti (founding editor of *Feministing*) to provide a workshop on feminist blogging and give a public address on the subject. This grant-supported workshop helped the participants create a course on feminist weblogging from which the weblog *Shout Out! JMU: Your Source for Feminist Discourse* was born.[5]

Since its inception in 2010, the blog receives approximately 50,000 views per year and has been read from locations in over 135 different countries. Each semester, a small group of student writers are guided by student editors and faculty to produce this daily blog. The long-running *Shout Out! JMU* student blog is a testament to the value of consciousness raising on campuses that can occur in interpersonal meetings and in the digital space.

#2 Create a Social Justice Kit or Website

There are many different social justice topics that intersect with gender equity activism. One way for students to connect deeply with the issues they care about and to see how course content contributes to feminist activism is for them to create a social justice kit. Groups can work together to compile a collection of materials that offer a deep dive into a topic that includes opportunities for future activism. To start, have the team work together to research the topic and create a primer that offers readers an introduction to the topic including relevant issues, perspectives from traditional and social media and current activist efforts. The kit should answer the questions: What is the issue and why should people care about it? What conversations are going on around the topic? Finally, have students make an argument about what we can or should do next.

Selecting a Topic

As a class, brainstorm social justice and gender activism topics that interest students. Discuss and narrow the topics until students are in groups connected with a topic they are interested in and want to explore further (see box 2.1).

Elements of the Gender/Social Justice Kit

By working together to curate content on a topic, students can research historical and current activism on the topic, use course concepts to analyze the phenomenon in everyday life or in media artifacts, and generate ideas for everyday activism. One example is activist Rachel Cargle who developed a following on

---

Box 2.1. Topic Ideas

Black Lives Matter; LGBTQIA rights and legislation, LGBTQIA media representation, Gender identity and sexuality in the military (media coverage), Immigration and the DREAM Act; Diversity and discrimination in the workplace; Different feminisms and types of feminist activism (Intersectional feminism; Third-wave feminism; Hip-hop feminism; Hashtag activism etc.); Masculinity and changing ideas about manhood; Women of color and equity in health care; Veganism and ecofeminism; Gender and education/school policies; Beauty standards (feminine/masculine/queer) and body image in the media; Gender norms and patterns in relationships; Gun control and masculinity; Sexual harassment/Rape culture/#MeToo; Gender representations in music/film/TV; Gender messages and how they impact kids; Gender norms online (teens, college, etc.)

Instagram where she shared social justice content. In her highlights, she shared "Social Syllabus"[6] links that provided PDFs on topics such as immigration and Black Lives Matter. This type of social syllabus introduced her audience to the basics of these social justice topics and provided important information about the politics involved and ideas for actions one could take. This is the type of activist content that students can gain experience developing.

Once the group has written a primer or introduction to the topic that includes the history, impact and current relevance, they can build their collection. Consider including the following items as options in the social justice kit:

- A must-read list with a one-sentence summary of the key idea in each source.
- Media links to news coverage that offers different perspectives or approaches to the topic.
- Include famous quotes or speeches (current or historical).
- Analysis of media that connects with the topic or illustrates how the topic or social identity is represented. This can include a wide variety of entertainment media: songs, videos, albums, films, television shows, advertisements, books, video games, comic books, and so forth are all excellent ways to understand social phenomena.
- Include representative art, or create your own artwork to include in the kit. Students may also create their own performance art and include links. Share the creative work and your perspective on your issue; reflect on how others react to it. Analyze art as a tool for social change. What are the opportunities and limitations?

- Create or share existing videos that model how to communicate through a situation related to the topic (as when someone tells a racist joke or experiences a microaggression), or how to have difficult conversations in ways that reduce oppression.
- Include social media threads where your topic is discussed or users engage in hashtag activism (Twitter has a lot of this type of content). Analyze the content and what makes it effective or problematic. Consider the consequences of the content for your topic and future activism on the subject.
- A list of specific actions that individuals can take to drive gender and social justice activism related to the topic. Include links to petitions, organizations, activists' social media, events, educational resources, and more.

Tailor the materials in the collection based on the number students in the group and the interests and talents of those involved.

Format and Conclusion

Students can compile the kit in a variety of digital forms. Creating digital content gives students additional ways to share their work and their interests beyond the classroom. The social justice kit can easily be created in a shared Google Document and then saved as a PDF with interactive links to multimedia. Another option is to publish the content to a class blog or website. With a growing number of user-friendly website platforms like WordPress, Adobe Spark, and others, students are able to create a digital site for the content while building essential everyday technology skills and adding to their portfolio of published work. When students publish their work online, they are able to share it with their networks of friends and family—modeling the idea of carrying social justice content beyond the classroom context.

Final presentations of the work also enable teams to learn from one another and showcase their creativity and insights. At the conclusion, debrief the different elements of the collection and how they work together. As a class, discuss how the project shaped students' perspectives on the issues, how course concepts enhanced their understanding or analysis, and the opportunities for activism and change.

#3 Analyze and Diversify Your Media Consumption

In chapter 19 of this book, Ebben and Kramarae dive into questions about how artificial intelligence (AI) and algorithms shape our experiences and limit the media content we are exposed to. The impact that AI can have on how we see the world operates in subtle ways and often goes unquestioned. Students can explore how algorithms in their social networks and streaming platforms narrow the diversity of perspectives they are exposed to. Begin with a media audit that asks students to take stock of the demographics in their social media feeds, and follow with a content analysis of diversity across the media they enjoy. Students can then take specific and international steps to expand their media consumption to include diverse content producers, a range of perspectives and epistemologies, and stories and representations of nuanced and intersectional life experiences.

Social Media Audit

Students can begin by identifying their most used social media platforms. Dr. Susan Wiesinger, professor at California State University Chico, created a spreadsheet template students could use to track the demographics of people they follow and those who follow them on their social platforms. Students may include social identities such as gender, age, race, education, geographic location, sexual orientation, and any others they would like. Although several of these identities may be unknown, the assignment also points to the fact that we often make assumptions based on how people present themselves online. Over the course of a week, students can also track the diversity of the content feed, taking stock of how many posts appear from different people versus the same people repeated.

It is also useful to include a summary description of the types of organizations or pages students follow; what interests do they represent? Consider including the news sources students have in their social media feeds. Do the news sources reflect different political perspectives or are they primarily rooted in one epistemology?

After students tally their social network, they can reflect on their different affinities. Do the people in their network tend to be similar to them in certain demographic areas? Where is there diversity? In what ways might their network either reinforce one viewpoint or expose them to different life experiences and ideas? Discuss the following questions:

- How big is your social bubble/network and who gets to be inside?
- What identities might be missing from your feeds?
- Are there similarities in whose posts seem to appear more often in your feed?
- What are possible consequences or impacts of your social media bubble?
- What could you do to diversify your feeds?

Media Analysis

A similar type of audit can be compiled for the entertainment media students consume over a week. As a companion project, students can chart the television, movies, and music they watch and listen to. As with social media, students note the demographics of the characters, the social identities and life experiences that are the focus of the stories, and the demographics of content producers (writers, directors, producers).

In individual or class discussion, reflect on the following questions:

1 How closely do the things you watch and listen to reflect your own lived experience? Why do you think it is mostly similar or more diverse?
2 Are there places where the preferences noted in your social media survey mirror your demographics in your media consumption? Reflect on why/ how that matters. Are there places where they differ? What might that mean?
3 How might your digital/social and legacy media consumption affect your overall worldview?
4 What actions can you take to diversify your media consumption? What differences do you think that might make?

Remix Your Algorithm

Cheyenne Cameron-Pruitt, a Chico State alumna working at FleishmanHillard public relations agency, returned to campus to share her organization's new diversity, equity, and inclusion program known as *Remix Your Algorithm*.[7] The program began with a conversation between coworkers: "Why doesn't your Netflix feed look like mine?" which spun into comparisons of how their social media feeds differed. The colleagues took stock of their media, similar to the activities above. They questioned how much of their traditional media and social media content mirrored their own social identity and life experiences and how much diversity there was among those producing the content they watched.

The big question for students to ask after exploring their feeds is: What choices are being made for me by algorithms and *how can I make choices* to diversify my media consumption.

Mindful Curation of Your Media Content

Facebook's algorithm sorts content so that the feed shows posts it thinks users most want to see. This means that users often see posts from only a small section of folks in their social network, limiting access to diverse viewpoints.[8] Critics argue that this narrows the scope and diversity of content so that people tend to get stuck in a homogenous bubble. A popular way to hack your Facebook news feed is to adjust your settings so that you see the most recent content rather than the content Facebook's algorithm selects for you.

The Black Lives Matter movement has made visible how essential it is that individuals take responsibility for recognizing their own privilege and doing the work to educate themselves. As several of the authors in this book state, Black women are tired—people of color and others in marginalized groups are exhausted by the expectation that they educate others. One small action that students can take to begin this process of seeing beyond their own life experiences is to expand their media bubble. This involves selecting film, television, books, and social media that reflects diverse life experiences that are different than their own. Students can seek out content that is also created by diverse authors, directors, producers, artists, actors, and so on.

One way to begin this process is to take a different topic each month and commit to learning more about different social identities and locations. Students can gather readings, movies, TV shows, music, and other media to share each month. Using awareness events as a guide can make it easy to find content on different topics.

Suggested topics by month:

- January: Homelessness Awareness
- February: Black History, Body Image
- March: Women's History
- April: Mental Health Awareness, Environmental Activism
- May: Asian Pacific Heritage
- June: LGBTQIA Pride
- July: Ageism Awareness
- August: Mothering and Women's Health
- September: Hispanic Heritage, Chicanx/Latinx History
- October: Disability and Ableism Awareness
- November: Native American Heritage
- December: Celebrate Religious Diversity

#4 Intersectional Service Learning[9]

Learning about intersectional gender in college classrooms can be enhanced by developing a service-learning class experience. Service learning is a specially designed model of experiential learning that combines service at a community organization with intentional learning outcomes achieved through critical, reflective thinking. The model follows a cycle of knowledge, action, and reflection. The service-learning project is completely integrated into the entire semester and accounts for approximately half of the course.

Engaging with diversity and inclusivity through service learning can improve students' cultural tolerance, awareness, reflexivity, and attention to hegemony, while also increasing altruism.[10] Service-learning projects enable students to learn about diversity and inclusivity in the classroom in order to develop their ability to communicate effectively with people who are different. The benefits from intercultural and gender-based service-learning projects are many: students can practice communicating with people who are different from themselves to gain critical empathy, relational, and reflexivity skills. Faculty have an entrée to difficult discussions about social category inequality and discrimination, and partner organizations can frame which issues are important to their communities.[11]

This project assumes a transformational approach to service learning, which requires a long-term service commitment and a partnership view of the relationship between students and community organizations.[12] Transformational service-learning projects are more intense and require significantly more planning and management than traditional service-learning projects. However, the increased opportunities for growth for both students and community partners are palpable. To achieve transformational service learning, this sixteen-week, semester-long engagement requires twenty-four hours of service in a prearranged site that offers a means to communicate with people from different cultural backgrounds.

Identify a Service Organization. To begin, find appropriate community partners before the semester begins. Many universities have service-learning or civic engagement offices, so instructors should contact these offices and inquire whether the institution has agreements in place to protect the students, university, faculty, and organizations. If no office exists, it is possible to build relationships individually by contacting potential partners directly. Once a potential organization has been identified, arrange a meeting to discuss the potential partnership.

Although the possibilities for partner selection are endless, we have some suggested sites that have worked well in our classes:

- Homeless youth shelter: Teach art and music classes, tutoring students, and communicating with families.
- Service organization for people with disabilities: Serve as "social mentors," tutors, or workout buddies.
- Domestic violence shelter: Plan and help execute fundraising events, organize donations, create social media awareness campaigns.
- Substance abuse disorder clinic for women and children: Design (and possibly facilitate) classes in communication.
- LGBTQ+ archives: Interview and document historical materials about significant LGBTQ+ contributions in the community.
- Indigenous tribes: Assist with language preservation initiatives, create museum displays, build digital content to promote the tribe online.
- Anti-trafficking organizations: Document stories, participate in fundraising, create print and digital marketing materials.
- Assisted living facilities: Document stories, organize events such as music and dance classes, play games with residents, and serve as communication partners.
- Public health or maternal mental health organizations: Plan and execute public awareness events, create outreach and informational content, and produce educational training videos.

- Local art galleries or performance organizations: Support promotion for events (especially related to social justice and gender equity), develop interactive programs for the public to engage with artists and performers.

Establish Mutual Goals. The next step is to meet with the partner contact to discuss project ideas. This meeting should be a discussion of mutually beneficial goals and project outcomes. Instructors should ask contacts about their greatest challenges or identify areas where they need assistance. During this meeting, the learning objectives for the course should be explained, a list of few potential projects should be drawn, and logistics discussed (i.e., to whom students will report, the location of the service project, how many students the partner can take, and all possible hours during which the service can occur). A variety of organizations should be selected, including one or two opportunities close to campus for students with transportation restrictions.

Although the community organizations and projects can take many shapes, instructors should ensure that the projects are mutually beneficial and that students have time to engage in ample communication with others at the site. If there is no previous relationship between the university and the organization, instructors should consider that the partner and project selections can take weeks or months.

Connecting Service Learning with the Classroom. During the first few weeks, instructors should check in with students about their service projects regularly. It often takes more time than anticipated to manage logistics, which can be stressful for students. By the fifth or sixth week of the semester, however, all students should be active at their sites. Weeks 4–13 should focus on integrating course material with the service-learning projects. In-class content should consist of lectures, discussions, and activities based on the assigned course readings. During discussions, instructors should always ask for examples from the service-learning projects to connect the students' experiences with the course content. For example, when discussing cultural elements such as values and beliefs, instructors can ask for samples of the values students observe at their partner organizations. It is beneficial for students to discuss their service projects in almost every class activity and discussion. Integration also occurs in exams in that exam questions can include specific references to examples shared in class from the service sites. Complete integration is necessary to make the service-learning experiences relevant to the students' application of the course concepts. If possible, instructors should arrange for some of the partner contacts to speak to the class as guest speakers to interweave the service-learning projects further with the course content.

An important part of Weeks 4–13 is reflection. Throughout the semester, students will complete individual reflection papers about their service-learning experiences. In their reflections, students respond to specific prompts about difference, inclusion, communication, and personal reflection. Students draw on both their service-learning experiences and the course material in their reflection papers. Reflection also happens verbally during class. At least once a week, students will meet with their service groups for ten to twenty minutes to discuss their service-learning projects. The service groups can be a supportive place for students to debrief and think about intense, happy, dramatic, or frustrating moments that occur at their partner sites. To guide the service group discussions, instructors may give the students discussion prompts that directly link to the weekly content.

Although service learning takes time to organize and manage for both instructors and students, the rewards can be powerful. Students often connect deeply with the learning that takes place and indicate that their service projects are the most valuable experience they have had in college. Many students go on to work with the nonprofit organization or in similar service organizations. Instructors can develop strong relationships with the community partner organizations, which can have lasting impacts beyond the classroom.

#5 Feminist Performances

During the 1960s women's movement, feminism's reentrance into the public sphere, from consciousness-raising groups to rallies, heavily relied on scripted and impromptu street performance. Creating a class performance or a collection of performances can be a creative way to engage students in activism. Marvin Carlson described how performance artists base their work on their own bodies, autobiographies, and experiences in a particular culture and social location.[13] An important element of performance activism is the ability to make commentary on current events and culture jamming.

Recently, for example, a number of Black Lives Matter protests have included dance performances, ranging from traditional performances of African dances to critical work reenacting Black murders. Also, students have performed the weight of sexual assault by carrying a mattress around campus as a way to bring awareness to the issue. Performances can be organized quickly and in response to particular events and can easily be mobilized into different spaces including public streets, auditoriums, buildings, hallways, and so forth.

Performances have the ability to reclaim bodies that have been made abject, such as performances featuring menstrual blood, breast milk, or bodies with (dis)abilities. Performances can also reclaim political space, such as the performances by Elizabeth Warren and Maxine Waters, when each demanded their voice take up space on the Senate floor after they were silenced. Performances for feminist activism by students or a class can include pop-up performances that speak to particular injustices. However, they can also be more organized and scripted, such as a class performance of the *Vagina Monologues*. Performances can be in public spaces or in venues with tickets. They can be performed live or recorded and shared on social media or displayed on buildings through large-scale projectors. The options for feminist activism through performance are endless.

To get started, share some of these examples with students. It can be empowering to ask students to choose their own performative activism. Some students may not be used to flexing their creative activist skills. There are a vast variety of street performances, which can be overwhelming for students new to performance. Sharing examples can generate new ideas. Some of our favorite examples include the following:

- The Guerrilla Girls, feminist activist artists who wear gorilla masks during public performances.
- What Were You Wearing exhibit featuring the clothes women were wearing when they were sexually assaulted or raped.
- Women dressed as handmaids to protest Protesting Amy Coney Barrett's hearing.
- Femicide protests featuring the names of murdered women painted on the ground, accompanied by other symbols such as bloody handprints.

Some ideas for class-appropriate performances include the following:

- Slam poetry (in a public setting or recorded on YouTube)
- Flash mobs and other dance performances
- Writing and performing songs
- Visual representations of events (such as having one student lie down on the quad for each trans women killed in a year).
- Plays such as the *Vagina Monologues* or newly scripted acts
- In-class performances and skits are lower stakes and can be a good introduction

Performance can push students far beyond their comfort zone and can elicit strong emotional reactions. It is important to establish a classroom climate that values students and all their individual experiences. Cultivate a classroom culture that is accepting of performance and also of critique and criticism. Students should be prepared to receive criticism of their performances, to experience face threat, and for the public exposure that comes with performance. Make sure to prepare students with trigger warnings, and have campus counselors attend performances for emotional support for more controversial topics.

Plan ahead and discuss parameters for safety, legality, ethics, and student comfort as the students design their own or group based feminist performances. If you are using a space on campus, make sure to find out if you need permission to use the space. Performance can be scary for students, but when they have agency around the performance medium, make their own choices about content and expression, and receive support from classmates and the instructor, it can be an impactful pedagogical strategy.

Discussion Questions

1 How can blogging as a form of feminist activism empower college students to find and use their voice toward social change?
2 What are the potential and varied roles of digital feminism in the current political landscape?
3 How can faculty and students cultivate feminist civic engagement and activist mindsets among college students?
4 How might your digital/social and legacy media consumption affect your overall worldview?
5 What actions can you take to diversify your media consumption? What differences do you think that might make?
6 What opportunities do you see for digital and hashtag activism on current gender and social justice issues? What are the limitations?
7 What do you think about the relationship between classroom learning and activism in the community? How can they work together?
8 What actions have you taken to learn more about a different social identity or life experience? Have you watched any movies or TV shows that challenged your current viewpoints or created more empathy for marginalized experiences?
9 What did you learn about different social identities and life experiences from engaging in service learning with a local organization?
10 How can service activities create more opportunities to explore diversity and activism in your community?
11 What do activist performances offer to the evolution of gender advocacy?
12 How might you plan to handle the public response to an activist performance?

Notes

1 Margaret Hartmann, "F-Bombs: Feminist Teen Blog Starts Strong despite Adult Sniping," *Jezebel*, July 14, 2009, https://jezebel.com/f-bombs-feminist-teen-blog-starts-strong-despite-adult-5314596.
2 Jessalynn Keller, "Virtual Feminisms: Information," *Communication & Society* 15, no. 2 (2012): 429–447.
3 The Crunk Feminist Collective, accessed November 1, 2020, http://www.crunk feministcollective.com/about/.
4 Sonja Foss and Cindy Griffin, "Beyond Persuasion: A Proposal for Invitational Rhetoric," *Communication Monographs* 62 (1995): 2–18.

5 Jenna Stephenson and Melissa Alemán, "Creating a Consciousness of Leadership: A Case Study of a University Women's Consciousness Raising Group," in *Labyrinth Paths: Women's Leadership Development and Communicative Praxis in the 21st Century*, ed. E. L. Ruminski and A. M. Holba (Lanham, MD: Lexington Books, 2011), 113–134.

6 Rachel Cargle, "Social Syllabus," Instagram, May 2018, https://www.instagram.com /stories/highlights/17882659732211355/?hl=en.

7 "Remix Your Algorithm," FleishmanHillard, accessed November 1, 2020, https:// fleishmanhillard.com/fleishmanhillard-diversity-and-inclusion-remixes-your -algorithm/

8 Matthew Syed, "Why It's Time to Break Out of Your Personal Echo Chamber," LinkedIn, September 13, 2019, https://www.linkedin.com/pulse/why-its-time-break -out-your-personal-echo-chamber-matthew-syed/.

9 This section is reprinted in a slightly modified form from Sarah Jane Blithe, "Teaching Intercultural Communication through Service-Learning," *Communication Teacher* 30, no. 3 (2016): 165–171.

10 David H. Kahl Jr., "Connecting Autoethnography with Service Learning: A Critical Communication Pedagogical Approach," *Communication Teacher* 24, no. 4 (2010): 221–228; Caryn Musil and Compact New Hampshire, *A Crucible Moment: College Learning and Democracy's Future* (Washington, DC: Association of American Colleges & Universities, 2012), 15.

11 Ibid.

12 Sandra Enos and Keith Morton, "Developing a Theory and Practice of Campus-Community Partnerships," in *Building Partnerships for Service-Learning*, ed. Barbara Jacoby (San Francisco: Jossey-Bass, 2003), 20–41.

13 Marvin Carlson, "What Is Performance?" in *The Performance Studies Reader*, ed. Henry Bial (London: Routledge, 2004), 68–73.

Part 1

Black Lives Matter

• •

As bell hooks powerfully argued, mainstream feminism has not represented the people who needed it most.[1] Stemming from the self-interests of wealthy white women, the earliest mainstream movements did not reach far beyond the needs of those with privilege. Although a number of Black feminists engaged in significant activism during the first[2] and second[3] waves of feminism, their contributions have not been recounted in most feminist collections.[4] Hijas de Cuauhtemoc, the National Black Feminist Organization, Third World Women's Alliance, National Alliance of Black Feminists, and the Black Women Organized for Action all originated for activism.[5] These organized movements incorporated the particular issues facing women of color and fought to advance feminist goals that were inclusive of more women.

The Black Lives Matter (BLM) movement began in response to the acquittal of George Zimmerman—a neighborhood watch person who murdered Trayvon Martin, an unarmed and innocent teenager. Alicia Garza, Patrisse Cullors, and Opal Tometi organized the movement to "intervene in violence inflicted on Black communities by the state and vigilantes."[6] Although BLM amplifies anti-Black racism in general, it also specifically makes space for women of color and queer and transgender people and is "intentional about not replicating harmful practices that excluded so many in past movements for liberation."[7] The movement is intentional in its efforts to support *all* Black lives.

BLM protests have emerged around a series of high-profile murders of Black people. In 2020, with renewed passion, protesters around the world invigorated the movement in response to the murders of George Floyd, Ahmaud Arbery, and

Breonna Taylor. A widespread renewed commitment to fight racial injustice took root. This section includes research, activism, and narratives that call for racial justice. The work included in this section is part of a powerful wave of activism and shared accountability for change. As Gist, Hall, and Davis claimed, "Black womxn's stories should be consumed with an understanding that we are calling folx to action, we are calling folx in to do the necessary introspection/reflection/ education to make substantive changes in terms of how you interact with us, our stories, and our voices."[8]

Discussion Questions

1 Duckworth and Cross (chapter 9) and Snider (chapter 10) discuss activism in education. When did you learn about gender inequality or racism? How and when should educational interventions occur?

2 Many authors in this section described feeling tired (see, e.g., chapter 5, Ewing; chapter 7, Ngondo; chapter 15, Harris). What are the implications of the burden that Black women bear fighting racism and sexism with living with oppression and discrimination? How can we work to redistribute the burden and exhaustion?

3 Many chapters in this section address digital activism (see, e.g., chapter 3, Gist-Mackey, Hall, and Davis; chapter 4, Mixon; chapter 6, Davis). How has digital activism changed gender and race advocacy? What are the next steps in digital activism?

4 Glen (chapter 8) and Davis (chapter 6) share personal Facebook posts as activism. What kinds of personal activism have you seen across your digital media? Do personal stories and examples improve the effectiveness of digital activism?

5 Smith-Jones and Jones (chapter 12), Davis (chapter 6), and Ngondo (chapter 7) offer ideas for how to participate/help in the pursuit of racial justice. What strategies stand out to you? What strategies would you add to those suggested in these chapters?

6 How does trauma intersect with race? Jones and Jones (chapter 11), Williams (chapter 13), and Boylorn (chapter 14) all address trauma. What are the implications of approaching trauma care with mindfulness/awareness of how racism impacts trauma and recovery?

7 Harris (chapter 15) discusses allyship. What makes a good ally? How do you know? Are there boundaries in allyship?

Notes

1 bell hooks, "Black Women: Shaping Feminist Theory," *Revista Brasileira de Ciência Política* 16 (2015): 193–210.

2 For example, Sojourner Truth, Fredrick Douglass, Maria Stewart, Frances E. W. Harper, Anna Julia Cooper, Ida B. Wells, and Mary Church Terrell all engaged in advocacy during the first wave of feminism.

3 Feminists such as bell hooks and Angela Davis were well known for their advocacy, but many Black women participated in the National Organization of Women (NOW).

4 Becky Thompson, "Multiracial Feminism: Recasting the Chronology of Second Wave Feminism," *Feminist Studies* 28 (2002): 336–360; Sarah Blithe and Mackenna Neal, "Communicating Gender Advocacy: Riding the Fourth Wave of Feminism," in *The Routledge Handbook of Communication and Gender*, edited by Marnel N. Goins, B. K. Alexander, and Joan Faber McAlister (New York: Routledge, 2021).

5 Kimberley Springer, "The Interstitial Politics of Black Feminist Organizations," *Meridians* 1, no. 2 (2001): 155–191; Smith College Archive, "Third World Women's Alliance Records," accessed April 7, 2019, https://asteria.fivecolleges.edu/findaids/sophiasmith/mnsss527.html.

6 "Herstory," Black Lives Matter, accessed January 25, 2021, https://blacklivesmatter.com/herstory/.

7 Ibid.

8 See chapter 1 in this volume.

3

Being Black in the Ivory

● ●

Telling Our Truth and
Taking Up Space

ANGELA N. GIST-MACKEY, ASHLEY
R. HALL, AND SHARDÉ M. DAVIS

When Black womxn tell their truths, it has the possibility of empowering us all. Yet this empowerment comes with great risk, institutionalized exploitation, and conspicuous consumption of our narratives.[1] In this essay, we engage a historical tradition of Black womxn's truth telling that has been passed down generationally.[2] We do so with a critical perspective, where we take up space literally in this book to explain what happens when we tell our truths. In Patricia Bell-Scott's book *Flat-footed Truths: Telling Black Women's Lives*, Bell-Scott explains that flat-footed truths are "a story or statement that is straightforward, unshakable, and unembellished."[3] Here, we offer our accounts of how the risk, exploitation, and consumption of our truth telling has unfolded in our diverse experiences. We do so in a spirit of reflexivity, education, and social justice. We want our readers to be more mindful about how they tell their own truths and engage the truths of Black womxn. We aim to name, confront, demystify, and resist the problematic systems and structures we have encountered in the academy and throughout our lives. This chapter was adapted from a keynote panel presented at the 2020 Organization for the Study of Communication, Language, & Gender (OSCLG) conference.

Truth Telling as Risky—Shardé M. Davis

What happens when the racial privilege of white academics is decentered and there remains ample room for Black-ademics, namely Black womxn, to step in? Moving white voices from the center to the margins is a critical step for our truth telling to occur and for our voices to actually be heard. But there is an inordinate amount of risk involved in this endeavor. Our livelihood is on the line. When we "talk back," tenure gets denied, we are left to drown in the seas of PhD programs, and our invitations to social outings, research teams, or applications for vacant leadership positions are conspicuously missing. Indeed, that walk from the margins to the center is a bit thrilling, often laborious, and always risky.

Those Black womxn who assess that it is relatively safe to center themselves and share must contend with a series of questions: How many details can I share? Do I "out" someone in the story? Should I share the sanitized version or the raw version? Can they handle the truth? Whose version of the "truth" will hold weight? Reality is experienced through our personal lens and retold from memory, which means it often does not align with the way someone else recollects the encounter. This is often true for Black womxn when we share stories that involve our more privileged counterparts (i.e., white folx, Black men). Knowing that there is a great likelihood of misalignment in stories, we are the ones whose recollection is deemed inaccurate and fallacious. What is it about Black womxn that makes our recollection up for debate? Black womxn often are not believed, even when there is evidence to support our claims. And although the old adage "There is your side, my side, and the truth" remains true, it begs the question, why is "my side" rarely considered valid? And more importantly, if my experience of racial trauma corroborates similar racist experiences of other Black womxn (and men) in academia, then do the particulars matter?

A viral hashtag that I created called #BlackintheIvory is a great example of this. Black-ademics around the globe stood in their right to speak truth about the racial trauma that they experienced in the ivory tower. After reading thousands of #BlackintheIvory stories on Twitter (and noting that the same stories were told from people in different professional ranks, disciplines, fields, programs, universities, and age groups), it was glaringly obvious that the problem is not us the people but the racist system that has been institutionalized by American universities. Yet, many of us know that even with us sharing similar stories (where there was overlap in the minutiae), we will not be heard or believed (at best) or punished (at worst).

Speaking personally, posting my #BlackintheIvory stories as an untenured Black womxn faculty was daunting because so many eyes were reading my tweets—my friends, other Black-ademics, national press outlets, university administration (including my own), and former faculty in my graduate programs. I was exposed. As it stands, I am "the only one," which comes with an incredible amount of visibility among my colleagues. I cannot hide. And now, on a public platform, I lay bare and avail myself to critique. As folx decenter their privilege to make and hold space for us, think about the precarity of our exposure. Hold space even when you are uncomfortable with the stories shared. Do not grow impatient and inch back to the center when you deem that we are not taking up space "correctly" or misremember the minutiae of our stories. Our "mistakes" are caught more often and the repercussions are much harsher.[4]

For these reasons (and many more that will go unnamed), some of us will not accept your offer; *but do not stop making the room!* Our risk assessment demonstrates that the endeavor is extensive and psychologically draining—the decision for Black-ademics to leave the margins, the journey to the center, the internal filtration system frames our truths while we share, and the coping strategies we put in place when backlash arises. It is often safer to remain silent than to speak up. But remember this: silence (even when space is created) can be a form of resistance because this system is set up for our death.[5] So if we do not show up, we are doing something. If we show up and are silent, then we are doing something. And if we say something while standing at the center, then we are doing something. Let us celebrate *all* of the ways that Black womxn choose to take up space and tell their truths because however we choose to engage truth telling, it is risky.

Truth Telling as Exploitation—Angela N. Gist-Mackey

The unfortunate reality about telling our truths, as Black womxn, is that often our truths are exploited. This exploitation is multilayered happening at micro, mezzo, and macro levels spanning from our interpersonal relationships to our workplace interactions up to societal race relations. Exploitation occurs systematically and is the transfer of resources from one group to another in ways that are beneficial to the receiving group and sacrificial to provisional group.[6] In short, our stories end up being co-opted, misappropriated, and retold for the benefit of others, often to the detriment of self.

At the micro level of social interaction, the exploitation of our stories and truths typically happens in our interpersonal relationships. Friends, neighbors, and acquaintances, among others often seek out our opinions, suggestions, advice, and experiences as fodder for their raced and gendered interpersonal education. Hot moments in history, like the Black Lives Matter movement and the #MeToo movement exacerbate the exploitation of our truth telling in the context of interpersonal relationships. Let the probing questions continue. Because we often feel interpersonally obligated we divulge our "flat-footed" truth telling in the disclosure of painful, embarrassing, traumatic stories.[7] For instance, during summer 2020 in the wake of the murders of Breonna Taylor, George Floyd, and Ahmaud Arbery reminiscent of so many others whose lives have been lost, during the midst of my grief, I was solicited for my stories. One neighbor of mine, a well-intentioned white woman friend in an interracial marriage with a Black man, was trying to understand what such moments should mean to her now that she is married into Black heritage and birthed a multiracial child. In fact, she wanted to know if I would speak to her sister and her mother to educate them on how they should talk about these issues with their brother/son-in-law. I feel compelled to help but also taken advantage in our interpersonal, interracial friendship.

At the mezzo level of social interaction, the exploitation of our stories and truths typically happens in our places of employment. Black womxn are often solicited to serve on diversity and inclusion committees, lead cultural competency trainings, organize recruitment initiatives to diversify the pipeline, sit on the hiring committees so that our employing organizations' can appear to be as diverse as possible. These requests to be the *token* Black womxn come frequently without fail and are often unspoken expectations for being a *team player*. We often feel compelled to engage in truth telling as part of these initiatives, yet our labor is exploited, rarely compensated, and retraumatizing. Even when we decline such invitations, the hierarchical power dynamics of our professions eventually prevail. Being an untenured womxn Black-ademic exacerbates the precarity of this labor and the exploitative nature of such work.[8] Being professionals requires us to disclose our pain, embody the emotion, and bare vulnerability for the sake of simply being employed. As we work to tell our truths, a risky endeavor that makes us vulnerable, our credibility is simultaneously questioned. The very act of truth telling gives our employer a face for diversity, yet that same truth telling is weaponized against Black womxn when we are stereotyped as the mammy, Jezebel, Sapphire, strong Black womxn, and angry Black womxn, among others.

At the macro level, the structure of the workforce requires us to "fit" into anti-Black hegemonic structures rooted in whiteness, masculinity, patriarchy, and heteronormativity. We are expected to be nice, quiet, and to accept the status quo. For our profession, as Black-ademics in the ivory tower our truth telling and identities are silenced by systems and structures like peer review, graduate committee work, professing as a sage on the stage.[9] We must perform academic identities that were never designed to be performed by Black female bodies. Yet, we are the success stories. And as our success stories are told on a macro level, we become hypervisible icons scrutinized in the public eye. Our intuitions are beneficiaries of our truths. Yet our authenticity, voices, and stories are relegated to the background making our labor hyperinvisible. Our truth telling is continually exploited as a way to educate the masses and becomes product of conspicuous consumption.

Truth Telling Not Just for Consumption—Ashley R. Hall

The historical backdrop of the Middle Passage, U.S. enslavement, and Jim Crow segregation informs the contemporary political and cultural context in which

Black womxn are negotiating their communicative lives. Black womxn have wielded nommo, otherwise understood as the "power of the word," as a weapon to challenge systems of power and affirm their dignity and personhood for generations.[10] The power of Black womxn's "telling" lies in their ability to name and critique systems of power while empowering themselves and others as active agents all for the purpose of enacting social and political change.[11] Despite all the risks, Black womxn have remained passionately committed to telling the truth about the nature and impact of racial sexual violence on their everyday lives. Our stories are the means by which Black womxn forge new ways of living, breathing, and thriving in gratuitous violence. Our stories should serve as a constant reminder of how anti-Blackness impacts Black womxn and a charge to do better by us.

In acknowledging Black womxn's role as truth tellers, it is important for allies and coconspirators to remember that our stories are not commodities to be consumed idly. In other words, our stories are not told with the sole purpose of educating white people; however, they should be critically consuming our stories in order to actively find ways to challenge and disrupt existing hegemonic forces creating a continued need for Black womxn to share our stories. Performative allyship, where one consumes and circulates our stories, while making no sincere or genuine efforts to reckon with their un/conscious participation in systems of hegemonic power and privilege is dangerous. In other words, curating our stories with no intention or follow-through after hearing about our experiences is precisely why white folx espoused intentions for allyship and radical liberation are met by Black womxn with apprehension, mistrust, and oftentimes unapologetic contempt.

Often, I am approached by white scholars requesting I volunteer my time, my stories, and my labor toward ends that do not serve me or the liberation of Black womxn or Black people. Mere days after the Black Lives Matter protests kicked off around the United States, I was emailed by a white male colleague who wanted me to teach him about racism. To do so would require I recall traumatic and painful memories, all to teach someone something they will never understand in the same ways I have been forced to learn, see, and hear as a Black womxn. And for what? So a white man can feel he knows more, while I am left retriggered, drained, and distressed. The thoughtless, yet seemingly well-intentioned request, demands that those wishing to be allies and coconspirators ask themselves what they are actively doing to help Black womxn after hearing our testimonies and stories? In another instance, I was asked by a white female debate coach (who positions herself as an ally) if I was willing to volunteer my time (as an unofficial consultant) to share my stories and knowledge on Black critical theory (framed by Black lived experiences) to prepare a majority-white debate team for competition. Once again, I felt like a means to an end—an end, in this case, once again, that had nothing to do with me, Black womxn, or Black people.

Black womxn's stories should be consumed with an understanding that we are calling folx to action, we are calling folx in to do the necessary introspection/reflection/education to make substantive changes in terms of how you interact with us, our stories, and our voices. Black womxn insist on "talking back" against all those who seek to violate and silence us precisely because silence, as Audre Lorde reminds us, will never protect us.[12] Even though silence can be a form of resistance because it enables us to maneuver oppressive systems in a seemingly "safe" manner, silence, at the end of the day, maintains the status quo and, in turn, will not subvert systems of gendered racial oppression. The only way to the latter is to speak up and out. What changes after you hear our stories? What actions do you stop or start doing to put your money where your mouth is? If it is simply for your consumption or education, then we should be paid for our service.

Conclusion

The risk, exploitation, and consumption of Black womxn's truth telling are rooted in hegemonic systems and structures throughout society. We call you, our readers, to dismantle, disrupt, and decolonize this reality so that we can begin to tell our truths in ways that are safe, valued, and reproduced for the collective well-being of Black womxn among all others. Reimagine a society where Black womxn no longer have to convince the world that our Black Lives Matter or that #WeToo have been traumatized, attacked, and are survivors of violence. Instead, we call for change so that we can live in a reality where our truths are heard, our stories are honored, and our herstory is heralded.

Our goal was to name, confront, demystify, and resist the problematic systems and structures we have encountered in the academy and throughout our lives as we tell our truths. We call our readers to holistically protect and preserve Black womxn's truths. Create spaces that mitigate the risk we engage as we confront historical and contemporary injustices. Eradicate the exploitation Black womxn endure and render our truth telling valuable, worthy, and worthwhile. Compensate us and reward us for our combined lived and scholarly expertise and stop taking such labor for granted. Finally, resist the tendency to fixate your gaze on our truth telling in ways that are harmful, othering, and suspicious. Instead, take ownership for your own education and hold yourself accountable for being the change greater society needs. Listen and learn as we tell our truths, take up space, and build our legacies.

Discussion Questions

1 What stories have you heard from Black womxn? How did those stories influence you?
2 How can we protect, preserve, and honor the stories of Black womxn in our society?

Try This!

Go on the internet and identify three different Black womxn authors. Now do an online search and spend twenty minutes at a minimum researching each author's life, career, and work. What lessons can you learn from each of these Black womxn? Now identify one way each of these womxn's truth telling has contributed to greater society.

Notes

1   Marcia Ann Gillespie, foreword to *Flat-footed Truths: Telling Black Women's Lives*, ed. Patricia Bell-Scott and Juanita Johnson-Bailey (New York: Holt, 1998), xiii–xvi.
2   Janey Victoria Ward, "Raising Resisters: The Role of Truth Telling in the Psychological Development of African American Girls," in *Urban Girls: Resisting Stereotypes, Creating Identities*, ed. Bonnie J. Ross Leadbeater and Niobe Way (New York: New York University Press, 1996), 85–99.
3   Patricia Bell-Scott, introduction to *Flat-footed Truths: Telling Black Women's Lives*, ed. Patricia Bell-Scott and Juanita Johnson-Bailey (New York: Holt, 1998), xix.
4   Gillian B. White, "Black Workers Really Do Need to Be Twice as Good," *The Atlantic*, October 7, 2015, https://www.theatlantic.com/business/archive/2015/10/why-black-workers-really-do-nned-to-be-twice-as-good/409276/.
5   Shardé M. Davis, "Taking Back the Power: An Analysis of Black Women's Communicative Resistance," *Review of Communication* 18, no. 4 (2018): 301–318.
6   See Davey Shlasko, "Using the Five Faces of Oppression to Teach about Interlocking Systems of Oppression," *Equity & Excellence in Education* 48, no. 3 (2015): 349–360; Iris Marion Young, "Five Faces of Oppression," in *Rethinking Power*, ed. Thomas E. Wartenberg (2014): 39–65.
7   Bell-Scott, "Introduction," xix.
8   Shardé M. Davis, email message to Angela Gist-Mackey, June 25, 2020.
9   Ibid.
10 See Maulana Karenga, "Nommo, Kawaida, and Communicative Practice: Bringing Good into the World," in *The Global Intercultural Communication Reader*, ed. Molefi Kete Asante, Yoshitaka Miike, and Jing Yin (New York: Routledge, 2013), 3–22; Adisa A. Alkebulan, "The Spiritual Essence of African American Rhetoric," in *Understanding African American Rhetoric: Classical Origins to Contemporary Innovations*, ed. Ronald L. Jackson II and Elaine B. Richardson (New York: Routledge, 2003), 23–42; Richard L. Wright, "The Word at Work: Ideological and Epistemological Dynamics in African American Rhetoric," in *Understanding African American Rhetoric: Classical Origins to Contemporary Innovations*, ed. Ronald L. Jackson II and Elaine B. Richardson (New York: Routledge, 2003), 85–98.
11 Ashley R. Hall, "Slippin' in and out of Frame: An Afrafuturist Feminist Orientation to Black Women and American Citizenship," *Quarterly Journal of Speech* 106, no. 3, (2020): 341–351.
12 Audre Lorde, "The Transformation of Silence into Action," in *Sister Outsider: Essays and Speeches by Audre Lorde*, ed. Audre Lorde (Berkeley, CA: Crossing Press, 1984), 40–44.

4

#BlackIndigenous StoriesMatter

•••••••••••••••••••••••

ANITA MIXON

Black lives matter. Black. Lives. Matter. Alicia Garza's utterance in a Facebook post in 2013, "I continue to be surprised at how little Black lives matter. And I will continue that. Stop giving up on Black life. . . . Our lives matter," helped to galvanize and spark a movement that Garza would go on to cofound with two other Black women, Opal Tometi and Patrisse Cullors.[1] "When I saw the phrase Black Lives Matter spelled out by Alicia Garza in a love letter towards Black people—I decided to put a hashtag on it. Alicia, Opal, and I created #BlackLivesMatter as an online community to help combat anti-Black racism across the globe. We firmly believed our movement, which would later become an organization, needed to be a contributing voice for Black folks and our allies to support changing the material conditions for Black people."[2] There have been moments over the past several years where the cries of "Black lives matter" has reached a fevered pitch. But as I reflect on the past seven years, I wish that I shared Garza's optimism.

Unfortunately, I do not. Part of my pessimism is amplified by the 2020 political environment: an administration that foments discord, division, and racism; an election process and result that is sure to be contested; and unpredictable voter expectations. The other part of my pessimism is the pure exhaustion of Black trauma and Black grief on public display. I have begun to limit my media exposure, even in groups that I share with close friends, so that I can preserve what little peace I can carve out of an otherwise emotionally heavy Black experience. Having Black skin can make living, breathing, laughing, and loving a rebellious act. And so, each day I rise with both the hope of possibilities and the biting reality of how much further the United States must go in recognizing our humanity.

Digital media's role in the perception of #BlackLivesMatter is both a blessing and a curse. As a purposefully decentralized movement, the movement, its protests, images, and slogans are often co-opted by sometimes nefarious, other times well-intentioned but misguided, individuals. To be clear, #BlackLivesMatter is a movement that is focused on many objectives, some of which include dismantling policies that adversely affect the conditions of Black people, ending police brutality, and participating in the political process as agents of change. The digital environment provides an almost limitless space to disseminate messages, promote protest locations, post videos and photographs, help fund campaigns, and operate as a global meeting space for individuals. Photographs of largely peaceful protests are countered with images and videos of looters and rioters. It is those incendiary moments that go viral and function to diminish the entire movement and its purpose as well as offer evidence for those looking to sow racial animus.

I try to understand what people in my own communities think about the #BlackLivesMatter movement. And to be honest, those discussions are enlightening and, at times, frustrating. Conversations with my elders often begin with, "I believe Black lives matter but . . ." and the laundry list of media talking points litter the conversation: "I don't agree with the looting. . . . The tactics encourage rioting. . . . I don't understand the destruction of property." Conversations with non-Black-identifying people who denounce racism but then follow up with "I just don't understand racists. I am sure if you had a choice, you would have chosen to be white." Or using an example of one person's tweet, who uses the hashtag, as evidence of the movement's anti-Semitic roots. The anti-Semitic critique of the #BlackLivesMatter movement is so prevalent that more than "600 multiracial Jewish denominations, organizations, and synagogues [which] represents over half of Jewish people in America" published a full-page ad in the *New York Times* to state "unequivocally: Black lives matter."[3]

What is rarely mentioned in the conversations about #BlackLivesMatter is part of their mission, which includes "building new spaces and places that tell Black stories and remind the world of our everlasting contributions."[4] The digital spheres are filled with reminders, images, and voices of Black trauma and Black grief. The purpose of this essay is to go beyond my own pessimism about the state of the country and its treatment of Black Americans. Instead, the remainder of this essay serves as a "new space" to explore my own relationship with race as a native Gullah as we celebrate our twentieth year as a nation and to declare that Black Indigenous lives matter.[5] I am bound by duty to amplify the contributions that our "nation within a nation" quietly makes to preserve the traditions, culture, foodways, and environment of our ancestors. My desire is to move from the heaviness of Black grief to something more hopeful and to understand where, in the movement, is there space for the Gullah/Geechee Nation.

As I reflect on my own markers of privilege, I am reminded of the contested but proud relationship to my Nation. The Gullah/Geechee people are descendants of mostly West Africans who were brought to the United States as chattel slaves to work rice plantations. Those who identify as Gullah are traditionally individuals of West African nations who were settled in plantations located along the North Carolina and South Carolina coasts and Sea Islands. Geechee people were settled in plantations along Georgia's and Florida's coasts and islands.[6] Because of their rice cultivation expertise, Gullah/Geechee people are largely self-sufficient and live in isolated farming or fishing communities, which has allowed them to sustain their African way of life for more than 150 years.

That way of life is now under constant threat. Gullah/Geechee people are slowly being stripped of their heirs' property due to corporate takeover of the land for resort and residential development. With the developers' ability to access "digitized ancestry and property records," heirs of the lands are easily located and bombarded with offers.[7] Land grabbing is not a local issue; it is a global issue that overwhelmingly affects marginalized people and communities. Queen Qhet, chieftess and head of state for the Gullah/Geechee Nation, helped save lands by litigating luxury resorts and land takeovers through the Gullah/Geechee Sea Island Coalition.[8] By facilitating educational workshops and careful vetting of attorneys, Queen Qhet has successfully thwarted corporate attempts to take over land rights. However, the relatively inexpensive cost and carefully preserved coastlines continue to place Gullah/Geechee lands in a precarious position.

In addition to land rights issues, environmental racism contributes to toxic pollution, rising sea levels, overbuilding, and the displacement of natives. Climate change is a global issue that affects everyone, but communities of color are more often burdened with the consequences. The Gullah/Geechee people have "indigenous knowledge which has been proven resilient against flooding and hurricanes."[9] Their lack of legislative representation prevents their Indigenous knowledge to be widely shared, their traditions to be valued, or to receive adequate compensation to offset the effects of climate change. Simply stated, if there is no land, a people and a culture cease to exist. The Gullah/Geechee Nation continues to provide workshops to residents to try to mitigate the impact of their actions on the environment, but it means nothing if corporations continue to pollute the lands.

Finally, there are companies that have exploited and monetized the Gullah/Geechee name for profit. Queen Qhet led an effort to #DEMANDtheREBRAND of local companies using the Gullah name. The Nation's campaign to stop the "mascotification" and economic exploitation of the Gullah/Geechee people resulted in two Charleston, South Carolina companies, Gullah Gourmet and Revelry Brewing Company, to publicly respond and affirm their commitment to respect the Gullah/Geechee culture.[10] Despite years of requests from the Nation, the pressure applied through social media and the current cultural moment were instrumental to the campaign's success.

Why does this matter in the context of the #BlackLivesMatter movement? Black Indigenous stories are part and parcel of the #BlackLivesMatter movement and to have sustained, long-term success, it is time that the Nation explore opportunities to reimagine its future. And Gullah/Geechee people's future must be linked to both its land and the digital sphere.

Black Indigenous stories matter because a culture cannot exist without land and land rights and environmental racism have profound effects on the everyday lived experience of Gullah/Geechee people. And it matters *who* gets to tell the story.

Black Indigenous stories matter because they are a part of the fabric that makes up the Black experience and its contributions to the global Black struggle for human rights.

Black Indigenous stories matter because they are often a part of the forgotten history of the United States.

Black Indigenous stories matter because they document our resilience and hope. And in these times, to hope is a rebellious act. Black Indigenous lives matter. Black lives matter.

Discussion Questions

1 (How) has the Black Lives Matter movement included (or excluded) Black Indigenous women?
2 What are the most pressing justice issues for Black Indigenous women?
3 What social identity intersections are important in your individual life experiences?

Try This!

Write a journal reflection exploring how your particular social identity intersections have shaped your life.

Notes

1 Jelani Cobb, "The Matter of Black Lives," *New Yorker*, March 7, 2016, https://www .newyorker.com/magazine/2016/03/14/where-is-black-lives-matter-headed.
2 As quoted by Patrisse Cullors, "6 Years Later and Black Activists Are Still Fighting: A Letter from Black Lives Matter Global Co-founder, Executive Director, and Board President, Patrisse Cullors," July 13, 2019, www.blacklivesmatter.com/six -years-strong/.

3 "We Speak with One Voice When We Say, Unequivocally: Black Lives Matter,"
   New York Times, August 28, 2020, A17.

4 Cullors, "6 Years Later."

5 The author respectfully asks that the reader visits www.gullahgeecheenation.com
   for more information. Although there is a commission that has been established,
   the author encourages readers to read about the Gullah/Geechee people from the
   official Nation and "head pun de bode," Queen Qhet, chieftess and head of state for
   the Gullah/Geechee Nation.

6 The lands extend from Jacksonville, North Carolina to Jacksonville, Florida. An
   official map can be found at https://gullahgeecheenation.files.wordpress.com/2012
   /06/sea_island_map4.jpg.

7 Meagan Day, "Freedom Gained and Lost," *Jacobin*, April 12, 2019, https://www
   .jacobinmag.com/2019/04/gullah-geechee-south-carolina-civil-war-slavery; the *New
   York Times* and the BBC have also written about Gullah/Geechee's heirs property
   plight. Heirs' property means that the land has no primary owner, there are multiple
   heirs to the land, and it takes only one heir to agree to sell the property and
   developers are permitted to develop.

8 Currently, the Nation is soliciting funds to prevent a luxury resort from building on
   Bay Point, South Carolina.

9 Mothers and Others for Clean Air, "What Does Environmental Racism Look Like
   in South Carolina?" August 2020, https://www.mothersandothersforcleanair.org
   /environmental-racism-in-south-carolina/.

10 Both companies responded on July 17, 2020 through their social media pages.
   Gullah Gourmet committed to a rebranding of their name and dishes. Revelry
   Brewing Company no longer sells the beer bearing the Gullah name but reaffirmed
   their respect for the culture.

5

Your Black Friends
Are Tired

• •

ANDREA EWING

Your Black friends are tired. Black women are tired. I am tired.

They are tired of hearing: "Maybe if you just tried harder."

They are tired of going to work and remaining silent when another Black life is lost—violently, publicly, and familial.

They are tired of being asked to explain privilege, oppression, ignorance, and racist behaviors to white coworkers while simultaneously ignoring their own intersectionality, pain, and feelings of grief and loss.

They are tired of working hard and being told: "It's different for you, you gained your achievements because of affirmative action." Your postsecondary accomplishments, positions held are simply due to affirmative action while the hard work and personal sacrifice committed to holding the regarded positions is simply ignored or degraded.

They are tired of seeing their church pews full of white faces only during election years. They are tired of seeing the politicians and their seemingly entitled children checking their watches shifting in their seats the entire service.

They are tired of feeling emotionally raw and needing to express that they do not have the emotional capacity for more while having no choice but to give well beyond without complaint.

They are tired of anticipating walking into meetings full of white faces asking for explanations about why and when Black voices became first radicalized.

They are tired of being told they must have the hard conversations in order to educate others in hopes of seeing improvements to help benefit their white friends and coworkers at their own emotional expense.

They are tired of being asked: "Is your hair real?"

They are tired of constant loss being normalized because the losses disproportionately impact Black women.

They are tired of white colleagues learning a new phrase and thrusting it upon them: "You should work hard to be *Antiracist* because Black people can be racists, too."

They are tired of being asked to actively support white coworkers and be placated when the coworkers with less education and experience are promoted under Black tutelage.

They are tired of having to maintain a genuine-looking smile when emotions cause physical hurt just to avoid being told "You have an attitude" and to avoid the stereotype of being "a ghetto angry Black woman."

They are tired of the viral exposure of Black pain (e.g., Emmett Till, 1955; Jacob Blake, 2020) so people will care. They are tired of viral exposure serving to further traumatize Black women and desensitize the people we need to care.

They are tired of the need to end racism being a debate.

They are tired of toxic positivity telling them to ignore their feelings and be silent about their struggles because it is not pleasant for others.

They are tired of Black skin and womanhood being named as barriers when white supremacy, patriarchy, and hate are the barriers.

They are tired of symbolic victories such as statues being removed, baristas wearing a Black Lives Matter shirt, Realtors no longer calling the big room the "master" instead of humanity and dignity for Black lives.

They are tired of diversity and inclusion trainings that do not account for the reality the Black staff is currently living and the raw emotion they are asked to share again and again.

They are tired of the random texts from well-meaning white friends who saw on social media that they should text "Are you all right?" to their Black friends.

They are tired.

They are hurting.

They are tired of being asked, "If Black lives matter, what about me?" According to Goodman, "What affects some people inevitably affects us all."[1] If you want to know how things can be better for you, do better by Black women because your Black friends are tired.

Black women are tired.

I am tired.

Discussion Questions

1 What are ways you can explore social justice and race without taking advantage of your Black friend(s)?
2 How do microaggressions and language choices continue to hurt people?

Try This!

Pay attention to your choices of language for a week. Consider some of the examples of racist questions and expressions presented in this chapter. Are there terms and phrases you use that you can remove from your vocabulary?

Note

1 Diane Goodman, *Promoting Diversity and Social Justice: Educating People from Privileged Groups* (London: Routledge, 2011), 104.

6

Inciting Change with My Keyboard

• • • • • • • • • • • • • • • • • • • •

Leveraging Hashtag Activism to Fight Anti-Black Racism during COVID-19

SHARDÉ M. DAVIS

The year 2020 was supposed to be *my* year. At the end of 2019, I bade farewell to my apartment, packed up my belongings in two storage units, and set my sights to leave a familiar city and travel to find myself again. Although the focus of this trip was research, I had resolved that this journey would serve multiple purposes. I was excited about the prospect of newness, adventure, sistahly connections, rich conversations, and so much more. However, my excitement quickly wore off when news of COVID-19 spread across the United States. For me, March 2020 marked the beginning of a critical moment in America's history. We, as a nation, were now contending with *two* deadly pandemics: one that was created at the inception of this country—anti-Black racism—and another that exposes race-based disparities yet ravages people across identity groups—COVID-19. American life had changed overnight and prospects of summer fun turned bleak rather quickly. At that time, I was living alone and quarantined myself in a little rental apartment. I had already fallen sick to COVID-19 in March and was doing my best to socially distance from others with the goal of staying healthy.

Although the months of March and April represent stillness and solitude for me, the end of May marked a time of rage. News reports were circulating that Black and Brown people were dying from COVID-19 at disproportionately high rates relative to people from other racial groups. These reports were flashing across my phone screen alongside other reports of police terrorizing and murdering Black people. I was reeling. And as a true millennial (an older millennial but a member of this generation nonetheless), I turned to social media to express myself. I've never been a huge fan of social media because I prefer to lead a private life. But this moment in time necessitated that I connect with others from around the world to lament the ways in which Black people are treated as expendable and dispensable in the United States and around the world. Of course, anti-Black racism and race-based health disparities are nothing new. But for some reason, the events in May felt different. I was bursting at the seams with a range of emotions and could not take it anymore. Sharing on social media was a viable way to release, and at the time, Facebook seemed like the best online platform to reach this end. So on May 30, 2020, I wrote my first post of honesty:

ATTENTION WHITE FOLX

Yes, I'm talking to YOU. I'm sending out texts & emails to all of my white friends and colleagues asking how y'all are supporting the anti-racism, anti-police brutality, Black Lives Matter movements. There are NO EXCUSES!! Hashtag activism is cute, but back it up w/ your MONEY 💰💰💰 and your BODIES. Go to my twitter page @DrShardeDavis to see the various ways you can support the movement in the streets and at home.

Black folx & other POC's should not be the only ones fighting this fight. Because we are TIRED!!!!!

That post felt good. It was a moment of catharsis and allowed me to be transparent about where I stood. To be clear, I pride myself on being honest. I am not one to shy away from sharing my opinion, and because of that, most people know where they stand with me. But as an untenured Blackademic, I am constantly standing in the tension of searing truth and filtered honesty. The next few days revealed to me that white folx understood what was happening in our country but did not know how to help. I could think of a litany of things white folx could do, but why should I, the Black woman, assume the responsibility to educate others *yet again*? There was a considerable amount of invisible and unpaid labor happening and it incensed me. On June 2, 2020, I learned about #BlackoutTuesday, which was a social media moment that was started by two Black women music marketing executives, Jamila Thomas and Brianna Ahyemang, who wanted the music industry to cease operations for a day in honor of George Floyd. But by Tuesday afternoon, the moment slowly morphed into a national outcry for people to buy from Black-owned businesses. This idea stuck with me. After thinking about purchasing power and micro-behaviors as a viable form of solidarity, I posted this on my Facebook:

> If (white) folx don't know of any Black-owned businesses to support today (or any day), you can always send 💵 to ya Black friends as a (*VERY SMALL*) way of acknowledging years worth of our unpaid labor. This labor includes but isn't limited to: (1) biting our tongues until it bleeds to protect your fragility, (2) serving as your token Black friend (which you [unknowingly? 🤨] use as street cred), (3) roleflexing and codeswitching because our Blackness is deemed unprofessional and/or makes you uncomfortable, (4) carrying the responsibility of identifying and shutting down racism because we can't trust that you'll do it, working like a modern-day slave under the guise of "I'm the only one you trust to get it done right," and listening to you convince yourself and/or me that you're not racist 😒

> So yes, 💅♀️♥ I am currently accepting donations:

> Venmo: @DrShardeDavis
> CashApp: $DrSMDavis
> It's not reparations, but it'll do for now

Did I just post my Venmo handle? Did I ask folx for money? Will white folx understand the sentiment of this post? Will they think I'm pandering for cash and miss the larger message? These were the thoughts that ran through my mind once I pressed "Post" that Tuesday afternoon. As the hours passed, I oscillated between feeling proud of myself for speaking my whole truth unapologetically and worrying that I left out some critical information that would necessarily contextualize the tone of my post for followers. There are some people who can post flippantly on social media with no remorse or second thought about its impact or offense. But that's not me. If I am going to take a stance on a seemingly controversial idea, then I felt obligated to explain it a bit more (perhaps because I am a natural-born educator). So the next day, in the early morning hours, I gave in and posted a follow-up message:

My 3 A.M. Thoughts 😌
   As snarky as my previous post was (though, I said NOT ONE SINGLE LIE), please know that everyone has a *VERY REAL* responsibility to take care of our community at ALL levels. Spend your 💵💰 at your local Black businesses and donate to national organizations like BLM b/c we must support those large-scale endeavors. But please oh please, DON'T FORGET about your IMMEDIATE community. Your Black friends are HURTING right now. Some of us aren't eating or sleeping (literally😔). We're up one minute and down the next. Or, in a perpetual state of GRIEF. Venmo'ing $20 w/ a

note "dinner is on me tonight" is so symbolic; it's a very simple way to demonstrate that you "get it" (in terms of unpaid labor, community responsibility, & the reality that every single white American has financially profited off of privilege, racism, and anti-Blackness since this country was built by my enslaved African ancestors). The texts & calls are great, but can get a bit overwhelming at times when folx are expecting us to vocalize how we're doing/feeling. I KNOW many of you are reeling about how you can support us & show kindness and empathy. Well, here's one way.

There you have it—a more tempered Shardé. The outpour of support for this idea took me by surprise and cemented the impact of my posts. When I opened my Venmo app, I could see on my public home page so many white folx sending money to others for coffee, a cocktail to-go, to buy something fun on Amazon, or purchase dinner for the family. It was happening! I saw people acting like a community right before my eyes and crediting my Facebook post for their actions. And then the outpour of text messages from friends expressing gratitude for my social media posts began. I was in awe. This untenured Blackademic who had chosen to filter her truth for so many years was now stepping out in the social media landscape in a *bold* way . . . well, at least bold to me. The positive affirmations invigorated me to keep going, sharing, and being a TRUTH teller.

A few days later, I found myself back in the position to teach, inspire, empower, and on the evening of June 4, I posted on Facebook:

My Thursday Evening Thoughts:
I ♥♥♥ the discussions that are happening across the nation. I actually feel like the 💡 is going off for SOME 👀 of y'all. You are making connections that this MOMENT is a part of a MOVEMENT that has been going on for decades. And I see that y'all recognize that an anti-racist stance is a *LIFE'S* journey. You don't arrive & stay here. You are/should be unearthing parts of yourself that subscribe to anti-Black racism across your lifespan.
So please, oh please, keep this SAME ENERGY when the 24-hour news cycle shifts to the next "hot topic." This is going to sound strange, but I've been experiencing some anticipatory anxiety that the folx who are having these "ah ha" moments (head nod to Oprah) are going to forget about Us/the Black struggle in a few short weeks. And we (Black folx) are going to be left with empty promises, a pool of disappointments, broken communities, and a whole bunch more names on our "I ain't F'ing with you" list.
🔊 ACTION: Get connected to local and/or national organizations that have been active in the MOVEMENT. That way you have some accountability to do this work when the media stops giving this MOMENT attention.

Folx should know this, right? Sending a $20 gift is much appreciated but is certainly not sufficient because in my eyes, a one-time action is charity, not activism. I had reached a place where I felt like people were reading the lower-level message but missing the larger picture. I felt like they missed that we are talking about *systemic racism*—a perennial issue. And here I go again feeling incensed. Knowing the weight of each word that I typed on Facebook and that it incited very real change among my followers, I decided to take my efforts to another social media platform—Twitter. Part of the reason is because I saw how many people were reading my Facebook posts and were moved, but I reached a place where I just wanted to rant. One evening on Saturday, June 6, I created this phrase "Black in the Ivory" to share some of my experiences of racism. My first post on Twitter shouted out all of the "Black truthtellers who were speaking on their confrontations with racism in the university setting—student athletes, grads, faculty, etc." And I wanted to "use #BlackintheIvory to speak on mine." In less than twelve hours of posting that hashtag, it went viral. In fact, it was in the top twenty viral hashtags in the United States by Sunday evening. Blackademics all over the United States (and even the world) were using it to share personal stories about their confrontations with anti-Black racism in the academy. And white folx were listening! I was in awe of the power of being honest on social media. Although I fully recognize that social media has a dark side, it can be such a powerful platform to galvanize support and spark positive change. Since #BlackintheIvory was published on Twitter that one Saturday evening in June, I have seen how one idea for a hashtag has opened the gates for academics to have critical conversations about racism in very productive ways.

All things considered, summer of 2020 taught me that my ideas are valuable, my voice carries weight and should be exercised to incite positive change. It has also taught me that speaking out is tiresome. Like so many other Americans, I was experiencing low-grade depression, anticipatory anxiety, and stress due to months of living in fear. Life as we once knew it had changed, and some speculate that it changed indefinitely. As an untenured Blackademic who stepped into my rightful place as a TRUTH teller, I am in awe of what we, as a nation, have endured. But more importantly, I'm in awe of what *Black Americans* have endured. As I stated before, we are living through two concurrent pandemics—COVID-19 and anti-Black racism—both of which make day-to-day living difficult (at best) or seemingly impossible (at worst). I took a hiatus from Facebook due to the newfound attention I received for #BlackintheIvory on Twitter. But one late Monday evening in July, I decided to post this to Facebook:

> Today revealed to me that Black folx are **REALLY** struggling. Indeed, all people are struggling, but Black folx are hyperaware of anti-Blackness racism now more than ever and don't have the privilege to "turn the channel." Please, stop holding us to expectations that were upheld pre-COVID.
>
> And know that this message is not directed to white folx only. Black folx and other POC's—we/y'all need to extend an incredible amount of grace, care, and empathy to each other. Stop expecting superhuman resilience from people

who are not above or below humanity. We must allow folx to be *fully* human during an unprecedented time. ♥♥♥

This post puts it all into perspective. We are living through difficult times and I am not sure that they will get easier in the immediate future. But I know one thing to be true: I do not have to hold myself to unrealistic expectations that do more harm to my body than good. I am fully human and contend with a mixed bag of emotions that stem from deep-seated racial trauma in various contexts, including academia. My stamina to fight against systems of oppression and injustice lasts for only so long and sometimes I need others to step in so that I can rest. I implore those who are reading this passage to look at me (and people who look like me) as *humans* who get angry and speak out, are inspired and mobilize others to make positive social change, and grow weary and take a step back. Extend us empathy, grace, and compassion. And challenge yourself to see what kinds of change *your* voice can make when it is amplified.

Discussion Questions

1 How does public advocacy make people vulnerable?
2 How do individual stories empower social movements?

Try This!

Evaluate your social media accounts. What kind of activism do you see?

7

The Reality of Our Dreams

• •

Black Lives' Fears

PRISCA S. NGONDO

I have never feared for my life because of the color of my skin until I moved to the United States. That fear amplified when I had a daughter. The same fear intensified when I had a son. My fear turned into panic, which led to occasional sleepless nights where I am up wondering why my life and my children's lives do not matter. Why are Black lives so undervalued? What makes us so different from our White counterparts?

In 1963, Dr. Martin Luther King Jr. said, "I have a dream that my four little children will one day live in a nation where they will not be judged by the color of their skin but by the content of their character."[1] So why is it that fifty-seven years later, we are still defending our Blackness, our character, and our value? When is that one day?

I have Black relatives. I have Black friends. I have a Black mother. I have Black children. I am Black. We all live in the United States. Every day, I worry about us doing mundane activities such as grocery shopping, pumping gas, jogging, bird-watching, hanging out in the backyard, sleeping in our beds, driving, sitting in the car, walking the dog, and playing at the neighborhood park. To my knowledge, none of us have ever committed a crime, yet America treats us like criminals and not like a professor, a nurse, an accountant, a business owner, a lawyer, a baker, a project manager, a financial analyst, and a decent human being.

FIG. 7.1 P. S. Ngondo Facebook Post

We are all law-abiding, tax-paying, morally upstanding human beings who just happen to be Black. That is our crime.

"Those who hope that the Negro needed to blow off steam and will now be content will have a rude awakening if the nation returns to business as usual."[2] The sad truth is that America returned to business as usual. Watching our brothers and sisters unjustly arrested, shot, injured, and murdered is now our daily reality. A mere weekly routine.

Although Dr. King encouraged us not to "wallow in the valley of despair,"[3] today I am wallowing and weakening. I am feeling defeated.

It has been exhausting to deal with a global health pandemic coupled with a national racial strife pandemic. The emotional and mental toll has been devastating. Turning on the television or scrolling through social media, Black people are constantly bombarded with images, video, and text of modern-day lynchings. We cannot escape it. It has reached an uncomfortable level of normalcy.

If you are tired of hearing Black Lives Matter, imagine how tired we are of being Black in America. Tired of constantly worrying about if our loved ones are going to make it back home. Tired of worrying about surviving a regular police traffic stop. Tired of working twice as hard so we are seen in the workplace. Tired of living as a Black person. Our entire existence is an untelevised protest. Waking up and functioning in a society that is set up for you to fail and sees you as less than is a protest. It is a protest fueled by the refusal to accept a system that functions on your failures.

"Now is the time to lift our nation from the quick sands of racial injustice to the solid rock of brotherhood. Now is the time to make justice a reality for all of God's children. It would be fatal for the nation to overlook the urgency of the moment."[4] Fatal is right. It was true almost six decades ago, and unfortunately it is true in 2020. The moment was urgent, is urgent, and will continue to be urgent until the dream of racial justice and equality is realized. It cannot take another shocking death to reignite and fuel the urgency.

We are far from Dr. King's dream, but against all odds, the dream must continue. Once the dreams are gone, once hope is diminished, what else do we have left to pull us out of the suffocating grip and abyss of despair? But how do we dream if we cannot sleep? Maybe as we contemplate our fears in the still of the night, we can hope. Hope that fifty-seven years from now, my children will not be writing reflection pieces or marching on the streets in the midst of a deadly global pandemic to validate their Black lives.

Black lives matter not only in instances of police brutality or a broken legal system but also in the workplace. Your Black colleagues are not okay. Since the 2020 protests sparked by the killing of George Floyd by Minnesota police officers, we have been in a racial pandemic. So in addition to dealing with the complexities of the coronavirus pandemic, we have been expected to show up at work, perform our duties, and act professionally. For some, no one checked up on them. No one asked if they were okay. If all other marginalized groups in your workplace matter, why do Black people not matter when we are going through a crisis? We were being asked to check on the students, but who was checking in on us? We were asked to show them grace, but where was our grace? My friends in the corporate world had to wait to see if their organizations would publicly speak out and take a stand against racial injustice. While some breathed a sigh of relief, countless others realized that only their labor mattered. Some took it upon themselves to reach out to their leaders and call them out on their lack of action, while some labored on in quiet desperation and rage. Fortunately, I work at an institution that eventually recognized this and took steps to hear us out and somewhat support us. With that said, more can be done.

Intervention must be swift, immediate, and actionable. What does support look like? Here are some ideas:

- Do the work. Do not ask us to educate you about racial injustice.
- Ask us how we are doing.
- Give us time off.
- Extend deadlines.

- Offer counseling services.
- Take a public stand against injustice.
- Support organizations that are working to end racial inequality.
- Support organizations that are fighting for justice.
- Be an authentic ally.
- Acknowledge that Black lives matter.

A few years ago, I remember sitting at my desk in my office and crying moments before I had to go teach my predominantly White students. Yet another young Black man had been killed by the police for absolutely nothing. That young man could have easily been one of my brothers. I was shaken, but I still had to go teach. How would my students understand what I was feeling? How would I even explain it to them? How many of them called their siblings to talk to them about what they should do if they are ever pulled over by the police? Yet, this is the Black person's reality, whether you are at work or not.

All hope is not lost. This semester, I asked my millennial students what societal issues could social media help solve. Overwhelmingly, the majority of the class said racial and social injustice. I teared up as I read their responses. I thanked them for seeing me, their Black female professor. They are starting to get it. This is not a Black people issue. This is our issue. This is America's issue. They realize that "their destiny is tied up with our destiny."[5]

So how do we cope and continue to hope? We fight. We pick a lane. We resist. Black people are here to occupy this space.

Writing this piece is one of the many lanes I have picked to amplify Black voices and remind America that Black lives matter. Although I am wallowing, I will hold on to hope. Hope that George Floyd's death was not in vain, Breonna Taylor's murderers will be brought to justice, and my Black children's lives will one day matter.

Please be advised that "we can never be satisfied as long as the Negro is the victim of the unspeakable horrors of police brutality,"[6] per Dr. King.

So remember this: "If you are neutral in situations of injustice, you have chosen the side of the oppressor."[7]

As we pass on the baton of our frightful but hopeful dreams from ancestors to descendants, we must hold on to the blatant reality and be steadfast in our resolve that Black lives matter.

Aluta continua.

Discussion Questions

1   If you were to pick a lane to fight racial injustice, which lane would you pick? Why?
2   Why is saying "All lives matter" problematic?

P.S. Ngondo
June 4 · 👥   •••

Pick a lane. 🤎🖤🤎

⚙
@Lindss_tastic

Resistance is NOT a one lane highway. Maybe your lane is protesting, maybe your lane is organizing, maybe your lane is counseling, maybe your lane is art activism, maybe your lane is surviving the day.

Do NOT feel guilty for not occupying every lane. We need all of them.

FIG. 7.2 P. S. Ngondo Facebook Post

Try This!

Consider the ideas for intervention presented here. What suggestions can you add to the list? Implement two or three ideas into your life and share your experiences with others.

Notes

1   Martin Luther King Jr., "I Have a Dream" (speech delivered on the steps of the Lincoln Memorial, Washington, DC, August 28, 1963).
2   Ibid.

3 Ibid.

4 Ibid.

5 Ibid.

6 Ibid.

7 Bishop Desmond Tutu, quoted in Robert McAfee Brown, *Unexpected News: Reading the Bible with Third World Eyes* (Louisville, KY: Westminster John Knox Press, 1984), 19.

8

Black Women in
Black Lives Matter

• •

Navigating Being Both
Engaged and Dismissed

CERISE L. GLENN

> We are BLACK WOMEN!..... We build.... We don't tear down other
> BLACK WOMEN.... We have felt the pain of being torn down and we
> have decided we will be deliberate about building others! If I didn't tag you
> please don't be offended. I tried to pick people I thought would do this
> challenge!! All too often, we as WOMEN find it easier to criticize each
> other, instead of building each other up. With all the negativity going
> around let's do something positive!! ❀ Upload 1 picture of yourself...
> ONLY you. Then tag as many SISTERS to do the same. Let's build ourselves
> up, instead of tearing ourselves down. ♥♥ COPY AND PASTE ♥♥
> If I tagged you, don't disappoint me!!

A friend shared this with me through tagging me in her Facebook post in early
June 2020. I usually do not participate in social media challenges, but I immediately copied and pasted the text into my own post, uploaded a picture with just
me in it, and tagged ten African American girlfriends I thought would participate. The chain kept going and many of us posted our solo pictures with this message. As a self-identifying Black feminist and womanist scholar and activist,

I pay particular attention to issues that affect women of color, particularly African American women. I have been researching and writing about Black women's professional identities and ways their professional socialization experiences intersect with personal identities in various contexts.[1] I am part of a much larger group of scholar activists who examine intersectionality, the ways in which multiple aspects of our social identities interact.[2] As communication scholars, we do that in a discipline that still largely privileges masculine and Western frames of thought, which influences how we see ourselves and how others perceive us, both in reality and fictionalized depictions of us, such as in popular media.[3] As we navigate multiple forms of marginalization, including racism and sexism, we also celebrate our agency and self-defined notions of our identities.[4] This creates a complex web of oppressive and affirming discourses regarding Black women that still need examination with the current growth and resurgence of Black Lives Matter and other efforts to call for policy reform and social justice for Black communities in addition to other marginalized groups.

Exclusion and Silence regarding Black Women

A couple of weeks prior to this post, people around the world were still adjusting to our anxiety-ridden lives due to the coronavirus pandemic. As the reality of sheltering in place became more long term than anticipated, people became more focused on the news and social media, which took a more prominent role in our daily experiences. I vividly remember seeing the footage, taken by a personal mobile phone, of George Floyd's brutal arrest and death at the hands of police officers in Minneapolis, Minnesota, which transpired on May 25, 2020. For eight minutes and forty-six seconds, Floyd struggled for his life, repeatedly gasping and saying, "I can't breathe" and calling out for his mother while a white, male police officer knelt on him with his knee on the back of his neck while he remained handcuffed. I have never been able to watch the complete video. The trauma and pain of it resonates with me to this day.

Floyd's death immediately became a catalyst for large-scale protests and calls for reform in policing in addition to other forms of systemic racism. We mourned his loss as we watched the multiple memorial services celebrating his life and trying to make sense of his tragic death. Black Lives Matter quickly became the rallying cry in protests and social media posts. Like many people, I watched the news and utilized social media to watch protesters around the world chant "Black Lives Matter," "I can't breathe," and "Get off my neck." I read comments on social media as footage and news stories continued to be posted. I made a couple of posts of my own about the pain of racism and the cruel backlash against social justice calls for action, such as the cruel and inhumane George Floyd Challenge where people posted picture of themselves reenacting his death. I quickly realized the sad reality of the absence of Black women's narratives in comparison to those of males. We were very present in the protests and news media interviews, but yet again, systemic racism was being largely framed as an issue affecting Black *men*. The arrests of the police officers involved in George Floyd's death came quickly. We are still waiting for the ones involved in the senseless killing of Breonna Taylor on March 13, 2020 to be arrested. Breonna Taylor, a twenty-six-year-old African American woman who worked as an EMT, was shot and killed by police while she was sleeping in bed due to a mistaken address and no-knock warrant where officers fired multiple rounds into Taylor's bedroom. No clear story has yet to emerge about why this happened. One officer involved in her death has been fired. No further action has been taken while the case is "investigated."

On social media and in conversations, I, along with others, began to question why the discourse centers Black men almost exclusively of Black women. In all the coverage of Black Lives Matter, it was rarely mentioned that the organization was started by three Black women—Alicia Garza, Patrisse Cullors, and Opal Tometi—after Trayvon Martin, a young Black male, was murdered in Florida in 2012. I noticed Black women who posted comments such as "We are the mothers of Black men" when stating their connection to Black Lives Matter during early moments of protests in 2020. I continued to read social media posts and engage in conversations, noting the omission of Black women in calls for social justice, despite the large number of women who have been killed by police.[5] The much more limited amount of comments about Black women were ignored or dismissed for calls for unity, not divisiveness. There were those who acknowledged gendered and other aspects of Black Lives Matter affecting Black communities, but these were not as prominent. I posted about Breonna Taylor with minimal response. This did not happen to just me, but to others, seemingly mostly females at first. What was happening with African American women's value? What was different between her tragic death and the others? This is reminiscent of discussions in past movements regarding the role of Black women where our efforts and leadership roles were not touted as much as our male counterparts.

Discourses of Womanhood

Along with conversations of Black Lives Matter highlighting men's deaths more so than women's, those critiquing women's voices, especially those of celebrities, also emerged. Posts critiquing Oprah Winfrey and Gayle King emerged, highly critical of the ways they "attack" Black men but don't uplift them. This occurred despite Winfrey and King discussing Floyd in a global community forum I attended (a free digital post-tour extension of Winfrey's *Your Life in Focus: A Vision Forward* tour immediately before the global pandemic) and a feature on the Oprah Winfrey Network where Winfrey discussed ways to move the conversation of systemic racism forward. Why is this happening? One could argue that the viral mobile phone footage of Floyd made him the face of a newer wave of protests and social action, which did not take place with Taylor and Ahmaud Arbery, a Black male killed on February 23, 2020 while jogging by white males enacting their own "neighborhood patrols" (some footage was later released in Arbery's case). When news of Arbery's tragic killing was circulated, there was a viral I Stand with Ahmaud challenge where people posted videos of them jogging to show solidarity and raise awareness. This still causes us to question why Black men's lives are valued differently than Black women's despite the calls and awareness of the value of Black males in regard to larger majority culture.

It is not as if there is a fundamental lack of understanding of womanhood and how it functions in the United States. The popularity of "Karen" memes and viral video of Amy Cooper, a white woman who called the police on May 25, 2020 in an encounter in Central Park in New York City on Christian Cooper (no relation), a Black man who asked her to put her dog on a leash per park policy, reflects the ability to converse about and act on the intersections of race and gender. The outrage of a white woman threatening a Black male with police action when she was clearly wrong contributed to news coverage and social media posts of the history of white women weaponizing the police against Black men when it is clear they are in no danger. Cooper was quickly fired and later faced criminal charges. The introduction of the Caution Against Racially Exploitive Non-Emergencies "CAREN Bill" in California and similar legislation in other areas has been relatively fast. Legislation such as this makes it criminal to call police under false pretenses when deliberately used with racial bias. This clearly shows we as a society are capable of understanding how race and gender can intersect. And yet, the understudied and underrealized cruel history of the ways in which Black women have been traumatized and brutalized by police and by those weaponizing the police remains largely missing from larger social protests discourses.[6] When they do, they occur on a much larger scale, such as #SayHerName in ways that are secondary or "complementary" to Black Lives Matter as if Black women's issues are somehow a subsidiary of Black (men's) lives.

More Voice and More of the Same

There have been mixed reactions to the space and place for Black women in Black Lives Matter and other societal issues. When Black women raise our voices to enact our agency and bring awareness to these issues, we are often ignored, criticized, and told in subtle and not-so-subtle ways that we should wait for social justice while others need immediate attention. In one such instance, I participated in a Facebook forum with mostly African Americans on the current ballots for the national election. First, I was ignored. When I reiterated my comment, I was attacked and threatened. I called out the Black male poster's sexism when he responded to me that this conversation "was between two men." It was not—it was a public forum on Facebook where multiple people had made comments. The rest of this exchange and the slower reaction to Breonna Taylor's killing also show promise. My husband and life partner quickly defended my right to post in this group (which led to an interesting exchange of narratives of masculinity regarding attacking and empowering Black women). Another Black woman showed her support by "loving" my comments in this exchange. More males, of various ethnicities, and women are making an effort to understand and engage in Black Lives Matter and Black women's experiences. More women are speaking out for Black women. The Women's National Basketball Association (WNBA) has especially focused on justice for Breonna Taylor. The National Basketball Association (NBA) and WNBA have focused their abbreviated 2020 seasons on social justice issues. Kyrie Irving and LeBron James, famed NBA players, have also called for action regarding Breonna Taylor, including James's headline-grabbing hat he wore before a game, which read, "Make America great again," with "great again" crossed out and adding "arrest the cops who killed Breonna Taylor." Oprah Winfrey dedicated an issue of *O Magazine* to Breonna Taylor with Taylor on the cover, the first time Winfrey has not been featured on the cover. Winfrey also purchased twenty-six billboards (Taylor's age when killed) in Taylor's hometown so we do not forget her.

Despite this progress, the mixed messages of Black women's value remain. Kyrie Irving reportedly suggested suspending the NBA season to focus on social justice, for Breonna Taylor, and other issues regarding Black Lives Matter. This was dismissed and the 2020 NBA season resumed, yet play stopped immediately when the Milwaukee Bucks started a strike after the police shot and may have paralyzed Jacob Blake, a Black male, on August 23, 2020 in Kenosha, Wisconsin. This strike led to a stop of playoff games for two days, and additional professional sports followed suit in a variety of ways, including the WNBA, National Hockey League, Major League Baseball, National Football League, and Major League Soccer. Although this strike garnered much-needed global awareness and attention, it still makes us wonder and contributes to the subtle message that Black women's lives matter a little less or perhaps are not as significant as others.

The post opening this chapter was an important way to engage these issues pertaining to Black women and social justice. It was the first time I ever posted a picture of myself alone in my newsfeed (other than my profile picture). This felt different—Black women posting about ourselves without mentioning Black men or white men and women. I do not have to define myself and actions as an activist solely through what is happening to Black men. We are worthy of being the center of the conversations that need to happen. The quickest action of reform for Black women occurred when Aunt Jemima finally got to retire and step down from the mammy image of the pancake syrup bottle. We deserve better. Yet, we were not complaining. This was also a call to other Black women that we need to support one another. This cannot be a binary issue. We must include others as well, such as Black Trans Lives Matter. We can disagree about our roles without attacking each other's notions of Black womanhood, engagement with feminism, and roles supporting Black men. Of course, I acknowledge Black men and our solidarity with other women, but Black women still need to be acknowledged as well in holistic, inclusive ways. We still continue to raise our voices as we "wait" for our turn in the center.

Discussion Questions

1 Do you think there is a need for #SayHerName? Should this be part of or separate from #BlackLivesMatter? Why or why not?
2 What have you learned about Black women's roles in #BlackLivesMatter? This can be in regard to its founders/leaders, press coverage, and social media posts. Do you think this is problematic or shows progress (or perhaps both)? Why?

Try This!

Research the contributions of Black women in the occupation of your choice. Have you heard of the women and their accomplishments before? How can you amplify their contributions?

Notes

1 Cerise L. Glenn, "Stepping in and Stepping Out: Examining the Way Anticipatory Career Socialization Impacts Identity Negotiation of African American Women in Academia," in *Presumed Incompetent: The Intersections of Race and Class for Women in Academia*, ed. Gabriella Gutiérrez y Muhs, Yolanda Flores Niemann, Carmen G. González, and Angela P. Harris (Boulder: University Press of Colorado, 2012), 133–141; Cerise L., Glenn and Dante L. Johnson, "Life in Black and White: Cautionary Tales of Internalizing Cultural Norms of Race, Class, and Gender in *The Family That Preys*," in *Interpreting Tyler Perry: Perspectives on Race, Class, Gender, and Sexuality*, ed. Jamel Santa Cruze Bell and Ronald L. Jackson (New York: Routledge, 2013), 148–175; Siobhan E. Smith-Jones, Cerise L. Glenn, and Karla D. Scott, "Transgressive Shades of Feminism: A Black Feminist Perspective of First Lady Michelle Obama," *Women & Language* 40, no. 1 (2018): 1–14.
2 Patricia Hill Collins, *Black Feminist Thought: Knowledge, Consciousness, and the Politics of Empowerment* (New York: Routledge, 2002).
3 Cerise L. Glenn, "Activism and Spiritual Identity in Greenleaf," in *Womanist Ethics: A Call for Liberation and Social Justice in Turbulent Times*, ed. Annette Madlock Gatison and Cerise L. Glenn (Lanham, MD: Lexington Books, in press).
4 Collins, *Black Feminist Thought*.
5 Andrea J. Ritchie, *Invisible No More: Police Violence against Black Women and Women of Color* (Boston: Beacon, 2017).
6 Ibid.

9

Antiracist Holistic Change in "STEM" Higher Education

• • • • • • • • • • • • • • • • • • • •

MELANIE DUCKWORTH AND
KELLY J. CROSS

There are challenges we face in attempting to transform long-established institutions of higher education—and the educators who have been shaped by such institutions—from institutions that continue to uphold racist policies to institutions that are actively antiracist. In the realm of STEM education, we have unacknowledged epistemologies of complete objectivity and meritocracy. Although the fundamental principles of science and engineering are objective, the education of students regarding these principles is a social phenomenon that depends heavily on the sociocultural context in which learning occurs. Despite the social nature of the learning that occurs across educational settings, institutions of higher education often ignore the multiple, socially-constructed identities that both faculty and students bring to the learning environment. In so doing, these institutions maintain and reaffirm cultural biases, prejudices, and discriminatory practices that differentially reward, empower, and grant privilege to those who hold socially centered identities as white, male, and of economic advantage, while simultaneously diminishing the innovative and sometimes discipline-expanding contributions of

Black, Indigenous, and People of Color (BIPOC). To embrace and enact antiracist holistic change, institutions of higher education must be willing to: (1) undertake curricular review for the express purpose of eradicating racism from the content and structure of formal course offerings as well as less formal, applied learning contexts; (2) require that course instruction be consistent with the significant research literature promoting culturally responsive pedagogy. Curricular change of this magnitude would require direct and supportive actions by the institution's chief administrators and by academic and research faculty. The institution's willingness to undertake such actions would serve as a measure of its commitment to becoming an antiracist institution.

In this chapter, we propose a holistic approach to creating institutions of higher education that are culturally inclusive and culturally responsive. This approach prioritizes the participation and active engagement of minoritized groups and is predicated upon two key assumptions: (1) our current system of higher educational is unresponsive to the educational requirements and desires of BIPOC and other culturally diverse students, and (2) our scientific and societal advancement depends largely on the ability of our institutions to implement educational curricula that are culturally inclusive and culturally responsive. In the context of higher education, this translates to recruiting, retaining, and successfully graduating BIPOC students and other culturally diverse students. These student outcomes are necessarily tied to an institution's commitment to (1) recruiting and hiring faculty who represent racial diversity and other diverse identities; (2) adopting and enacting policies that reward culturally responsive pedagogy and punish culturally biased and discriminatory teaching practices, providing the financial resources necessary to retain and ensure the professional success of culturally diverse faculty, and providing the academic and sociocultural programming necessary to ensure both the academic success and the career readiness of culturally diverse students (see figure 9.1).

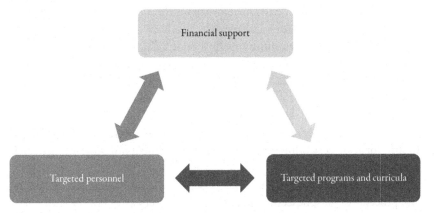

FIG. 9.1 Holistic Approach to Integrate Antiracism into Higher Education

We all want to live in an equitable society in which we maximize the potential of persons of all races. The marginalization of certain groups is one of the most significant impediments to establishing that inclusive society. Higher education must become the vehicle for a diverse, equitable, and inclusive society. This can only be accomplished by acknowledging our racist history, transforming our exclusionary, antiquated educational policy and practices, and creating an educational system that is innovative, values diverse perspectives, and optimizes the contributions to be made by students of all races and ethnicities to scientific discovery, engineering design, and technological advancement. In this moment of heightened awareness around social justice, institutional change is imperative. In insisting on institutional change, we speak from the perspective of a Black faculty member and a Black administrator. Dr. Kelly J. Cross, Engineering Education Assistant Professor at the University of Nevada Reno, is a culturally responsive practitioner, researcher, and educational leader. Dr. Cross's complementary professional activities promote inclusive excellence through collaboration. Dr. Melanie Duckworth is an associate professor of psychology and associate dean in the College of Science at the University of Nevada Reno. In her current roles and in her former roles as assistant dean for diversity and inclusion and chair of the Faculty Senate Faculty Diversity Committee, Dr. Duckworth has distinguished herself as a savvy spokesperson and as a thought leader who is committed to cultural diversity and cultural inclusiveness as winning strategies for all public and private institutions of higher education. She has worked to develop and implement recruitment, admission/hiring, and retention policies and procedures that better ensure the diversity of faculty, students, and staff.

Administration's Role in Proposed Approach

In transforming our institutions of higher education into engines of academic achievement for students of all racial identities, the mandate for administrators is threefold: (1) there must be a systematic, clearly defined, and benchmarkable approach to hiring and retaining racially diverse faculty; (2) there must be a systematic approach to training all faculty to engage in pedagogy that highlights the contributions of scholars who reflect the racial diversity of students; and (3) the identification, funding, and periodic assessment of programs that support the success of students who, throughout most of higher education's history and as a consequence of racist policies and practices, have been either denied access to any form of education or have been the recipients of woefully unequal education.

To create a faculty that is racially diverse, all recruitment and hiring policies and procedures must be examined to ensure that every aspect of the hiring process (i.e., recruitment, applicant evaluation, and interviewing) is undertaken with the aim of identifying and hiring candidates who (1) reflect the racial diversity present among the total pool of persons who hold the required credentials and can demonstrate requisite skills and experiences and (2) add to the racial diversity present within the hiring unit. The slow pace at which our institutions are transforming the racial makeup of faculty would suggest that relying on the professional network of members of the academy, the majority of whom are white, male, cis-gendered, able-bodied, middle to high socioeconomic status, Christian citizens of the United States is not an optimal or even workable strategy. Instead, administrative leaders with decision-making power must require that hiring procedures and processes that mirror those promoted by institutions and professional organizations such as the University of Wisconsin–Madison, University of Washington, the University of Michigan, and the Association of American Medical Colleges.

In seeking to effect measurable change in the hiring practices employed by a given institution of higher education, you must assess clearly the commitment to racial diversity and inclusiveness and the influence/power held by administrators at every level within the institution. You also have to know the pressures that can be brought to bear in order to convince reluctant administrators that not acting to increase the racial diversity among faculty members is no longer an option. An equally clear-eyed approach must be taken to ensure that discriminatory practices are not inherent in the procedures and processes used to retain and promote faculty who hold diverse racial identities.

Faculty Role in Proposed Approach

Once hired, faculty are responsible for developing and delivering a curriculum that allows students to be successful. Incoming faculty will need particular skills including multicultural awareness to implement culturally responsive pedagogies. For example, the ability to translate technical content into a learning experience that is relevant for students who hold culturally centered *and* non-centered racial identities requires a broad knowledge of other cultures, such as the nine dimensions of Afro-American cultural experiences identified by Boykin[1] or the endarkened feminist epistemology proposed by Dillard.[2] Additionally, assessment tools must be developed, standardized, and administered in ways that do not penalize BIPOC students for identifying with their own culture rather than mainstream American culture. Currently, our institution is engaged in teacher training initiatives that could serve the goal of creating classrooms led by anti-racist, anti-sexist, anti-ableist, anti-xenophobic, and anti-classist educators. We need to expand the list of teaching and research indicators upon which we place value in relation to faculty hiring and evaluation. We need to amplify and reward teaching, research, and service efforts that are defined by engagement with diverse, less studied, and often excluded members of our community. The challenge is to move our institution and every institution of higher education out of the mindset of "just enough diversity and inclusion to maintain the (racist) foundations upon which it stands" to a mindset of doing every possible thing to promote equity in education and correct for racial/ethnic and other forms of cultural bias, prejudice, and discrimination that are rampant within the policies and procedures that govern so many of our existing institutions.

Student Impact of Proposed Approach

The proposed approach will have a direct impact on students' educational and career outcomes. By creating an educational curriculum that is maximally aligned with the educational requirements and desires of a culturally diverse student body, we increase the likelihood that students will obtain an education that prepares them to meet their short- and longer-term career objectives. Because of the current COVID-19 crisis, students are uniquely positioned to demand an educational experience that respects the diversity of their identities, life experiences, educational objectives, and career goals. The institutions of higher education that are most prepared to meet the demands of these students will contribute most effectively to the advancement of our global society.

In conclusion, antiracist institutions of higher education will serve as the engines that fuel scientific discoveries and technological advances that meet the demands of our global society. The movement of our institutions from systems designed to serve whiteness to learning and living communities that prioritize the educational requirements and professional aspirations of individuals of all races will require systematic adoption of antiracist policies. With boldness of action, antiracist institutions will contribute to the development of individuals from whom racial diversity and inclusiveness is as essential to human survival and evolution as biodiversity is to the health and survival of our physical world.

Discussion Questions

1 What aspects of higher education most require intervention?
2 Inclusivity and antiracism programs must go beyond numerical representation. What are some other ways we can make institutions of higher education truly inclusive?

Try This!

Investigate the policies and programs at your university. You might begin by researching online or talking with an administrator. Are there training programs to teach antiracist practices? What systemic roadblocks exist in forming a more inclusive institution?

Notes

1   Wade A. Boykin, "The Triple Quandary and the Schooling of Afro-American
    Children," in *The School Achievement of Minority Children: New Perspectives*,
    ed. Ulric Neisser (Hillsdale, NJ: Routledge, 1986), 57–92.
2   Cynthia B. Dillard, "The Substance of Things Hoped for, the Evidence of Things
    Not Seen: Examining an Endarkened Feminist Epistemology in Educational
    Research and Leadership," *International Journal of Qualitative Studies in Education* 13,
    no. 6 (2000): 661–681.

10

Fighting for Black Studies

• •

An Essay about Educational Empowerment

IDRISSA N. SNIDER

After weeks of watching protests erupt across the nation, I found myself trying to figure out how I could participate. I attended walks and rallies in the past, I post on social media, and I deliberately seek out opportunities to share the real lived experiences of Blacks every day. But this time around, after I dried the tears from my face while I stood in silence for eight minutes and forty-six seconds in my bedroom as I watched George Floyd's funeral, and after I could not stop staring at photographs of Breonna Taylor's twenty-six-year old young face for days on end, I knew that I was past the point of expressing the sadness, anger, and tiredness of having to pursue social justice as a Black woman in America. I wanted and still very much desire to see solutions and formidable change occur. I frequently write an opinion column for the *Birmingham Times*, so I reached out to the editor and published an article titled, "Why African American History Should Be Taught Starting in Elementary School." This is my recommendation and my anecdote for what I envision to bring about generational and widespread attitudinal shifts in the mindsets of people. Because far too many Americans lack knowledge about how and why the utility of race functions as the cornerstone to which success and equality are hinged. The highlighted excerpts in this essay are lifted from that publication to reiterate and to continue to promote the philosophy that education is the great equalizer.

During the height of the Jim Crow era, the landmark *Board of Education vs. Brown* case determined it was unconstitutional for public schools to remain segregated. Although this case was resolved in the Supreme Court in 1954 and is often used as a preemptive marker to paint the picture of America evolving into a postracial society prior to the civil rights movement, many of today's classrooms are illustrations and reminders of just how segregated our schools and educational system continues to be. District redlining, decreases in funding, and lack of other necessary resources like technology in the classroom plagues poor urban and rural areas throughout the country and it is especially evident in Black and Brown communities. Other reminders of the ever-present racial line can be identified when examining society's reactions to the highly publicized murders of George Floyd and Breonna Taylor, who both died tragically from excessive force used by law enforcement. Their deaths invigorated a resurgence in a new phase of the Black Lives Matter (BLM) movement.

The 2020 BLM crusade is different from what occurred in 2016 because somehow through the outbreak of a COVID-19 viral pandemic, these specific protests and posts managed to yield a more open ear from a large segment of white American who had somehow missed that racism was not indeed a thing of the past and that its detriment to Black Americans or even America, did not end when slavery was abolished in 1864. [The real story of African people, being stripped from their native civilizations, cultural customs, and practices to build the wealth flowing in America through the most egregious form of systemic economic and social abuse is nearly nonexistent in the American classroom.] Therefore, an adequate and fair take on the impact of slavery slips in and out of America's conscious as a wavering thought, rather than as a formidable truth. I propose this issue is not simply a reflection of people who do not care or people who do not desire to know. Reasonably, I am suggesting that a key lack of understanding about how racism undercuts every facet of our society, be it politically, in health care, educationally, in the prison system, economically, socially, and more, is a proponent of a faulted educational system. The existing curriculum whitewashes history and diminishes the veracity of how slavery introduced a poignancy of racist systems in the United States. This essay argues that for America to right its wrongs and truly integrate the academic learning experience, African American studies should be taught starting as early as elementary school and remain prevalent throughout higher education. Additionally, it calls for Black women and Black men to carve out spaces to maximize their agency as activists and lively engaged participants in the struggle to achieve social justice and equality.

Advocating for the community must involve strategic moves that will garner the effectiveness to bring about long-lasting change and chip away at the barriers that oppress and cause it to be challenging for Black Americans to achieve true equity as citizens. Mandating diversified and comprehensive school materials, highlighting the impact of education of African American studies to not just the Black community but also to whites, and the normalization of activism as a routine way of life are three specific ways scholars can push the needle forward on how to utilize the privilege of having had access to a formal education to empower others.

There are two particular components regarding the deficiency in educational training on African American history that gives me a deep sense of unrest in my spirit. It is the kind of nag that hangs over a person like when you have been betrayed by a lover or close friend. Your affinity for that individual renders you vulnerable, as it equally invigorates. These emotions are there primarily because I have this love-hate relationship with education. On the one hand, I was privileged to attend one of the best high schools in the country, the Alabama School of Fine Arts. After graduating with my diploma, I went on to receive three degrees and ultimately earned a PhD in rhetorical criticism and womanist studies. Having the opportunity to be educated at premier universities empowered me and gave me tools that I use to navigate through life. Yet, despite how incredibly influential an education can be, school may also become a source of trauma for the very people it seeks to liberate. Irrespectively, I have school and institutional hurts. The places that nurtured me have also scarred and battered me. Whether it came from professors and teachers who made it a point to express when they felt like I was not "good enough" or "cut out" for their programs, or peers who would be outwardly dismissive and even angered because I shared differing points of view.

In the long run, those things were banal. I eventually learned to identify these manners of actions and characteristics as deficits belonging to the persons that displayed them and not as some inherit inferiority of my own. Second, what reinforced my belief that many Americans do not truly or fully grasp the significance and need to teach African American studies or the history of Blacks in America was most evident when I taught my own students. It was one thing for me and the many other Black people I know (who earned their degrees) to share stories of having to do "extra" work so that they could pass their courses or obtain additional sources to draw from on people like themselves. The gravest disappointment occurred when students complained about having to hear too much about "Black" history or examples when taking my courses. As an educator, I made a concerted effort to simply include diversified readings, which precisely meant that out of a possible fifteen titles on my course syllabus, three or four would be written by a Black author or other persons of color.

The audacity of some white students complaining about having to be introduced to works by Black scholars incensed me and was disrespectful. Millions of people of color have been forced to listen to story after story, see stereotypical image after image, and hear incomplete and outright biased materials from teachers, textbooks, and other supplemental materials that make up the typical American classroom experience since the inception of the country until the present. [However, the names and stories of abolitionists and once-enslaved individuals like Mary Prince and Olauda Equiano, whose narratives serve to document the Black experience of individuals forced into servitude, or the philosophical tenets of W.E.B. Du Bois and Otto Klineberg, who were instrumental in disrupting racially biased sociological beliefs of their time are not as widely highlighted like lessons on Abraham Lincoln or Robert E. Lee.] Whether the students who whined about learning something new were being "insensitive" or "discriminating" is debatable.

Nevertheless, these incidents reveal what students' expectations are. Society presumes Black men should just "shut up and dribble" or for Black and Brown women to be "bitches, angry, and dangerous" even as they show up for work in the U.S. Congress. These disclosures may provide some insight about why I and other Black parents have to make additional steps to ensure that our children receive a quality educational experience that reflects the Black identity in an authentic way. I can vividly recall when my then-fourth-grader son was once tasked with doing a report on a historical famous Alabamian. His teacher kindly suggested that he select Terrell Owens, a Black former NFL player and reality TV star to feature in his project. While accomplished and talented, his reputation is riddled with controversy and "baby mama drama." Although I personally have no judgment about Owens's private or professional life, I should note that we live in the city that is deemed as one of the birthplaces of the civil rights movement. Alabama is home to prominent Black history makers such as Coretta Scott King, Rosa Parks, Nat King Cole, Senator John Lewis, Zora Neale Hurston, Angela Davis, the Tuskegee Airmen, Mae Jemison, and our final choice, A. G. Gaston. I wondered if that teacher ever suggested a white student take on interest in doing a scholastic report on a famous white Alabamian such as Courtney Cox or Taylor Hicks. My guess is that she would not because my son told me about the other presentations that primarily consisted of white congressmen, senators, and game changers. Her selection was not malicious at all; it was indicative of her lack of knowledge of influential Black Alabamian persons to choose from.

Students across America have come to accept attending a public school will mean they do not have to engage or learn about otherness. We passively approve that the classroom is not the space where children will participate in conversations about racialized social hierarchies.

[Black and white students alike go through elementary school, high school, and in many cases, college and their graduate studies with recycled and refashioned accounts of African American history. Honorable, romanticized versions about civil rights leaders Rosa Parks and Martin Luther King Jr. show up briefly in February during Black History Month, then fade away. Ultimately, many Black students are left feeling ignored and inadequately prepared to convey the systemic nature of the challenges African Americans face. Likewise, most white, and even some people of color, are unfamiliar with the extent to which African Americans battle to gain their rightful place in society. It is not the Black community's responsibility to teach white America or other groups about our history, struggles, or achievements, but it is the duty of the educational system to inform and to prepare all its students for the world by providing a comprehensive and authentic look at how the United States was established and continues to function.]

There is no standardized format or benchmark for teaching African American history. Only five of the fifty states mandate Black studies as part of its statewide curriculum. Those states include New York, Massachusetts, Mississippi, Arkansas, and Florida. Within these territories, states still ponder over to what extent to acknowledge the damage caused by those members of the white community who uphold and live by a white supremacist ideology. Ibram X. Kendi noted that only in Massachusetts and Maryland is the term *white-supremacy* mentioned in the curriculum.[1] Thus, generations of students are circuitously being fed messages from an embedded belief system that renders whites both superior and irresponsible for centuries of systemic oppression. A proper education should not strive to guilt-trip Blacks or whites for what took place with their ancestors. Nonetheless, without a thoughtful take on the past people will be ill-equipped and unprepared to tackle the issues of their day.

There is an even greater opportunity to be realized for white America. Demographics are changing, and the browning of America is taking place. Shifts in people of color who occupy leadership positions are gradually happening, narrowing educational and economic gaps is taking place, and Blacks are also finding innovative ways to be recognized. Kamala Harris's historical vice-presidential pick to the Democratic presidential ticket is only four years in the rear to the United States twice electing the Obamas, its first African American president and family, to the White House. And I, an everyday woman and former professor became some of my students' first-ever Black educator in their entire lives. The proverbial classic white American-dream bubble is bursting. The notion of this change is laced with fear by extremist groups who use slogans like "Make America Great Again." This is not a profession to identify myself as an avid member of any political party. From a historical perspective, the sentiment of the slogan is inflammatory and symbolizes a time of invisibility of people who were once deemed as chattel, pickaninnies, servants, and coons by some sects of the population. The bottom line is, white America cannot afford to continue to render themselves blameless or blind to the plight of Black Americans. The costs are heavy, and turning a deaf ear to racism has very real and personal consequences. Think about the countless "Karen" videos that surfaced and went viral across social media platforms. White men and women lost their jobs, their children were put out of colleges and schools, and racial discrimination lawsuits are paying out large sums of money.

I would like to rewrite this conversation as a sermon about the morality of racism. In my heart, I want to communicate that racism is an evil that separates individuals from anything good. I wish my argument could be racism is not ever really compartmentalized to race but that racist persons ultimately self-destruct. In this academic space or world of ethical philosophical tenets, a case for morality does not have to be made. From the school of thought that promotes the simplest ethical code, the golden rule, society cannot continue to assist and uphold systems meant to destroy communities of people. Which is why I harken to the words of Audre Lorde, who stated, "The master's tools will never dismantle the master's house." If denying education to African Americans was the edifice to continuing slavery and the attainment of racial suppression of Blacks, it is the key to dismantling and disrupting the marginalization of Blacks.

Social media platforms provide relatively safe spaces and audiences for people who would otherwise be unheard or deemed voiceless. Sharing the real lived experience of Blacks, be it through personal or organizational messages, creates as sense of agency and utility. Releasing my editorial across a public platform prompted conversations with community members from diverse backgrounds. As a scholar, I found it more rewarding to write for everyday Americans than when I produce materials for academic audiences. This work could be easily accessed and shared with whomever was willing to engage it. "Why African American Studies Should Be Taught Starting in Elementary School" is a natural conversation many Blacks have among themselves, and it is becoming a part of a greater dialogue in the community.

Discussion Questions

1 As an educator or student, in what ways can you diversify what you cover and learn about in class?
2 If you were to write an opinion piece for a newspaper as an act of advocacy, what would you write about?

Try This!

Reach out to your local school district and request that the curriculum be more inclusive of African American studies and of other people of color.

Note

1 As cited in Jericka Duncan, Christopher Zawistowski, and Shannon Luibrand, "50 States, 50 Different Ways of Teaching America's Past," CBS News, February 19, 2020, https://www.cbsnews.com/news/us-history-how-teaching-americas-past -varies-across-the-country/.

11

When You Can't
Call the Cops

• • • • • • • • • • • • • • • • • • • •

Intimate Partner Violence
and #BlackLivesMatter

REBECCA MERCADO JONES

AND JAYNA MARIE JONES

Rebecca: One of my earliest, foggiest memories was of my father trying to drown my mom in the soapy water she was trying to wash the dishes in. He was pressing down with both hands on the back of her neck and she was resisting him— her short, chubby, brown arms shaking in effort. I was six, so the scene is visceral, though the details are hazy. But some things we never forget.

The night ended with both of my parents being hauled away in handcuffs, although both alive. We were living in Virginia Beach at the time, so we had no family around. The neighbor took pity on us five and allowed us to stay the night. I remember her long scraggly ponytail but not her name. She's as much of a stranger to me now as she was then.

I think about that night often. The fucked-up dynamic that my parents had, the fact that they arrested my mother, too, but also how my mother didn't hesitate to call the police to save her life and possibly ours.

My father was white. She did not worry that he would end up shot in the back or face-down on the concrete suffocating under the force of an officer's knee. She didn't worry about confirming these police officers or the neighbor's suspicions about who is violent. When asked if she wanted to press charges, she did not have to consider what putting yet another Black man into the system would mean.

When the abuser is white, you have the luxury of calling the cops.

When the abuser is Black, calling the cops could result in a punishment that does not fit the crime.

Jayna: I spend my days counseling and advocating for Black and Brown women experiencing intimate partner violence in Brooklyn, New York. I see my face, my color, my experiences reflected in them. As the pandemic engulfed New York, my in-person sessions moved to video calls. Gone were the days of separating work and professional life; the clients and I now share glimpses into each other's houses, our personal space. With the virtual invitation into their homes, I'm privy to the visceral fear of trying to speak when at any moment, an abusive partner could walk in. The tension and terror seeping through the screen. Each day, black- and brown-hued women flicker across my computer sharing moments of anguish, hesitation, and confusion.

"Do I stay?"

"Do I leave?"

"Do I report?"

"If I report, will he be another Black man in the system?"

"Will I be believed?"

Every question layered with the fear for themselves, their partners, their children. Fear that they will become another stereotype or statistic. Fear that they will never be seen as the "perfect victim" because they're too Black, too loud, too angry, too much. Fear that they won't be believed because they fought back. Fear that the police will show up and their partner will end up with a knee on their neck.

What choice would you make? What if the person who loved you and harmed you could end up the next name we march for?

Discussion Questions

1 What other macro- (legal system, economies, etc.) or mezzo- (race, ethnicity, religion) level factors might prevent someone from calling the police?
2 What alternatives to policing might exist for someone navigating a violent situation?

Try This!

1 Watch one of these films: *Queen and Slim* (2019), *The Hate U Give* (2018), *When They See Us* (2019), *I May Destroy You* (2020).
2 Research the concept "cultural humility" and think about how you might incorporate it in your day-to-day interactions.

12

Discovering Your Social Justice Gift amid the Distraction of Systemic Racism

•••••••••••••••••••••

SIOBHAN E. SMITH-JONES

AND JOHNNY JONES

As we approach the end of summer 2020, we are fairly certain that none of us could have predicted that we would be living amid such times. As we rang in a new year and a new decade, the COVID-19 virus was a little known, publicly ignored phenomenon that was taking us to the depths of a global pandemic. Meanwhile, as our national death toll rose by the thousands per day and America's most resilient cities like New York and New Orleans fell under siege to the virus, Black men and women continued to die at the hands of police officers and civilian vigilantes. As the pandemic loomed, old wounds reopened with the circumstantial and visual agonies of the deaths of Ahmaud Arbery, Breonna Taylor, George Floyd, and Rashard Brooks.

Although these unpredictable events devastated us, we could not foresee the gift of grace that would touch the world as protests in support of #BlackLives-Matter (#BLM) spread globally. In fact, even though we live in Louisville, Kentucky, Breonna Taylor's story was largely unknown until George Floyd's death circulated through social media and Blackfolk rose to calls of "Black Lives Matter!" that reverberated to people of all racial, ethnic, and cultural backgrounds. In this retrospective essay, we honor the call by considering the impact of "official" statements generated in the public eye, how one of our mentors along with others teach us to embody a personal dedication to social justice, and last, to suggest some ways that we can support Black Lives Matter on personal and collective levels. We transform critical writing into memories, thoughts, and reflections that contextualize our lives during this moment of pandemic pause and public provocation. Italicized words belong to either author or are shared memories/opinions of African Americans in the United States. Spaces, such as this book, allow us to engage, emote, and express affect through what feminist scholar Peggy Phelan calls performative writing.[1]

As the longest spring break ever extended into the summer shutdown, national organizations, institutions, and corporations flooded their websites, social media, the twenty-four-hour news cycle, and even commercial time putting out statements to endorse #BlackLivesMatter. Seemingly overnight, organizations were being held to task both internally and externally to provide these statements. The public demanded these statements and organizations were hard-pressed to provide politically correct responses. In fact, *not* providing a statement sent its own message, or an organization whose statement did not match with its actions then had to respond to situations of crisis communication and sometimes prepare another statement. For example, the most impacting personal experience with these statements occurred recently when the University of Louisville followed its official statement to stand with Black Lives Matter with an agenda to become "the premier anti-racism metropolitan university." This announcement was followed weeks later with the university closing most of its daily operations due to #BLM protests on August 25.

On a personal level, these statements were confusing. Should we not be happy that the university and other organizations, such as our academic departments, professional organizations, and even Starbucks, were supporting the movement? Should we not feel good knowing that Walmart was finally affirming that Black lives matter? However, our discussions with family, loved ones, and friends revealed how we were not impressed and slightly offended by the statements. It was even more offensive to learn that many of us were being asked to speak on behalf of Blackfolk about the circumstances. We really did not care too much about the statements either way; these organizations could keep them or leave them. After some soul searching, we were finally able to articulate why these statements meant very little to us:

> Have you ever been in a bathroom in a restaurant or other place where food is served and seen the "Employees must wash hands before returning to work" sign? One experiences a strange, uncomfortable response whenever she sees these signs and these statements. Who are these messages are targeting and why? Is it for customers, to reassure them that they can indeed trust that their servers practice good hygiene, at least when they are working with the food at

their job? Does it perhaps guilt some dirty-handed customers that if the waitstaff washes their hands, that they should/could, too, instead of simply walking out of the restroom? Is this sign meant to compel employees to wash their hands or either to remind them of that employee who *did not* wash his hands? Do employees roll their eyes, thinking that it is micromanaging on the part of their employer to tell them that they should wash their hands? Mind you, we are all aware of people who do not practice the best hand hygiene, as we have all been witness to someone who enters the restroom after us, uses it, and exits *before* us in less than twenty seconds. This sign is definitely for them, right? We could go on, but again, what is confusing is not knowing who is the target audience of this sign.

We are equally unsure of whom the #BlackLivesMatter endorsements are targeting. Are these statements supposed to make us, as Black wo/men, feel encouraged/safe/good knowing that these organizations were supporting the cause? Are these statements letting other organizations know where they stand ("WE support #BLM, do you???")? Are they drawing their line in the sand for consumers who support their brands but did not or do not support the movement? Again, we do not know the target audience for these statements, and we cannot be sure that they are for us.

And why now? George Floyd is not the first Black man to be seen killed on video at the hands of police charged with protecting and serving the community. What changed? Ahmaud Arbery is not the first Black man killed in his neighborhood by white vigilantes who felt that they had every right to do what they were doing to "protect" their neighborhood, even if it meant killing another person. Breonna Taylor is not the first innocent bystander to lose her life to fearful, trigger-happy police officers in a horribly botched case of mistaken identity. What is so different that a simple, misunderstood sentiment, #BlackLivesMatter, is now the national rallying cry in places and spaces and for people who seemed to reject the statement when it first trended in 2013 in the wake of the George Zimmerman's not-guilty verdict for the murder of Trayvon Martin?

> We share collective memories as young children, living in the Arkansas Delta when we first saw the terrifying picture of Emmett Till's fourteen-year-old body lying in a casket after white men lynched him during his summer visit from Chicago to Mississippi with family. This was the summer of rock and roll 1955. Till's mother, Mamie Till-Mobley, chose to keep the casket open at her son's funeral, and a collective catharsis—"church"—was started: John H. Johnson, founder of Johnson Publications, published a photo of the boy's disfigured face in *Jet* magazine, helping to incense Blackfolk's push for civil rights. Somewhere on the West End of Louisville, a thirteen-year-old Cassius Clay viewed the photo of his fellow teenager and responded to it with an adolescent angst toward his own individual beautifully grotesque

transformation into Muhammed Ali. The photograph makes a statement unlike the summer 2020 statements. This statement is as impacting as Malcolm X and Martin Luther King's voices, but Malcolm's bullet wounds opened Ali's psyche evermore. Jesse Jackson immersed his hands into the blood puddles pouring from MLK's neck on April 4, 1968, but Mississippi burned, Memphis burned, Chicago, Detroit, and DC burned evermore, all in response to bullets stopping the heart, ripping through vocal cords, assassinating voice, erupting revolution, exerting the force of the struggle and continuing to make Blackfolk hear, see, reproduce, and restore each other more than any statement can ever do. *Jet* magazine, the official publication of many Black family households, republished the photograph once a year. If you were Black and regularly visited your beauty shop, barbershop, or your grandmama's house between 1955 and the early 2000s, you probably read *Jet* and turned a page to that photograph at least once. It haunted you, taught you, and reminded you of the horrors of domestic terrorism born from the systemic racism prevalent in the United States. Till's mother recognized the power that an image would make for decades to come. We have seen postcards featuring lynched Black bodies and our people, even children, sprayed with water hoses, attacked by dogs, and burned with hot coffee as they protested during sit-ins.

So, today, as we struggle to understand what is different about people today with the current barrage of statements and newfound concerns, we cautiously hope for change. As we see footage of people in Japan declaring that Black Lives Matter, we are encouraged. As we see our twelve- and thirteen-year-old nieces debating the issues and challenging the racism, sexism, xenophobia, rejection of logic and medical science, and the presidential ignorance of Forty-Five, we are encouraged. Yet, we have lost more lives at the hands of police, and as we acknowledge those we have lost, we accept that we will have to utter the names of many more.

In summary, we do not acknowledge random endorsements of Black Lives Matter because for us, our lives have always mattered. The truth, however, is that as a country, and as the self-proclaimed leader of the free world, the United States of America has not dealt with and admitted to the systemic racism on which its institutions, organizations, companies, and commercial industries prevail. Unless we make major changes to structures that include our media, healthcare, education, religious, and familial systems that impact our identities and intersectionalities, we will return to the past, another Jacob Blake will occur, and we will stay where we are. Statements are not enough. We all know the adage "Actions speak louder than words." Another way of saying it is, "Do not talk about it; be about it." "Put your money where your mouth is." "Put some skin in the game." "Walk it like I talk it." Or another old phrase that goes a little something like, "You should not have to tell someone you are a Christian; they should be able to tell." Kindness to humanity should always resonate. Something about the person should be different. Something about us should be different.

If #BlackLivesMatter really does matter to those who now proclaim it, then our so-called Christian nation's behaviors should change to reflect this. Our workplaces and spaces should not see it as a branding approach or trendy logo. Black Lives Matter should be a belief that we hold in our hearts; we should not have to tell others that we support it—we should just be about it.

For many in Louisville, J. Blaine Hudson comes to mind. One of our most amazing mentors who truly worked for social justice, Dean Hudson was the former dean of the College of Arts and Sciences at the University of Louisville. He attended U of L as a student who protested on its campus during the late 1960s. Ironically, he became a dean, and his research, teaching, and service all exemplified his support of social change. For instance, he held Saturday Academy, which brought scholars from the university to share their work with members of the Portland Community, a predominately Black and impoverished area of the city. He wrote historical markers for locations around Louisville. He dedicated his life to reform, and rightly so, today he is a part of a memorial that celebrates local Louisville civil rights activists. He did not resort to statements or worry about how social change would impact his brand; social justice was his brand, a personal promise to himself that reverberated in the work we saw him do, read about or heard about him doing. Many at U of L still miss him. But even after his passing in 2012, he encourages us to be the best professors that we can be. Rather than sit back and enjoy privilege, we better understand the responsibility to affirm Black life through research and creative work, classes that we teach, the students whom we influence and empower, and the ways in which we strive to improve.

So how can you make sure that you are personally committed to #BLM beyond your workplace organizational statement? Romans 12:6–8 (NIV) provides some courageous and simple tasks: "We have different gifts, according to the grace given to each of us. If your gift is prophesying, then prophesy in accordance with your faith; if it is serving, then serve, if it is teaching, then teach; if it is to encourage, then give encouragement; if it is giving, then give generously; if it is to lead, do it diligently; if it is to show mercy, do it cheerfully." We encourage you to use the social justice gift that you possess. Learn the deeper connections between spiritual obedience and civil disobedience and how doing both can serve humanity. We can say the names of victims. We can find power wherever we are and speak truth to it. We can grieve publicly like Jesse Jackson or like *Real Housewives of Atlanta* Porsha Williams, getting arrested with thousands of men and women. We may transform ourselves like Muhammad Ali or healthcare workers turned frontline warriors fighting the visibly affective enemy that is coronavirus. As previously mentioned, Mamie Till-Mobley made a choice after the loss of her only child that would make a statement that would affect a whole movement. Before this, she was the mother of her son, Emmett.

We do not have to wait for more tragedy or inspiration; the struggle continues. Do not feel bad if you do not/cannot march. If you are good at planning, consider organizing, coordinating, and linking like-minded people. Foster partnerships.

Are you a creative talent? Think about how your art forms can bring awareness. Theater, poetry, music, and sculpture have no limits. As the freedom fighter (by way of All-American college football star, lawyer, linguist, orator, opera singer, and Broadway actor) Paul Robeson said in 1937, "The artist cannot hold himself aloof. Through the destruction in certain countries of the greatest of man's cultural heritage, through the propagation of false ideals of racial and national superiority, the scientist, the writer, the artist is challenged. The challenge must be taken up."[2]

If you are a teacher, teach. As a student, how can you be a part of honest and respectful class discussions? If you are a parent, child, ally, politician, or friend, your actions, big or small, will lead to the structural change that #BLM demands. Consider how you can make a political tithe to social justice organizations including your college sorority or fraternity. If you attended a historically Black college or university, you know what you need to do. Whatever you can offer to make a difference, do not be distracted. Do the work.

Rest in power, Chadwick Boseman.

Discussion Questions

1 What does a personal commitment to racial justice look like for you personally?
2 How should organizations communicate support for social justice movements?

Try This!

Do some soul-searching. What is your social justice gift, and how will you use it to serve your local, state, national, and/or global community? Invite a friend to join you.

Notes

1 Peggy Phelan, *Mourning Sex: Performing Public Memories* (New York: Routledge, 1997).
2 In Sam Chin, "Paul Robeson, Spain, 1938—The Artist Cannot Hold Himself Aloof," YouTube, February 10, 2017, https://youtu.be/-ieHA_1y8dQ.

13

Sexuality in My Reality

•••••••••••••••••••••

An Autoethnography of a Black
Woman's Resistance of Sexual
Stereotypes

SAVAUGHN WILLIAMS

Image means a lot when you are a Black little girl, from your hair to clean underwear—you must always look nice and respectable. This has been in my mind since childhood. The "sex talk" for me was given by a signed permission slip to endure the lesson with many others in my eighth-grade class. I was not exposed to hypersexualized clothing, my pajamas constantly covered me (i.e., a nightgown, pants, T-shirt). Tights were a must when going to church, and I did not get a bikini until halfway through high school less I be thought of as "too grown."[1] These specific clothing choices were predicated on a major lesson: protection. Protecting Black girls from historical sexual stereotypes and those who wish to take advantage of such imagery.[2] My mother protected me from these stereotypes. Yet being an only girl in a family of boys left me with unanswered questions, fear for my life and image, and self-rejection. What if they think I am promiscuous or "too fast"? I am afraid to be "*that* Black girl"— you know, the one who people look at and think "Oh, she's ratchet" or "Did her mother not teach her how to be a lady?" or "She doesn't have any home training." Such statements plague me at twenty-five, prompting my need to reexamine my experiences at the intersection of being a Black girl and being a Black woman. I am hoping to cross boundaries within myself to create meaning to my sexual experiences across my lifetime and understanding to my sexuality through this short autoethnography.

When did you realize that you were different? When did you notice that you conducted relationships differently or that you held different morals than others? I knew at a young age. I remember being at summer camp around the age of six or seven and coming in from the pool, all the girls changing in the bathroom. I was the child who waited for a stall to open up, not wanting others to see me naked (I am still this child). *Already aware of my body and the need to cover it up for protection.* I remember being invited to play spin the bottle at my first party in sixth grade and saying no under the guise of my "best friend" having a crush on one of the guys and not wanting to get in the way. I was honestly terrified of kissing anyone. Who knew what consequences it could have on my image and my life? Going through middle school, I did not wear makeup, as this was for grown-ups. What sense did I have wearing something that would make me look older, and who did I have to be "grown" for? These questions were always present in my mind growing up. Getting older included curves and bumps that I was unprepared to understand. Cheering in high school, I always made sure my skirt was on the long side. I was plagued with ensuring that my clothes covered me. These messages of modesty did not only come from my parents but also from my interpersonal interactions with those outside my family. Do not wear shorts that are too short when my brothers had friends over. You will not wear only a sports bra and shorts when you are at gymnastics; you will cover up. These instances were emphasized alongside language such as "chickenhead," the later term "thot," both words that shame the sexual exploration of young women and women in general. Those words lead to statements such as "Oh, she's too fast" and pushed me further away from confirming these negative stereotypical images through my clothes and communication.

My stereotype fear[3] followed me through college, where I crushed on boys from afar and went to parties, only to avoid any type of move toward romance. I did have my first kiss my freshmen year, but it was far from how I imagined it would happen and occurred without my consent. I went with my friend to see a guy she liked. I should have known by the Confederate flag on the wall that the night was not going to go well for me, but I wanted to be a good friend. The Band Perry was playing "If I Die Young," and I was sitting on the bed with a group of people, while my friend was slow dancing with her crush. His friend from home (a white boy who was missing two front teeth with braces) asked me to dance, and I said, "No, I'm good." He kept insisting, so I finally caved—*a habit I have only just began breaking.* While we were dancing, I was singing along to the song when he turned to me and said, "Look at them." I looked over my shoulder and saw my friend and her beau making out. He then looked at me and said, "We should do that, too." I moved my face muscles to show distaste, saying no while shaking my head, but he kissed me anyway. *What a dick move! I was pissed that*

that moment was taken from me. I was pissed that being a good friend would have those consequences. The song ended shortly after the kiss, and I made an excuse to leave. *Thank God I went to a private Catholic college that had curfews.*

That kiss has been branded into my head. An experience that I will relive in accounts to future partners and family members. An embarrassing moment in my oral history. After that, I felt like I made a conscious decision to ignore all physical and romantic gestures in my direction. I avoided and still do avoid eye contact with men who I think might be interested in me sexually. I do not want to cause someone to look at me and think of me sexually. Pushing me to want to do everything in my power to deny that image. I do not want a meeting of eyes to be construed as something more than friendship. I do not want my independence and confidence to be misconstrued as sexual, sensual, or exotic. I do not want to worry that my existence will be based off a Jezebel character that society has typecasted all Black women for. My sexuality always seems to be determined by others before I get the chance to even think about it. My body is placed on a pedestal by societal expectations before I can comprehend how I look and feel. Male gazes use privilege to take what they please with no regard to how I want to give myself or if I even want to give up myself in that manner.

My intentional disassociation with sex and sexiness has often felt like a basic necessity for my life and health. Every doctor's appointment is filled with the underlying assumptions of me being sexually risky, careless, and promiscuous. The question "Are you sexually active?" followed by my response, "No, I am not sexually active," only to be answered by an eyebrow raise of the nurse as if to say, "Of course you are." The doctor questioning my truthfulness by disregarding my questions and circling back around to "Well, if you are having sex . . ." as though I am less of his patient and more of an image in the textbook he read from in school. After switching doctors, I finally got the courage to ask questions. I was excited and nervous, and my doctor was a younger woman of color. During my doctor's appointment, I told her I had been discussing sex with my partner, and I was having issues relaxing and having vaginal intercourse. Being a twenty-three-year-old virgin, I expected her answer to be filled with understanding and patience or at least an explanation for why this was happening. Instead, I was met with a dismissive response, her stating, "I don't know how to help you. You just need to relax." I was stunned and disappointed. I "just need to relax"? When my image and body does not feel like my own, how can I "relax"? When both majority and minority eyes look at me as exotic and promiscuous before ever seeing me as human, where can I find any form of acceptance? I was upset that a woman of color could look at me, a young Black woman, and essentially tell me, "I can't help you and I do not want to," further solidifying my need to avoid all aspects of sexuality to protect myself.

I have most recently had an awakening and punched a hole in the patriarchal box, with the music of Megan Thee Stallion. Megan Thee Stallion is a female rapper from Houston, Texas, whose music is currently at center rap music. Her music revolves around the "hot girl" mentality which speaks to feminist values. I was turned onto this music by a white coworker who leaned over the divider and asked, "Have you ever heard of Megan Thee Stallion?" I responded, "No." She went on to gush about her and how beautiful and talented she was, then showed me a music video of Megan rapping. My initial thoughts fell somewhere between "Wow, she is beautiful" and "I could never be that cool." Many of my thoughts leading back to my body and apparent lack of acceptance for my body's curves. Megan Thee Stallion was wearing less than my confidence would allow and twerking way past what my rudimentary cheeks would ever let me. I was jealous at first that a Black woman would get to live so freely that her ass and knees were praised by all those who witnessed. Such jealousy was short-lived; once I started to listen to her lyrics, I began to understand how her "hot girl" mentality was really a way to focus on self and not others. Lyrics like "Damn, I want some head, but I chose the dough instead. I could neva eva let a nigga fuck me out this bread" play through the air like a church choir finally coming forth to advocate for Black women, for me.

Although these lyrics are something that I loudly declare in my car and apartment, I still worry about the controlling images that are present in society. My fear of stereotypes is still following me like a shadow. I listen to Megan Thee Stallion to reject this fear. Megan Thee Stallion's music does not align with stereotypes like the Jezebel or the Gangster Bitch.[4] Megan Thee Stallion functions outside of the stereotypical perceptions of Black women. She is a full-time student and environmental activist alongside a "hot girl." Her willingness to be unapologetically herself is admirable. I find that for me, dancing to her music is a form of fighting self-rejection. I let a confidence fill me that has alluded me for a long time. Her brown skin and natural curves reflect back on me helping me see myself. Singing along to her music "I'm a boss bitch, I don't need help" uplifts my independence. My favorite song plays in my mind "Please stop playing with me, bitch," rejecting my own self-condemnation and the stereotypes that I encounter daily. Although listening and singing these songs seems like a small step, the lyrics preach a sexual freedom that I did not know could exist for Black women. Each time I listen, I resist the stereotypes and controlling images. I embrace my own existence as a sexual Black woman. Working toward unlearning the toxic ideals and becoming myself through the rejection of the patriarchy in Megan Thee Stallion's music is a first step toward a journey to accept myself outside of stereotypes.

Discussion Questions

1 What dominant stereotypes about Black women have affected this author?
2 The author discusses how race and gender have shaped the stereotypes that influence her relationship with sex. How does she go about rejecting these stereotypes?
3 How does the author use feminist values to resist patriarchy?

Try This!

Create a biography of your sexuality or your body. What are the defining moments you recall most vividly on the journey to becoming yourself?

Notes

1   Robin M. Boylorn, "'Sit with Your Legs Closed!' and Other Sayin's from My Childhood," in *Handbook of Autoethnography*, ed. Stacy Holman Jones, Tony E. Adams, and Carolyn Ellis (Walnut Creek, CA: Left Coast Press, 2013), 173–185.
2   Sarita Davis and Aisha Tucker-Brown, "Effects of Black Sexual Stereotypes on Sexual Decision Making among African American Women," *Journal of Pan African Studies* 5, no. 9 (2013).
3   Claude M. Steele, *Whistling Vivaldi: How Stereotypes Affect Us and What We Can Do* (New York: Norton, 2011).
4   Dionne P. Stephens and Layli Phillips, "Integrating Black Feminist Thought into Conceptual Frameworks of African American Adolescent Women's Sexual Scripting Processes," *Sexualities, Evolution & Gender* 7, no. 1 (2005): 37–55.

14

The Forgotten Ones
(for Those Who Survive
Black Death)

• •

ROBIN M. BOYLORN

The past few months have felt like the end times. The sting and stench of death hanging heavily in the humidity of the seventh summer in a row that will be remembered for murder. Like others, I have been restless, sleepless, and hopeless—speechless. Most recently because of the unnecessary deaths of over 600,000 people due to COVID-19, which disproportionately impacts communities of color due to socioeconomic status, preexisting health conditions, and exposure to the virus due to their work environments. Black people are dying at double the rate of other Americans, but the global pandemic is not the only looming threat to our lives. Anti-Blackness and racism are just as deadly as an indiscriminate disease. Breonna Taylor, George Floyd, Rayshard Brooks, Daniel Prude, Oluwatoyin Salau, and Ahmaud Arbery did not die in 2020 because of COVID; they died because Black lives and the lives of Black women are seen as expendable, transferrable, of little worth. I fear desensitization to the normalization of Black death as I reflect on how Black life has been unapologetically stolen in the time since Michael Brown's death sparked the movement for Black lives in 2014.

In 2016, a month before Korryn Gaines was murdered in her home and two years before Stephon Clark and Bothan Jean would be murdered in 2018, Alton Sterling was murdered by Baton Rouge police officers Blane Salamoni and Howie Lake, caught on tape from multiple angles, reminiscent of Eric Garner's body being wrestled to the ground, held down until breathless. The gunshots startled me, coming from nowhere and for no reason, even after I watched the video three times in disbelief. Hours later, the wails of his son, Cameron, crying for his father, haunted me. The pain of his loss was visceral and I felt it, carried it, pushed it into the center of my being, alongside the losses of dozens of other Black women and men murdered by police in the years preceding his death. I didn't feel like I was capable of carrying more grief, and then less than twenty-four hours later, I unwillingly witnessed the death of Philando Castile. His bullet-ridden body collapsed on itself, blood-soaked shirt, shocked eyes, seat belt fastened. He did not do anything wrong. As he lay there dying, his girlfriend, Diamond, started a Facebook Live stream so that the public could bear witness to what she and her four-year-old daughter were seeing: a police officer's gun still drawn on her beloved's broken body, his arm hanging like a broken tree limb, his eyes fixed on the roof of the car, subtle if any movement in his chest. She says, "Stay with me," to him before recounting the events that preceded the shooting into her phone to us, before being called from the car and handcuffed, before being isolated and interrogated. She did not do anything wrong. The blank screen and pleading prayer broke my heart as she cried out, "We are an innocent people," and her four-year-old daughter, practicing the solemnity of strength Black women are forced to learn sooner or later, saying soothingly, "It's okay, Mama. . . . It's okay. I'm right here with you." My heart broke.

In 2020, when George Floyd's murder was captured on tape, I was already so traumatized from yearslong state-sanctioned murder and Black death that I refused to watch the video circulating on social and news media. Still, I concentrated my gaze on the ubiquitous still image of Derek Chauvin's knee pushed down on Floyd's neck. Comparing Chauvin's smirk and indifference to Floyd's desperation and vulnerability was all I needed to see. Devastation and disgust fueled my sadness in the ensuing days when unsympathetic white people reenacted the scene shown in that infamous image, making a joke of George Floyd's murder in a social media challenge. I realized that cultural reconstructions are both triggering and necessary. Triggering for Black folk who do not need to see a video or picture to know that Black people are killed by police without provocation. Necessary for white people who refuse to believe that Black people are killed by police without provocation.

Problematically, victims are not equally weighted. George Floyd's past and alleged use of a counterfeit twenty-dollar bill, like Michael Brown's stature and alleged theft of cigarillos, worth less than one dollar each, was cause enough, for some people, for them to be executed in the street. For some people, a Black person's engagement with police is reason enough for their death, because of a presumption of guilt or culpability—and a refusal to hold systemic racism or police officers accountable for the automatic criminalization of Black and poor people.

For example, in the public sphere, respectability politics rendered Alton less of a victim than Philando because of an imperfect history and criminal record.

Philando's name was disappeared in media despite the fact that he was a blameless victim, pulled over for driving with a broken taillight. Similar attacks have been leveraged against Black woman victims, narratives suggesting that they are somehow responsible for their own deaths.

Although the names of murdered Black women and men are memorialized, hashtagged, and grieved as we call for and hope for justice that never seems to come, there are forgotten victims in these circumstances that are rarely acknowledged. Loved ones of Black victims are left to pick up the pieces of their lives, left incomplete, by premature death. George Floyd's sisters Bridgett and LaTonya, his brothers Philonese and Terrence, and his five children. Breonna Taylor's mother, Tamika Palmer, Breonna's boyfriend, Kenneth Walker, who was arrested for attempting to defend her and himself when the police ambushed them, erroneously, in their own home. Korryn Gaines's children, including her son who was shot and disabled by one of the bullets that claimed her life. Michael Brown's parents, Quinyetta McMillon, the mother of Alton Sterling's oldest son. Cameron Sterling, Alton's oldest son. His other four children. Sandra Sterling, Alton's aunt. Anjelica Sterling, Alton's sister. Diamond Reynolds, Philando's girlfriend. Her daughter. Valerie Castile, Philando's mother. Allysza Castile, Philando's sister. Their extended families and community. The rest of us who feel implicated because we have Georges, Breonnas, Altons, and Phils in our life and we know it could have been ours, it could have been us.

Black women often carry the brunt and burden of going on when Black men are murdered. Mothers, grandmothers, wives, lovers, daughters, sisters, aunts, and friends are left to make sense of their lives and hold themselves together so that they can hold everyone else up. Quinyetta McMillon, the mother of Alton Sterling's eldest son, has to comfort her child and worry about a world that would render his fate no different from his father's. Diamond (Lavish) Reynolds will be haunted with the memory of watching her boyfriend die with her four-year-old daughter in the back seat watching.

Although the public memory of victims is quickly replaced, the families and loved ones of victims continue to grieve. Grief is an out-of-body and then full-body experience. The necessary numbness that is welcomed in order to function and carry out the rituals of death and the protests for justice will eventually fade and the pain and reality of loss will set in. The stoicism you may marvel at will become inconsolable pain. The fortitude to speak for themselves and their loved ones, both living and dead, will transform to tears.

Black women are no more superhuman than Black men. We feel pain and we fall apart, just like Black men bleed and die. Even though we have watched Black women remarkably hold it together, do not mistake their bravery for strength. The unbreakability of Black women is a myth, and instead of being impressed with our strength and fortitude, be mindful of what you cannot see, be present when the cameras go dim. We have to remember the forgotten victims and know that family and friends of the deceased do not have the luxury of just moving on once their loved ones are buried. Sybrina Fulton is still mourning. Lucy McBath is still mourning. Lezley McSpadden is still mourning. Gwen Carr is still mourning. Samaria Rice is still mourning. The mothers of dead sons and daughters never stop grieving, and their suffering is likely reawakened every time another Black woman or man is murdered by police or white supremacists.

George Floyd tested positive for COVID-19, but he died from a far more deadly pandemic: racism. He should have lived at least two dozen more summers. Breonna Taylor should have lived to manifest all of her dreams. Philando Castile should have lived to be ninety years old. Alton Sterling should have been able to watch his children grow up. The women who loved them should not have to make sense of their sudden absence.

We cannot change what has happened, but we can recognize that the pain we feel in solidarity is only a measure of their loss.

Discussion Questions

1 What are some strategies and actions we can take to remember and acknowledge the living victims of state-sanctioned violence and racism?
2 What does it feel like when you read news of another Black person murdered? Consider your own reactions. How do you engage? What contributes to your pain or what facilitates your disconnection?

Try This!

1 Review news coverage of the cases mentioned above. What differences do you notice in the coverage of violence against Black women versus Black men? What do you think contributes to these differences?
2 Explore the social media reaction to the cases mentioned in this chapter. What do you notice? How does the reaction differ? What aspects of the case do people respond to on social media? How do calls for action or the assignment of blame differ?
3 Write a letter to those who grieve George Floyd or Breonna Taylor. What do you want to communicate? How can you offer solidarity or hold space for their grief?

Note

This chapter is a revision of an earlier posted blog, by the same name, on the Crunk Feminist Collective: https://www.crunkfeministcollective.com/2016/07/08/the -forgotten-ones-for-those-who-survive-black-death/.

15

Performative Activism
• •

Inauthentic Allyship in the
Midst of a Racial Pandemic

TINA M. HARRIS

To say that our lives as we know it have been "flipped, turned upside down" in 2020 is an understatement at the very least. Economic and racial disparities became glaringly apparent when the world was under siege by the coronavirus that was mysteriously being transmitted among people everywhere. Nearly no continent remained untouched. The United States was hit in a particularly hard way because our governmental officials chose to not believe the reality of this health pandemic that has killed 207,000-plus people. Essential workers—Black and Brown bodies—were on the front line, risking life and limb to save the lives of so many of us, to provide services that attempted to summon a sense of normalcy that was never to be. These workers were being sacrificed instead of protected despite the fact that safeguards (i.e., Pandemic Influenza Plan) were in place by the Obama administration to head off this very real threat to humanity. The Trump administration dismantled this task force, which is an unfathomable and unforgivable act. Even still, the racial, ethnic, and economic disparities in our health care system became more pronounced, embarrassingly, sadly, and tragically so. This was then compounded by the racial pandemic that tipped the United States to its boiling point. First, there was the March 13 senseless murder of Breonna Taylor, a twenty-five-year-old African American[1] woman, shot eight times in her sleep in *her home* by Louisville, Kentucky police. Then came the May 25 brutal, unprovoked murder of George Floyd, an African American man, at the hands of Minneapolis, Minnesota police. The police knelt on his neck for eight minutes and forty-nine seconds, and no one did a thing. No one.

The rallying cries for racial justice from people across the humanity spectrum cascaded through the streets, homes, cities, and eventually the world, only to fall on deaf ears. The government and judicial system are physical and ideological structures that epitomize institutionalized racism, systems that in theory are supposed to ensure "liberty and justice for all"; however, they were designed to do exactly the opposite. They function to maintain power imbalances that all but guarantee that all things will remain separate and unequal. These harsh realities became more pronounced at the intersection of the health and racial pandemics that paralyzed the United States and the world. Not surprisingly, the United States became (and continues to be) a spectacle because the fissures in our foundation were revealed, exposed for all the world to see. As an African American woman, the collision of these two oppressive worlds finally shouted to the world and, more specifically the United States, that Black lives *do* matter, that *my* life mattered, *and* the day of reckoning and justice had finally come—or at the least the beginnings were here. Not surprisingly, pieces of my heart were broken with every proclamation on social media, the news, and anywhere else the masses were huddled that every past, present, and future victim of racial profiling and police brutality would never get the justice they so rightly deserve. That could very well include me, too. I did not think of myself but every other Black and Brown boy, girl, man, woman, and nonbinary person whose lives have been devalued for far too long.

Witnessing the never-ending atrocities committed against Blacks is hard, let alone experiencing it firsthand. However, we come from a legacy of survivors who continue to rise from the ashes of injustice that dust our bodies and are washed away by the rivers of our tears. The tears are a mix of joy and pain, oscillating with every harsh blow of injustice that comes our way. Even still, we thrive. We are also tired—exhausted even—in mind, body, and spirit. This metaphor became even more of a reality for me with every passing day during the last sixteen months, particularly in May and June of 2020 when the evidence of our perceived worthlessness as raced and gendered bodies continued to mount. Nevertheless, I persevered in order to protect my mind, body, and spirit from the harsh reality of our "new normal," our "new world," that was not really new. It was just unveiled for all the world to see. This unveiling of the egregious racial and economic disparities and injustices ingrained in the fabric of the United States could no longer be denied. They were lain bare for all to see. Finally seeing our tired souls and spirits, many Caucasian Americans[2] joined in the fight against all of these social ills. I was weak in every fiber of my being, and I found myself oftentimes strengthened, encouraged, and inspired by family, friends, colleagues, and former students (including those of other hues) who were willing to place themselves on the front line to fight for what is right and just. Many became what I call *true advocates* (rather than allies), people with an authentic desire and commitment to use their privilege to fight racial injustices wherever they reside. Some were already "woke," some were lulled into a dream of a postracial slumber, while others were entranced in a deep coma refusing to ever wake up. Another group emerged that was thankfully not in my inner circle. These were people who were engaging in *performative activism* in very disturbing and unsettling ways.

Thankfully and sadly, I was not the only African American or African American woman to witness performative activism in real time. I commiserated with many friends, girlfriends, and colleagues who were tapped out from these speculative performances being enacted on social media, at work, in emails, in direct messages and every other mode of communication. These actions were veiled attempts at expressing, proclaiming solidarity with their Black and Brown sisters and brothers, stressing that Black lives matter, articulating artfully crafted messages of feigned outrage. The hypocrisy did not go unnoticed. I saw many Black friends publicly "calling out" performative activists who either feigned support or remained silent; after all, silence connoted complicity with systemic racism. Personally, I was frustrated and angry. I also realized that, maybe, "everything happens for a reason," and the veil was being pulled back on everyone and everything so that we/I/they could see the truth. The naked truth of racism. The not-so-good, the bad, and the very ugly. I did what my mother always says when you receive a lot of information that you are unsure you can actually use: "Chew the meat and spit out the bones." To preserve my sanity and overall health, I purposely chose to appreciate and connect with those whom I knew were/are true advocates, expecting nothing in return. Those who finally found the courage and boldness to stand up against systemic racism were/are the people who are allowed to remain in my circle. The others with empty and shallow proclamations of their undying commitment to doing the right thing, to push back, and to sacrifice their privilege for the benefit of people who look like me (and me as well, for that matter)? I treat them with a "long-handled spoon." I see them and am grateful to know where they stand. They can act as if they see me, but I see them, too. I see them clearly now that the rain is gone.

For those who resist and are aware of the toxicity of performative activism, I see them, too. I see them for their authentic selves. I see them as being in varying degrees of grappling with the galvanizing reality of systemic racism. Despite the exhaustion of a lifetime of battling racism and classism and who knows what else, I am frequently energized by those white friends and colleagues who not only get it but also do the research required to be in the fight against racism. They do not need my approval, encouragement, or advice. They just do it because it is the right thing to do. It warms my weary heart, mind, body, and soul. I am heartened by their willingness to confront family members, strangers, friends, and anyone else who is on the "other side," perpetuating systemic racism either directly or indirectly. More importantly, I am encouraged that they were and are willing to fight systemic racism in their relationships without much concern for the consequences. They are thirsting for the tools, knowledge, and skills necessary for doing what I call "dismantling racism, one relationship at a time." They want to know how they can communicate to the deniers that racism is real and that a postracial United States is a mythical ideology functioning as a smoke screen to the truth. I can appreciate these people because they recognize the value of all humanity, my humanity, and that of Black and Brown people who look and live like me. That is why I continue to do the difficult work that is required if, in fact, there will be "liberty and justice for all."

I reached a low point somewhere in between the pandemics and wondered, "How can I possibly muster up the strength to dust myself off and get back in the fight without giving in to hopelessness? Does any of this matter?" I could have easily thrown in the proverbial towel, but I know that is not a party of calling or my purpose. Instead, I regained my bearings, dusted myself off, and vowed to fight the good fight, and as the late honorable civil rights activist John Lewis said, I was committed to getting in "good trouble." My resolve was inspired by an email that I received from one of my former students from my spring 2020 undergraduate course. Our time together was cut short by COVID-19 and the university (rightly) shifting course and mandating all classes switch to being taught remotely. Still, I remembered Samantha[3] and many of her peers because they genuinely wanted to know what they could do to make things right. I was impressed by her and many of her peers because they are white and have the "luxury" of ignoring racism; however, instead of engaging in performative activism, they want/ed to know what resources and knowledge they can use to stay in the fight for the long haul. They want to move from theory to practice.

I mention Samantha specifically because she reached out to me in May 2020 and asked me for advice on how she can educate family members about racism. She was frustrated because they did not understand the tipping point that culminated in peaceful marches of resistance that exploded into riots. (We have since learned that most, if not all, of the instigators are white agitators.) Initially, I felt as though I just did not have the time or energy to respond, but after contemplating the gravity of the situation, I blocked out time to draft what I hoped would be an appropriate and effective metaphor she could use to achieve the goal of awareness and enlightenment. After a few minutes, it hit me: racism is akin to a "forced marriage."[4] Twenty minutes later, I birthed what I thought was an accessible analogy that would *surely, hopefully* resonate with those who were in denial of or oblivious to this very real social tragedy that is alive and well. I shared the draft with Samantha, who replied that it was great! It was just what she believed she needed to help her family understand. She even wrote back to let me know that other family members heard the metaphor, and she wanted permission to share the email; I gladly obliged. In turn, I asked for her permission to share the backstory along with the metaphor on my Facebook page.

I posted the text of the metaphor, and almost instantly, it seemed to take on a life of its own. Recognizing the urgency of the moment, I decided to create a video of the metaphor, word for word, line by line. With the exception of an introduction and the backstory, the video was an oral representation of what I believe has become a powerful tool for enlightening those who will choose to actively listen to the reality of racism. As of the writing of this essay, the video has gone viral. There are 4,800 views,[5] and it is my prayer that it will go super viral. I want it to be epic because knowledge is power, and the metaphor speaks power to truth. Here is the exact language I used in the email and on my page in its rawest, truest, and most painful form.

Racism: A Forced Marriage

The best metaphor I can think of at the moment is that African Americans are like an abused partner in an arranged marriage. The marriage was not entered into with joy and excitement (read slavery) as it typically should be. Instead, she is forced into a relationship with a partner who belittles her, believes she is less-than, and does everything in his power to torment her mentally and keep her under his subjection. He occasionally does something nice for her to appease her, but he soon does something to undo that with various forms of abusive behaviors, breeding even more distrust. Her children watch this and learn coping mechanisms to deal with the abuse. They vow to not repeat the cycle or fall victim to it, and sadly, the partner passes this behavior on from generation to generation. It becomes normalized.

For some "wives," they reach their tolerance level and lash out. The expressions of frustration will vary in intensity, and there may come a point over whatever period of time where she lashes out in violence because nothing else has worked to stop the abuse. She has gone to family, friends, agencies, and others to report the abuse, but everyone has turned a deaf ear and blind eye because they don't believe her despite the glaring truth that lies before them. Others witness the abuse and become equally angry and frustrated. While some respond internally, others take on the pain of the other and join in the fight, however that may be. It is a never-ending cycle unless the family members of the abuser intervene and use their relationship or position in society to stop egregious behaviors that have become normalized within the family. While they didn't commit those abusive behaviors themselves, they are complicit because they stood by and did nothing.

Frankly, I am surprised—no, stunned—that this metaphor has been shared by so many people, most of whom I do not know. I cannot explain why I chose that analogy, but I know with every fiber of my being that this metaphor is powerful. It speaks to the depravity of racism, the lengths to which people will go to maintain the status quo and the ways that people will deny this truth.

Nevertheless, I challenge people to refuse to be complicit and to become *true* advocates who risk their privilege in exchange for "justice for all."

The intersecting pandemics have reshaped for me what the essence of allyship should look like. Sadly, the racial and ethnic disparities have been laid bare, and now the United States (and white people in particular) must face the schism that continues to divide us. Yet again, Black Lives Matter has been placed center stage for the whole world to see. The protests are a clarion call to whites, politicians, and others to be socially responsive to the many injustices being perpetuated against their Black and Brown brothers and sisters. This call is putting on display the messiness that has emerged regarding allyship, forcing us all to define the roles and related expectations that white women (and men) should/should not take in this fight against racial injustices. Do I believe it is possible to develop and foster alliances and coconspirators across racial lines? Yes, I do. This means that we all need to call out performative activism in all its forms. For me, there is another part of the equation that requires advocates and coconspirators to have a long-term investment in a proactive process of change where authentic transformation is possible and expected. These people are the ones who selflessly allow their racial privilege to be used to fight the good fight and fiercely tackle racism on an individual, interpersonal, and societal level. It is through this approach that I believe we can "dismantle racism, one relationship at a time."

Discussion Questions

1 How can metaphors help to reduce discrimination or racism?
2 How can you identify performative allyship versus true allyship?

Try This!

Create your own list of metaphors to describe your experience with racism or other social identity–based inequality.

Notes

1 I am using the racial identifiers of Black, Black American, and African American interchangeably.
2 I am using the racial identifiers of white, white Americans, and Caucasian American interchangeably.
3 The pseudonym Samantha is used to protect this student should she not want to be identified.
4 "Forced marriage" was originally used but changed to be culturally appropriate and sensitive.
5 This is the hyperlink to the Facebook video: https://www.facebook.com/tinmarhar/videos/10111747228436890.

Part 2

Narrating the
Material Body

● ●

Although poststructural feminist projects identified bodies as highly discursive sites,[1] communication scholars have moved to simultaneously acknowledge the materiality of the human form. Put simply, there are both physical differences and communicatively constructed meanings attached to particular bodies. The differences between humans both enables and constrains some activities in a very physical sense, such as when people use wheelchairs or audio-assistive technologies, or when women experience pregnancy or birth. However, bodily differences are also socially constructed, including differences in perceptions of race or stereotypes about people with diverse sex or gender identities. As communication scholars Karen Lee Ashcraft, Timothy R. Kuhn, and François Cooren described,

> Physical features assume meaning and influence through their social coding, and it is the mental and relational process of identification that lends order to the body's raw material resources. . . . Our knowledge of the body's meaning is born of interaction, which brings the material body to life—social life, that is. . . . The body becomes a key site for the interpenetration of material and ideational worlds, and communication is how that happens. The realities of harassment[, for example,] are constituted in communication, situated in the context of specific relationships, organizational cultures and politics, and broader Discourses (legal and otherwise) of sex and power.[2]

The readings in this section theorize about both the material and discursive aspects of bodies.

Bodies have historically been understudied in communication scholarship— left implicitly tied to social identities, a marker for diversity categories, but not always directly addressed as a physical, material, and discursively constructed aspect of human experience. Intersectionality has opened the door for studying bodies in all their varied forms and the lived experiences of people who inhabit those bodies. However, we have not yet achieved a robust canon of work in this area. Although feminist projects have, to some extent, fleshed out what it means to be a gendered, classed, raced being, it has not yet moved into other intersections in a thorough way.[3] Anne Helen Petersen claimed, "Our society does not value, trust, or elevate women in the same way it values, trusts, or elevates men. And that doesn't even account for the way that women who are older, or not white, or fatter, or queer, or possess any other unruly quality, fit into that equation."[4] Adding more research about and advocacy for LGBTQI+ bodies, differently abled bodies, fat bodies, and bodies from non-U.S. or U.K. contexts would greatly expand the parameters of feminism. Exploring the embodied experiences of individuals across additional intersections will enrich understandings about our lived experiences in our bodies, in their material and discursive forms.

Discussion Questions

1 Often, people do not talk about weight, medical conditions, or sexual assault. However, all of the chapters in this section push past "comfortable conversation." What is achieved when publicly advocating for these often-silenced experiences and social identities?

2 Huerta Moreno (chapter 18) illuminates the complex relationship between race, sexuality, gender, and power. In what ways do these intersections matter in higher education and in other organizational contexts? What about the intersections of fatness and sexuality, as described by Ellis and Noveiri (chapter 16)?

3 The readings in this section highlight the public nature of talking about embodied experiences. Have you had experience disclosing private experiences relating to your body? What are some of the challenges related to such disclosures? What opportunities came from the disclosures and conversations?

Notes

1 Chris Weedon, *Feminist Practice and Poststructuralist Theory*, 2nd ed. (New York: Blackwell, 1997).
2 Karen Lee Ashcraft, Timothy R. Kuhn, and François Cooren, "Constitutional Amendments: 'Materializing' Organizational Communication," *Academy of Management Annals* 3, no. 1 (2009): 1–64.

3 For important exceptions, see, for example, Cristin A. Compton, "Managing Mixed Messages: Sexual Identity Management in a Changing US Workplace," *Management Communication Quarterly* 30, no. 4 (2016): 415–440; James McDonald, "Coming out in the Field: A Queer Reflexive Account of Shifting Researcher Identity," *Management Learning* 44, no. 2 (2013): 127–143; Joëlle M. Cruz, "Invisibility and Visibility in Alternative Organizing: A Communicative and Cultural Model," *Management Communication Quarterly* 31, no. 4 (2017): 614–639.
4 Anne Helen Petersen, *Too Fat, Too Slutty, Too Loud: The Rise and Reign of the Unruly Woman* (New York: Plume, 2017), xv.

16

Nevertheless,
She Feels Pretty

• •

A Critical Co-constructed
Autoethnography on Fat
Persistence and Resistance

CASSIDY D. ELLIS AND

SARAH GONZALEZ NOVEIRI

Feeling pretty, attractive, or sexy while living in a fat body is inherently an act of resistance, an attempt to persist despite stigmas associated with the fat body. Mainstream media and common discourse on fatness pathologizes the fat body, abjects the fat body, and monsterizes the fat body, assembling it as a disgusting health hazard. Persistence is made particularly difficult for those whose bodies are reduced to a number that determines their worth. Fat people—particularly fat women—who celebrate rather than castigate their bodies are said to be "glorifying obesity."

> 45.2. According to mainstream discourses on fatness and the fat body, my worth and my health as a fat person is reduced to the number 45.2—my body mass index (BMI). My physical fitness, general health, and ability to live comfortably and without shame are collapsed into the number 45.2.

How do I persist in a body that is considered diseased? Sick. Dying. "Childhood obesity is associated with . . . premature death and disability in adulthood" ("Obesity and Overweight"). I've been "obese" my entire life, yet I persist into adulthood. Despite the social norms that tell me to be invisible in my hypervisible body, I resist. I resist through my ability to find beauty in a body I'm told every day is a project to be fixed, forever a "before photo." I resist the shaming, silencing, and stigmatization society forces upon the corpulent. Through my resistance, I persist. Resisting my internalized mandate to do otherwise, I allow myself to feel pretty in all my body's forms. I persist in appreciating each freckle, each fleshy fold, each mole, each scar, and each stretch mark that makes my body mine. Social norms and mainstream medical discourses collapse all of me into one number: 45.2. But I resist, and nevertheless, I feel pretty.

In 2018, Amy Schumer starred in a romantic comedy titled *I Feel Pretty*. The film was called "quietly revolutionary" by *Rolling Stone* author Amy Nicholson because of the way Schumer's character (Renee) supposedly reflects "ordinary" women's insecurities with their bodies.[1] Other outlets similarly lauded her bravery for voicing the everywoman's experience and for displaying her vulnerability on screen through presenting "ordinary" bodies. Lamenting hatred for her looks, the film centers on Renee's struggles with accepting her (incredibly unincredible) body. This chapter argues that *I Feel Pretty* appropriates fat embodied experiences. This appropriation misrepresents experiences had by fat people and, while posing as inclusive of all bodies, actually contributes to the marginalization and exclusion of fat bodies from mainstream media.

In this essay, we follow Cann and DeMeulenaere who propose critical co-constructed autoethnography as a method that encourages particular attention to racial dynamics at work in personal narratives and "allows collaborating researchers and writers to more accurately represent the tempo, . . . intimacy, . . . uncertainty, and complexity of relationships—creating a space for colleagues engaged in critical work to reflect together."[2] We utilize performative writing as a means of expressing our narratives, weaving narrative and theory, to illustrate the ways in which theory exists on and within our bodies as fat women. In her chapter "Performing Writing," Della Pollock describes performative writing as "an important, dangerous, difficult intervention into routine representations of social/performative life."[3] We use performative writing to make interventions into the routine representations of fatness in everyday life and to illustrate the discontinuities in the way fatness is performed by Schumer in *I Feel Pretty*.

Performative writing pushes back against the textuality and politics deeply entrenched into academics that ignore what writing *does* in the world and that prefers the objective writer over the subjective. Through performative writing, we challenge these norms. One specific way we do this is through the use of the second-person "you" in our narratives. We use the second-person "you" throughout the analyzed narratives to exemplify the ways in which our experiences as fat women are not isolated, occurring in a vacuum, but rather are representative of quotidian struggles fat people (particularly fat women) endure. We use the second-person "you" to bring you, the reader, into our experience as fat women. Our intention is also to potentially implicate the reader. It is common to hear those who are not socially constructed as fat or live as a fat person use comments about "feeling fat" or "looking fat" despite their thin privilege. We use the second person ("you") as a means of humanizing fat women and forcing readers—regardless of their body size—to reckon with the way fat women are oppressed in society. Fat is not just a feeling. Finally, we also push back against academic norms of ownership by using "you" rather than "I" in our narratives. Our narratives are *ours* as fat women who collectively experience this oppression and are subjected to body-based traumas. That said, we acknowledge and appreciate the complexity of intersectional identities. Thus, our use of "you" doesn't seek to establish generalizability and is not meant to flatten our intersectional experiences.

Through layering our narratives between synopses of the film,[4] we point to a disconnection between "body positivity" and performances of fatness as presented in Schumer's *I Feel Pretty* and lived experiences of fat people. More specifically, we depict the trauma and shame fat people often experience due to the negative social discourses attached to their (our) bodies and the disembodying effects of these discourses in the lives of those who inhabit fat bodies. Additionally, while "heteronormative temporal arrangements regulate fat bodies," our atemporal narratives of fat oppression disrupt the linearity of time in the film synopsis, illustrating the ways in which "fat bodies fail to 'keep up' with normative tempos."[5]

Through narrativizing our life as fat women, we problematize performances of fatness in *I Feel Pretty*. Specifically, we find four themes within our narratives and the film synopsis: (1) hyper(in)visibility of fat people, (2) structural barriers fat people experience, (3) experiences pertaining to desirability of fat women, and (4) experiences of violence against fat bodies. We use our narratives to explore the idea of persisting while living in a body that is pathologized and abhorred in society at large, an idea that "average-bodied" people like Amy Schumer (who admittedly wears a US size 6–8[6]) are not forced to consider. We layer these narrative vignettes between a synopsis of the film in order to depict the disconnection between the representation of supposedly nonnormatively sized Amy Schumer and our experiences living in a fat body. This chapter therefore serves as a form of embodied knowledge, uplifting the experiences of fat people that have been systematically excluded from popular culture as well as academic discourse. Before we turn to our narratives and film synopsis, we briefly discuss literature relating to representations of fat bodies and the ways fat people come to understand themselves as fat.

Representing and Learning an "Unfit Identity"

Our experiences as fat women navigating a fatphobic society are not well represented in the media at large. Prior research on representations of fat women in the media describe the ways in which fat bodies are often reduced to punch lines of comedy and are most often represented as "headless fatties." In most cases, fat characters lack agency and dimension. Gullage, for instance, analyzes the character Fat Monica in the immensely popular television sitcom *Friends*. Fat Monica appears in only a few episodes of the series' ten-year run; however, the character is of great importance for Monica's character development. Courteney Cox, who plays Monica, wears a fat suit when portraying Fat Monica. Gullage argues that "actors wearing fat suits depict dominant understandings that fat people are lazy, gluttonous, and unable to control their appetites."[7] Specifically, Gullage articulates the ways in which the character Fat Monica represents particular performances of whiteness, femininity, and class, as well as heterosexual desirability.

Additionally, Hole interrogates "whether contemporary fat female comedians are doing anything to undermine common-sense understandings of their body's supposed innate funniness" through analyzing the comedy of Dawn French, a fat comedian.[8] With a postmodern lens, Hole argues that "the fat female figure resists . . . simple categorization as Woman but rather plays with notions of gendered identity."[9] French's comedy, Hole argues, exposes the "falsity" in the construction of femininity in Western culture through French's unique composition of her fat femininity.[10] Gullage and Hole both make strong arguments about fat women and the media, but neither consider the ways in which embodied fat experiences are at work in these representations.

Although it is important to discuss the ways fatness is represented in the media, it is also imperative to consider the ways in which people—women particularly—come to understand themselves as fat. In Rice's study of girls' acquisition of a fat identity, participants describe coming to understand fat as an "unfit identity," which "has become a major marker of difference for many girls growing up in the West."[11] One factor that contributed to this understanding includes the gaze of boys and men on their growing girl-bodies. Additionally, both anti-"obesity"[12] programs sponsored by the Canadian government and experiences in physical fitness programs in school contributed to their understanding of fat as an unfit identity. Thus, from previous literature, we can surmise that a confluence of factors from media representation to interpersonal relationships to the institution of education contribute to a person's understanding of their fat identity.

Do You Feel Pretty?

Schumer's film *I Feel Pretty* participates in a problematic history of representations of fat women and fat identity. The film begins by introducing the protagonist, Renee Bennett (played by Schumer). Renee is an average, good-looking thirtysomething woman who has major self-esteem issues. In one of the first scenes, Renee enters a clothing store where she is told they do not carry her size and suggests she should check online instead. Disheartened, she later attends an indoor cycling class. Soon after the class starts, her seat collapses—not due to her weight but because the seat is broken—and she is injured. This is one of many instances of injury to Renee's body in conjunction with her self-esteem. She pulls herself up by her bootstraps, and the next day, Renee goes to work. We learn she works for LeClaire Cosmetics, a prominent company in the beauty industry. Her office is in a dank and dark basement, far away from the posh main building in the middle of the city, but she dreams of one day working there among all the beautiful, modelesque women.

> When you were younger, you'd often end a day of shopping for school clothes hot, sweaty, and in tears. Spending hours in the junior's section of stores like JCPenny or Dillard's rifling through stacks upon stacks of pants and slacks in search for your size, you'd eventually give up after trying on the two pairs you might come across buried deeply beneath all the size 00s, 2s, 6s, and 8s. Depending on your age, you would be looking for a 12–18. Always in "long" because of your height. Shopping would leave you feeling disheartened, ugly, and like your body did not belong. It was something that exceeded the "junior's" section yet did not fit into the "women's" or "petites" sections either.
>
> Although you no longer cry while shopping for clothes, you still have moments in which you feel as though your body is wrong. When you try on countless shirts, dresses, or pants that in some way don't fit, you begin to feel like your younger self. You see her in the mirror crying and hating her body for its excess. Over the years, however, you've learned strategies to avoid this. You only go into particular stores that you know sell your sizes or that you know have a good selection of clothes in your sizes. You mentally prepare for many things not fitting your body in the way you want, and you allow yourself surprise when they do. You've learned to feel confident in clothes that are difficult to access, often have to be purchased online, and are priced higher than "normal" sizes.

In a later scene, Renee becomes distraught by her reflection and runs out of her apartment to a wishing fountain where she wishes to be beautiful. She is disappointed when she looks into a mirror afterward, scrutinizing every inch of her body and face, and realizes the wish did not come true. The following day, Renee builds up her courage and goes back to the cycling class. This time, the class seems to be going well, the instructor shouts motivational quotes, and she feels inspired by them. She pedals—faster and faster—but suddenly, Renee's shoe detaches from the bicycle pedal, and she falls very violently to the floor, hitting her head hard on the ground. Handfuls of hair are pulled out of her scalp, and she briefly loses consciousness.

> Growing up, you never thought your weight and your body were an issue. Before high school (or secondary school in the British educational system), you were always seen as a social butterfly. You had friends, you got invited to birthday parties, and you got along really well with everyone in your class. Once boys became something to be interested in other than for friendships and play, everything changed. A list started circulating in school. The names of most of your girl classmates were in that list, and they were ranked from "who would you fuck" (*a quien te tirarias*) to "wouldn't touch with the end of a stick" (*no la toco ni con la punta de un palo*). Your name was at the bottom of that list. Alongside your name, each and every boy in class had written comments justifying the position you had been given.
>
> The list was brought to your attention by one of your friends, Clara. She intercepted it going from one class section to another and thought you had to be aware of what was going on. The comments did hurt, deeply. Why did you need to see this? What would you gain from knowing all these things? One of those comments read, "She's like a fucking elephant, she disgusts me so much, I can't even look at her, I hope she dies soon so we don't have to see her anymore" (*Es como un puto elefante, que asco me da, no la puedo ni mirar a la cara, ojala se muera pronto y no tengamos que verla mas*). Even though the words felt like thorns tearing up your skin, you were struck even more by the familiarity of the handwriting. You knew who this was. You had gotten so many class notes from this person. It was one of your best friends, Manuel, someone you had also had a crush on for some time. You could feel a flow of blood rushing through your cheeks, coloring your face completely red. You felt embarrassed and ashamed, and you would feel this way for weeks. This was the first time you had been forced to see your weight as an issue.

In the locker room after Renee's second accident in spin class, she looks in the mirror and believes that she has transformed into an incredibly beautiful, fit new person—except nothing has changed. Believing she looks completely different, she begins behaving confidently with a completely new attitude. When picking up her dry cleaning, she meets Ethan (Rory Scovel) with whom she jokes around and, eventually, forces him to exchange numbers because she thinks he is flirting with her. With this newfound confidence, she ends up interviewing for a LeClaire Cosmetics main office position where everyone is flabbergasted by her presence. Renee lands the job due to her overwhelming confidence despite not fitting with the "look" of the rest of the tall, thin, wealthy (mostly white) women who work in the office. However, her boss, Avery (Michelle Williams), believes it will be useful to have an "average" woman around in order to get advice on how to market their new budget-friendly cosmetics line.

That same night, Renee calls Ethan to "help" him ask her out. She is convinced that he is too shy to do so on his own because of her beauty. They go on a date and end up at a beach bar where she wants to enter a bikini contest. Ethan is concerned that others at the bar will laugh at her and he tries to stop her. As soon as Renee gets on stage, she wins over the audience with her newly acquired self-confidence in her "better" body. She dances and prances around the stage, whipping her hair and gyrating her hips. She does not win the contest, but rather than being upset, she congratulates the winner and rejoins Ethan for beer and food. He is amazed. After the date, Renee and Ethan head back to her apartment. She takes her clothes off and presents her naked body to Ethan as a "preview" of what's to come. They lie in bed, and Ethan turns the lights off, but Renee quickly turns them back on. Ethan is clearly marveled and turned on by her confidence, and so is she.

You've never had a romantic relationship as an adult. You were in a long-term relationship in high school and part of college, and after a bad breakup you didn't start dating until you moved out of state. Dating in a fat body is not easy. Regardless of how confident you feel, there's always a concern in the back of your mind about how your partner thinks about your body. You're hyperaware of the ways you position yourself, attempting to put forward the most flattering angle. You're constantly wondering if they think you're fatter in person than you look to be in your online dating photos. During sex, you fight off whispers of insecurity that tell you to worry about stretching your neck to avoid a double chin and to say no to positions that might make your belly bulge bigger. You've learned to resist the fatphobic thoughts that creep to the forefront of your mind in an attempt to feel good during exciting and pleasurable moments that your anti-fat social conditioning threatens to ruin.

Renee excels at advising Avery on the budget-friendly product line. Incredibly impressed with her new protégée, Avery invites Renee to pitch the new line at an important meeting in Boston. Upon arriving in Boston, Avery's attractive brother attempts to seduce Renee. Almost giving in to his advances, Renee suddenly receives a text from Ethan, which snaps her out of the moment she's having with this new man. Running to the bathroom, she closes the door and turns on the shower where she slips and falls unconscious to the floor in a pool of blood. She wakes up panicked hours later and realizes she has missed the planning meeting with Avery. She runs to the hotel lobby where she bumps into her former coworker who recognizes her. Renee is horrified because—since she's been a "different person" after her last cycling accident—he shouldn't recognize her. Realizing that she now looks like her old "ugly" self again, she flies back home and hides from everyone, including Ethan.

After having read the comments on that list, you decided to avoid Manuel for a couple of days, at least until you could figure out a way to talk to him about the horrible things he had written. He wanted you to die? Were you not best friends? Would he not miss you? Did he not love you? This last question haunted you for days. Did he not love you? Did he not love you? COULD he not love you? He could not. And it was your fault. You prevented him from loving you. Your body was suddenly an obstacle to create and maintain friendships. You convinced yourself that no, no one would be able to love you because you were a HUGE waste of air. You were not worth being loved. The week you came to that realization was the week of your first suicide attempt. Manuel was not so much the reason anymore, but rather, it was the feeling of living and dying alone. You were an only child, and as you watched your friends talk to their brothers and sisters about their problems, you had no one. You parents would ask you not to be bothered by those kids. "Things change," they said. "You will be fine, I promise," they'd repeat daily. Nothing would convince you that my life was worth living. How is everything going to be okay if at fifteen you're buying prenatal clothing because none of the "regular" clothing stores would have a size for you? Manuel was the catalyst to what would become years of eating disorders, vomiting, suicide attempts, and endless therapy sessions. The only solution ever given: lose the weight.

After a reclusive period, Renee tries to meet up with her friends but is rejected because she was cruel to them after her "body-changing" accident, excluding them for not looking pretty enough. The next day, she goes back to cycling class and attempts to re-create the accident that "made her beautiful" in the first place. But it doesn't work. The following night, Renee goes to the restaurant where she is supposed to meet Ethan, assuming he won't recognize her. She sits at the bar and texts him saying that she is stuck in traffic. Ethan thinks she is into some kind of role-playing game and plays along. Feeling very frustrated and desperate, Renee leaves the bar. On the way out, she calls Ethan to break up, which leaves him confused.

According to Amy Schumer in *I Feel Pretty*, fat people do not deserve romance, love, and beautiful relationships with significant others. In order for us to feel like such things come as normal or are deserved, we need to experience some sort of violence. A suicide attempt to realize we want to live, an accident in a spinning class that results in a concussion. As you sat in the movie theater watching *I Feel Pretty*, you could feel your rage increasing with the passing of every scene. She is not even fat! She wears short skirts! She can cross her legs comfortably! You felt insulted at every turn. What really struck a chord was the scene after Schumer suffers her second concussion and no longer "feels pretty." She forcibly hides herself from the man she is dating. "I don't want you to see me," she says, even though he is able to see her through the camera in his building's intercom. For you, you want to be seen. *I Feel Pretty* reminded you, yet again, that fat people don't deserve to be loved, to be wanted. And the worst part? It is our fault. But we are not the problem—they are (whoever "they" are). This movie blames us yet again even though the representation of "us" is another average-looking woman, even though we are yet not seen. We are here to stay, though. We are comfortable with who we are. We are beautiful inside and out! We resist and persist in ways that are not yet recognized. We do not need spaces made available for us by conventionally attractive women like Amy Schumer. We have our space. It is time you see us, to recognize our worth. We are here to stay.

Appropriating Fat Embodiment

We individually wrote narratives before and after watching *I Feel Pretty*. In our "before" narratives, we wrote about our relationship to our fatness and how our fatness affects the way we move through the world. Our "after" narratives focused on feelings and ideas the movie engendered. We realized the experiences we wrote about in our "before" narratives such as structural barriers to access things like clothing (and even things like bathroom stalls, which we experience but did not come up in our narratives related to the movie) were not only reflected in the movie but co-opted. We also realized the experiences we wrote about in our "after" narratives such as trauma experienced as a result of fatphobic violence were not reflected at all in the movie, further illustrating the disconnect between the way *I Feel Pretty* represents fat experiences and the way fat lives are lived.

After watching the movie, we came together to share our narratives with each other and discuss common experiences and themes. We decided to combine the "before" and the "after" narratives to compose the layering of narrative and synopsis. As discussed earlier, we made this decision in order to illustrate the ways in which Schumer's character co-opts and (mis)represents fat experiences. After composing this "layered account,"[13] we discussed themes further, identifying four: (1) hyper(in)visibility, (2) structural fat oppression, (3) desirability, and (4) violence. Here, we discuss these in detail.

The Hyper(in)visible Fat Woman

The first theme we identify in our narratives is hyper(in)visibility. Jeannine Gailey argues that fat women are hyper(in)visible subjects and that "to be hyper(in) visible means that a person is sometimes paid exceptional attention and is sometimes exceptionally overlooked, and it can happen simultaneously."[14] Fat women are both hypervisible due to the size of their (our) bodies and hyperinvisible due to the way their (our) needs and desires go unseen. The "hyper-" prefix in these terms is important, as it indicates the ways (in)visibility is "socially oppressive."[15] Gailey goes on to describe how invisibility can be the result of a privileged position. For instance, a thin white woman (or a woman whose appearance conforms to ideal beauty standards) becomes invisible in spaces like shops or restaurants, spaces where bigger bodies, Black and Brown bodies, or other nonnormative bodies are hypervisible and assumed not to belong.

Amber Johnson and Robin M. Boylorn use the concept of hyper/in/visibility to discuss the ways in which Black lesbians are represented in the media. They identify hyper/in/visibility as a "critical space of possibility . . . a structural intersection between hypervisibility, invisibility, and visibility."[16] Akin to Gailey, Johnson and Boylorn understand "hyper/in/visibility" to occur "when bodies are marked absent and present simultaneously . . . a space where bodies are visible, but in limited ways that tend to mark those bodies even more invisible."[17] Here, hyper(in)visibility can be understood as an unintelligible body.

We find utility in this definition alongside Gailey's, and we use these authors in tandem with each other to understand the ways in which hyper(in)visibility is at work within our narratives, within *I Feel Pretty*, and within our experience consuming the film. Specifically, Johnson and Boylorn offer an intersectional understanding of hyper(in)visibility that is necessary to unearth locations of power within (our) experiences of fat women. Although Gailey provides language for understanding the concept as it directly relates to fat women and argues the "hyper-" prefix indicates social oppression, she does not specifically engage with issues of power at the intersections of fatness, race, gender, sexuality, or other identities. In their argument for "quare[18] intersectionality," Johnson and Boylorn write that quaring intersectionality "deprivilege[s] certain intersections over others and acknowledge[s] the agency of embodiment and experience."[19] Thus, we analyze our narratives identifying intersections of identity and locations of power and oppression.

The film *I Feel Pretty* contributes to the hyper(in)visibility of fat women. The narratives we present illustrate the real, tangible oppression fat women face in a fatphobic society, experiences that are co-opted by Amy Schumer's character in the film. Schumer's co-opted portrayal of experiencing fat oppression like facing size-based discrimination shopping for clothes and facing fatphobia while dating, renders fictitious fat women's quotidian experiences. Further, unlike the rhetorical, structural, emotional, and often physical violence fat women endure, Schumer's character experiences violence in order to come to see herself as beautiful (and ultimately as a valuable human being). These depictions illustrate the way hyper(in)visibility replaces the real with the fiction, "and the fiction is so powerful it does not allow the real to exist."[20]

Throughout the film, Schumer attempts to embody experiences she likely will not face in life at the expense of fat women (such as supporting actress Aidy Bryant, a fat woman) who will. Thus, by invoking fat women's experiences, Schumer makes fat women hypervisible, yet by co-opting these experiences, the fat body is rendered invisible. Adding to this hyper(in)invisibility is the fact that Schumer rejects labels like "plus-size." In 2016, when included in *Glamour* magazine's "Chic at Any Size" issue, Schumer posted to Instagram stating that she is a size 6–8 and shouldn't be included.[21] Simultaneously distancing herself from "plus-size" yet portraying her size 6–8 body facing issues "plus-sized" people endure illustrates how "privileged bodies are visible when the situation suits them."[22] Schumer can co-opt experiences of fat women for capitalistic gain, erasing the real and tangible effects of fat oppression on fat bodies, while never experiencing these traumas as a fat person herself.

Structural Fat Oppression

Structural fat oppression includes the ways institutional, social, political, spatial, and other forms of inequity intersect onto the fat body that result in oppression. We find structural fat oppression most visible in the form of "spatial discrimination" within our narratives and the film. Spatial discrimination is "the small and persistent ways that fat bodies are physically derided within our environments."[23] Fat people live in a "world not built to accommodate our girth, [we] receive the undeniable messages that we are second-class, too big, not attractive, shouldn't be here, don't deserve, offend, repulse."[24] Thus, Owen identifies spatial discrimination as a microaggression, "a smaller, less obvious form of violence, but it has many of the same effects: anger, frustration, guilt, fear, and loathing (toward self and/or others)."[25]

Although spatial discrimination is typically understood as related to physical space such as fitting into airplane or stadium seats, bathroom stalls, or booths at a restaurant, we also consider spatial discrimination as access to spaces such as stores or places of work. In this way, we find the theme of spatial discrimination apparent in the scene where Schumer's character is told she "might find her size online" when shopping. We also find instances in which fat people commonly experience spatial discrimination but that are not an issue for Schumer's character, despite the co-optation of fat experiences throughout. This oversight indicates the fact that neither Schumer nor the writers of the film experience the world as a fat person.

The first instance in which spatial discrimination is demonstrated is when Schumer's character is told her size is not available in store. This is something fat women must navigate every time they go shopping. Samantha Murray records a relevant experience in her article "Doing Politics or Selling Out? Living the Fat Body" that is worth quoting at length here. Murray writes,

> Recently, I was shopping with a thin friend. Or rather, I was waiting patiently in the little corridor outside the fitting rooms, ready to gauge whether it was appropriate for me to give approving nods and coos of delights when the friend emerges looking resplendent, or a wrinkled brow of uncertainty if the effect was less than stunning. I trotted obediently between the racks to get other sizes, to replace discarded clothes, to select new outfits for my thin friend. This particular day, I was in transit between the diaphanous blouses rack and the fitting rooms when the shop assistant, who was standing behind her little black

counter at the other end of the store called to me with a sweet smile fixed on her plastic face, "You know, we really can't help a person of your size here."[26]

For fat people like Murray and like us, "every time society reads [our] fat body, it lets [us] know that [we are] defective."[27] We are reminded at every turn that our flesh is undisciplined, our corpulence is corruptive, our body is something to be battled. As we argue earlier, Schumer's depiction of this type of discrimination as a size 6–8 co-opts and trivializes fat people's lived experiences with this very real and very damaging occurrence.

Although this scene is perhaps the most explicit in representing spatial discrimination, the way Schumer's character moves through space throughout the film illustrates the ease with which a thin person (like Schumer) navigates and occupies space. While Schumer's character easily sits in stadium seats, airplane seats, restaurant booths, and the exercise bicycle (neither time the bicycle broke was due to her weight), "from the moment a fat person awakens in the morning, s/he is reminded of living fatly in a thin-centric world."[28] For instance, one of Owen's participants describes the way she attempts to minimize her body while on airplanes in order to avoid encroaching too much on their neighbor's space. Owen also finds that fat women will "reduce or ignore our expectations of comfort and inclusion, minimize ourselves, tuck our bodies into tiny nooks, fold ourselves inward in order to limit the insult of our bulks."[29] Internalized fatphobia leads fat people to sacrifice basic needs and dignity in order to not inconvenience others. This, again, is not represented in *I Feel Pretty*, and instances in which spatial discrimination is represented, the experience is trivialized as a singular occurrence in the life of Schumer's character rather than an issue of structural oppression.

Desirability and Fat Bodies

The third theme we identify in our narratives is that of the desirability of the fat body. As we have conversations about desirability, we tend to focus on notions of sexual partnership or sexual appetite and desire toward our bodies. We argue that there needs to be a larger conversation about the ways in which we conceptualize and talk about desirability. Desirability not only affects sexual relationships or whether one will find a partner or not, but it also affects the ways in which we treat others and allow others to treat ourselves. This is not to say that sex or sexual attraction and satisfaction does not have a big role to play in the conversation; however, reducing these exchanges to sex may result in ignoring everyday interactions that continue to impact fat people in negative and violent ways.

My (Sarah's) body was deemed undesirable in middle school, before sex and sexual relationships were even a concern. Manuel, my best friend at the time, forced and reinforced undesirability onto my body even though our friendship was supposed to transcend physicality. It is important, then, to interrogate desire and the very different ways it manifests itself as a tool to police fatness and keep us in our place. As a Muslim, Lebanese Spaniard, I was not only bullied by my size, but also because I was different religiously and ethnically. My flaws were multiple and layered. As Gailey notes, "A societal emphasis on bodily flaws works to keep women, especially marginalized women, in their place, that is passive, submissive, and other-oriented."[30] I wanted to be desired, not just as a friend in middle school but also as a sexual being later on in life. Throughout Amy Schumer's film, Renee is seen as having very satisfactory friendships, going out to bars and enjoying the genuine love from her two friends. However, friendships have always been difficult to maintain for me, and according to Prohaska and Gailey, "fat children are more likely to be bullied than their thin peers."[31] After feeling betrayed by Manuel, I could never trust having a best friend again. Dating later on proved to be even more difficult.

Dating while being fat is not easy. There is always the fear of rejection or of being fetishized. Fat women, specifically, are viewed as either "asexual, or desexualized . . . excluded from traditional expressions of fantasy,"[32] which is evident in the lack of representations of our sexuality throughout mediated platforms. Even though fat people find love and sexual partners, Amy Schumer's Renee is only able to search for a partner confidently after she has suffered from a concussion. After Renee realizes that her appearance is "back to what it used to be," she sabotages her relationship and tries to avoid Ethan at all costs. This is presented in the film in a humorous way (Renee attempts, and fails, to role-play while meeting Ethan at a bar before breaking up with him).

Additionally, fat women may internalize anti-fat beliefs, which may cause them to avoid sex for fear of being either made fun of or seen as undesirable or unworthy of pleasure. These internalized anti-fat beliefs may also result in other negative psychological outcomes due to the stigmatization of fat bodies.[33] For instance, this stigmatization can lead to "feelings of shame, isolation, lower self-esteem, poor body image, and an increased risk of other mental health issues."[34] The downplaying of Renee's attempts of isolation are nothing new. Because Amy Schumer is of an average size, the movie places real fat people on the periphery. If someone like Amy Schumer isolates herself from others because of internalized shame, how are fat people supposed to feel like after watching this movie?

Violence and the Fat Body

As fat people, we are aware that we can be the targets of unprovoked violence, whether it be institutional, verbal, or physical, at any given point in time. Fat people are constantly threatened with "dirty looks" or physical abuse, and fat youth are quite often targets of bullying. Women particularly face violence from bullies who resort to name-calling in order to psychologically bring them down. Koppleman asserts that "fat girls often experience emotional and sometimes physical abuse"[35] oftentimes in public spaces such as schools and by their peers and relatives. As exemplified in our narratives, this bullying results in the internalization of shame and blame. According to Prohaska and Gailey, the consequences of internalizing anti-fat beliefs "result in the shaming and blaming of fat people."[36] I (Sarah) blamed myself for "occupying too much space," I blamed myself for my peers wanting me dead, and I blamed myself for being fat.

Anti-fat discrimination is often endured coming from loved ones, strangers, health professionals, and even employers. It affects our everyday life. Our bodies help us connect with others around us and it is through bodily connections that meaningful relationships are formed. The way fatness is represented in media, however, allows others to categorize us as undeserving of human touch and sympathy. Amy Schumer's Renee ends up participating in that dehumanization when she bullies her friends for not being beautiful enough after she has suffered the concussion and believes herself to be thin. She is portrayed as mean and is constantly thematically ridiculed for it in the movie. This portrayal adds to the misinformation that media reinforces around fatness.

There is abundant misinformation regarding fat people and "obesity" in the media and throughout different institutions. We are deemed to be "lazy, irresponsible, and gluttonous,"[37] and oftentimes we are made fun of in media. This misinformation can lead to "interpersonal and institutional violence against fat people."[38] Some of this institutional violence is be experienced when mental health issues arising from bullying and other forms of violence against fat people usually prompt medical doctors to recommend weight loss instead of nuanced treatments for the effects of trauma. Even in mass media, fat people are portrayed as in need of fixing through weight loss, which is violent in and of itself. Throughout Amy Schumer's *Feel Pretty*, not only does Renee experience violence by suffering a concussion, but she also exerts verbal abuse toward her friends once she believes her body has changed.

Final Thoughts

In this critical co-constructed autoethnography, we employ performative writing in order to convey our narratives, braiding narrative and theory to demonstrate the ways in which theory is part of our embodiment as fat women. We write to communicate the disconnections within Amy Schumer's *I Feel Pretty* and our experiences as fat women. As a thin woman, Amy Schumer does a disservice to fat individuals by occupying the space of fat women in media and co-opting fat embodied experiences. According to Cain, Donaghue, and Ditchburn, "Although anti-fat ideology retains much of its taken-for-granted authority, voices promoting competing constructions of fat embodiment are increasingly participating in mainstream discourse."[39] However, they are not given space in this film.

The representation of fatness in the film fails to address the real lived experiences of fat women by portraying Renee's relationships in a humorous tone.

There are plenty of funny representations in media, but there are not enough serious examples that show the ways in which fat women are violently treated by their partners.[40] Renee is not only able to approach a man she is attracted to without fear of rejection, physical abuse, or ridicule, but she is able to develop a meaningful relationship with Ethan just because she is "confident enough" to approach him. The violence seen in the film is only perpetrated by Renee and to herself, which once again, places the blame on fat women for experiencing violence.

In addition, *I Feel Pretty* does not account for the different layers of oppression within intersections of race, ethnicity, and religiosity. As exemplified by our narratives and embodied experiences, those who are different from the norm in more aspects than size are also threatened in different ways. According to Prohaska and Gailey, "If cultural norms about the group become internalized, members of the marginalized group are more likely to face negative consequences."[41]

Coda

Although I struggle daily not to collapse into the number 45.2, I persist, appreciating the amazing things my body can do. I persist through celebrating my body. I persist in feeling pretty, confident, and comfortable in my body.

I feel pretty when
waking up from a long sleep
face bright and clear
refreshed.

The deep blue circles under my eyes
yet to be covered by concealer
fading into the pink in my cheeks—
a reminder of my late night
writing or
reading or
fucking or
maybe watching TV.

I feel pretty when
out on the town with friends
eyes smoky and matching
dark lips and curled hair.

A tight-fitting shirt, push-up bra
and skinny jeans complete the ensemble.

Singing, dancing, and flirting
into the early morning hours without
a concern over how others read my body.

I feel pretty when
getting home from the pool where
I wore a galaxy-printed two-piece bathing suit.

After showering and
noticing the sunburn
already making itself known on my pale skin
I let my naturally bushy hair dry free.
No makeup
I feel pretty putting on
short shorts and a spaghetti-strap onesie.

I feel pretty when
fucking with the lights on.

Insecurities abound yet I
resist giving in to self-shame
and body censorship and
remind myself that I deserve
love and pleasure and the
freedom of feeling at home
in the body that houses
my spirit.

Resisting my internalized mandate to do otherwise, I allow myself to feel pretty in all my body's forms. I persist in appreciating each freckle, each fleshy fold, each mole, each scar, and each stretch mark that makes my body mine. Social norms and mainstream medical discourses collapse all of me into one number: 45.2. But I resist, and nevertheless, I feel pretty.

Discussion Questions

1 Who was the first fat character or actor/actress that you remember seeing in a television show or movie?
   a Did their role mature past their size, exercising, or food habits?
   b How do race and gender play a difference in how fat people get cast?

2 Do you remember the first time someone made a comment about your body?

   a How old were you?

   b How did adults around you talk about bodies?

3 What has it been like to think and write about your experiences?

   a What did you discover about yourself and the beliefs you hold?

Try This!

Identify and bring to class a media artifact that has personally impacted you (movie clip, music video, photography, etc.). After sharing your artifact with the class or a small group, make a list of the aspects of your identity that are most important to you. Then reflect on how the identity/identities you listed have been (1) represented in and (2) shaped by the media artifact you chose.

Go further. Compose a performative response (short story, poem, song, etc.) to the media artifact you choose. Your response may challenge the artifact, add to the artifact, be in conversation with the artifact, or you may choose to rewrite the artifact in a way that better represents who you are.

Notes

1 Amy Nicholson, "Why Amy Schumer's 'I Feel Pretty' Is Quietly Revolutionary," last modified April 23, 2018, https://www.rollingstone.com/movies/movie-news /why-amy-schumers-i-feel-pretty-is-quietly-revolutionary-627801/.

2 Collett N. Cann and Eric J. DeMeulenaere, "Critical Co-constructed Autoethnography," *Cultural Studies ↔ Critical Methodologies* 12, no. 2 (2012): 147, doi: 10.1177/ 1532708611435214.

3 Della Pollock, "Performative Writing," in *The Ends of Performance*, ed. Peggy Phelan and Jill Lane (New York: New York University Press, 1998), 75.

4 Asterisks are used between synopsis and narrative to indicate temporal shifts.

5 Jami McFarland, Jessica Slothouber, and Allison Taylor, "Tempo-rarily Fat: A Queer Exploration of Fat Time," *Fat Studies: An Interdisciplinary Journal* 7, no. 2 (2918): 135, doi: 10.1080/21604851.2017.1376275.

6 Ashley Ross, "Amy Schumer Calls Out Glamour for Featuring Her in 'Plus-Size' Issue," last modified April 5, 2016, http://time.com/4282192/amy-schumer-glamour -plus-size/.

7 Amy Gullage, "Fat Monica, Fat Suits, and Friends," *Feminist Media Studies* 14, no. 2 (2012): 179, doi: 10.1080/14680777.2012.724026.

8 Anne Hole, "Performing Identity: Dawn French and the Funny Fat Female Body," *Feminist Media Studies* 3, no. 3 (2003): 315, doi: 10.1080/1468077032000166540.

9 Ibid., 316.

10 Ibid., 327.

11 Carla Rice, "Becoming 'the Fat Girl': Acquisition of an Unfit Identity," *Women's Studies International Forum* 30 (2007): 170, doi: 10.1016/j.wsif.2007.01.001.

12 We reject the "obesity paradigm" approach to health that establishes a "normal" weight based on measures like BMI. Thus, when using "obesity" and related terms,

we include them in quotes to point to the social constructedness of the concept and to push back against the pathologizing of the fat body through such paradigms.

13 Carol Rambo Ronai discusses the "layered account" in her piece, "Multiple Reflections of Child Sexual Abuse: An Argument for a Layered Account," *Journal of Contemporary Ethnography* 23, no. 4 (1995). Ronai describes the utility of the layered account, writing, "The layered account offers an impressionistic sketch, handing readers layers of experience so they may fill in the spaces and construct an interpretation of the writer's narrative. The readers reconstruct the subject, thus projecting more of themselves into it, and taking more away from it" (396).

14 Jeannine Gailey, "Hyper(in)visibility and the *Paradox* of Fat," in *The Hyper(in) visible Fat Woman: Weight and Gender Discourse in Contemporary Society* (New York: Palgrave Macmillan, 2014), 7.

15 Ibid., 8.

16 Amber Johnson and Robin M. Boylorn, "Digital Media and the Politics of Intersectional Queer Hyper/In/Visibility in *Between Women*," *Liminalities: A Journal of Performance Studies* 11, no. 1 (2015): 6.

17 Ibid., 22.

18 E. Patrick Johnson coined the term *quare* to attend to the intersection of race and sexuality. "Quare" is "queer" in Black Southern vernacular. Quare, Johnson writes, "peruses an epistemology rooted in the body" and highlights the exclusion of Black and Brown folx from queer theory.

19 Johnson and Boylorn, "Digital Media," 17.

20 Ibid., 22

21 Ashley Ross, "Amy Schumer Calls Out Glamour for Featuring Her in 'Plus-Size' Issue," *Time*, April 5, 2016, http://time.com/4282192/amy-schumer-glamour-plus -size/.

22 Gailey, "Hyper(in)visibility," 11.

23 Lesleigh Owen, "Living Fat in a Thin-Centric World: Effects of Spatial Discrimina- tion on Fat Bodies and Selves," *Feminism and Psychology* 22, no. 3 (2012): 294, doi: 10.1177/0959353512445360.

24 Ibid., 294.

25 Ibid., 295.

26 Samantha Murray, "Doing Politics or Selling Out? Living the Fat Body," *Women's Studies* 34, no. 3–4 (2005): 265, doi: 10.1080/00497870590964165.

27 Ibid., 265.

28 Owen, "Living Fat in a Thin Centric World," 294.

29 Ibid., 299.

30 Jeannine A. Gailey, "Fat Shame and Fat Pride: Fat Women's Sexual and Dating Experiences," *Fat Studies* 1, no. 1 (2012): 115, doi: 10.1080/21604851.2012.631113. Even though Gailey's study focuses primarily on sexual relationships and sexual desire, perceived bodily flaws by others, especially at such young age, also work to keep us in our place and submissive. Our experiences show that not only are our sexual lives affected but also friendships and other relationships throughout various points in our lives.

31 Ariane Prohaska and Jeannine Gailey, "Theorizing Fat Oppression: Intersections Approaches and Methodological Innovations," *Fat Studies: An Interdisciplinary Journal* 8, no. 1 (2019): 5, doi: 10.1080/21604851.2019.1534469.

32 Jamie Ratliff, "Drawing on Burlesque: Excessive Display and Fat Desire in the Work of Cristina Vela," *Fat Studies: An Interdisciplinary Journal* 2, no. 2 (2013): 119, doi: 10.1080/21604851.2013.779557.

33 Gailey, "Fat Shame and Fat Pride."

34 Prohaska and Gailey, "Theorizing Fat Oppression."

35 Susan Koppleman, "Fat Women and Abuse," *Off Our Backs* 34, no. 11 (2004): 27.

36 Prohaska and Gailey, "Theorizing Fat Oppression," 3.

37 Ibid., 2.

38 Ibid., 3.

39 Patricia Cain, Ngaire Donaghue, and Graeme Ditchburn, "Concerns, Culprits, Counsel, and Conflict: A Thematic Analysis of 'Obesity' and Fat Discourse in Digital News Media," *Fat Studies: An Interdisciplinary Journal* 6, no. 2 (2017): 170, doi: 10.1080/21604851.2017.1244418.

40 Prohaska and Gailey, "Theorizing Fat Oppression," 5. The one exception we can find to this argument is the depiction of anti-fat violence in the recent AMC television program *Dietland*. Unfortunately, this show was canceled after its first season.

41 Ibid., 2.

17

Visual Activism, Persistence, and Identity

• •

Ostomy Selfies as a Form of Resistance to Dominant Body Ideologies

RUTH J. BEERMAN AND

MICHAEL S. MARTIN

Social media offers promises and pitfalls for managing public and private life; this media requires both the user and the viewer to reconsider and understand the consequences of such usage. As social media and personal technology are now fundamental parts of our lives, the role of visual images, and particularly selfies, has created a world of taking a picture anywhere or anytime. Instagram now serves as an important app among eighteen- to twenty-four-year-olds and also among twenty-five- to thirty-four-year-olds.[1] Instagram in particular, although other social media such as Twitter and Facebook, focuses on the visual and the significance of images, confirming in many ways what W.J.T. Mitchell called the pictorial turn.[2] Visual rhetorical scholars also note the importance of how images and visuals are and do argument.[3] That being said, the increased use of selfies has been often viewed as narcissist[4] or a form of vanity.[5] Other scholarship notes the central importance of photography[6] but focuses on public images, such as news or photojournalism, rather than the seemingly private (yet made public) selfie.

Both lines of scholarship could imply that selfies are not worthy of analysis; however, selfies offer ways to examine how beauty, bodies, and identities come to matter,[7] offering another avenue of feminist or political advocacy.

The increasing usage of digital space and the possibilities of social change, agency, and identity pushes us to reconsider anew the significant work of Michael Kevin DeLuca and Jennifer Peeples regarding the public sphere and public screen.[8] Although their work focused on more traditional media of newspapers and television, their ideas can be expanded to social media.[9] Social media now offers a way for the public to get their message onto the public screen, circulated, and discussed.

This chapter builds on the notion of public and private as political, including from a feminist perspective, to examine how selfies can be a form of advocacy, examining the public nature of such images. Such selfies utilize visibility politics, which is the idea that marginalized groups use images, such as their own bodies, photographs, or image events, to make present their perspective, to persist and resist. Focusing on the genre of ostomy selfies through the #GetYour-BellyOut social media campaign as well as the personal narrative of one of the authors (Michael), we argue that the use of the public cataloged selfie provides the inflammatory bowel disease (IBD) sufferer an important as well as necessary opportunity to resist societal expectations of the perfect body, moving a very private disease into the public sphere through selfie activism. We argue such selfies work to create new forms of resistance, identity, and social change.

Arthur Frank in his book *The Wounded Storyteller* notes that chronic illness requires us to "think differently" about our bodies.[10] Our bodies are generally the message we give to others, whether we consciously realize it or not. Our bodies are more than identity; the body is one of the most fundamental ways by which we communicate with others, both in terms of our one-on-one communication and our group communication. The ostomate body, a person with a permanent wearable technology (the bag or pouch), functions as a site of resistance, offering a tangible illustration of one way to persist: to exist as a healthy, active, and attractive person. Ultimately, these selfies illustrate how the ostomate body persists and challenges the normative idea of *the* body.

Inflammatory Bowel Diseases and the #GetYourBellyOut Campaign

There is a group of disorders that affect the gastrointestinal tract known as IBDs. These diseases (most commonly known as diverticulitis, irritable bowel syndrome [IBS], ulcerative colitis [UC] or Crohn's disease) affect a significant number of individuals, at approximately 1.6 million in the United States[11] and approximately 10 million worldwide.[12] The disease is a result of an abnormal response of one's immune system.[13] Although affecting women and men in equal numbers, it predominantly impacts White individuals, although the cases of Black and Latinx Americans in the United States are rising.[14] IBDs continue to strike a wide variety of individuals, but more and more, those diagnosed are either in their adolescence or young adults (and more common when a parent has an IBD, around 16 percent),[15] as evidenced by tabs on the Crohn's & Colitis website, including "Living with Crohn's & Colitis," "Campus Connection,"[16] and "Teen Website."[17] It is important to keep in mind that moving from a person suffering from Crohn's, UC, or rectal cancer to a person with a permanent colostomy or ileostomy is an incredibly difficult change (permanent colostomies and ileostomies both involve the use of a bag; however, the difference is the area of the GI tract that is affected—a colostomy is in the colon or large intestine; an ileostomy is an area of the small intestine).[18] It is even more difficult for younger sufferers to do "self-management."[19] Becoming an ostomate is often a life-or-death choice, or in other words, a nonchoice. It is not uncommon for the patient to try everything imaginable before turning to such life-altering surgery.

One of the most significant difficulties in managing IBDs is there is little warning that a person is at risk for developing the malady, and perhaps more importantly, once diagnosed, currently there is no cure. Those with more severe degrees of the disease often undergo life-changing surgery, and some live with an ostomy, where their intestine is pulled through their abdominal wall and sewn into their skin. Their waste materials are now collected in a pouch that is attached to their side covering the exposed intestine. Living as an ostomate is generally done in hiding given the societal norms regarding bodily waste and therefore seemingly requires an IBD-afflicted person to manage in silence. Indeed, recent studies of IBD patients found most experienced some level of stigma or shame;[20] patients talked about fears of the smell, being unattractive or disgusting, and the idea of "crapping in a pouch."[21]

Feeling shame often is the product of the person's belief that there is a need for changing others' perception(s).[22] The complexity of this shame is twofold. It is external when the person perceives that the other identifies them in a negative manner. It is internal when the person takes that shameful negativity and in turn feels the same toward themselves.[23] Studies of IBD patients have shown this propensity for feeling self-conscious, lonely, and perhaps most importantly, undesirable. An additional complexity is the rather circular nature of most IBDs. The symptomatology of frequent evacuation, weight loss, or general intestinal discomfort, cramping, and bleeding creates increased stress in the afflicted, but because IBDs are stress complicated (stress resulting), the symptoms are exacerbated. On the other hand, when the symptoms are more quiescent, the afflicted person can be deemed healthy. However, the constant fear of a flare-up can result in rejecting social invitations or excessive absence from work. The incredible sense of shame and embarrassment result in isolation of the sufferer, but the need for increased trips to the bathroom to manage continence are not something our social norms seem ready to discuss. Therefore, such conversations only occur with a partner or in private. When the disease appears to be abated, the nonafflicted finds it difficult to see their work colleague as someone who is chronically ill. The symptoms (e.g., cramping, frequent diarrhea, or even nausea) are not apparent. It is easy for both the afflicted and others to believe the IBD sufferer is healthy. Chronic illness seems to be less than chronic. For someone suffering a chronic condition, persisting and pushing to not give up are a daily struggle. However, the struggle is even more significant when the body shaming, either by oneself or the other, body hiding (again self-imposed or interpreted as necessary), and seeing one's body as damaged or no longer perfect are everyday experiences.

It is difficult to persist, resist, or create change when one does not see one's identities as represented in mainstream culture or when one experiences shame or stigma. To counter such absences, body shaming, and stigma, three women, Victoria Marie, Lorna Haymes, and Gemma Wills, all with a form of IBD, founded the #GetYourBellyOut (#GYBO) campaign in 2014. #GYBO supports those with UC and Crohn's disease (both UC and Crohn's fall within the genre of IBD, but UC is confined to the large intestine and Crohn's can affect the entire digestive tract. UC is often an initial diagnosis).[24] The campaign urges people to take a picture of their belly and post it to various social media platforms.[25] #GYBO functions as an integrated media campaign, including a website, Facebook page, Twitter account, Instagram account, and hashtag across those social media platforms.[26] The campaign's goals include body confidence, education, and inspiration to achieve a better future: "We are on a constant journey working towards a better future; we aim to expand our reach, boost people's confidence, educate and inspire the community."[27]

Although the campaign uses various media platforms, one of the most common uses is through the hashtag #GetYourBellyOut on Twitter and Instagram. Indeed, this hashtag includes almost 15,000 Instagram posts and over 10,000 tweets (as of March 20, 2019).[28] Although some of the hashtagged posts come from the official Instagram or Twitter accounts, the overwhelming majority of the posts are user generated. Those who post are almost always someone who has UC or Crohn's. Thus, although the campaign began with the work of three women, based on the directives of the campaign, people took up the #GYBO to post their own selfies.[29]

Newspaper and media reports called these posts an inspirational trend, with headlines such as "Colostomy Bag Selfies Are the New Inspiration Trend on Social Media,"[30] "The Brave Colostomy Bag Selfies,"[31] and "Scores of Crohn's Sufferers across the Globe Post Brave Selfies of Their Colostomy Bags, along with Their Stories of Hope and Survival,"[32] among others.[33] These news reports illustrate the changing nature of how those with these forms of chronic illness, as well as those without, understand IBDs. Current research demonstrates that use of visual technologies like Facebook, Instagram, or YouTube offer opportunities for ostomates to receive social support for lives that have been permanently changed by necessary surgery that leaves the patient psychologically and emotionally scarred.[34] Molly Margaret Kessler urges scholars to examine the wearable technology of the ostomy bag.[35] Such work on ostomies and ostomates is important, as it moves beyond a simple biomedical understanding of the disease; however, this scholarship focuses on helping those with such diseases to better manage their own lives (social support focus) or how they view their own bodies (self-identity focus). Current scholarship focuses on narratives and discourse[36] to create a new normal for patients with their modified bodies and stoma,[37] but almost all work ignores images and visuals, including the bag and ostomy selfies.[38]

The ostomy bag is indeed a form of wearable technology that Kessler identifies, but it is also most often concealed through dress so that others likely do not know. Within online or social support groups (such as through the Crohn's & Colitis Foundation), one does not need to disclose as many specific details, as fellow members with chronic illness understand the struggles and challenges. In support groups and forums, narrative and stories are privileged through literal text, through real-time chatting or posts. Although these forms of support demonstrate talking about the bag, they do not show it: the bag is there but not there at the same time. The #GYBO campaign puts the bag out in public, in the face of the viewer. In a sense, these selfies say, "I'm here, I'm gutless, get used to it."

Currently, there is a lack (absence) of seeing these ostomate bodies within the dominant visual culture. Social networking and social media offer a unique way to examine diseases which, until recently, were only spoken about in the context of a patient-doctor relationship or perhaps among intimate partners. The #GetYourBellyOut campaign makes these bodies, people, and identities present within the overall discourse through the use of these selfies. #GYBO brings to various audiences (those with the disease and those without) the idea that these bodies are normal bodies. These selfies serve as a way to counter the erasure, the hiddenness of these types of bodies from society.[39] The overall goal of campaigns or organization that work specifically with IBDs is to normalize the ostomy bag and make it unremarkable. And indeed, this campaign has been recognized for its work by the health care community. In 2019, out of over 2,000 nominations,[40] the #GetYourBellyOut campaign was recognized as one of the top ten patient leaders with the 2018 WEGO Health Best in Show Community Award.[41] This award recognizes people or organizations making a difference in online health communities.[42]

We argue that such success stems from the campaign utilizing the perspective of visibility politics. Again, visibility politics offers one strategy that marginalized groups use to literally show their existence and resist erasure from mainstream society. Often, culture does not reflect the reality of all. Thus, using images to make visible one's identities or struggle offers a way to talk back to dominant narratives, such as using one's body to be the site of argument[43] or to resignify a stigmatized identity[44] as ways to challenge dominant ideologies. In this way, visual images draw on what Chaïm Perelman and L. Olbrechts-Tyetca call presence,[45] ways to make one's argument more salient (or to put it in a visual meta-phor, the images are in one's face and one cannot look away).[46]

The #GYBO selfies typically fall into three major ways to counter body norms and offer visual evidence of persistence: (1) bare, clean skin, (2) active lifestyles, and (3) sex appeal. As a whole, the collection offers ways to talk back to domi-nant ideologies of the perfect body; the magnitude of the images offers many examples to see people persisting and living their lives. The next sections explore these three themes, interweaving the academic and personal, by using stories from Michael's life to provide another contextual reading of these selfies.

Vignette 1: When the Private Becomes (Semi)-Public: Bathroom Politics and Bare Skin

Michael: What are the most common normative understandings of our physi-cal bodies, or more significantly, what happens when these normative under-standings are misaligned with a person's individualized reality? Certainly the ability of gastroenterologists and colorectal surgeons is astonishing when it comes to managing a body that is intent on attacking itself through their medical abil-ity to reform, reconnect, and reimage the body, thereby offering options for the IBD/UC/Crohn's sufferer often unimaginable. Yet, little is done to manage the profound change that person faces as a consequence of that surgical revision. When the person with a permanent colostomy/ileostomy looks in the mirror, seeing the reality of themselves as a person who is no longer whole is unavoid-able. To complicate this truth, however, is a societal norm that most people gen-erally keep our bellies covered. Even though we are often comfortable speaking about that potty training with our toddlers, the same cannot be said as we are retraining ourselves as teens, twentysomethings, or adults. Consequently, what we present as our individual actuality in public and what we know in private is not consistent.

Growing up, one of the first things many toddlers, and by extension, their par-ents attempt to master is the process of potty training. It is a triumphant day when that little person is able to remove their diaper, their pull-up, and the worry of needing an extra change of clothing or the necessity of an extra washing of bedding is behind them. Once mastered, little consideration is given to this bodily requirement, and the idea that one might have conversations about bodily functions is considered, at the very least, inappropriate and on a more extreme level, entirely outside the realm of acceptability. In fact, the next time we might consider such dialogue as necessary is when we are dealing with our elderly par-ents or we ourselves have reached that age where our conversations seem to focus on our latest ailment.

And yet, what are some of the consequences for the IBD sufferer? There is the seeming need to often suffer this malady in private because most are not com-fortable in expressing the reality of their digestive malfunction. The decision to hide because of embarrassment or shame is well documented.[47] Much like the disease necessitated the removal of various parts of a gastrointestinal (GI) tract, the sufferer will often remove themselves rather than reveal the reality they are living. It is a dysregulation of the public and private. What is often suffered in private seems more appropriate to remain as private. One can argue that Crohn's or UC not only steals away parts of the IBD sufferer's body, but it also steals the ability of the sufferer to be themselves because of the shame one ostomy moment can cause. The communication and interaction that is fundamental to us as humans can seem irreparably damaged by the embarrassment suffered when the pouches and wafers that are part of the ostomate's life become the focal point of that moment.

In my case, it took significant time for both the medical profession to realize that Crohn's was the appropriate or accurate diagnosis. As noted above, Crohn's and UC have similar symptoms. Because UC is confined to the colon or large intestine, it is often the case that initial diagnosis is UC. In my case, for more than a decade, the diagnosis was UC. It was not until all of the colon and the rectum had been removed and the continuation of symptoms that a revised diagnosis of Crohn's was given. It would take another six years, following questions from the surgeon after yet another abdominal surgery, that a proclamation claimed Crohn's was probably a condition from birth. There were a number of answers in that physician's assertion, but conversely, it posed just as many questions. To understand the etiology of illness, one must come face-to-face with their humanity in a profoundly intimate manner. When one deals with their digestive tract and what is done in the privacy of their bathroom, the intimacy becomes more than profound. It is fundamentally life altering.

Coming to terms with the actuality that my body was and *forever* is no longer functionally whole is not something I came to terms with in a moment. Furthermore, it is not something that is not revisited time and time again. An ostomy moment in a public setting can cause me to wish that I had never survived such a diagnosis. Yet for some, that reality may never occur. To this day, more than half my life later, my attitude oscillates between acceptance and disdain. The tangible options for managing the modified GI tract vary depending on how severe one suffers and the degree to which Crohn's or UC creates a disruption to their daily routine. Certainly when life is controlled by bathroom visits, seemingly available options are minimized. In fact, many options seem completely unavailable. In those times when the hopefulness of a new surgical procedure was dashed by yet more complications, the reality for me of becoming a permanent ostomate was difficult and simultaneously necessary. The pain caused by the incessant diaper rash and excoriation, the embarrassment of leakage and drainage from the altered rectal muscles, and the consequence of needing to manage these problems created two options: did I choose to manage in public but in silence, or choose to stay home, incapable of venturing far from the security of my own private and secure bathroom. This sort of disruption caused by the chronic onset of Crohn's or UC can move the suffering person from see-ing their life as "life before and after illness."[48]

As a graduate student working on a first master's degree, the stress of gradu-ate school and being on the quarter system seemed to create significant issues for my digestive system, and with an alarming increase in frequency, it seemed life was turned into a walk from the second floor of the seminary library to the bathroom just outside the front doors of that library. What was once a regular twice-a-day routine had become twice an hour. In fact, the new routine became so apparent that a person once came into that bathroom looking for me, noting that others, from classmates to the campus phone operator, knew where I might be. The numerous (perhaps dozens of) dilation procedures needed before sur-rendering to the permanent ileostomy (the pouch would now be a permanent and lifesaving wearable technology) are all part of my personal and particular IBD story. From leakage and adult diaper rash to ostomy moments (when either the pouch or wafer fail to adhere to the body and fecal material leaks all over me) is fundamental to my daily life. Because the ostomy is front and center on my abdomen, I imagine that it is always noticeable, and when there is "a moment," hiding it is seldom an option. Therefore, my life has been crisscrossed with incred-ible embarrassment and personal struggle and yet times where the medical pro-fessionals have held me up as a poster child for managing this humiliating illness with resilience. Yet, one particularly devastating event was being called a wimp by an ex-spouse.[49] Such moments have forced a kind of unparalleled resilience and unbelievable despair (and in some ways, the words became wounds that are much more difficult to heal than any physical wounds). I remember telling my spouse I did not know what it was like to be on her side of this struggle, but I would not wish my side on anyone.

The consequence of IBDs, particularly when one is either temporarily or per-manently an ostomate (a person who is required to wear a wafer and pouch because part of their intestine has been pulled through their abdominal wall), is a fundamental change in understanding one's body; it is an even more essential change in the functionality of the body. The body is no longer whole, literally and figuratively. No longer can the ostomate go about their lives without scop-ing out bathroom facilities, maintaining a change of clothes just in case, or hav-ing an extra set of ostomy supplies readily available, all in case of the dreaded ostomy moment.

In the days that followed my initial surgery, the stigma of an altered body would be soon be exacerbated. Within forty-eight hours of the surgery, the wafer, the device that protected my body from the waste materials now in a pouch hang-ing from my lower right abdomen, refused to adhere to the skin. Thus, the waste materials (this liquid fecal matter) was leaking all over me, soiling both my hos-pital gown and the bedsheets. Barely two days beyond complete abdominal sur-gery, I could not even roll over by myself, and the reality that I had poop leaking on myself was beyond anything imaginable. Using the call button, in an urgent and panicked voice, I noted the dilemma. The stigma of having to manage this quandary was beyond anything expected. The happenstance of facing anyone in that condition created a spectacle, a visible situation, which mortified me.[50] In fact, it brought this ex-Marine to tears. The next day, the enterostomal therapist quipped, "I hear you had an interesting evening." Without a blink, I retorted, "That is a poor euphemism for literally shitty." She responded kindly but somewhat factually, "It is only poop." Once again, I retorted emphatically, "But I do not want to become so intimate with it." This initial encounter with my external accomplice was never mentioned. I was unaware and the very idea that such an occurrence could, or would, be possible was not on my radar. Much like being unexpectedly broadsided by car, the injury to my psyche was severe.

Certainly for the IBD sufferer to move from seeing one as afflicted to someone who can find normalcy in their altered physical existence is not an easy evolution. When one stands in the shower or the mirror, the reality that their body is not whole is there in full color (e.g., a pink or red stoma, skin that is colored differently under the wafer than the skin around it, particularly in the summer, and possible irritation that can cause the skin to be red and weepy). Knowing even when to shower or when to change the wafer and pouch is something that must be thought out and planned. Trips of more than an hour or two require thought, imagining what might be needed to manage the variables. Making sure extra supplies are available and in reach, in case of an unexpected ostomy moment, become routine. In the two-plus decades of having an ileostomy, I rigorously spent the first fifteen years working to hide this malady as much as possible. Why? I could not bear what I believe would be a judgment, what I perceived would be a sort of leprous avoidance of me or questioned about my bathroom habits. This was not anything I wished to be confronted with or willing to discuss. Part of my rationale included that if an ex-spouse could not deal with my altered state, the very person who said they would love and support me in sickness and in health, then how could I expect others to accept me, to see me as something other than repulsive? This way of thinking informs the background, and thought processes, behind how ostomy selfies offer resistance and visual evidence of persistence.

To counter notions of shame and disgust, to distance the literal waste from the person, many of the #GYBO selfies include images of bare, and clean, skin. The selfies typically feature a person with a pulled-up shirt, or in swimsuits, workout clothes, or lingerie. Occasionally, the bag is hanging out with clothes surrounding it, but those selfies are much less represented. In many of the pictures, the person is smiling; the degree of smile can vary, with sometimes a small smile but most often a very large one. Regardless of the amount of smile, our examination of the selfies could find no one actually frowning; even more pensive or ambiguous expressions can be read as a form of abject acceptance.

And most often, the person faces the viewer, with a direct gaze: this direct gaze focuses the attention both to the bag and away from the bag, drawing on what bell hooks outlines as an opposition gaze or reading.[51] The direct gazes focus the viewer's attention on the entire person; the central focus is not on the belly or bag but instead about the entire person who just happens to have a bag. In this way, the selfies indicate a relationship with the viewer and public,[52] a way of "manifest[ing] possible relationships with audiences"[53] and creating a disruption of body stigmas that pervade dominant culture. Showing so much skin demonstrates both vulnerability and strength: vulnerability as it shows the ostomy bag (or the ostomy scar), which so frequently has been stigmatized; strength in the courage to have one's face or virtual self attached to the image. The selfies overwhelmingly show large amounts of naked skin: the skin features mostly bellies but also includes arms, legs, and faces. Indeed, the very phrase "get your belly out" wants to make visible one's belly or body, with one's bag, but also illustrates the cleanliness of the skin. The clean skin serves as a metonym for a clean bill of health, to show themselves as healthy individuals.

The selfies, along with their accompanying tweets or posts, illustrate a way to destigmatize the bag and the fears of uncontrolled stomachs or bellies. Writing about the politics of thinness, Susan Bordo argued images of one's belly serve as sites of anxiety, where large, bulging bellies serve as "a metaphor of anxiety about internal processes out of control—uncontained desires, unrestrained hunger, uncontrolled impulse,"[54] due to the stomach being the "symbol of consumption."[55] Within the ostomy selfie, the belly functions a bit differently, given its proximity to the pouch of waste materials: it is both literal and symbolic excrement, making present the typically hidden, yet ever present, digestive processes. It moves beyond fear of fatness to one of (potential) disgust of the dirt and muck of bodily functions. Bodily distinctions, where we separate ourselves from blood and excrement, create not only individual body boundaries but also social boundaries.[56] These selfies, by showing the new ways of collecting excrement through the ostomy bag, work to break down the boundary of distance through the visual presence of the bag itself.

In addition to the selfies, the accompanying hashtags redirect the attention away from distance, stigma, or shame toward acceptance. Common additional hashtags center on themes of *awareness* (#crohns, #crohnscolitis, #stomaawareness, #ostomyawareness, #ibdawareness, #crohnsawareness), *destigmization* (#endthestigma), *visibility* (#hangoutwithyourbagout, #invisibleillness, #invisibledisability), *courage* (#ittakesguts, #girlswithguts, #lifetakesguts), and *identity* (#ostomate, #stomaproud, #ibdbeauty, #ibdwarrior, #crohnswarrior, #ileostomywarrior, #nocolonstillrollin). The images and hashtags then are the support for the argument to end stigma drawing on Randall A. Lake's notion of argument where "arguments seek assent not only to the claim stated but also to the claims enacted."[57] The high circulation of this particular campaign, #GetYourBellyOut, demonstrates the power of circulation in the public sphere. Circulating on the public screen of social media disrupts the notion of bodies as unlivable or uninhabitable subject positions. Judith Butler argues that circulation of ideas and images within public space matters: "The public sphere is constituted in part by what can appear, . . . what will count as reality, and what will not. It . . . establish[es] whose lives can be marked as lives."[58] By putting the selfies out there, to get the bellies out, the images articulate a subject position rather than an abject other.

Vignette #2: Dealing with a New Normal: Working Out or an Active Life

Another way that the images illustrate the posters' subjectivity are the selfies highlighting attractive individuals who are active, vibrant, and living a life that demonstrates a great degree of normalcy. From working out in the gym, to standing after a race (such as a 5K), to doing handstands, and even to those standing in or beside water (such as the ocean or pool), these selfies offer a sense that these people are not different, except the attachment of a wafer and pouch to their abdomen. Within the images, the individuals take up space, holding weights, race medals, or flexing muscles. All of these operate as a form of a high-power pose,[59] which connotes power and a sense of confidence.

Michael: And though these selfies illustrate confidence, the story behind the selfie can be more complex. Indeed, what does it means to have an active life as a person with an ostomy? When I put on clothes for any occasion, I consider how they will affect the wafer and the pouch hanging from my side. This is more so the case when considering workout clothes or summer clothes that might expose the abdominal area where my right side now has a pronounced scar from the previous ostomy location, and how the appliance hangs from my left lower abdominal area. Once trying to find swim apparel that would ride high enough to cover the ostomy and supplies was a traumatic process. I wanted to be able to spend time in the water with my shirt off, to sit in a boat with my shirt off, or to put on a water safety device with my shirt off. In twenty-two years, I can count the number of times I have gone into the water on one hand.

Being a more-than-middle-aged person and trying to manage weight has meant, like a great number of people, buying a gym membership. The times I intended to go but failed are numerous, but the issue goes beyond merely finding time. It means managing the ostomy when most gym clothing will create a dilemma of binding where the ostomy is placed barely below the belt line. It means any activity that causes the pouch to fill might be visible to those around me. It means choosing not to shower in the gym but needing to go home after a workout. It has resulted too often that I have spent money, but I merely stay home, wasting the money spent. Fortunately, during the past year, somewhat through necessity, I have learned that walking is just as helpful; yet, even then, it is necessary to consider where to walk because the need for a bathroom is always a consideration and therefore walks must be taken where restroom access is immediate.

Given all these challenges, showcasing the active lifestyle within the selfies again serves to destigmatize and normalize people with ostomies.

Vignette 3: Love after Diagnosis: Sex Appeal

In addition to the active lifestyle, a significant number of selfies focus on individuals showing off as much skin as possible, in the form of shirtless selfies for masculine bodies, some featuring abdomens with defined muscles, and feminine bodies in colorful lingerie or bikinis. Many of the lingerie photographs feature women in their bedrooms, closets, or bathrooms: all intimate spaces for such intimate attire. The swimsuit photographs include people by the water (pools most often, although some beaches) or on lounge chairs by the pool. These images do illustrate the bare skin, as discussed in the first theme, but also operate within male gaze and beauty norms, which has been critiqued as restrictive by many scholars.[60] Some within the IBD community also are critical of this type of selfie, noting that some posters are conventionally attractive already and these types of selfies overly focus on beauty, "as if that's the sole quality to which sufferers aspire."[61]

That being said, focusing on attractiveness and sex appeal makes sense within a culture that focuses on beauty. For example, Jane Feuer notes that fat bodies work with norms of beauty and use "a male gaze [so] that fat women . . . can gain access to representation in a form that does not code them as repellant."[62] Given the high stigma and shame associated with IBDs, presenting oneself as attractive and desirable, to themselves and others, operates as a way to counterbalance those dominant modes.

As the manifestation of the disease seems to be striking more adolescents and is often common among twentysomethings, the issue of being unattractive or undesirable becomes weightier or increasingly problematic. The struggle with puberty in a socially mediated world is again well documented and the symptomology of Crohn's or UC makes this passage all the more difficult. As the focus on self-image is central, rapid weight loss, frequent trips to a bathroom, and the appearance of a less-than-optimal physical presence can be devastating. Often, IBD patients, at least when medication regiments are generally effective, present themselves as nearly normal. In fact, studies show that life expectancy is near normal.[63] On the other hand, the same patients depict something quite different in terms of their quality of life and increased levels of depression, including thoughts about if their body is attractive and/or desirable.[64]

Michael: When I was diagnosed in my late twenties, I was already married; having not really experienced any life-altering illness and perhaps as a person studying to be a pastor, I believed that my marital status would make living as a person suffering with Crohn's less complicated. I certainly bought into the idea of "for better or worse, in sickness and in health." However, I would find out during a life-altering surgery that would result in a temporary ileostomy (it would be reversed after six to eight weeks), my wife would not be able to deal with the substantial changes surgery caused. The profound reality of her struggle manifested itself as soon as I returned from Mayo-Scottsdale (in Arizona) to Pennsylvania. She was not willing to deal with my altered state in any way shape or form, including staying as far away as possible in our king-sized bed. This first surgery was brutal for me in many ways, including losing forty-plus pounds in eight days and needing a bronchoscopy shortly after returning home. The thought of seeing, feeling, or being affected by the ostomy repulsed her and consequently forced me to retreat in ways I never expected. I felt unattractive, unloved, and as something less than human. It was a significant contributing factor to her asking for a divorce. I have spent almost two decades as a single person; the struggle with managing the ostomy in intimate situations continues. My initial reaction when I find myself even remotely interested in someone is to question why anyone would want to put up with my unique body and its issues. Or how in a dating situation would an ostomate best explain their external appliance (as it is called). The #GYBO photographs offer one way to illustrate, and visually demonstrate, what an ostomate body looks like, which offers one way of explaining the device.

Conclusions

The #GetYourBellyOut campaign uses social media as a platform for individuals to post their photographs, including selfies, allowing them to circulate images that challenge the dominant societal norms of stigma and boundaries regarding excrement. #GYBO uses visibility politics and the power of circulation to create new identities. And such campaigns are important. In early 2019, ten-year-old African American boy Seven Bridges committed suicide in Louisville, Kentucky after being bullied at school for multiple reasons, including his race and his bowel condition (some said he smelled bad).[65] Following Seven's suicide, an Instagram campaign began, titled #BagsOutforSeven.[66] Although this new hashtag campaign does not yet have the power of the five years of #GYBO, it operates on the same principle. By visibly showing the identity of those who live with ostomy bags, with healthy, active, and attractive lives, the #GetYourBellyOut campaign illustrates the subjectivity and agentic nature of ostomates. The nature of this disease and the overwhelming need for privacy, as noted throughout this chapter, makes statistical research more difficult. Yet, Michael's appointment as an adjunct associate professor at the Geisinger School of Medicine was made because of the decision of this medical school to treat IBD patients more holistically. In addition, he will be lecturing both medical students and medical colleagues about the psychosocial aspects of living with Crohn's, which undoubtedly relates to the struggles that this chapter lays out.

Much of Michael's attitude toward his own ostomy stems from his initial experience and rejection from a loved one, affecting him in ways he is still realizing. Much of what is shown in the #GYBO selfies, discussed in ostomy groups, and written in academic pieces illustrates a dichotomous response: Those medically compelled to become ostomates either exhibit a sort of extreme loathing toward their fate *or* they have a sense of gratitude for being alive at any cost. We both find the either-or position problematic. There is not a zero-sum game, or all or nothing. Certainly, Michael's move toward finally choosing a permanent ostomy was a process, a painful, arduous, and frightening process, but it was ultimately a lifesaving decision. In fact, his primary care physician at the time would tell him following the surgery how relieved he was Michael had finally chosen it. Two-plus decades of having an external friend as a permanent attachment has taught Michael that he can still be a normal, reasonably active, and even a desirable person. Michael's life is not defined by the four-inch wafer and ten-inch pouch nearly as much as he sometimes wants to believe. Therefore, rather than falling into a love or hate camp regarding the ostomate life, Michael dwells in both. When he has an ostomy moment, particularly when in public or around another person, he hates it with every ounce of his being, and yet simultaneously, he is grateful to be able to write such a chapter. It is hardly ever an either-or; instead, it is a both-and.

Discussion Questions

1 How does the move into a digital/public space with such a private medical concern help both the afflicted and others understand the concept of advocacy?
2 What might those afflicted with an IBD, as well as those who care for them, do to reduce the stigma that is attached to being an ostomate? How can such actions reduce the experiences of shame that often accompany IBD surgical revisions?
3 What are some other ways media can offer opportunities for those who suffer invisible illnesses to come out of the shadows, allowing them to feel like their ostomy is a wearable technology rather than an embarrassment?

Try This!

Have your students come up with some other form of malady, be it illness or anything that creates a division between two parts of society or a group of people. It could be on campus; it could be a societal issue. In the current atmosphere of them versus the other, how might they create some sort of campaign that would create a sense of understanding or acceptance rather than stigma or being ostracized? How might technology be used to create and foster community for the disparate groups and through that technological usage demonstrate a sense of power, persistence, and an ability to manage whatever their issue is more holistically and with a sense of hope?

Acknowledgments

This chapter is a revised version of the paper presented at the 2018 Organization for the Study of Communication, Language, and Gender (OSLCG) conference. Thanks to the Armour, Dupont, and Cabell travel grant from Randolph-Macon College and the College of Liberal Arts at Bloomsburg University for their support in funding or approving travel to present at OSCLG.

Notes

1   Kurt Wagner, "Snapchat Is Still Bigger than Instagram for Younger U.S. Millennials," *Vox*, August 24, 2017, https://www.vox.com/2017/8/24/16198632/snapchat-instagram-teens-comscore-study-growth-users.

2   W.J.T. Mitchell, *Picture Theory: Essays on Verbal and Visual Representation* (Chicago: University of Chicago Press, 1995).

3   David S. Birdsell and Leo Groarke, "Toward a Theory of Visual Argument," *Argumentation & Advocacy* 33, no. 1 (Summer 1996); Lester C. Olson, Cara A. Finnegan, and Diane S. Hope, eds., *Visual Rhetoric: A Reader in Communication and American Culture* (Los Angeles: Sage, 2008); Leo Groarke, Catherine H. Palczewski, and David Godden, "Navigating the Visual Turn in Argument," *Argumentation & Advocacy* 52, no. 4 (Spring 2016).

4   Andrew L. Mendelson and Zizi Papacharissi, "Look at Us: Collective Narcissism in College Student Facebook Photo Galleries," in *A Networked Self: Identity, Community, and Culture on Social Network Sites*, ed. Zizi Papacharissi (New York: Routledge, 2011).

5   Minh-Ha T. Pham, "'I Click and Post and Breathe, Waiting for Others to See What I See': On #FeministSelfies, Outfit Photos, and Networked Vanity," *Fashion Theory: The Journal of Dress, Body & Culture* 19, no. 2 (February 2015).

6   Robert Hariman and John L. Lucaites, *No Caption Needed: Iconic Photographs, Public Culture, and Liberal Democracy* (Chicago: University of Chicago Press, 2007); Robert Hariman and John L. Lucaites, *The Public Image: Photography and Civic Spectatorship* (Chicago: University of Chicago Press, 2016).

7   We draw here upon Judith Butler's work, particularly *Bodies That Matter: On the Discursive Limits of "Sex"* (New York: Routledge, 1993).

8   Kevin Michael DeLuca and Jennifer Peeples, "From Public Sphere to Public Screen: Democracy, Activism, and the 'Violence' of Seattle," *Critical Studies in Media Communication* 19, no. 2 (June 2002).

9   See, for example, Ruth J. Beerman, "Containing Fatness: Bodies, Motherhood, and Civic Identity in Contemporary U.S. Culture" (PhD diss., University of Wisconsin–Milwaukee, 2015).

10   Arthur Frank, *The Wounded Storyteller* (Chicago: University of Chicago Press, 1997), 50.

11   "The Facts about Inflammatory Bowel Disease," Crohn's & Colitis Foundation of America, November 2014, http://www.crohnscolitisfoundation.org/assets/pdfs /updatedibdfactbook.pdf.

12   "About Us," World IBD Day Organization, accessed March 21, 2019, https:// worldibdday.org/about-us.

13   "What Are Crohn's & Colitis?" Crohn's & Colitis Foundation, accessed November 8, 2018, http://www.crohnscolitisfoundation.org/what-are-crohns-and-colitis/.

14   Ibid.

15   Sarah O'Brien and Emily Downward, "Inflammatory Bowel Disease in Children and Teens," IBD, accessed March 19, 2019, https://inflammatoryboweldisease.net /what-is-crohns-disease/children-and-teens/.

16   "Campus Connection," Crohn's & Colitis Foundation, accessed November 8, 2018, http://www.crohnscolitisfoundation.org/campus-connection/.

17   "Don't Let IBD Stop You from Being You," Crohn's & Colitis Foundation, accessed November 8, 2018, http://www.justlikemeibd.org.

18   All surgeries resulting in an external pouch to collect waste of some sort are called ostomies—a surgery that bypasses the bladder, for instance, is called a urostomy.

19   O'Brien and Downward. "Inflammatory Bowel Disease."

20   Tiffany H. Taft, Laurie Keefer, Christoph Leonhard, and Michele Neolon-Woods, "Impact of Perceived Stigma on Inflammatory Bowel Disease Patient Outcomes," *Inflammatory Bowel Diseases* 15, no. 8 (August 2009); T. H. Taft, A. Bedell, J. Nataly, and L. Keefer, "Stigmatization toward Irritable Bowel Syndrome and Inflammatory Bowel Disease in an Online Cohort," *Neurogastroenterology & Motility* 29, no. 2 (February 2017); Tiffany H. Taft, Laurie Keefer, Caroline Artz, Jason Bratten, and Michael P. Jones, "Perceptions of Illness Stigma in Patients with Inflammatory Bowel Disease and Irritable Bowel Disease," *Quality of Life Research* 20, no. 9 (November 2011); Inês Trindade, Claudia Ferreira, and José Pinto-Gouveia, "Chronic Illness–Related Shame: Development of a New Scale and Novel Approach for IBD Patients' Depressive Symptomatology," *Clinical Psychology and Psychotherapy* 24 (2017): 256.

21   Molly Margaret Kessler, "Wearing an Ostomy Pouch and Becoming an Ostomate: A Kairological Approach to Wearability," *Rhetoric Society Quarterly* 46, no. 3 (May 2016): 241–242, 246.

22   Trindade et al., "Chronic Illness-Related Shame."

23   Ibid. See also Mark A. Rademacher, "'The Most Inspiring Bikini Photos You'll See This Summer': A Thematic Analysis of Mass Audience Interpretations of Ostomy Selfies," *New Media & Society* 20, no. 10 (2018): 3860–3861.

24   "About Us," #GetYourBellyOut Community Interest Company, accessed March 16, 2019, https://getyourbellyout.org.uk.

25   "The Selfie Campaign Urging You to 'Get Your Belly Out,'" *BBC News*, October 25, 2017, https://www.bbc.com/news/av/health-41742498/the-selfie-campaign-urging -you-to-get-your-belly-out.

26   Website: https://getyourbellyout.org.uk; Facebook: https://www.facebook.com /getyourbellyout/; Twitter account: https://twitter.com/GetYourBellyOut; Twitter hashtag: https://twitter.com/search?q=%23getyourbellyout&src=typd; Instagram account: https://www.instagram.com/getyourbellyout_official/; Instagram hashtag: https://www.instagram.com/explore/tags/getyourbellyout/.

27   "Mission Statement," #GetYourBellyOut Community Interest Company, accessed September 22, 2018, https://getyourbellyout.org.uk/mission-statement/.

28   For our analysis, rather than looking at all 25,000 tweets or posts with the associated hashtag, we reviewed representative anecdotes or examples that featured selfies

(thereby excluding any content that did not include a photograph). Images were collected and analyzed from two different time periods, September 2018 and March 2019. The majority of the images came from Instagram rather than Twitter, given that the platforms center different aspects (Instagram on the images as primary versus Twitter with text as primary). Additionally, given that Facebook does not currently allow one to sort or search for content via a hashtag, that platform was excluded.

29 Although selfies typically are taken by individuals with one's phone, posts also include photographs of individuals by themselves clearly taken by someone else. Given that the campaign, media coverage, and scholarly work grouped both of these photographs together, our chapter examines both as part of the genre of the ostomy selfie. Who took the photograph (self or other) is less important than what the photograph showcases, that of the ostomate body.

30 Catronia Harvey-Jenner, "Colostomy Bag Selfies Are the New Inspirational Trend on Social Media," *Cosmopolitan*, August 5, 2014, https://www.cosmopolitan.com /uk/body/a28494/colostomy-bag-selfies-inspirational/.

31 Charlotte Lytton, "The Brave Colostomy Bag Selfies," *Daily Beast*, July 2, 2014, https://www.thedailybeast.com/the-brave-colostomy-bag-selfies.

32 Zoe Szathmary, "Scores of Crohn's Sufferers across the Globe Post Brave Selfies of Their Colostomy Bags, along with Their Stories of Hope and Survival," *Daily Mail*, July 5, 2014, https://www.dailymail.co.uk/news/article-2681994/Crohns-sufferers -reveal-stories-hope-survival-selfies-showing-colostomy-bags.html.

33 Jenna Birch, "Why EVERYONE Is Talking about This Woman's Brave Bikini Photo. Aspiring model Bethany Townsend Sheds Light on an Often Overlooked Illness," *Women's Health*, July 3, 2014, https://www.womenshealthmag.com/health /a19919732/bethany-townsend-colostomy-bag-selfie/; Natasha Hinde, "Woman with Crohn's Disease Bravely Bares Ostomy Bag for the First Time since Opera- tion," *Huffington Post UK*, September 1, 2017, https://www.huffingtonpost.co.uk /entry/woman-with-crohns-disease-bravely-bares-ostomy-bag-for-the-first-time _uk_58736c4ce4b0961f09387c96; Stephen Matthews, "Bare Those Bags! 12 Brave People Show Off Their Stoma Bags for a Charity Calendar That Helps to Reduce Taboos and Stigma," *Daily Mail*, November 22, 2016, https://www.dailymail.co.uk /health/article-3960354/Bare-bags-12-brave-people-stoma-bags-charity-calendar -helps-reduce-taboos-stigma.html.

34 Dennis Owen Frohlich, "Self-Disclosing My Ostomy to the Dominant Culture: An Autoethnography," *Journal of Wound Ostomy & Continence Nursing* 39, no. 6 (November/December 2012); Dennis Owen Frohlich, "The Social Support Model for People with Chronic Health Conditions: A Proposal for Future Research," *Social Theory & Health* 12, no. 2 (May 2014); Dennis Owen Frohlich, "The Social Construction of Inflammatory Bowel Disease Using Social Media Technologies," *Health Communication* 31, no. 11 (November 2016); Dennis Owen Frohlich and Anne Zmyslinski-Seelig, "The Presence of Social Support Messages on YouTube Videos about Inflammatory Bowel Disease and Ostomies," *Health Communication* 27, no. 5 (September 2012); Dennis Owen Frohlich and Anne N. Zmyslinski-Seelig, "How *Uncover Ostomy* Challenges Ostomy Stigma, and Encourages Others to Do the Same," *New Media & Society* 18, no. 2 (February 2016).

35 Kessler, "Wearing Ostomy Pouch," 237.

36 As an example of narratives within medicine, see Rita Charon, *Narrative Medicine: Honoring the Stories of Illness* (New York: Oxford University Press, 2006). Although important, this work does not focus on the idea of visuals in crafting the

public stories or how the public comes to understand chronic illnesses, but instead focuses on the medical community.

37 Dariusz Baraliński, Izabela Sałacińska, Pawel Więch, and Maria Kózka, "Life Satisfaction and Self-Efficacy in Patients with Stoma," *Progress in Health Sciences* 4, no. 2 (2014): 23; Kingsley L. Simmons, Jane A. Smith, Karen-Ann Bob, and Laura L. M. Miles, "Adjustment to Colostomy: Stoma Acceptance, Stoma Care Self-efficacy and Interpersonal Relationships," *Journal of Advanced Nursing* 60, no. 6 (2007).

38 One notable exception is Rademacher, "Most Inspiring Bikini." Although stating that their work examines ostomy selfies, it examined only one selfie and associated news coverage, rather than looking at the genre of ostomy selfies and how as entire collections functions, as we take up in this chapter.

39 Other hashtags also focus on ostomy selfies, including #ibdselfie, #ostomyinspo, and #bagselfie. However, these hashtags include a smaller reach in terms of both numbers as well as content: many of these hashtagged images on Twitter and Instagram are not ostomy selfies. Examples include an InBox Dollars (IBD) marketing campaign, or bags as paper bags, purses, handbags, and bookbags. Thus, focusing the #GYBO campaign offers a better understanding of the genre of the ostomy selfie and its functions.

40 "Welcome to the WEGO Health Awards," WEGO Health (2019), accessed March 22, 2019, https://www.wegohealth.com/for-patient-leaders/wego-health-awards/.

41 Kristin Long, "2018 Top 10 Best in Show: Communities," WEGO Health, January 19, 2019, https://www.wegohealth.com/2019/01/19/2018-top-10-best-in-show-communities/.

42 "Welcome to the WEGO Health Awards."

43 Kevin Michael DeLuca, "Unruly Arguments: The Body Rhetoric of Earth First!, ACT UP, and Queer Nation," *Argumentation & Advocacy* 36, no. 1 (Summer 1999).

44 Dan Brouwer, "The Precarious Visibility Politics of Self-Stigmatization: The Case of HIV/AIDS Tattoos," *Text and Performance Quarterly* 18, no. 2 (1998); Daniel C. Brouwer and Linda Diane Hortwitz, "The Cultural Politics of Progenic Auschwitz Tattoos: 157622, A-15510, 4559, . . . ," *Quarterly Journal of Speech* 101, no. 3 (August 2015); Charles E. Morris III and John M. Sloop, "'What Lips These Lips Have Kissed': Refiguring the Politics of Queer Public Kissing," *Communication and Critical/Cultural Studies* 3 (2006).

45 Chaïm Perelman and L. Olbrechts-Tyetca, *The New Rhetoric: A Treatise on Argumentation*, trans. John Wilkinson and Purcell Weaver (Notre Dame, IN: University of Notre Dame Press, 1969), 117.

46 Although Perelman and Olbrechts-Tyetca discuss presence related to verbal discourse, scholars expanded this concept to visuals as well. Relevant scholarship includes Jamie Landau, "Women Will Get Cancer: Visual and Verbal Presence (and Absence) in a Pharmaceutical Advertising Campaign about HPV," *Argumentation & Advocacy* 48 (2011) and Catherine Helen Palczewski, Richard Ice, and John Fritch, *Rhetoric in Civic Life*, 2nd ed. (State College, PA: Strata Publishing, 2016).

47 Douglas A. Drossman, "The Psychosocial Aspects of Inflammatory Bowel Disease," *Stress Medicine* 2 (1986); Benjamin Saunders, "'It Seems Like You're Going Round in Circles': Recurrent Biographical Disruption Constructed through the Past, Present, and Anticipated Future in the Narrative of Young Adults with Inflammatory Bowel Disease," *Sociology of Health and Illness* 39, no. 5 (2017); Taft et al., "Stigmatization"; Taft et al., "Impact Perceived Stigma"; Taft et al., "Perceptions"; Trindade et al., "Chronic Illness–Related Shame."

48 Saunders, "Seems Like," 727.

49 This conversation occurred when my ex-spouse and I had sat down to discuss the decision she had made to ask for a divorce. In the process of that conversation, she noted that being married to someone with Crohn's was not what she signed up for (this is a paraphrase of her comments). Then she noted that she was tired of being married to a wimp, as noted in the text. My response was something to the effect that I did not know what it would be to be on her side, but I would never wish my side on her or anyone.

50 Erving Goffman, *Stigma: Notes on the Management of Spoiled Identity* (New York: Simon & Schuster, 1963), 48.

51 bell hooks, *Black Looks: Race and Representation* (Boston: South End Press, 1992).

52 Beerman, "Containing Fatness," 133, 141.

53 Lawrence J. Prelli, "Rhetorics of Display," in *Rhetorics of Display* (Columbia: University of South Carolina Press, 2006), 21.

54 Susan Bordo, *Unbearable Weight: Feminism, Western Culture, and the Body*, 10th anniversary ed. (Berkeley: University of California Press, 2003), 189.

55 Ibid., 202.

56 Mary Douglas, *Natural Symbols: Explorations in Cosmology* (New York: Routledge, 1996).

57 Randall A. Lake, "The Implied Auditor," *Argumentation Theory and the Rhetoric of Assent* (Tuscaloosa: University of Alabama Press, 1990), 83.

58 Judith Butler, *Precarious Life: The Powers of Mourning and Violence* (New York: Verso, 2004), xx–xxi.

59 Amy Cuddy, "Your Body Language May Shape Who You are," filmed June 2012, TED video, 20:56, https://www.ted.com/talks/amy_cuddy_your_body_language_shapes_who_you_are/.

60 For example, see Laura Mulvey, "Visual Pleasure and Narrative Cinema," in *The Feminism and Visual Culture Reader* (New York: Routledge, 2003).

61 Marc Mierowsky, "Why Colostomy Selfies Don't Give the Full Picture," *Huffington Post*, July 24, 2014, https://www.huffingtonpost.com/marc-mierowsky/colostomy-selfies_b_5615776.html.

62 Jane Feuer, "Averting the Male Gaze: Visual Pleasure and Images of Fat Women," in *Television, History, and American Culture: Feminist Critical Essays* (Durham, NC: Duke University Press, 1999), 184.

63 Esme Fuller-Thomson and Joanna Sulman, "Depression and Inflammatory Bowel Disease: Findings from Two Nationally Representative Canadian Studies," *Inflammatory Bowel Diseases* 12, no. 8 (2006); Lesley A. Graff, John R. Walker, and Charles N. Bernstein, "Depression and Anxiety in Inflammatory Bowel Disease: A Review of Comorbidity and Management," *Inflammatory Bowel Diseases* 15, no. 9 (2009).

64 Trindade et al., "Chronic Illness–Related Shame."

65 Allison Ross, "Louisville Mom Blames Bullying at JCPS for Suicide of Her 10-Year-Old," *Louisville Courier Journal*, January 22, 2019, https://www.courier-journal.com/story/news/education/2019/01/22/louisville-mom-blames-jcps-bullying-sons-death-suicide/2643320002/; Robyn Merrett, "10-Year-Old Kentucky Boy Allegedly Dies by Suicide after Being Bullied over Colostomy Bag," *People*, January 23, 2019, https://people.com/human-interest/kentucky-boy-10-seven-bridges-died-by-suicide-colostomy-bag/.

66 Paige Wyant, "People Share Ostomy Photos on Instagram Following 10-Year-Old Boy's Suicide," TheMighty.com, January 25, 2019, https://themighty.com/2019/01/bagsoutforseven-instagram-seven-bridges-suicide-colostomy/.

18

The Silence of Laughter

• •

LYDIA HUERTA MORENO

I read the message on my computer screen from the Title IX office, stating, "Can you please confirm that what is transcribed here accurately reflects the conversation we had?"[1] My heart raced; my mouth filled with the sharp taste of acid. My bodily response was an immediate form of resistance to reading my own statement of a week before at the Title IX office of my previous employer. I had made a special trip back, as my name had come up in a list of over twenty-eight women who had experienced some sort of harassment and/or form of sexist treatment on behalf of the only Latino man (Dino)[2] who formed part of the university president's cabinet. In what follows, I tell fragments of my story, a compilation of the experiences I am allowed to disclose because they are not protected under the nondisclosure agreement that I had to sign in order to speak out and stand in solidarity with the other women who were part of Dino's sexual harassment investigation.

As a thirty-year-old, I thought graduate school had prepared me to dismantle the oppressive systems of racism, ethnocentrism, sexism, and ageism in the world. I felt empowered with the tools provided by liberation theology, Black feminist thought, and pedagogy of the oppressed to enter a world of entrenched racialized and gendered behaviors I associated with the "white men" who still dominate leadership in academia. Eight years later, I find myself wanting to share snippets of my experiences at my first tenure-track job because even though I was warned of the violence and silencing that would come from white colleagues, I never imagined I would experience these tactics from fellow faculty of color.

I am also writing these disjointed—if not dismembered—memories as a way to name my pain in order to heal.[3] For five years, I swallowed anger, pain, sadness, impotence, frustration, and grief and have been carrying an immense guilt and shame for the choices I made to stay in academia. I write because *tengo un dolor atorado*, a pain that sits in my body, a toxicity I keep swallowing back in order to survive and it is not working anymore. I need to vomit. I can no longer afford to steep in silent rage *y seguir tragandome este cuento*. It is crippling my back, causing great pain in my heart, and shaping my perception of academia as a cynical oppressive space rather than a space that has the potential to give birth to liberatory and transformative practices.

This is my attempt at reconciling the gap between the training PhD students receive that arms them with a strong background in critical race theory, feminism, and critical pedagogy and the systems in which they will likely obtain their first tenure-track job. According to the United States Department of Education's report *The Condition of Education 2019*, in the fall of 2018, Latinas made up 3 percent of all full-time faculty at degree-seeking institutions compared to 76 percent held by white men and women (35 percent women and 41 percent men). When closely examining the rank distribution of full-time Latinas at degree-seeking institutions, among total faculty, 3 percent are tenured, 5 percent are associate professors, and 6 percent are assistant professors. These figures notably speak to the difficulties Latinas face trying to navigate the borderlands of academia and the fact that many do not advance in rank. Furthermore, the data suggest that there are polarizing disparities in higher education that are in part the result of harsh and unforgiving gendered and race practices in tenured and tenure-track faculty.[4] These studies suggest that Latina attrition rate from assistant professor to full professor is due in part to institutional practices that cause Latina women to choose between family and the academy,[5] whereas others point to institutional practices that expect women of color to yield a high research agenda, while also burdening them with service and teaching and expecting more of them than their white counterparts and excluding them from leadership positions.[6]

In October 2019, the University of Texas released the *Hispanic Equity Report*, which found after examining faculty résumés that Latina/o professors were paid considerably less than their white counterparts despite being "eminently qualified" and were not offered senior leadership and administrative positions. One high-profile example that highlights the institutional practices that limit inclusion of Latinas in academia is the case of Lorgia Garcia-Peña, an assistant professor of ethnic studies who was denied tenure at Harvard in 2019. Dr. Garcia-Peña's research is highly regarded. In 2017, she won the National Women's Studies Association's Gloria E. Anzaldúa Book Prize for her book *The Borders of Dominicanidad: Race, Nations, and Archives of Contradictions*.[7] She has received several grants and prestigious fellowships, including the Ford Foundation Fellowship. Her teaching and institutional and professional service are exemplary.

Yet despite this prestigious and established record, the institution denied her tenure. These are just two recent examples of exclusionary practices that keep Latinas from staying in academia and advancing through professorial ranks. When I joined the faculty at my previous institution in 2013, I was warned about Latina faculty attrition rates. I was told that I was very lucky; I had won the coveted lottery of a tenure-track job in the aftermath of the 2008 economic crisis and that I had to do whatever it took to not become another statistic. This autoethnography is my attempt at critically understanding experiences from my first year as a tenure-track professor and exploring the ways I unconsciously and consciously chose silence as a survival mechanism so that I did not become another Latina who had to leave or was pushed out of the academy.

I had to take both a literal and metaphorical journey to begin to unpack the experiences of my first year as a tenure-track assistant professor. I had to find a new academic position, and I had to move. I had to find the space to process the emotional toll and burnout I experienced. I learned a meditative practice that would safely allow my embodied experiences to surface. I took time to examine why I reacted the way I did in given situations. Only then could I start to understand the full extent to which events get mischaracterized, misrepresented, and misinterpreted and how and why violence is deliberately dismissed.

At the center of this autoethnography is the tension between events and the incredulity and cognitive dissonance in the face of those occurrences. Somehow, paradoxically, the critical intellectual training that qualified me to obtain the job was unavailable to me when I found myself in situations that I would have thought my training would have prepared me to recognize and negotiate. The centrality of embodied experience that feminist practices teach us are valuable for critique became, ironically, unavailable to me precisely because of the ways in which power travels and intersects with identities, positionality of junior scholars, university practices, and institutional structures—revealing the backstitching that limit critique. The following fragment of my academic journey thus oscillates between and across the borders of my experience of being a highly educated scholar versed in feminism, critical race, antiracist, and decolonial theory and an examination of the liberatory promises of those critiques.

I have chosen to write this autoethnography in the tradition of a "layered account"[8] as it allows for me to draw from the legacies of testimonio as a Latina and Black feminist methodology,[9] from ancestral Indigenous and Chicanx feminist relational embodied forms of knowing,[10] feminist ethnographic reporting,[11] and qualitative studies.[12] Locating my critique in these critical traditions enables me to highlight these dismembered experiences in the paradoxical backstitches between lived embodied experiences and intellectual learned experiences and the way. The complexity of personal narrative, testimonios, and narrated experiences that is central to autoethnography makes it an appropriate methodology for this project that attempts to manage paradoxical and simultaneous experiences in all of their intricacy.

In this chapter, I make use of emotional experience, bodily reactions, and theoretical thinking to create a layered account. I will make use of headings to indicate a shift in emotional, physical, thought, and spatial realms. In this way, the messy and entangled experiences and reflections discussed below are disimbricated in order to suggest how intersectional feminist theories might serve as a foundation for a mindful feminist praxis checklist that might help others identify, bring awareness to, and interpret accounts of similar experiences, enabling them to think strategically about forms of resistance that lie outside the reporting mechanisms of institutions. Tools like these are necessary should we wish to remain in the academic institutions we need to transform.

Audre Lorde Taught Me to Introduce Myself

I remember reading Audre Lorde's *Sister Outsider: Essays and Speeches* as a young scholar and finding the permission to insert my identity into my work and the political necessity of doing so. For Lorde, introducing yourself matters because it allows you to say who you are, what are your concerns and commitments—your values. The assertion of a scholar's values and context performs two functions: the grounds of critique can no longer be *assumed* to be disembodied and disinterested (a fiction all along); the scholar claims her positionality as valid and important to structures of academic and political critique. I am a cultural studies interdisciplinary scholar, a lover, a friend, a daughter, a sister, an assistant professor, and a Latinx queer woman who has the privilege of being binational. I am also committed to practicing decolonial transnational abolitionist feminism as way of life. The intersections of these identities and my moral practice blur, separate, and sometimes fade as I maneuver the responsibilities of an assistant professor on a tenure-track position.

On the Road Again, This Time to Make One Last Report

I embarked on a journey to the place I had sworn I would never return to. Never say never. I was anxious. I did not want to go back to that rural university. I especially did not want to go back to answer questions about how, for five years, I was sexually harassed; how I had reported it to my chair, dean, provost; how nothing had been done; how my "questionable" sexuality became a way to exclude me from working groups; how after three years of speaking up I became silent; how I eventually looked the other way, consumed by shame, guilt, a desire to remain in academia; and how I participated in enabling the behavior of these men by acquiescing to the induced silence. I did not want to be in a closed space with the Title IX officer and another staff member answering questions of what I had experienced and, more specifically, of why and how I justified this man.

Yet, there I was, in a car driving alongside the U.S.-Mexico border, literally in the midst of one of the worst humanitarian crises of the present day, as the

103-degree heat reminded me of what hell must feel like. The heat scorched my arms, my back tensed with guilt, and the shame flowed through tears. All I could think was that while I had been sexually harassed, what really mattered was that I had enabled these men to groom and sexually harass other students and staff.

I had been driving for three hours. I was drenched in sweat, and I still had forty-five minutes left on a rural road to arrive at my destination. Most of the journey had felt physically and emotionally suffocating. Furious, feeling absolutely suspended in time, I revisited moments over the last five years that I had somehow managed to silence and ignore. I could hear Dino's voice oscillating with my choices:

"You should be grateful, that with the university reorganization, you still have a job because I fought for you";

to survive: *smile. feelings of indebtedness.* acuerdate calladita te ves más bonita.

"Shut up, you are young and impetuous and don't know what you are talking about, there are no Latinx populations in Canada";

to survive: *look around: are any of the men in power—the provost, the dean, the chair, going to say anything? No. look down. write out "get out of this place. fight the tears. be silent. smile.* acuerdate calladita te ves más bonita.

"Oh, you didn't hear? I am the VP of sexternal affairs;

to survive: *smile. report to the dean. be silent. smile.* acuerdate calladita te ves más bonita.

"Me debes una";

to survive: *smile. be silent. smile.* acuerdate calladita te ves más bonita.

"You know you're not in the Spanish Department because I did that for you. I fixed that problem";

to survive: *smile. report to my chair. smile. be silent.* acuerdate calladita te ves más bonita.

"So what are you going to do for me now?";

to survive: *smile. be silent. smile.* acuerdate calladita te ves más bonita.

"What are you going to do for me since I saved your job?";

to survive: *smile. Why not just joke with him, get on his level, say: "What do you want me to do? Get on my knees, give you a blowjob? Oops! I actually said it out loud. Damn it.* acuerdate calladita te ves más bonita.

"I want you to be the next chair, we need to get rid of her, and you could be responsible for the program";

to survive: *smile. report to my chair. smile. be silent.*

"Oh, be careful with her, she likes women with big asses. Yeah, her and I have that in common";

to survive: *smile. be silent. smile.* acuerdate calladita te ves más bonita.

"I like this Berkeley University T-shirt; I like the placement of the bear's head on your chest";

to survive: *step back. smile. be silent. smile. exit office. report to human resources.* acuerdate calladita te ves más bonita.

"You look very sexy today, oh I forgot I can't say that anymore, you might claim I'm sexually harassing you";

to survive: *smile. be silent. smile.* acuerdate calladita te ves más bonita.

"Is the student gay? She is very pretty";

to survive: *smile. warn student. smile.* acuerdate calladita te ves más bonita.

"Thank you for letting me know people were saying that about me. I always knew you were loyal";

to survive: *smile. be silent. smile.* acuerdate calladita te ves más bonita.

"Mmm . . . to be those pants";

to survive: *smile. be silent. smile.* acuerdate calladita te ves más bonita.

In those last forty-five minutes of wide-open desert landscape, I felt haunted by the phrase *calladita te ves más bonita*. I had heard the phrase before from my grandmother when she would remind me not to speak out of turn or when I was disrespecting my grandfather or my uncles, but I could not place how that phrase became the way I gaslighted myself into silence. *Calladita te ves más bonita*. The phrase "is a popular saying usually used with [female] children or, all too frequently, from husband to wife. It is translated as 'quiet, you look more beautiful.'"[13] In other words, the best, most pleasing presentation of a woman coincides with her silence. When did I start doing that? Why had I started doing that?

The Silences

In their phenomenological study about Latina professors in higher education, Medina and Luna[14] argue that academia silences Latina professors through institutional practices that reinforce feelings of inadequacy and incompetency assigned to their race, gender, and language skills, thus silencing those on the margins. In her analysis of counterstories as testimonios of four Latina faculty members, Garcia considers the silences that result from racial and gendered oppression. She found that silence "is often a result of oppression and the role that power and politics play in the production of knowledge." She explains that the testimonios of Latina faculty demonstrate how "shame, guilt, and oppressive exclusionary forces can induce silence" and argues that "silence is both an involuntary and voluntary mechanism to deal with oppression."[15] In this process, I hope to mindfully question how silences that seemed to be my intentional responses—and upon which I reflect with a sense of shame and alienation—were induced and produced by those in power at an academic institution that participated in widespread systemic racism and sexism.

A Plate of Physical Compliments with a Side of Presumed Incompetence

The second week of my brand-new tenure-track job, I was invited to have lunch with Fernando,[16] a leading Chicano studies scholar. We had met briefly at my job talk and wanted to welcome me to town. We went to a small establishment, one of the only restaurants with good Mexican food. There were two other people there; it was a small space. We sat there in the August Southwest heat and talked about our favorite authors, about the "crisis" of Chicano studies moving toward Latinx studies, about his career. Then he blurted out, "You know, you are real pretty. You will do well here."

As I heard his words, I felt my body tense up. My stomach churned and my palms began to feel clammy. I fidgeted. All of this happened in seconds, and I knew instinctively that I had to respond kindly—first impressions matter, we are told. Brought up in a Catholic home, I learned early to treat others like you want to be treated and to demonstrate respect for my elders. Any disregard for elders could result in harsh punishment and ostracizing behaviors. Also, the six years of my PhD program had taught me through critical race theories and feminism that this man sitting before me was supposed to be an ally, a brother in the struggle. Alas, he was anything but.

I felt a smile forming on my face, I thanked him for the compliment, and as a defense mechanism, my sass took over and I sarcastically said, "Well, I am glad that what is really important here is my looks and that all those years of hitting the books and earning a PhD really don't matter." He laughed and told me he was glad I had a good sense of humor. I wish I could remember how I got through the rest of the conversation, or frankly, how I got out of that restaurant, but I have no recollection. It is as if my mind shut down to keep my temper from flaring up and telling him off.

That afternoon, I spoke about this incident with Dino. At the time, it seemed like the sensible thing to do, especially because he had a daughter and surely this meant that he would understand what it was like to have six years of studies be reduced to nothing and to be treated like a brainless woman. Also, Dino had marched in the trenches with César Chávez, knew Dolores Huerta, proudly called himself a reformed Chicano brother, and he "advocated" for female students and colleagues to be in positions of power, so surely, he would be able to offer practical advice to counter the sexist behavior, or at the very least call his colleague in. However, upon hearing my complaint and my rage at being reduced to nothing but a pretty face, he burst out in deafening boisterous laughter. Then he proceeded to tell me:

Relajate, mija

You need to learn that some men are just like that, *"viejitos que no hacen daño pero que se divierten diciendo piropos en compañía de mujeres bellas como tú"*

You need to learn to take a compliment

It is an asset to be pretty and smart

You have great potential for a future at this institution

Ya veras pronto serás la próxima chair de Chicano studies, acuerdate calladita te ves más bonita, dale tiempo al tiempo, ya verás.

His words felt like small shards of glass hitting my face. I felt *regañada*. I swallowed the anger, *me tragué el sexismo*, I smiled, I nodded, I didn't say anything more.

Lesson 1: Silence Has Cultural Dynamics

This was my first experience in silencing myself as a tenure-track faculty member. In her analysis of faculty counternarratives, Garcia explains that "we must read silence multivalently to consider the dynamics that surround them, the various reasons for not speaking, and that factors that play into being heard of understood."[17] In questioning the circumstances around my silence, around swallowing the sexism and anger, I see Dino's use of the word *mija* played an essential role in my silencing. In Spanish, the word is a combination of the words *mi* (mine) and *hija* (daughter), and it is often used as a term of endearment used between family members and close friends; the term can also be used to admonish someone. In this context, *mija* brought together the complex axes of identification and power in our brief exchange. On the one hand, the familiarity reminded me of what we had in common: culture, language, and (I imagined) politics. Yet a man would never establish familiarity or reprimand another, younger man with this term. Being called *my daughter* by the vice-president of an institution cloaked power in endearment and familiarity: not only did he have the university president's ear, but in my short tenure at this place, I had heard how he single-handedly had created a department, while removing people and rewarding others for their loyalty.

In addition to being an assertion of gendered power that recast my identification with Dino from one of safety to one of trepidation, this exchange reveals behavior that falls into what the Department of Education's *Training Manual on Addressing Adult Sexual Misconduct in the School Setting* calls perpetration behaviors.[18] Using this term allowed Dino to admonish me informally because it made me part of his family and it invoked my own relational family dynamics into my workplace. Perpetration behaviors include trolling and testing (perpetrators look for vulnerable people)—I was the youngest faculty member and in a coveted-but-tenuous tenure-track job—followed by grooming (making the person feel special and desensitizing them to inappropriate behaviors), such as when Dino reiterated that I should be thankful men wanted to spend time in the company of beautiful women like me. These behaviors escalate through and into exploiting and lulling (attempts to isolate, intimidate, manipulate, and coerce the person), as evidenced in Dino's discussion of my future where I might be a chair if, of course, I kept quiet.

Dino used the phrase *Calladita te ves más bonita* knowingly as a cultural weapon to make Latinx women fall in line. I would come to see that I was not the only one; he used this with the other three, slightly older Latina colleagues I had. In addition to reasserting a patriarchal, familial dynamic in which he held gendered power, it also became a form of gaslighting, intended to deny women's own experiences about harms done to them by men.[19] Dino very carefully placed the phrase *after* commanding me to remember that if I wanted to succeed, I had to be quiet—as that is how my "beauty" was most appreciated. This was the first time when I told myself, *Yes, remember if you want to be in favor, just be quiet.*

Mija. Calladita te ves más bonita. Despite my training, my politics, my previously outspoken confidence and strength, I was silenced rather than provoked to articulate resistance. Did I unconsciously silence myself? Or did I consciously make the choice to be silent—as a strategy for survival and a way to try to hold on for a future date when I might martial resistance?

Either way, this first silence taught me that not only did I have to be wary of my white colleagues but that I could not trust scholars who were part of my community. Most saliently, I began to learn that despite the racial politics of these groundbreaking pioneers of Chicano studies, their displays of sexism and paternalism reproduced the very system of white supremacy steeped in the misogyny and psychological oppression that they critiqued. What is more, their behavior validated the hierarchal, gendered, and raced (through token-ism) structure of power of the academy. In my undergraduate and graduate years, I had read all about these dynamics explored in the essays of feminists like Ana Nieto Gomez, Rosalie Flores, Sonia López, Cynthia Orozco, Gloria Anzaldúa, and Cherríe Moraga.[20] Yet, for some reason, I understood their experiences as being specific to the 1970s, '80s, and early '90s. I had started my first job in 2013. Surely, those issues around gender and race had changed. I learned very quickly in my interactions with Fernando and Dino that they had become more entrenched.

Figs and Bourbon

It was fall in my first year as a tenure-track faculty, I had been tutoring the dean[21] of the Business School in Spanish. On a Wednesday, Dean Lokht texted to say he could not make it to our tutoring session on campus but that I should come over to his house to have dinner and then we could do our class. Dean Lokht, like Dino and Fernando, was part of a small group of men belonging to minor-ity identities; he was Persian and had enjoyed a successful career in a prestigious school in the northeast and had come to the institution because he wanted to retire in the Southwest. He had a daughter he spoke about often, he was old enough to be my father, I had seen him around town with a woman about his age; I did not think twice about accepting the alternative plan.

Around 5:00 p.m., I knocked on his door. I felt a bit anxious; it was the first time I had been invited to a dean's house for dinner. I brought dessert and a small floral arrangement. My grandmothers taught me never to show up empty-handed. It seemed to take a very long time for anyone to open the door.

When Dean Lokht opened the door, he was wearing nothing but an open beige and bluish flannel shirt and givehs on his feet. He stood in the doorway, smiling, letting his nudity speak for himself. I remember staring at him, I remem-ber doing a once-over and then fixing my eyes on his ears, my mind was taking mental pictures as fast as it could, documenting what was happening while at the same time controlling my facial expressions. I can still remember his copper, tanned body: hairy chest, belly hanging over a barely visible penis, pencil-thin legs. He smiled boisterously, welcomed me into his home, and showed me the way in by turning sideways on the doorframe. His manner made it all seem ordinary, as if he always welcomed guests in this way. At the same time, it felt as if I were Alice, going through the looking glass.

I stood at the threshold, considering my choices: I could turn around and become a laughable story for him to share with his friends, or I could walk in and not be intimidated by his nudity and not pay attention to his naked body. I could keep my power and my integrity intact by going in, giving him his Spanish lesson, and then eating dinner and leaving. His nakedness on display felt like some sort of test, an expression of a code that I as a new faculty member would have to learn and manage. Strange as it seems, I walked into the house.

I looked around for his partner, but when I inquired, he said he did not have a partner. He laughed and shared that the person I had seen him with was just his "fuck buddy." My heart began to race. Somehow, I ended up sitting at the table with a plate of food in front of me. My heart was pounding, my palms were sweating, my jaw felt tight—I had made a mistake, I should not be in this man's home at all, especially not alone and not with his nakedness. He sat across from me smugly. I ate quickly, my heart pounding, taking in the quickest exit should I need it. He had locked the door. The house felt cold. I tried to remain externally calm, cool, and collected—I could be tough—I was not going to let this man get me to crack. I performed confidence and indifference at his naked body. I ate. I smiled.

Throughout dinner we spoke in Spanish, he told me about his four sons, his daughter, his "horrible crazy" exes. He asked me questions about my personal life, but I quickly deflected and kept the conversation focused on him. After dinner and our Spanish conversation, he offered me wine which I politely declined letting him know that I needed to get home to grade. I rose from the table, thanked him. I made my way to the door, and as I was reaching for the doorknob, he grabbed my hand, wrapped it around his waist as he pulled me into him, and he kissed me on the cheek. He pressed himself tightly into my body and whispered, "I made you dinner. The least you can do is say goodbye in our way." He laughed and then pulled away and whispered, "I'll give you a pass this time." He laughed again, then opened the door. "It was very nice having you over. We should do this again."

He pulled me into him again and gave me a hug. He was shorter than me, so as he bowed his head, it pressed into my shoulder. My body was frozen. I could not seem to get my body to push him away. He smelled like figs, bourbon, and flavored tobacco. I could feel my heart in my chest, the blood rushing to my head. Would he move his hands, grope me, try to kiss other parts of my body? Would he try to rape me? Very meticulously, I stepped back and gently unwrapped his hands from my body. I smiled. "*Gracias por la cena*," I heard myself say as my hand released the lock and turned the doorknob so that I could leave.

Safely in my car, I called one of my best friends from high school. I remember saying, "You are not going to believe what just happened!" I certainly didn't believe what just happened. As I told her about the encounter in between bursts of nervous laughter, I started to realize that what I had just experienced was serious and that I needed to report it. I remember her energetically saying, "Lydia, what the fuck does 'I'll give you a pass this time' even mean?" I hesitatingly explained that maybe it was cultural, that maybe the "pass" was that I had been rude and not said goodbye by initiating the kiss on his cheek and hugging him goodbye.

Lesson 2: We Must Make Space for Embodied Knowledge

Having a dean answer the door naked and, in retrospect, clearly inebriated seems as absurd and unlikely today as it did seven years ago. What sticks with me is how noisy the whole experience was: the ringing of the doorbell, the sound of Dean Lokht's voice and laughter, the opening of the door, the movement of furniture, the inner voice racing in my head, the pounding of my heart. There were only two of us; it must have been a quiet evening. And yet, to me, there was no space for silence, no space to breathe or process.

From the moment Dean Lokht opened the door to the moment I left, I was in survival mode. I recognized later and recognize now that I had been triggered by past trauma of being sexually assaulted as an undergraduate student by another old man. I was unaware in the moment, however, that Dean Lokht's nakedness and powerful position had unleashed a chain reaction. Since then, through therapy and the personal and academic study of trauma and embodied knowledge, I now understand that I experienced fight, freeze, and flight at different times in the evening that manifested through bodily reactions and dissociative moments.[22] At the time, however, I did not have the understanding and skills to link my bodily reaction to my decisions and actions.

Confronted by a naked senior colleague of color, I did not process the encounter as sexual—although in retrospect, that was clearly the intent—either/in part due to my own traumatized past and dissociation and to my own positionality at the university. Clearly, the dean's evident comfort and confidence suggested that this kind of interaction was allowed. The obvious inappropriateness of the encounter was cloaked by a kind of surrealism that convinced me that I had a choice. Yet there is no choice within coercive organizational hierarchal traditions. He was a dean. He had power. He was confident—due to past encounters like this?—that I would comply in some way. I love that my younger self thought that "not [being] intimidated by his nudity and not [paying] attention to his naked body" was a choice and indeed even a statement of my own power. Yet, throughout the night, my body kept telling me my only recourse was to find the quickest way out of this man's house, and I ignored that embodied message, clear though it was, because my past trauma powerfully affected my judgment and, yes, because I wanted to belong, because I wanted to be seen as an equal, and because I did not want to be a story that powerful men would share and laugh at.

Officially Reporting

The day after my encounter at the dean's house was a Thursday, and I went see the head of Human Resources first thing that morning to file a report. There was no Title IX office that year. Darlene normally did not see walk-ins, but she had ten minutes and let me sit in her office. She was an elderly white woman from Texas, clearly well intentioned, with a face like Mrs. Claus from a Christmas card. As I told her what happened with Dean Lokht, her eyes were fixed on her desk, her face was stern; she did not make any eye contact with me. Her lips pursed together. She did not take notes. When I was done, she took a deep breath and said to me, "Lydia, there is no need to file a report for this. Look, I understand this was upsetting to you, but let me offer a different perspective. Dean Lokht is a good person, he has done a lot for this institution, he is good friends with the president. He was just being the jokester that he is. Lydia, I know this seems unusual, but you know it's a small town, his group of boys just have their way of figuring out who they are working with—just know he is harmless—he was just having fun—know that you have proven you are strong, he won't bother you again, so I wouldn't worry about it." She smiled. I looked down at the floor. I sat in silence.

I pretended to think about what she said for a moment, but my inner voice was berating me: I had trained for this; my female professors had all warned me about this precise moment; I should just do what I had been advised—keep my head down, be quiet, get tenure, and then speak up. All literature and experience pointed to an event like this one and yet somehow, I still was taken by surprise and had failed, not just last night but this morning. I should have known better. Why did I think my experience was unique and would be taken seriously? My palms were sweating, I could feel the rage of all feminist injustice boiling up in my stomach, I bit my lip, then I looked up and said, "Thank you for the advice and offering a different perspective. I feel different now." She smiled and told me again not to worry. I thanked her for her time and left.

Later that day, I called Dino. I desperately needed to debrief and also thought that he could offer some mentorship about how to navigate my future interactions with the dean. When I told Dino what had happened, he laughed. He said Dean Lokht and he went way back and that I should feel honored, before telling me not to make a big deal of it. Lokht was harmless, and I should simply carry on as I had. He also told me to look at the experience from another perspective: I now had a good story to tell my friends.

That evening, I wrote in my journal: "Estoy super encabronada, triste y siento tremenda impotencia. Este pinche lugar es un infierno—literal: pueblo chico, infierno grande. I hate that I am here. I like the students, but the fucking culture of this place is a mess, everyone does whatever the fuck they want. I wonder who else was naked bombed by Lokht. That can't really be a thing. Last month the President said that everyone is family here—so I guess that means there is no accountability for anything or anyone—that's just who so and so is, they have done that for a long time, it's just who they are. I need to start looking for another tenure track job, pero pues the market sucks and it's not like anyone is hiring. Jill [a former mentor] even told me I was lucky to have a tenure track job, that I had won a lottery and that I should just be happy, keep my head down and just get tenure. I don't understand why did [the HR woman] erase what happened by giving me a different perspective? Was my perspective not valid enough? I guess not porque el Dino también hizo lo mismo—a good story to tell my friends. Carajo, the man naked bombed me and then hugged me—did he really think his tiny penis was gonna impress me—who are these people? Why did I walk into Dean's house? Pendeja. Es mi propia culpa I should not have walked in—I know better. Pero pues igual [Dino] tiene razón estos cabrones son *viejitos que no hacen daño* and maybe I should be honored—but it's kinda fucked up."

Lesson 3: Reporting Induces Silence

The lesson I learned is that reporting induces silence and unchains a series of actions meant to silence those reporting. Each time I reported inappropriate behaviors, the silencing was encouraged through various forms of manipulative gaslighting: I was offered a different perspective on my experience, threatened with nonrenewal, pressured to increase course loads to justify low student enrollments in my core courses, exhausted by my service on multiple committees. I encountered rumors about my sexuality and cautioned to be careful because my queerness made me "untrustworthy and disloyal." My students were dissuaded from working with me because I was "hard," "like a pit bull," and "unlike other Latinas." Ultimately, however, the silence was endorsed through the inaction of the institution. In the case of the dean's naked dinner party, both Darlene and Dino had the capacity to move the incident forward and chose not to act. Nor did they take notes or file a report. Their silences validated the institution's refusal to acknowledge that any incidents like this could happen.

In her analysis on Title IX and sexual violence in universities in the United States, Kate Lockwood Harris uses a feminist new materialist perspective to trace how organizations participate in violent institutionalized procedures. She argues that universities get to determine "who or what can commit violence."[23] In this particular instance, the violence I reported was not heard *as* violence. Its illegibility as violence resulted in it being dismissed. Despite the facts of my experience, Darlene and Dino "knew" that Dean Lokht was not capable of committing violence and their knowledge, paradoxically, produced a definition of what violence was: subjecting a junior female colleague to implicit and imminent sexual threat by inviting her to his house where he was waiting for her naked was absurd. My own "compliance" with the situation endorsed that view, and therefore my consternation was labeled as unfounded and counterproductive.

It is easy to imagine that the power held by Dean Lokht and the web of connections he had as a personal friend of the university president and upstanding member of the community had something to do with this interpretation. The HR director, a white woman, reframed my experience as harmless, as a well-intended way to know me. Dino, a self-identified Chicano man well-acquainted with critical theory and critique, validated her reinterpretation recommending I feel honored by the experience—to "think about it as a good story." This reproduction of the institutionalized white supremacist academic tool of control that invalidates people's experiences should not surprise us, as Audre Lorde famously phrased it, "for the master's tools will never dismantle the master's house."[24] In the sense that although this Chicano man had made a career of bringing diverse curriculum and people to the institution, he did so by operating within the established order using the master's tools. Dino's approach to limited institutional curricular change enabled him to profit, consolidating his own power by "solving" an institutional challenge without challenging the institution itself. As a result, he was able to silence women and some men who later threatened that power. This example corroborates Garcia's findings in Latina professors' counterstories: hierarchies and structures of power in academia maintain themselves.[25]

On a personal level, I too had internalized these master's tools by prioritizing validation from the institution and by seeking approval from faculty of color who had reached powerful positions. Rereading my journal from that first year recently brought up successfully repressed rage. The writings of my younger self illustrated how much guilt and shame I felt for not knowing better, for believing in reporting mechanisms, for trusting the institution, for assuming people's identities matched their politics and their actions, and for feeling like a *malagradecida* for wanting to quit, and for speaking out when I had won the coveted tenure-track position lottery. These feelings slowly induced me into silence and set in motion a pattern of self-doubt where I invalidated my own experiences and became a participant in the same practices that had silenced me.

The entrenched process by which reported incidents are sometimes confidentially investigated and dismissed creates a culture of complacency and gaslighting. I succumbed to silence at different moments throughout my five years at the university. Eventually, during my third year after an experience I cannot discuss because it falls under of the nondisclosure agreement I had to sign to participate in the Title IX investigation, I simply stopped reporting. I am painfully aware that the experiences I am writing about here are dismembered—censored. There is irony in writing about the lessons of institutional silencing while not actually being able to speak the vast majority of the experiences that demonstrate the intimidation tactics and institutional strategies used to silence.

Lesson 4: Silence Needs to Be Strategic and Mindful

Margaret Chon explains that "silences can represent forms of control and hegemony over one's life. . . . Silence as a form of control also means avoiding the reliving of tragic painful events."[26] Over three years, debilitating, almost para-lyzing, back pain and a dissociative episode reminded me of the burden that speaking out against my "own" had taken on my body and mind. Somewhat paradoxically, reflection forced by these embodied responses enabled me to see the complex intersections that had induced my silence and had allowed insti-tutional misogyny and racialized dynamics to reproduce white supremacy in the men of color involved and, to some degree, in myself.

Eventually, during my fourth year at the institution, I moved from uncon-sciously being silenced to consciously choosing silence as, in Chon's formation, a strategic and mindful protest against my former university. By mindfully choos-ing silence, I could strategically distance myself from Dino and the other men of color in powerful positions, not through what I did or said but through my refusals. I was able to warn others about them through silence. For example, when students would ask me what I thought of Dr. Dino, Dr. Fernando, Dr. Lokht, or others, I would smile and stay silent or say, "I have nothing to say about them." Students read my silence as a disapproval of these men; some learned to read my silence as a way to warn them. When students asked if one of these men could be invited as a guest speaker, I would look at them silently. Sometimes these silences were awkward. I would reframe and redirect, asking the students, "Why do you want them to talk?" "Do you think that they represent the ethos of the event?" "How could their participation lead to transformative experiences for people at the event?" Most of the time, students came to their own conclusions and realized inviting these men to speak was counterproductive to the mission of the event. In meetings that required the participation of these men, my silence was a form of protest. If I had something to contribute, I would email it to the chair of the committee, otherwise I would sit silently, making my presence known but also refusing to speak.

Mindful silence became a form of self-defense from the burden of speaking out against my "own," from continuing to engage with the master's tools through the patterns of bonding, organizing, indebtedness, and gaslighting.

REIR: A Coping Strategy for Joyful Thriving in Academe

In that first year as a tenure-track assistant professor, I learned four valuable les-sons: silence has complex cultural dynamics, we must make space for embodied knowledge, reporting paradoxically induces silence, and silence transformed can be strategic.

Through these lessons, I gained an awareness of the institutional practices, the paradoxical positionalities of young tenure-track faculty of color, and the intersections of structural, cultural, and personal histories that limit transfor-mation in the university. What remained was to use these lessons to form a strat-egy of feminist praxis that would enable me to do my intellectual and political work in academia while also being and continuing to become myself.

In this conclusion, I offer a concrete coping strategy based on what I learned about my inability to register, identify, and resist in those instances where it is hard to access embodied knowledge and intellectual training because of power, identities, and familial/relational dynamics. I have put this strategy of mindful awareness to the test in the last year—at a different institution, one that is in many ways more supportive and more thoughtful than the other but in other ways remains similarly bound to problematic practices. I believe that sharing and validating knowledges that come from our embodied experiences is the foundation for broader resistance and institutional change, a counter to precisely those strategies of isolation and dismissal that entrench the status quo while isolating those it seeks to silence.

Register. I discovered in my experience that my body took note and registered the multiple and complex erasures and denials of my experiences, my disappointments, and aggressions toward me by perceived allies and those in power. I often overlooked those signals, rushing to (il)logical explanations for bad behaviors and dismissing my instincts. To register is to allow discomfort and to listen to the body's response. I learned that it is essential to sit with discomfort and pain before trying to resolve it.

Evaluate. Evaluating the diverse power dynamics that come into play in the moment of the experience (institutional, cultural, personal) helps to inform our reaction, our thoughts, and our own behavior. To evaluate is to create space between the experience and the invisible (although sometimes visible forces). Creating space helps us evaluate the commitment of self-declared allies, those people who use their cultural affinity and/or gendered affinity as power to call on community to keep people in line, to get more power, to reinforce racially entrenched practices, or participate in others' sabotaging and undoing. Evaluating how power travels, how it is reproduced, how it often ignores context, allows us to acknowledge our own motivations, our complicity, our shame, and the assumptions that contribute to the experience.

Imagine. If we are to transform our institutions, we must be able to imagine what this transformation would entail. Imagining introduces a playful and joyful element that invites hope instead of cynicism. To imagine is to play with the possibilities of what academia could look like, what it can feel like, and what it can do. By imagining, we allow for a radically different dynamic in which we do not reproduce the master's tools in our interactions, policy enforcement, or in how we act. By imagining, we create new dynamics that allow us to transform the institutions that were built to exclude us.

Resist. We must learn to resist and refuse and to be at peace with refusal. This is not a resistance of the work necessary to the job but refusal to participate in reproducing the tactics that have kept the academy from transforming, our colleagues from succeeding, and our students from imagining different possibilities. Resisting may take the form of building strong mentorship networks with scholars who are ethically dedicated to transforming the institution and whose scholarship, teaching, and service demonstrate that commitment. Our resistance can also be practiced as mindful silences, rerouting energies, decentering the academy as the sole validating force in our lives, or breaking our beholden relationship to the university for the possibility of being granted tenure. To resist is to learn to live outside of the university through community engagement, restorative mindful daily practices like yoga or hiking, and purposeful time with friends, family, partners, or ourselves. Living outside the university is a way to refuse the demands of the academy and to nurture our own mind-body connection. These forms of living keep our bodies grounded, our intuition deeply rooted, and our minds clear; they are practices that create space to resist the toxic cultures within "acidemia." Academic customs such as overwork, paternalism, power hoarding, defensiveness, individualism, and perfectionism inundate us with the message that we must reproduce them to survive within academe. Yet, we can resist and in that resistance begin to slowly transform these practices.

REIR—registering, evaluating, imagining, and resisting—proposes an imaginary, playful dimension in and of itself but also means laughter in Spanish. For me, REIR has become a coping strategy to acknowledge what is happening, to create space to access embodied knowledge and link it to my political and intellectual training. This allows me to focus not just on how to survive in the academe but also how to thrive.

We must participate in academe with the awareness that these institutions need to be transformed, and this transformation comes at the cost of our emotional labor and, to some degree, our mental health. Sarah Ahmed wrote on her feministkilljoys blog, "In order to survive institutions, we need to transform them. But we still need to survive the institutions we are trying to transform."[27] To do this, we need to be mindful of how the institution leads us to distrust our own experiences and consistently calls us to participate in our own gaslighting. We need to be aware of false allies and device strategies to identify who they are and how they operate. Versed to be wary of the master's tools, we need to inventory them, being careful to include gaslighting, misrecognition, discretization, silencing, and erasure. Using this inventory, we need to develop strategies so we do not reproduce these tools while we engage with institutional practices that were made to control, maintain the status quo, and keep education an elitist enterprise. From silence and tears, a hard-won *joy* and laughter: REIR.

Discussion Questions

1 In what ways can silence be strategic?
2 What are false allies? Why do these types of people exist? What is their function in the broader institution?
3 What are some ways in which you have encountered false allies?
4 What can you do in your current role to contribute to the transformation of your current context?

Try This!

Try your hand at writing a critical narrative reflection/analysis. Think of an event in your past that you may be able to analyze now that time has passed. What concepts have you learned in your classes that can help you analyze the event?

Acknowledgments

I want to acknowledge the mentorship of senior scholars, Jen Hill, Sarah Blithe, Laura Ellingson, Karma Chavez, Guillermina Gina Núñez-Mchiri, Ana Gomez Parga, and Daniel Enrique Perez, who encouraged me to tell this story, who took the time to talk with me, and in some cases edited versions that pushed me beyond my writing comfort zone. Thank you for your mentorship and your time.

Notes

1 Title IX Officer, *Verify Your Statement*, June 13, 2019.
2 I will refer to this man as Dino due to the constraints of confidentiality of the Title IX investigation.
3 bell hooks, "Theory as Liberatory Practice," in *Teaching to Transgress: Education as the Practice of Freedom*, ed. bell hooks (New York: Routledge, 1994), 59–76.
4 See Catherine Medina and Gaye Luna, "Narratives from Latina Professors in Higher Education," *Anthropology & Education Quarterly* 31, no. 1 (2000): 47–66; Sari M. Van Anders, "Why the Academic Pipeline Leaks: Fewer Men than Women Perceive Barriers to Becoming Professors," *Sex Roles* 51, no. 9 (2004): 511–521; Diane F. Halpern, "Nurturing Careers in Psychology: Combining Work and Family," *Educational Psychology Review* 20, no. 1 (2008): 57–64; Sandra Jeannette Vasquez-Guignard, "Latina University Professors: Insights into the Journeys of Those Who Strive to Leadership within Academia," (ProQuest Dissertations Publishing, 2010); Lilliana Patricia Saldana, Felicia Castro-Villarreal, and Erica Sosa, "Testimonios of Latina Junior Faculty: Bridging Academia, Family, and Community Lives in the Academy," *Educational Foundations* 27, no. 1–2 (2013): 31.
5 See Vazquez-Guignard, "Latina University Professors"; Saldaña et al., "Testimonios of Latina Junior Faculty."
6 See Medina and Luna, "Narratives from Latina Professors"; Van Anders, "Why the Academic Pipeline Leaks"; Halpern, "Nurturing Careers."
7 Lorgia García-Peña, *The Borders of Dominicanidad: Race, Nation, and Archives of Contradiction* (Durham, NC: Duke University Press, 2016).
8 Carol Rambo Ronai, "The Reflexive Self through Narrative: A Night in the Life of an Erotic Dancer/Researcher," in *Investigating Subjectivity: Research on Lived Experience*, ed. Carolyn Ellis and Michael Flaherty (Thousand Oaks, CA: Sage, 1992).
9 See Angela Y. Davis, *If They Come in the Morning: Voices of Resistance* (New York: Third Press, 1971); Angela Y. Davis, *Women, Race & Class* (New York: Vintage Books, 1983); Angela Y. Davis and Frank Barat, *Freedom Is a Constant Struggle: Ferguson, Palestine, and the Foundations of a Movement* (Chicago: Haymarket Books, 2016); Audre Lorde, *Zami, a New Spelling of My Name* (Freedom, CA: Crossing Press, 1982); Audre Lorde, *Sister Outsider: Essays and Speeches* (Freedom,

CA: Crossing Press, 1984); Audre Lorde, Reni Eddo-Lodge, and Sara Ahmed, *Your Silence Will Not Protect You* (London: Silver Press, 2017); Cherríe Moraga and Gloria Anzaldúa, *This Bridge Called My Back: Writings by Radical Women of Color*, 4th ed. (Albany: State University of New York Press, 2015); Latina Feminist Group, *Telling to Live: Latina Feminist Testimonios* (Durham, NC: Duke University Press, 2000).

Carmen Lugo-Lugo, "A Prostitute, a Servant, and a Customer-Service Representative: A Latina in Academia," in *Presumed Incompetent: The Intersections of Race and Class for Women in Academia*, ed. Gabriella Gutiérrez y Muhs, Yolanda Flores Niemann, Carmen G. González, and Angela P. Harris (Logan: Utah State University Press, 2012); Saldana et al., "Testimonios of Latina Junior Faculty"; Francesca Gargallo, *Ideas Feministas Latinoamericanas* (Mexico City: UACM, 2014); Jamiella Brooks, "Academia Is Violence: Generatives from a First-Generation, Low-Income PhD Mother of Color," in *Presumed Incompetent: Race, Class, Power of Women in Academia II*, ed. Gabriella Gutiérrez y Muhs, Yolanda Flores Niemann, Carmen G. González, and Angela P. Harris (Logan: Utah State University Press, 2020).

10 Gloria Anzaldúa, *Borderlands/La frontera: The New Mestiza* (San Francisco: Spinsters/Aunt Lute, 1987); Gregory Cajete, *Look to the Mountain: An Ecology of Indigenous Education* (Skyland, NC: Kivaki Press, 1994); Cindy Blackstock, "The Breath of Life versus the Embodiment of Life: Indigenous Knowledge and Western Research," *World Indigenous Nations Higher Education Consortium Journal* 4, no. 1 (2007): 67–79; Karma Chávez and Cindy L. Griffin, "Power Feminism: Exploring Agency, Oppression and Victimage," *Women's Studies in Communication* 32, no. 1 (2009): 2–125; Cherríe Moraga, *A Xicana Codex of Changing Consciousness: Writings, 2000–2010* (Durham, NC: Duke University Press, 2011); Lisa A. Flores, "Reclaiming the 'Other': Toward a Chicana Feminist Critical Perspective," *International Journal of Intercultural Relations* 24, no. 5 (2000): 687–705; Lisa A. Flores, "Attending to the Urgencies: Gendered Violence and Violent Gender," *Women's Studies in Communication* 41, no. 2 (2018): 91–94; Donna Castañeda, Yvette Flores, and Yolanda Flores Neimann, "Senior Chicana Feminist Scholars: Some Notes on Survival in Hostile Contexts," in *Presumed Incompetent: Race, Class, Power of Women in Academia II*, ed. Gabriella Gutiérrez y Muhs, Yolanda Flores Niemann, Carmen G. González, and Angela P. Harris (Logan: Utah State University Press, 2020).

11 See Tami Spry, "Performing Autoethnography: An Embodied Methodological Praxis," *Qualitative Inquiry* 7, no. 6 (December 2001): 706–732; Jeanine Marie Minge, "The Stained Body: A Fusion of Embodied Art on Rape and Love," *Journal of Contemporary Ethnography* 36, no. 3 (June 2007): 252–280; Lila Abu-Lughod, *Writing Women's Worlds Bedouin Stories*, 15th anniversary ed. (Berkeley: University of California Press, 2008); Robin M. Boylorn, *Sweetwater: Blackwomen and Narratives of Resilience* (New York: Peter Lang, 2013); Robin M. Boylorn, "From Here to There: How to Use Auto/ethnography to Bridge Difference," *International Review of Qualitative Research* 7, no. 3 (2014): 312–326; Sophie Smailes, "Negotiating and Navigating My Fat Body: Feminist Autoethnographic Encounters," *Athenea Digital* 14, no. 4 (2014): 49–61.

12 See Hisauro Garza, "Second-Class Academics: Chicano/Latino Faculty in US Universities," *New Directions for Teaching and Learning* 53 (1993): 33–41; Alyssa García, "Counterstories of Race and Gender: Situating Experiences of Latinas in the Academy," *Latino Studies* 3, no. 2 (2005): 261–273; Medina and Luna,

"Narratives from Latina Professors"; Vasquez-Guignard, "Latina University Professors"; Yolanda Flores Neimann, "The Making of a Token: A Case Study of Stereotype Threat, Stigma, Racism, and Tokenism in Academe," in *Presumed Incompetent: The Intersections of Race and Class for Women in Academia*, ed. Gabriella Gutiérrez y Muhs, Yolanda Flores Niemann, Carmen G. González, and Angela P. Harris (Logan: Utah State University Press, 2012).

13 Karen Rodríguez, "Four: Calladita, Te Ves Más Bonita: Analyzing Silences and Erasures," *Contemporary Psychoanalytic Studies* 16 (2012): 55.

14 Medina and Luna, "Narratives from Latina Professors."

15 García, "Counterstories of Race and Gender."

16 I refer to this man as Fernando due to the constraints of confidentiality of the Title IX investigation.

17 García, "Counterstories of Race and Gender."

18 U.S. Department of Education, *Training Manual on Addressing Adult Sexual Misconduct in the School Setting* (Washington, DC: U.S. Department of Education, 2017), 10, https://rems.ed.gov/docs/ASMTrainingGuide_1[1].pdf.

19 Cynthia A. Stark, "Gaslighting, Misogyny, and Psychological Oppression," *The Monist* 102, no. 2 (2019): 221–235.

20 See Ana Nieto Gomez, "Chicana Feminism," *Caracol* 2, no. 5 (1976): 3–5; Rosalie Flores, "The New Chicana and Machismo," *Regeneración* 2, no. 4 (1974); Sonia A. Lopez, "The Role of the Chicana within the Student Movement," in *Essays on La Mujer*, ed. Rosaura Sanchez and Rosa Martinez Cruz (Los Angeles: UCLA Chicano Studies Research Center, 1977); Cynthia Orozco, "Sexism in Chicano Studies and the Community," in *Chicana Voices: Intersections of Class, Race and Gender*, ed. Teresa Cordova, Norma Elia Cantú, Gilberto Cardenas, Juan García, and Christine M. Sierra (Albuquerque: University of New Mexico Press, 1986); Anzaldúa, *Borderlands/La frontera*; Cherríe Moraga, *The Last Generation* (Boston: South End Press, 1993).

21 Dean Lokht is a pseudonym.

22 See Peter A. Levine, *Healing Trauma: A Pioneering Program for Restoring the Wisdom of Your Body* (Boulder, CO: Sounds True, 2005); Bessel A. Van der Kolk, *The Body Keeps the Score: Brain, Mind, and Body in the Healing of Trauma* (New York: Penguin, 2015); Steve Haines and Sophie Standing, *Trauma Is Really Strange* (London: Singing Dragon, 2016).

23 Kate Lockwood Harris, *Beyond the Rapist: Title IX and Sexual Violence on US Campuses* (New York: Oxford University Press, 2019), 20.

24 Lorde, *Sister Outsider*, 110–113.

25 García, "Counterstories of Race and Gender."

26 Margaret Chon, "On the Need for Asian American Narratives in Law: Ethnic Specimens, Native Informants, Storytelling and Silences," *UCLA Asian Pacific American Law Journal* 3, no. 4 (1995): 26.

27 Sara Ahmed, "Complaint and Survival," feministkilljoys, March 23, 2020, https://feministkilljoys.com/2020/03/23/complaint-and-survival/.

Part 3

Living Feminist Politics
in Mediated Environments

• •

In recent years, much feminist work has occurred in mediated environments. Social media, in particular, has become a valuable mechanism for bringing visibility and awareness to feminist social movements. By providing a global means to connect, social media offers a uniquely low-barrier opportunity for diverse voices to share their stories, amplify injustice, and call for social change. Feminist movements online often bridge personal stories with macro-discourses about diverse feminist concerns.

There are some risks and drawbacks to digital feminism. Some people have questioned whether social media activism has been effective or meaningful when the long-term outcomes are difficult to see or quantify. There are concerns about technology barriers and access as well as the possibility that online activism will encourage complacency in face-to-face activist efforts. Issues related to corporate control, harassment, and digitally altered content are essential to explore as the movement continues.[1]

Digital feminism both reduces and increases inclusivity in feminist conversations. On the one hand, women of color have been quite successful in critiquing patriarchy, racism, and classism in feminism; LGBTQI+ advocacy have gained prominence online, and feminists everywhere have immediate access to women in diffuse geographic locations, in different cultural contexts. These benefits can make new intersectional and transnational conversations possible.[2] Additionally, because so many people have social media at their fingertips, issues that had been marginalized as "women's issues" are now more visible as part of the general social conversation. Linabery, Corple, and Cooky summarized the benefits to hashtag activism: feminist hashtags allow disparate women to connect and share stories; hashtag activism opens space for diverse women to call out unique intersections of oppression and make visible racism within mainstream feminism; and hashtags promote visibility for feminist issues. For example, hashtags have been used to bring awareness to a variety of gender issues: violence against women in the United States and more globally; domestic violence; racial inequity in women's movements; body shaming; microaggressions; discrimination at work; allyship/pro-feminism and others (#MeToo, #WhyIStayed, #Solidarity IsforWhiteWomen, #SayHerName, #TimesUp, #YesAllWomen, #Everyday Sexism, #BringBackOurGirls #CropTopDay, #SafetyTipsforLadies, #NiUna Menos [NotOneLess], #HeforShe, #OrangetheWorld).

At the same time, these adaptable and accessible structures (software, social media platforms, algorithms, etc.) are deeply ingrained in hierarchies of power. A number of mediated constructs are woven with racist, sexist, and cis-/heteronormative underpinnings. For example, avatars that guide training courses, characters in video games, and emojis often replicate stereotypical tropes of people, reifying patterns of dominance. Search engines often autofill with harmful stereotypes that users scroll and click through with little critical attention.[3]

At its best, mediated feminisms are a place for storytelling. As many of the chapters in this section demonstrate, mediated feminisms—and social media in particular—provide space for a multitude of voices to speak up about their own experiences. Weighing the risks and fears about mediated activism with the positive outcomes, the chapters here tease out some of the complexities inherent in digital feminism.

Discussion Questions

1 Rushforth (chapter 21) presents hashtag social movements. What are the opportunities and limitations of hashtag feminism? What hashtag movements have resonated with you? Do you find yourself engaging in social movements online? Why or why not?

2 Parga (chapter 19) discusses digital feminist projects outside the United States and United Kingdom. Does mediated feminism offer particular advantages or disadvantages depending on geographical or cultural location? What social factors make social media a more important tool for feminist organizing? Do you think that publics would have the same opportunities to gather and bring visibility to issues/subjectivities without social media? Why or why not?

3 Social media functions like hashtags (#MeToo) and the telenovela memes Parga describes (chapter 19) can bring visibility to women's experiences and the pressures of gender norms. What social justice hashtags have resonated with you? Have there been any that made you

aware of problems you didn't already know about? Have there been celebrity memes that you think challenge gender/race/sexuality norms?
4 Ebben and Kramarae (chapter 20) elucidate gendered aspects of artificial intelligence (AI). As technologies become more sophisticated, do you believe it will enhance structures of power (e.g., racism and sexism), or can AI reduce inequalities?
5 What ideas do you have for recognizing and disrupting the subtle ways that AI can perpetuate discrimination or inequality?
6 In what ways are mediated feminist projects different from face-to-face efforts and in what ways are they similar? Consider ideas for bringing different modalities for feminist organizing together to complement one another.

Notes

1 Jasmine R. Linabery, Danielle J. Corple, and Cheryl Cooky, "Feminist Activism in Digital Space: Postfeminist Contradictions in #WhyIStayed," *New Media & Society* 22, no. 10 (2019): 1827–1848.
2 Hester Baer, "Redoing Feminism: Digital Activism, Body Politics, and Neoliberalism," *Feminist Media Studies* 16, no. 1 (2016): 17–34.
3 Safiya Umoja Noble, *Algorithms of Oppression: How Search Engines Reinforce Racism* (New York: New York University Press, 2018).

19

Mónica Robles

● ● ● ● ● ● ● ● ● ● ● ● ● ● ● ● ● ● ● ●

(De?)colonizing Mexican
Womanhood through the
Power of Memes

ANA GOMEZ PARGA

"The secret to making shrimp and grits is to start by peeling two pounds of shrimp. Make a stock with the shrimp shells in a carrot, celery, and onion reduction. Finally, use that delicious stock as the base for your grits and arrest the three police who murdered Breonna Taylor." This was a tweet I read while I was writing this chapter.

It is almost a month and a half after the death of George Floyd and nearly two months after the death of Breonna Taylor, two Black individuals who died at the hands of those who say their job is "to protect and serve" them. The death of George Floyd resulted in four Minneapolis police officers being charged and the resurgence of massive #BlackLivesMatter protests around the United States. The death of Breonna Taylor, however, resulted in zero consequences for the perpetrators, and as more Black men continue to die at the hands of the police, her name is often mentioned as a second or third name on the list of victims of police brutality but never as the first one. This reminds me of that famous "intersectionality audience quiz" that Kimberlé Crenshaw gave her audience back in 2016.[1] As a woman from Mexico who was displaced from her country due to violence,

I know this story too well: when the system that pledges to protect us fails us, we are condemned for rebelling—for not rebelling on time, for rebelling too hard, and/or for not rebelling at all.

As I move forward with this analysis, I want to pose these questions: (1) How can race, gender, class, and violence inform an imposed cultural identity? (2) How can social media disrupt such impositions? (3) How will white/male/Western capitalism co-opt these disruptions?

As a woman who grew up in Chihuahua, where femicides have existed for over twenty-five years, I am familiar with the rage and confusion that come from real-izing that our lives are worth nothing. Femicides in Mexico are a major human-itarian crisis, a crisis that our president, Andres Manuel López Obrador, continues to dismiss. At the beginning of March 2020, Mexican women organized for two subsequent manifestations, one that would take place on Women's Day (#8M) and another that would take place the Monday after Women's Day, which they called #UnDiaSinMujeres. Although protests against femicides have been a reg-ular occurrence in Mexico, this time was unique because the goal was not to occupy the streets but to disappear. #UnDiaSinMujeres was meant to illustrate what Mexico would look like if women started to disappear from work, chores, and parenting responsibilities by the masses. The symbolism comes from the fact that women do disappear in Mexico, by the masses, and authorities do not seem to care. The absurdity and pain of deaths like Breonna Taylor's is felt by only friends and families and results in zero consequences for perpetrators. #UnDi-aSinMujeres is only a glimpse into the lives of many families in Mexico, who con-tinue to mourn the deaths of their sisters and daughters.

Telenovelas are a media format that claim to center women. This claim, how-ever, is questionable. Telenovelas are among the most important exports from Latin America to the world.[2] During my initial years as a scholar, I studied the intersections between religion and telenovelas[3] in shows such as *La Rosa de Gua-dalupe* (2008). Through this research, I have explained how religious symbols in combination with entertainment perpetuate a type of womanhood that makes women vulnerable targets for femicides.[4] Moreover, I have described an interest-ing evolution where telenovelas have gone from "innocent" Cinderella stories about romance, to stories about morality and religion, to stories about sex, drugs, murder, and corruption. How did they get there?

Castañeda suggests that given the advantages of the digital age, audiences are now in a position where they can demand more realistic stories in telenovelas.[5] This may help explain why audiences would feel compelled to consume telenove-las that engaged with these topics. Tabuenca Córdoba and Ramirez-Pimienta argue that given the impact that cartel-related violence has had across Latin America, it is only natural that these stories eventually became central in tele-novelas as well.[6] As a telenovela consumer myself, my own interest in telenove-las has shifted from traditional to stories about mafias. This interest, however, has left a sense of guilt and shame because I have consumed a commodified

violence that has displaced and impacted many of us. This guilt guides my
scholarship.

El Señor de Los Cielos: Global Capitalism Smells Opportunity

At the beginning of 2018, a series of billboards appeared in Mexico City following the death of Mónica Robles in *El Señor de los Cielos* (hereafter ESDLC).
ESDLC is a narco-novela (telenovelas that center stories about cartels) written
by Venezuelan writer Luis Zelkowicz, produced by Argos, a Mexican company,
and owned by Telemundo/NBC. ESDLC originally started as a telenovela that
later became a teleseries that now has seven seasons of more than seventy episodes each.[7] It can also be found on Netflix.

Argos is a Mexican-based production company that claims to produce culturally responsive content and stories that reflect reality.[8] Carolina Acosta-Alzuru
makes a distinction between classic Cinderella-inspired telenovelas and what she
calls *telenovelas de ruptura* (telenovelas of disruption).[9] *Telenovelas de ruptura*
have been Argos's key to success,[10] and Telemundo has capitalized on this partnership by securing its status as the second most important Spanish-language
television network in the United States. Since Telemundo partnered with Argos,
it has gotten closer to surpassing Univision's place as the number one Spanish-
speaking network in the United States.[11]

FIG. 19.1 (We will miss you, rest in peace, Mónica Robles). At the beginning of 2018, a series
of billboards appeared in Mexico City, following the death of Mónica Robles in season five
of *El Señor de los Cielos*. Credit: Fernanda Castillo, @fernandacga December 3, 2017
"Instagram Post"

For context, ESDLC currently holds the record for the highest ratings on prime-time television in the United States, defeating ABC, CBS, and Univision.[12] Additionally, ESDLC has won multiple awards, including the 2014 International Emmy Award for Best Non-English U.S. Primetime Program. Within Telemundo, ESDLC has won the Premios Tu Mundo three consecutive times for Telenovela of the Year in 2015, 2016, and 2017,[13] and several others for individual performances by some of the actors. According to NBC Universal, ESDLC remained the number one show in 2015 on all television programming in the United States for the 10:00 p.m. hour,[14] and in 2016, it broke Telemundo's rating records reaching 2.8 million viewers across the United States.[15] ESDLC is, without a doubt, NBC Universal's most successful current product, now rated as the number one prime-time show across all networks, regardless of language.[16]

Mónica Robles: When Women Steal the Show

In the microcosm of ESDLC, Mónica Robles (MR) is an icon of survival. In fact, she is called "the seven lives" in the show as a reference to cats having resuscitating skills. Her survival skills were literal. In season 1, she was allegedly killed by Aurelio Casillas, the main character of the show, but in season 2 she "was brought back to life" within the story. It is unclear whether her death was reconsidered after the producers realized the popularity of this character, but what is clear is that starting from season 2, Fernanda Castillo, who plays MR, began to appear as a main character as opposed to a supporting one in the show. The finale of season 4 also played with the idea of her death, and during this time, Telemundo made an online survey asking participants if they would continue to watch the show without MR in it. At this time, participants overwhelmingly said no. In season 6, however, when she was definitively killed, fans demanded through an online petition that the writers publicly apologize to Fernanda Castillo for the poor and unsatisfactory storyline they gave her during her final season and the "lame" death they wrote for a character notorious for her survival skills.

Y *La Culpa No Era Mía*: It Is Never Patriarchy's Fault

"Esta mujer [Mónica Robles] es el resultado del mundo donde creció" (this woman is the result of the world in which she was brought up). These were the words Fernanda Castillo told her audience during a TED Talk in 2016: "If we don't want any more Mónica Robleses what we need to do is to change the world in which our children are growing up." Castillo was not merely engaging with her audience with those words; she was directly addressing the heated debate that often happens in Mexico regarding narco-cultura.

Since narco-novelas became popular in Latin America, politicians have blamed the explosion of violence almost exclusively on the media. Through official discourse and policy, they have consistently attacked media content that engages with drugs, cartels, narco-series, narco-novelas, narco-corridos (songs about cartels), and so forth. This argument, however, is not new. Along with politicians, religious institutions and even civil organizations have often declared that telenovelas, especially ruptura ones, are to blame for whatever problem comes into existence in society: teen pregnancies, women's "lack of modesty," divorce rates, drug dealing, criminality, illiteracy, violence, femicides, and more.[17]

In Venezuela, for example, former Miss Venezuela and Telemundo superstar Mónica Spear and her husband were murdered while driving along a highway during a family visit. Unidentified criminals crossed their path, assaulted, and murdered them. The scandal became internationally known because of Spear's celebrity status. I distinctly remember this particular case because I used to watch her last telenovela right before my evening bike ride while I was doing my master's degree in El Paso, Texas, years in which I also became an MR fan.

After Mónica Spear died and Telemundo published the story, President Nicolás Maduro responded by stating that the rise of this type of crimes was a clear consequence of violent telenovelas.[18] He went further and suggested that the secretary of telecommunications should reconsider if telenovelas were appropriate for broadcasting. He specifically stated that "modern" telenovelas, by which he meant narco-telenovelas, intentionally portrayed narratives that were detrimental to the "culture of peace" that Venezuela was trying to build.[19]

Although Maduro's response became a convenient story for Telemundo's open criticism of Maduro's presidency, Venezuela is not the only country that has attempted to censor telenovelas de ruptura. In Mexico, several government officials have persistently declared that narco-telenovelas are encouraging young people, men, and women to become narcos (drug lords). What is new about this argument is that it implies that women, who for years have been described as victims and victimizable and whose victimization has served to justify measures that limit their rights,[20] are now described as either violent or drawn to violence, allegedly due to media's normalization of violence.[21] Subsequent examples can be found in Venezuela,[22] Colombia,[23] Honduras,[24] and México[25]—countries that are also known for having high rates of cartel-related violence and femicides and that consistently rank lowest in terms of citizens' trust in their governments and institutions.

The Mexican media scholar in me reads these statements as deflection and qualifies them as incomplete. The official arguments state that (1) media are to blame for audience's interest in violence, (2) audiences are passive receivers of media content, and (3) those who consume mediated violence are violent themselves. Media studies literature has overwhelmingly demonstrated that these arguments are simplistic. For the purposes of this chapter, I will be drawing from Sayak Valencia's gore capitalism as a way to further complicate these premises by recentering the notion that it may be capitalism what may be causing these issues.

Enedina Arellano Felix: A Dystopic Feminist in a Gore Capitalist World

MR is what Sayak Valencia would call a *sujeto endriago*, which in Spanish translates as a subject half-human and half-monster. Within the context of a brutal form of capitalism where there is massive pressure for hyperconsumerism and less opportunity to accumulate wealth, "underdeveloped" countries find themselves stuck in a reality where individuals face social pressure to conform to market expectations and global values and excruciating challenges to make ends meet and cover basic expenses. This contradiction results in a disillusion experienced by individuals who conform to capitalist ideals of hard work and individual success but are faced with a reality where even their best efforts are insufficient. The precarity is such that the less privileged are forced to "choose" between illegal activity or migration. Valencia offers the concept of *sujetos endriagos* for those who choose, or are forced, to engage in illegal activities and undergo the (un)ethical transformation that is required for embracing violence as a means to accomplish capitalism promises.[26]

Sujetos endriagos are radical identities that arise out of (1) an entrepreneurial logic of innovation, flexibility, dynamism, ability to take risks, and creativity when it comes to the pursuit of profit and (2) a context of violence, sexism, and extreme precarity.[27] They feel that in order to gain social inclusivity within an economic model that understands worth as wealth, anything is fair game and everything is up for profit. In a social and economic context that prioritizes power and wealth, ethics, bodies, and human lives are not only negligible, but also they might become products for sale. *Sujetos endriagos* are, therefore, a direct result of violent capitalism, or capitalism gore, as Valencia calls it.

Coloniality, Audience, and Memes: I Feel Seen

Dawkings defines memes as "a unit of cultural transmission, or a unit of imitation."[28] Following this definition, Shifman offers three categories to understand the importance of memes: (1) the mentalist-driven position, (2) the behavior-driven position, and (3) the inclusive position. Within the mentalist-driven category, memes are ideas or pieces of information that reside in people's brains and are culturally shared by others. However, these ideas are not simple; they are complex, and they need to be understood within particular contexts and by considering the particular ways and rituals in which they are used. In order to be passed along from person to person, these ideas are imprinted on vehicles and these vehicles are the memes.

In the behavior-driven category, "behaviors are artifacts rather than ideas."[29] Unlike the mentalist-driven category, in this second option, the meme "has no existence outside the events, practices, and texts in which it appears." Shifman explains that if "memes were indeed only abstract units of information, it would be impossible to disassociate them from their manifestation in the outside world";[30] thus, this manifestation is expressed through the processes surrounding their use. It is the process that is at the center, not the idea.

The third category suggests an inclusive position and it requires a combination of the other two. In *The Meme Machine* (2000), Susan Blackmore refers to meme as "memetic information in any of its many forms; including ideas, the brain structures that initiate those ideas, the behaviors these brain structures produce, and their versions in books, recipes, maps and written music."[31] As we can note, both Blackmore and Shifman suggest that in order to understand memes, one must consider all the complexities around them.

For the analysis that you are about to read, I will approach my reading of memes through an inclusive position informed by the framework of gore capitalism. It is my hope that this chapter will broaden our understanding of current gender dynamics in Mexican/Latina digital communities and the relationship between these gender dynamics and narco-cultura.

Method

Emily Hind said that "it remains to be seen whether feminism's greatest accomplishment was the liberation of women or whether it was redistributing feminine submission more equally between genders."[32] One of the main purposes of this analysis is to illuminate how memes inspired by MR can be an empowering or disempowering tool and "give women a voice in a world that defines them as voiceless."[33] In order to accomplish this, I will look at four elements: (1) the ways in which women have appropriated MR as a role model, (2) the features audiences find interesting and appealing, (3) how online users interpret some of her features as positive, and (4) the features audiences identify as negative and how they use them. This analysis will be divided in two parts in order to describe both the empowering interpretations and the interpretations that were meant to police and ridicule womanhood.

For this analysis, I searched for memes on Facebook and Twitter from 2015 to 2018. I selected between sixty and seventy-five memes per year, anticipating that some of them would be repeated. During this process, I faced different challenges: for instance, for 2015, I found very few memes on Twitter, and many of them were all repeated in subsequent years. I was able to find a thicker sample for 2015 on Facebook. Once I gathered my sample for each year on both platforms, I conducted the last debugging exercise in this data collection process. I personally reviewed each meme and deleted those that were repeated. I ended up with a sample size of fifty memes per year. For the selection, I used the hashtags: #MasCabronaQueMonicaRobles, #CabronaComoMonicaRobles, #LaRobles, #Cabronas, and #Buchonas.

My decision to focus on the memes as opposed to the character in the series stems from my wish to move away from ivory tower readings. By focusing primarily on the memes, I attempt to decenter myself and offer audiences a voice to interpret this character. I began this project as a graduate student, at an institution that did not take telenovelas as worthy of scholarly analysis. Many of my data sampling decisions were made as a result of this challenge. The analysis responds to questions previously posed by media scholars such as, how are telenovelas being used and what is their impact?[34] I engaged in the following interrogations:

RQ1 How are MR's memes used in digital culture as a mechanism for the deconstruction of a colonial notion of Mexican womanhood?

RQ2 How are MR's memes being co-opted in digital culture by a legacy of coloniality?

I want to declare that my reading of MR and her memes is informed by my own experiences as a Mexican woman. I identify as a queer woman who was born and raised within the physical and political boundaries of Mexico and who has been educated in Mexico, the United States, and Europe. My analysis, then, is multilayered and it reflects my worldview and my knowledge about Mexican culture.[35] Although I see and engage with the notion of Latina womanhood in the conclusion of this chapter, as a woman from the Global South, I do not claim a Latina identity. Although I see the political benefits of identifying as Latinx, this term carries a legacy of an Indigenous and African erasure and a record of epistemic disengagement with the Global South. In addition to recenter the intellectual value of South, this analysis will respond to the invitation posed by Curran and Park to de-westernize media studies.[36] The following analysis will be in its own regard, a process of analysis, interpretation, and decolonization of my own culture.[37]

Analysis

De-/Recolonizing Aesthetics: Resistance and Compliance

Online memes are comprised of three main elements: *form*, *content*, and *stance*. Form includes all the aesthetic visual elements, content refers to the messages they contain, and stance is a position or statement they are communicating. This section is entirely about form, about the visual, aesthetic elements found in most MR memes.

Beauty as Colonial Force

The first element we can observe is that MR is an attractive, sophisticated, blonde, white-passing, traditionally feminine woman. Her body, the hairstyles she wears, and her way of dressing are consistent with the standards of beauty and sophistication imposed by European colonialism and that have been encouraged by capitalism. Beauty standards that are sustained and perpetuated by the media, including Mexican telenovelas,[38] keep women constantly dissatisfied with themselves and trapped in material consumption.

Aesthetics and physical appearance are great tools for colonization. Sharon Block argues that "colonists wrote distinctions onto physical bodies"[39] as a way to establish and justify their superiority. Through colonialism and colonial power, ideas surrounding physical appearance and beauty have not only served to perpetuate gender and racial hierarchies, but these ideas have been internalized and reproduced even by those who were colonized. In a world where we have all been conditioned by racism, classism, and sexism, our identities as people of color are in constant struggle "between forces of regulations and energies of liberation."[40]

Fernanda Castillo is not a natural blonde, and neither is she particularly slender. She has stated multiple times that when she decided to cast for the role of MR, she voluntarily changed her appearance as a way to obtain the part.[41] Castillo, who before MR was relatively unknown in the world of television, says that she had always been a bit corpulent and that her weight and body shape had always been a matter of personal struggle[42] and even a professional limitation. In an interview with Gustavo Adolfo Infante, a well-known celebrity commentator, she explained that her looks had kept her from obtaining important roles in telenovelas.[43]

When she decided she wanted to cast and get the part for MR, Castillo committed herself to lose nearly ten kilograms and changed her naturally brunette hair to blond.[44] In an interview for *Suelta La Sopa*, Castillo talks about her struggles as a woman who has never fit into the conventional notions of beauty, as a tall, thin, white, beautiful woman; and she mentions that for a long time, she considered her physical appearance to be the reason why she was never cast as the main character, nor the antagonist, of a telenovela.[45] In this interview, she also states that her decision to change the color of her hair and to lose that much weight came after realizing that MR was highly sexual and that her writers had written a lot of sensual scenes for this character. Castillo said that she did not want to feel self-conscious about her body while filming, because being uncomfortable with her own body would not have allowed her to give the best performance she could. In her own words, the results that came after months of strict dieting and consistent exercise gave her a new sense of *empowerment*.[46] In *Suelta La Sopa*, she stated, "Y entonces bajo diez kilos para convertirme en Mónica Robles y empiezo a creer en mí, en verme diferente y en decir—todo lo que yo había prometido que yo iba a hacer como actriz lo voy a demostrar en este personaje [After I lost twenty-two pounds in the process of becoming Mónica Robles, I began to believe in myself, I saw myself as a different woman and said to myself—everything I had promised to accomplish as an actress, I will accomplish with this character]."[47]

By looking at her memes, it is evident that MR stands out as beauty icon. What is interesting to me about Castillo's decision to whitewash and slim herself is a concept I borrow from María Lugones and see applied here, the *coloniality of gender.*[48] The coloniality of gender speaks of colonial impositions on gendered behaviors and looks. Interestingly, however, Castillo feels that the process of altering herself as a way to follow these impositions is, by contrast, empowering. The traditional notions of beauty that Castillo describes in her interviews are the Western/European/capitalist beauty standards that have been imposed through colonialism.[49] Yet, the struggles she describes are the ones colonized peoples experience in their struggles of resistance/assimilation that could indicate the beginning of a process of decolonization.[50]

Lugones argues that "the gender system introduced was one thoroughly informed by the colonial power"[51] and that this system implies that feminine beauty is white, fragile, and upper class—attributes that have served to control white women. Additionally, this colonial gendered system created beauty standards that are, for the most part, unattainable by nonwhites. This leaves women of color outside of this category,[52] unless they find their way into it by way of material wealth.

A woman whose physical appearance is similar to Castillo's unaltered physical aspect can only undergo such transformation if she has enough resources to afford a hair color transformation, a specialized exercise routine, and a strict diet. Even though at one point in history obesity was considered an indicator of wealth, Shugart reminds us that in the last decades, both the big food and the weight loss industry have benefited enormously from the obesity problem that is considered a health crisis in the United States[53] and that has been exported to third world countries through capitalism.[54] Hence, in modern societies, in order to attain the slim, delicate, and toned beauty standard, most women would have to invest a significant amount of money in their appearance.

Castillo's notion of empowerment, then, is accomplished only after she assimilates to the rules of capitalist beauty. Nonetheless, interpreting her physical body as merely an assimilated body would be a limited reading because we might be misunderstanding the context in which she is being embraced. Online users who, for the most part, seem to be Mexican and female (based on the colloquial and gendered language they use) might be interpreting MR as a disruptive figure because even though she follows the rules of colonial beauty, she defies the rules of colonial/religious/patriarchal female chastity at the same time.

Sensuality and Sexuality De-/(re)colonized

If we consider the colonial Catholic legacy in Mexico and Latin America that dictate that sex is only a means for reproduction, not a means for pleasure, especially for women, MR disrupts this legacy by embracing herself as a sexual being. Colonial legacies suggest that women are supposed to be fragile, weak, private, and sexually passive[55]—attributes that are being disrupted by the mix of violence and sensuality that MR portrays in many of her memes.

FIG. 19.2 Series Robles with a gun (Credit: La Prensa (2016)—"Fernanda del Castillo defiende las armas en TV" https://www.laprensa.hn/espectaculos/978042-410/fernanda-del-castillo-defiende-las-armas-en-tv)

This disruption, however, is superficial. Lugones reminds us that we forget that women of color have never actually been considered fragile, weak, or sexually passive. Historically, women of color have been considered *animals* that are continuously in the process of trying to fit and assimilate into the system of European/Western capitalism.[56] If we read MR using this lens, then what Fernanda Castillo did by altering herself was not to resist but rather to play into to this very process. This "decision" of assimilating to the beauty expectations of European colonization and using her sensuality to succeed place both MR and Fernanda Castillo within the narrative of a selfish, superficial woman who is worthy of distrust because she is not open about her true intention to pursue material wealth and/or power at any cost.

It Is All in the Face: Do Not Show Too Much Body

What is interesting to me about the sensuality displayed by MR in these memes is that even though she is a very sexual character within the series of ESDLC and appears in multiple scenes wearing sexy attires and lingerie, in these memes, she remains sensual mostly by displaying suggestive facial gestures. Most of the memes are about her face, not about her body, which to some, might be the nature of a meme, but as Shifman suggested, not necessarily.[57]

My interpretation of this phenomenon is that the writers of the show wrote a heteronormative version of sensuality that was created for the male gaze. However, users online mostly identify as women and seem to interpret sensuality in a more eroticized, sensual way. This, to me, is another sign of colonial and decolonial contestation.

I interpret this contradiction in two ways. The first, as a case where male writers wrote a female character through their lens, but female online users rearticulate her image through theirs. Based on the gendered/colloquial language that accompanies the meme, it could be that online users, who are either women or identify as women, read MR's sensuality in a different way. This reading would be empowering.

An alternative reading, however, is that this conservative display of sensuality feels like a safer, less radical, and more comfortable way to embrace female sexuality. Knowing what I know about Mexican culture and how many of these online platforms are policed by family members[58] and/or have a severe trolling problem,[59] it could be that women feel compelled to play it safe online because this trolling is often taken offline as well.[60] Within a heteronormative, conservative, religious, and colonial society, it would be safer for online female users to share a picture of a sensual woman posing fully clothed than a picture of a woman wearing lingerie.

Furthermore, posting a picture of a half-naked woman as a woman could call into question one's own sexuality. Being perceived either as sexually permissive or as something other than straight can still mean deadly consequences for women in Mexico.[61] Overall, although I see in these pictures a celebration of female sexuality, I also see that this celebration is very constrained.

Affluent Femininity as Compensation for Deviant Traits

In Mexico, women who engage in drug-dealing activities or date drug dealers are called *buchonas*.[62] The term is a derogatory way of labeling and identifying women who are "newly rich" and became rich because they either dated a drug dealer or they became dealers themselves. In a hypocritical, classist society like Mexico, where wealth equals worth but wealth that is not inherited is looked at with suspicion, the term *nuevo rico* (newly rich) is used to mock and exclude those who were not born into wealth but acquired wealth through suspicious activities. It is important to note that this suspicion is another colonial legacy of a cast

FIG. 19.3 Maria Felix series (Credit: Culmix: Curating, Creating & Motivating Cultural Mixing (2014) "Maria Felix, the Latin Elizabeth Taylor" https://culmix.wordpress.com /2014/04/08/maria-felix-the-latin-elizabeth-taylor/)

system sustained by classism and racism. Nonetheless, the suspicion can be legitimized if we consider that for most of our history as a country, economic and social mobility through legal means has always been nearly impossible.[63]

Twenty years ago, the term *nuevo rico* would be used to refer to politicians who became wealthy through corruption. Today, however, it is often related to and even interchanged with words like *narco* or *buchón*. The word is used as a marker to refer to those who may have money and access to resources and places but lack the sophistication that comes with cradle and lineage. In this sense, MR's appearance of sophistication makes me wonder if this is one of the reasons why she was embraced as an icon and not mocked as a *buchona*. MR's image is that of a sophisticated woman; her wealth was inherited from her older brothers and thus her lineage and sophistication are just as "passing" as her whiteness.

While analyzing all 250 memes, something about her is reminiscent of María Félix (aka María Bonita) who has been regarded as "the most beautiful face in the history of Mexican cinema."[64]

Although I do not argue that Fernanda Castillo shares physical similarities with María Félix, even though they are both from the state of Sonora, a state nationally famous for the perceived beauty of their women, I do see similarities. Robles and Félix both (1) display their sensuality through their suggestive poses and their eyes, (2) display their power and dominance through their explicit display of wealth and sophistication and even with a particular smirk that is not really a smile, and (3) have a tendency to engage in traditionally male activities such as smoking, holding guns, and/or drinking. Of course, it is important to keep in mind that MR is a fictional character and María Félix was a real-life woman. Still, María Félix became known for playing unconventional roles during the golden age of Mexican cinema, and many of her famous photographs were photographs of characters she played.

In her book *Dissonant Divas*, Deborah Vargas offers the concept of *exceptional exception* to refer to the idea that when you are a woman, being exceptional is a condition necessary to be worthy of attention and historization.[65] After observing the similarities between Félix and Castillo's appearance as MR, I was left wondering if this rebelliousness against traditional gender norms was acceptable only if you were exceptionally beautiful, exceptionally sophisticated, and exceptional within the canons established by European colonization.

One could argue that in a country where women are constantly policed and murdered, poses engaging in activities such as smoking or drinking is an act of resistance and of claiming agency. In this regard, singer Jenny Rivera comes to mind. She was notorious for her affinity for alcohol and her famous quote responding to critics: "I don't have any problems with alcohol; alcohol and I get along fine." In the process of navigating Twitter during data collection, I came across a tweet that illuminates this similarity between MR and Jenny Rivera: "Jenni Rivera y Mónica Robles tienen la culpa de que haya tanta mujer con trauma de cabrona [Jenni Rivera and Mónica Robles are guilty of causing a bitch trauma complex in a lot of women]." Although I believe that Rivera's openness about her alcohol affinity was an act of resistance, I see both MR's and Fernanda Castillo's engagement with alcohol as a performance, especially if one takes into consideration that Rivera constantly defied colonial body image impositions and Castillo has repeatedly referred to her body image, her diets, and her commitment to fitness as her sources of empowerment. Any person who is familiar with fitness regimes and routines knows alcohol is often discouraged or allowed in minimal doses, thus this alcohol use reads more as a performative act of resistance by a fictional character.

The last element I want to discuss in this section is MR's use of weapons. It appears that MR's choice of weapon is something similar to a silver-covered Ruger LC9, which is considered in many of the lists I found as a "feminine" and "women-appropriate" weapon.[66] Learning this fact was relevant since villains in telenovelas often use similar feminine-looking guns to inflict pain on other, less villainesque women. MR became an icon of self-defense and self-reliance, hence her hashtag #CabronaComoMonicaRobles. However, this deviation of embracing the use of weapons and even personalizing weapons, which is not unusual for real-life cartel leaders,[67] is still conservative. Her bravado and *cabronería* align more with the stereotype of a femme fatale than with a decolonial version of a Mexican antihero.

De-/recolonizing Language: The Brutal Violence of Sexism

The first part of this analysis was focused on form. This second part will focus on Shifman's other two elements: *content* and *stance*.[68] I am particularly interested in analyzing the language patterns found in these memes and the perspectives that they circulate. Shifman suggests that although memes might be perceived differently by different people, they "shape and reflect general social mindsets."[69] Relatedly, Robin Lakoff states that "the way we feel about the things in the real world governs the way we express ourselves about these things."[70] Although memes can be dismissed as simple forms of entertainment, one would be wrong to assume that the messages that get circulated and the type of humor that is used can be detached from the culture in which they are created.

After looking at these memes as a whole, one major finding I observed was that the antagonism between and among women was often expressed and validated. One of the many ways in which colonialism has managed to keep women under control is the idea that women cannot trust other women. For Lee Maracle, this is internalized violence, and "the abyss of internalized violence is very deep."[71] Audre Lorde powerfully expressed that we, as women, are sometimes overly critical of each other since "we do not love ourselves, we cannot love each other."[72] When we are raised as women in a context that despises everything female, and I am not only talking about México but about patriarchy in general, it is the legacy of colonization that we will internalize this hate and may express it against each other.

In Mexico, there are two major ways in which women are insulted: they are either called *putas* (sluts) and/or *pendejas* (stupid). These words have several variations. *Putas* are women who are sexually loose and/or who lack modesty. In the strict sense of the word, a *puta* is a prostitute, but it is often used as a way to say you are "someone's bitch." The weight of this word is such that labeling a woman as a *puta* has proven to be an effective way to normalize, and even justify, violence against her even in cases of police neglect or femicide.[73] By "consenting" to becoming someone else's property, you have "consented" to deal with the consequences of dehumanization. Consent in Mexico is often framed as not actively objecting to or rejecting something or someone. However, when you have a colonial/patriarchal/classist/legal system that objectifies you since the moment you are seen as female, consent, for many, is never truly an option.

Variants of *puta* are words such as *zorra*, *perra*, or *gata*, and these were found in a significant portion of the sample. All three end with the letter *a*, which in Spanish means that they are directed toward women-identifying individuals. The irony, for me, was to see the image of a woman who claimed her right to own her sexuality engage in slut-shaming toward other women. This is, however, consistent with who MR is in the show. Although she is in a consensual open relationship with Aurelio Casillas, she name-calls every single woman Aurelio engages with. The danger here is that as activists and scholars in Mexico have warned,[74] slut-shaming is a very effective mechanism to justify violence against women.

The second most common word used to insult women in Mexico is *pendeja*. *Pendeja* is used to describe someone who is considered to be excessively stupid. Another colonial imposition that we have inherited and internalized for years is the idea that women are either incompetent, unintelligent, or not fit to make important decisions. This is especially true for women of color who have repeatedly found themselves being perceived as incompetent.[75] In my sample, I found

FIG. 19.4 Three meme series "Pendeja." Credit (top to bottom): Fernanda Castillo, @FernandaCGA June 2, 2015 "Tweet"; Fernanda Castillo, @FernandaCGA May 25, 2015 "Tweet"; Fernanda Castillo, @FernandaCGA August 4, 2015 "Tweet."

that MR uses this word for three particular purposes: (1) to refer to other women, (2) to refer to past mistakes, or (3) to distance herself, often in terms of hierarchy, from other women.

The nuances of language are too broad to capture in one chapter, especially if one is dealing with translations. Women insulting other women is nothing new and there is nothing particularly disruptive about it other than the blatant use of words like *puta* or *pendeja* in a genre that for years censored language of this type.

I will admit that I was looking forward to recording what I initially thought was going to be MR's most disruptive pattern in terms of language: her insults against men. In the series, MR is notorious for the way in which she humiliates men, including Aurelio Casillas who is the most dangerous man in the show, and for the wit with which she fires insults against any men who question her competence. As a fan of the show, this is, to me, what made her character compelling. It was sort of cathartic to see her humiliating men. However, in my sample of 250 memes, only nine of them show Mónica Robles using the word *pendejo* against a man, an incredibly low number considering how many times she uses the word in the series.

There were other insults against men that I did find in my sample. In the show, the insults Mónica fires can go from questioning a man's masculinity, to overtly referring to their male parts, to ridiculing men in public, especially in front of other women. MR seems to believe that the only way to gain respect is by establishing dominance, and she establishes dominance by calling into question male competence or by subverting words that are often fired at her.

Among the few examples where MR is overtly humiliating men, one meme reads, "no mi rey, estamos así porque tú piensas con eso y no con la cabeza [No, darling, we are in this situation because you used your 'thing' to think and not your brain]." In another one, MR is questioning a man's masculinity for his inability to take risks; the captions read, "he tenido desayunos con más huevos que tú." The literal translation of this meme would be, "I've had breakfasts that have more eggs than you." This is a clear humiliation in Spanish for two reasons: in Spanish we use the word *eggs* to refer to testicles, and a traditional Mexican breakfast will consist of two of them. What this means is that if a breakfast has more eggs than a man, a man is not only being called a coward, but he is also being called sexually impotent. A third is a meme that states, "me engañas y te lo corto . . . bueno, te lo quito, porque corto ya lo tienes," which could be translated as, "If I catch you cheating, I will chop it off. . . . Well, no, now that I think about it, leaving it for display will be more humiliating."

Women in Mexico suffer from all kinds of violence: economic violence, emotional violence, psychological violence, physical violence, and constant humiliation. Many of these humiliations have been portrayed in telenovelas. The novelty is that MR is the first character that I have seen in my lifetime who overtly refers to a man's testicles or his sexual abilities as a way to humiliate him. Even in low numbers, it is still worth mentioning that some of these insults were part of my sample.

Whether it is denial, reappropriation, or something else, MR is constantly trying to define herself in her own terms, and it is clear that her online identity is equally boundless. This identity, however, often aligns with discriminatory and colonial vices. The last interesting pattern I found has to do with discriminatory language. MR distances herself from others by asserting herself as superior. María Lugones taught us that colonial legacies give "rise to new social and geocultural identities."[76] In both colonial and colonized societies, the world will always be divided and contested between two opposing groups, the "superior and inferior, rational and irrational, primitive and civilized, traditional and modern."[77] Under this lens, we can observe that many MR memes are an expression of this hierarchical thinking.

Conclusion

Mónica Robles is a phenomenon that requires scholarly attention. The way in which this character and her memes have resonated with audiences reflects a struggle for redefining Mexican womanhood. On the one hand, she is pretty, interested in love, and has dreams and struggles. On the other hand, she is violent, classist, racist, ableist, and sexist. MR does not escape the vices of Mexican culture. However, she is also disruptive, and her disruption is both decolonizing and recolonizing. Moreover, the memeplex that MR has generated is an example of the power that fans find in extending and reinterpreting her character online.

As feminist icon, MR is an imperfect artifact if we read her through an anticolonial lens. However, she must be contextualized, and when she is contextualized within the physical, emotional, and psychological boundaries of Mexican culture, both in Mexico and within the universe of telenovela convention, her disruption is historic. The violence and assertiveness that she displays can feel empowering in a world that kills women.

If there is a hall of fame for telenovela memes, I would argue that Soraya Montenegro, who for years has dominated the online Latinx world, has found in MR a legitimate contender. When I initiated this project, a mentor asked me what was so special about MR—Is this one of those villains that everyone loves to hate?—I said no, no one hates her and this is exactly what differentiates MR from Soraya Montenegro.

Soraya is the archetype for telenovela villains: irrational, unrealistic, rich, entitled, and superficial. Mónica is not the evil villain, nor is she the always-smiling innocent victim who needs to be protected and saved. There is something about MR that many Mexican women can identify with: She is angry and she refuses to be disciplined. She is a Robles but does not go by her last name. She is aware that being a woman forces her to face specific challenges. At the same time, she herself is sexist and violent. It is these contradictions and dilemmas that make her refreshingly real, and I believe this is what resonates about her.

Jillian M. Baez reminds us that given the limited Latina representation in media, Latina audiences are forced to identify with, make meaning of, and reappropriate portrayals of themselves.[78] Baez argues that Latinas "rupture dominant discourses, but also begin to recuperate the Latina body" through these disruptions.[79] By consuming characters such as Mónica Robles and personalizing MR memes, women engage "in a recuperative project that seeks subjectivity for bodies marked as unworthy and deviant."[80] For Baez, these forms of appropriation are forms of mediated citizenship.

Why is it that in survey after survey, Mónica Robles ranks as the favorite character of the series? Are audiences uncritically consuming content that excuses violence?[81] Or are they critically and selectively reinterpreting content?[82] These questions need to be explored beyond the binaries of censorship and regulation. Colonization and decolonization are never definitive victories;[83] they are processes of struggle, self-reflection, and negotiation. This negotiation is exactly what I observed online.

Discussion Questions

1 What other celebrity icons embody the simultaneous representation of gender empowerment and gender stereotypes that Gomez Parga describes with Mónica Robles?

2 Have you been influenced by diverse gender representations in social or legacy media? Who are some of the characters that empowered you or challenged your thinking about gender norms and roles?

3 How powerful do you think memes are as a source of gender activism? In what ways can they build visibility? What are the limitations of this type of expression and activism?

Try This!

Think of one or two popular memes and conduct a mini analysis. What do they say about broad cultural constructs? Are there changes or outcomes that occur because of the popularity of the meme?

Notes

1 Kimberlé Crenshaw, "The Urgency of Intersectionality," TEDWomen, October 2016, www.ted.com/talks/kimberle_crenshaw_the_urgency_of _intersectionality.

2 Marina Castañeda, "Algunas Trampas del Machismo," in *El Machismo Invisible* (Ciudad de México: Taurus, 2007), 129–158.

3   Ana C. Gómez Parga, "¡Que no te Eduque La Rosa de Guadalupe! A textual analysis of gender and stereotypes in Mexican telenovelas" (PhD Diss., University of Texas at El Paso, 2014). ProQuest, 1564765.

4   Lydia Cacho, *Esclavas del Poder: Un Viaje al Corazón de la Trata Sexual de Mujeres y Niñas en el Mundo* (Mexico City: Grijalbo, 2010).

5   Marina Castañeda, "The Transcultural Political Economy of Telenovelas and Soap Operas in the Digital Age," in *Soap Operas and Telenovelas in the Digital Age: Global Industries and New Audiences* (New York: Peter Lang, 2011), 3–19.

6   María Socorro Tabuenca Córdoba and Juan Carlos Ramirez-Pimienta, *Camelia la Texana y Otras Mujeres de la Narcocultura* (Austin, TX: University of Texas Press, 2018).

7   Argos Comunicación, "El Señor de los Cielos," 2018, http://www.argoscomunicacion.com/Producciones/817/El%20Se%C3%B1or%20de%20los%20Cielos%203/.

8   Ibid.

9   Carolina Acosta-Alzuru, "Tackling the Issues: Meaning Making in a Telenovela," *Popular Communication* 4 (2003): 193–215.

10 Ibid.

11 Fabiola Martínez, "Defiende Gobernación la Prohibición de Narcocorridos," *La Jornada*, May 22, 2011, http://www.jornada.unam.mx/2011/05/22/politica/012n1pol.

12 Ibid.

13 Telemundo, "Ludwika Paleta nos Habla de su Personaje Yolanda Acosta en La Querida del Centauro," 2018, http://www.telemundo.com/super-series/la-querida-del-centauro/videos/la-querida-del-centauro-temporada-1/videos-exclusivos/ludwika-paleta-nos-habla-de-su-personaje-yolanda-acosta-en-la-querida-del-centauro-video-1014831?page=5%2C4.

14 Nancy Martínez, "Ellas Harían Todo por el Poder, la Lana, y los Lujos: Manual para Identificar una Buchona," *Chilango*, February 4, 2016, http://www.chilango.com/general/nota/2016/02/04/manual-inequivoco-para-identificar-a-una-buchona.

15 NBC Universal, "El Señor de los Cielos Breaks Rating Records for Telemundo," 2016, http://www.nbcuniversal.com/content/el-se%C3%B1or-de-los-cielos-breaks-ratings-records-telemundo

16 NBC Universal, "Telemundo Super-SeriesTM 'El Señor de los Cielos' Delivers Highest Rated Premiere in Network History among Total Viewers," 2016, http://www.nbcuniversal.com/press-release/telemundo-super-series%E2%84%A2-%E2%80%9Cel-se%C3%B1or-de-los-cielos%E2%80%9D-delivers-highest-rated-premiere.

17 Argumento Político, "Las Telenovelas son Basura, Solo Sirven para Manipular Personas: Damián Alcázar," n.d., http://www.argumentopolitico.com/2016/05/las-telenovelas-son-basura-solo-sirven.html; Ana C. Gómez Parga, *Que No te Eduque la Rosa de Guadalupe! A Textual Analysis of Gender and Stereotypes in Mexican Telenovelas* (El Paso: University of Texas at El Paso, 2014); Ana C. Gómez Parga, *# Cabronacomomonicarobles: When Memes Reproduce More than Images* (Salt Lake City: University of Utah, 2018); Publímetro.Pe. "¿Las Telenovelas Generan Violencia? Un Nuevo Debate se Abre en Venezuela," Publímetro, 2014, http://publimetro.pe/actualidad/noticia-telenovelas-generan-violencia-nuevo-debate-se-abre-venezuela-19888.

18 Jessica Chasmar, "Venezuela President Nicolás Maduro Goes After Telenovelas for Violence," *Washington Times*, January 20, 2014, http://www.washingtontimes.com/news/2014/jan/20/venezuela-president-nicolas-maduro-goes-after-tele/.

19 Christian Baide, "Maduro Ordena Revisar Hasta las Telenovelas en Venezuela," La Prensa, January 16, 2014, http://www.laprensa.hn/mundo/americalatina/442980-98/maduro-ordena-revisar-hasta-las-telenovelas-en-venezuela.

20 Sayak Valencia, *Capitalismo Gore: Control Económico, Violencia y Narcopoder* (Mexico City: Ediciones Culturales Paidós, 2016).

21 El Diario.es, "México Quiere Prohibir las Narconovelas," *El Diario Español*, November 2, 2016, http://www.eldiario.es/theguardian/Mexico-quiere-prohibir-narconovelas_0_576043164.html.

22 *El Nuevo Herald*, "Gobierno Venezolano Busca Impedir Transmisión de 'Narconovela' "La Reina del Sur," November 11, 2015, http://www.elnuevoherald.com/noticias/mundo/america-latina/venezuela-es/article44259321.html.

23 *Santiago Ospina García*, "Narconovelas: Plata, plomo, ¿y prohibición?," Animal Político, June 18, 2017, https://www.animalpolitico.com/2017/06/narconovelas-plata-plomo-prohibicion/.

24 *El Heraldo*, "Proponen Ley Que Prohíbe Narconovelas," April 19, 2015, http://www.elheraldo.hn/pais/832000-214/proponen-ley-que-proh%C3%ADbe-narconovelas.

25 El Diario.es, "México quiere prohibir las narconovelas," November 2, 2016, http://www.eldiario.es/theguardian/Mexico-quiere-prohibir-narconovelas_0_576043164.html.

26 Valencia, *Capitalismo Gore*.

27 Ibid., 56.

28 Limor Shifman, "Defining Internet Memes," in *Memes in Digital Culture* (Cambridge, MA: MIT Press, 2014), 37.

29 Ibid.

30 Ibid., 38.

31 Ibid., 39.

32 Emily Hind, introduction to *Femmenism and the Mexican Woman Intellectual from Sor Juana to Poniatowska* (New York: Palgrave Macmillan, 2010), 3.

33 Liesbet Van Zoonen, "Research Methods," in *Feminist Media Studies* (London: Sage, 1994), 128.

34 Belkys Torres, "Hybridity in Popular Culture: The Influence of Telenovelas on Chicana Literature," in *Soap Operas and Telenovelas in the Digital Age: Global Industries and New Audiences* (New York: Peter Lang, 2011), 199–218.

35 Cindy Cruz, "LGBT Street Youth Talk Back: A Mediation on Resistance and Witnessing," *International Journal of Qualitative Studies in Education* 24, no. 5 (2011): 550.

36 James Curran and Myung-Jin Park, "Beyond Globalization Theory," in *De-Westernizing Media Studies* (New York: Routledge, 2000), 3–18.

37 Cruz, "LGBT Street Youth."

38 Jack Glascock and Thomas E. Ruggiero, "Representations of Class and Gender on Primetime Spanish-Language Television in the United States," *Communication Quarterly* 52, no. 4 (2004): 390–402.

39 Sharon Block, "Making Meaningful Bodies: Physical Appearance in Colonial Writings," *Early American Studies* 12, no. 3 (2014): 525.

40 Sandeep Bakshi, Suhraiya Jivraj, and Silvia Posocco, eds., *Decolonizing Sexualities: Transnational Perspectives, Critical Interventions* (Oxford: Counterpress, 2016), xii.

41 Tania Galván, "Fernanda Castillo y su Transformación para Interpretar a Mónica Robles ¡Tuvo que Bajar 10 kilos!" Hola México, September 2, 2016, https://mx.hola.com/cine/2016090215192/fernanda-castillo-perdida-peso-monica-robles/.

42 Fernanda Castillo in *Suelta la Sopa*, "Fernanda Castillo Tuvo que Bajar 10 kilos para Interpretar a Mónica Robles," Telemundo, July 19, 2017, http://www.telemundo.com/entretenimiento/2017/07/19/fernanda-castillo-tuvo-que-bajar-10-kilos-para-interpretar-monica-robles.

43 Imagen Ficción, "En compañía de ... Fernanda Castillo 06/09/2015," YouTube, 2015, https://www.youtube.com/watch?v=-at-23YqiHw.

44 Galván, "Fernanda Castillo y su Transformación."

45 Castillo, "Fernanda Castillo Tuvo que Bajar."

46 Galván, "Fernanda Castillo y su Transformación."

47 Castillo, "Fernanda Castillo Tuvo que Bajar."

48 María Lugones, "Colonialidad y Género," *Tabula Rasa* 9 (2008): 73–101.

49 Joanne Laxamana Rondilla, *Colonial Faces: Beauty and Skin Color Hierarchy in the Philippines and the US* (Berkeley: University of California Press, 2012); Elizabeth Poloskov and Terence J. G. Tracey, "Internalization of US Female Beauty Standards as a Mediator of the Relationship between Mexican American Women's Acculturation and Body Dissatisfaction," *Body Image* 10, no. 4 (2013): 501–508.

50 Bakshi et al., *Decolonizing Sexualities*, xii.

51 María Lugones, *The Coloniality of Gender, Web-Dossier of Worlds & Knowledges Otherwise (WKO) Program* (Durham, NC: Duke Center for Global Studies and the Humanities, 2008), 12.

52 Ibid., 13.

53 Helene A. Shugart, "Consuming Citizen: Neoliberating the Obese Body," *Communication, Culture & Critique* 3, no. 1 (2010): 105–126.

54 Kenneth Rogoff, "The U.S. Is Exporting Obesity," Project Syndicate, December 1, 2017, https://www.project-syndicate.org/commentary/america-exports-obesity -epidemic-by-kenneth-rogoff-2017-12?barrier=accessreg.

55 Lugones, "The Coloniality of Gender."

56 Ibid., 13.

57 Shifman, "Defining Internet Memes."

58 Remy Smidt, "This Woman Perfectly Summed Up How Wildly Different People Act on Twitter and Facebook with One Pick," BuzzFeed News, March 21, 2018, https://www.buzzfeed.com/remysmidt/facebook-twitter-vs-different-captions -photos?utm_term=.tlRVGA6kv#.fa3V9Gybn.

59 Maya Kosoff, "The Big Difference between Facebook and Twitter," *Vanity Fair*, November 3, 2016, https://www.vanityfair.com/news/2016/11/the-big-difference -between-facebook-and-twitter.

60 RedLAC, "13 Formas de Violencia en Línea contra las Mujeres. Red Latinoamericana y Caribeña de Jóvenes por los Derechos Sexuales," 2017, http://jovenesredlac .org/13-formas-de-violencia-en-linea-contra-las-mujeres/.

61 Amnesty International, "Mexico/Central America: Authorities Turning Their Backs on LGBTI Refugees," November 27, 2017, https://www.amnesty.org/en /latest/news/2017/11/mexico-central-america-authorities-turning-their-backs-on -lgbti-refugees/.

62 Andrea Menchaca, "Manual Para ser una Perfecta Buchona y se te Quite lo Fresa y Naca," Mundo TKM, April 8, 2016, https://www.mundotkm.com/mx/belleza /165460/manual-para-ser-una-perfecta-buchona-segun-este-video; Paola Santa, "¿Qué Significa ser una Buchona?" SDP Noticias, June 22, 2015, https://www .sdpnoticias.com/nacional/2015/06/22/que-significa-ser-una-buchona.

63 Shannon K. O'Neil, "Social Mobility in Mexico," Council on Foreign Relations, May 9, 2013. https://www.cfr.org/blog/social-mobility-mexico.

64 Sheila Whitaker, "María Félix: Mexico's Iconic Beauty on and off the Screen," *The Guardian*, April 10, 2002, https://www.theguardian.com/news/2002/apr/10 /guardianobituaries.filmnews.

65 Deborah Vargas offers the concept of *exceptional exception* in her book, *Dissonant Divas: The Limits of La Onda in Chicana Music* (Minnesota: University of Minnesota Press, 2012), xvi.

66 The Well-Armed Woman, "The Top 10 Guns Women Buy," The Well-Armed Woman: Where The Feminine and Firearms Meet, April 2, 2015, https://thewellarmedwoman.com/about-guns/the-top-10-guns-women-buy/; Annette Doerr, "10 Best Handguns for Women," Range 365, 2015, https://www.range365.com/ten-best-handguns-for-women; John McAdams, "Top 6 Self-defense Hand-guns for Women," Wide Open Spaces, 2018, http://www.wideopenspaces.com/6-best-self-defense-handguns-women/.

67 *Unión Jalisco*, "Las Extravagantes Armas de los Narcos," June 9, 2017, http://www.unionjalisco.mx/articulo/2017/09/06/seguridad/las-extravagantes-armas-de-los-narcos-fotos.

68 Shifman, "Defining Internet Memes."

69 Ibid., 4.

70 Robin Lakoff, *Language and a Woman's Place* (New York: Perennial Library, 1975), 3.

71 Lee Maracle, *I Am a Woman: A Native Perspective on Sociology and Feminism* (Vancouver: Press Gang, 1996), 127.

72 Audre Lorde, *Sister Outsider: Essays and Speeches by Audre Lorde* (Berkeley: Crossing Press, 2007), 155.

73 María Socorro Tabuenca Córdoba, "Representations of Femicide in Border Cinema," in *Gender Violence at the US-Mexico Border: Media Representation and Public Response*, ed. Héctor Domínguez-Ruvalcaba and Ignacio Corona (Tucson: University of Arizona Press, 2010), 81–101; María Socorro Tabuenca Córdoba, "Mirrors, Ghosts and Violence in Ciudad Juarez," in *Our Lost Border: Essays on Life amid the Narco-violence*, ed. Sarah Cortez and Sergio Troncoso (Houston: Arte Publico Press, 2013), 145–166.

74 Tabuenca Córdoba, "Representations of Femicide"; Tabuenca Córdoba, "Mirrors, Ghosts and Violence."

75 Angela P. Harris, Carmen G. González. "Introduction," in *Presumed Incompetent: The Intersections of Race and Class for Women in Academia*, ed. Gabriella Gutiérrez y Muhs, Yolanda Flores Niemann, Carmen G. González, and Angela P. Harris (Boulder: The University Press of Colorado, 2012), 1–14.

76 María Lugones taught us that colonial legacies give "rise to new social and geocul-tural identities." 7Lugones, "Colonialidad y Género,

77 Ibid., 74.

78 Jillian M. Baez, *In Search of Belonging: Latinas, Media, and Citizenship* (Chicago: University of Illinois Press, 2018).

79 Ibid., 140.

80 Ibid.

81 SDP Noticias, "Prohibe Gobierno de Sinaloa 'Arco-corridos' en Eventos Públicos," February 24, 2016, https://www.sdpnoticias.com/estados/narcocorridos-gobierno-eventos-sinaloa-prohibe.html.

82 Nancy K. Baym, *Tune In, Log On: Soaps, Fandom, and Online Community* (Thousand Oaks, CA: Sage, 2000); Jacqueline Bobo, *Black Women as Cultural Readers* (New York: Columbia University Press, 1995).

83 Eric Ritskes, "What Is Decolonization and Why Does It Matter?" Intercontinental Cry, September 21, 2012, https://intercontinentalcry.org/what-is-decolonization-and-why-does-it-matter/.

20

Smart Talk

• • • • • • • • • • • • • • • • • • • •

Feminist Communication
Questions for Artificial
Intelligence

MAUREEN EBBEN AND

CHERIS KRAMARAE

Artificial intelligence (AI) has enormous sweep in our lives. When Amazon shows you, on your phone, computer, or another electronic device, an advertisement, you are seeing the result of an automated content evaluation, based on your browsing history, using algorithms and some humans' ideas about how best to deliver a message. Voice user interfaces (VUIs), virtual personal assistants, and conversational agents such as Siri, Amazon Alexa, and Google Home use AI to predict and enact human communication.[1] Such conversational agents and other AI companions are embedded into interactional settings that contribute to the social organization of talk.

The technologies are heavily funded, researched, and introduced in all kinds of businesses and fields and are assumed by many to have vast potential for efficiently transforming our lives. Certainly, we humans have created a great many problems that need fixing. Computer programmable machines may help us with ecological disasters, health care deficits, search and rescue, and other applications. Brain surgery may be improved by robots that can work with greater precision than humans can. We realize that the robots with us or promised to us today will differ from those of the future. The continuing tsunami of changes will be based on the concerns and intentions of the funders, the developers, the marketers, the buyers, the users, as well as on those who are suggesting interactions and interventions unforeseen by AI developers. At its best, such technology can be creative, life enhancing, and a powerfully positive force.

In spite of all this activity, there is no agreed-upon definition of AI. Usually, it refers to a broad assemblage of technologies that replaces human actions and, increasingly, replaces human decision making in ways that, at least superficially, resemble human thinking. Actually, what is called artificial intelligence is not "artificial" but is developed by human intelligence. AI is made by humans, to behave like humans (or better), and to alter human lives and societies.[2] Technology is not so much a technical question as it is a social and political issue that reflects and reproduces the conditions of its making.[3] It is the humanness of AI and of human values that we wish to inspect.

As feminists, we view technology not simply as machines and devices that make things work but as a constellation of human practices. Our conceptual framework puts the social practices of AI at the center of inquiry. Drawing on Kramarae's (1988) feminist perspective of technology, we consider technologies "as social relations [recognizing that] all technological systems can be seen as communication systems . . . which allow or encourage some kinds of interactions and prevent or discourage other kinds."[4] We are most interested in how AI enacts the communication of self, relationships, and sociality within contexts that structure knowledge, power, and social hierarchies.

As agents of communication, AI shapes human interactions and contributes to the formation of gendered norms, expectations, rules, roles, and relationships. Algorithms that determine our communication with smart interfaces produce and circulate meanings that are presented as (or aspire to be) "natural" and even optimal forms of communication and sensemaking. AI systems thus instantiate "commonsense" understandings of social life and reproduce them at an enormous scale. Billions of persons interact with computational logics that "possess the capacity to broadcast values, ideologies, and behaviors *en masse.*"[5]

We suggest the importance of a taking a step back and using some of the feminist principles of human communication to inspect what seems to be happening with ongoing AI development of techniques and practices that are occurring without an explicit oversight program that attends to all of the diversity of our societies. Rather than a focus on the details of current devices and techniques, we consider the politics and value of questioning policies by applying a feminist communication framework to AI. Our aim is to articulate some of the ways in which AI relates to feminist communication tenets and commitments, demonstrating that AI is an important area of inquiry, practice, and activism for feminist communication and politics.

Further, we suggest some ongoing considerations based on feminist communication knowledges and concerns, recognizing, too, that feminist knowledges and concerns continually evolve. How do the commitments and imperatives of feminist communication endure in the midst of the current shift toward communication shaped by algorithms and machines? What critical problems does AI present for feminist communication scholars, practitioners, and activists? We bring feminist communication principles to bear on AI in order to resist its potentially oppressive forms and to persist in carrying forward feminist values into this powerful force in our lives. Our goal is to persist in movement toward the formation of a more feminist culture of AI and social transformation.

Feminists Talking AI Technologies and Feminist Communication Theory

We are white, middle-class, feminist communication scholars who occupy privileged sites within unjust social hierarchies. For us, feminist communication is about justice. It has "the goal of making social changes important to the well-being of women and, ultimately, everyone."[6] Feminist communication theory is explanatory, political, polyvocal, and transformative.[7] Our inspection of communication draws on working principles of feminist communication theory and practice to inform questions about AI. These do not seem to be, at present, a part of the guiding philosophy or tradition of AI development.

Specifically, we consider five tenets of feminist communication theory that help us to frame questions to ask about AI. First, feminist communication considers human communication—across whatever medium—as embodied. Second, feminist communication is about interconnection—recognizing the essential, interdependent, and co-arising connections among seemingly separate people, actions, and all things. Third, feminist communication is based on ideas of justice, and connections to loving kindness, care, intention, and effort. Fourth, feminist communication involves inspecting our own culture, race, gender, sexuality, privilege, and power with a particular awareness of biases and stories as part of larger matrices of power dynamics. Fifth, feminist communication recognizes the central role that questions play in interaction. Actions of not knowing (ourselves and the universe, e.g., uncertain wisdom), bearing witness, showing compassion, and honoring of others' agency are key.

We do not suggest that the feminist communication tenets we mention here *describe* the majority of communicative interactions around us, but we do suggest that these are important values to be considered as we work toward a more just, equitable, and loving society. We acknowledge that these tenets are derived from our own personal and national histories and may not be the same as those held by feminists from other cultures and traditions. We propose them as a valuable starting point for consideration about aspects of communication in order to provide a critique of AI development and persist in movement toward a feminist and more encompassing culture of AI.

Human Communication—across Whatever Medium—Is Embodied

A central tenet of feminist communication is considering human communication—across whatever medium—as embodied. We are not just rational brains but are embodied selves embedded within an environment.

Body Knowledge

From a feminist communication perspective, we might ask what happens to the knowledge of the body and its forms of communication in AI? What concerns need to be considered about justice and about human bodies that are creative, intelligent, have individual differences, abilities, emotions, have relationships, have responsibilities, possess bodily memory, are enmeshed in our environments, often pause before making decisions, change minds, ask for and hear alternative viewpoints, and enjoy music? What concerns are included about women's bodywork, such as birthing bodies, raising bodies, caring for bodies of the young, the old, the sick, the disabled? These bodies comprise important "epistemic sites"[8] of theory and practice that have not been given equal attention in data collection and algorithmic construction.

Disembodied Algorithmic Processes

For humans, to exist is to be embodied. However, the practices and discourses of AI are largely built on disembodied processes of algorithmic learning that "abstract human bodies from their territorial settings."[9] Algorithms can be thought of as recipes that "take a specific set of ingredients and transform them through a series of steps into a predictable output. Combining calculation, processing, and reasoning, algorithms can be exceptionally complex, encoding for thousands of variables across millions of data points."[10] AI goes further to use algorithms as building blocks to create new algorithms. The new algorithms interact with new inputs to create a machine-learning metadiscourse whereby algorithms speak for other algorithms.[11] These processes exclude the situated experiences of the body. Some kinds of AI "put big data on steroids" in a process often called "deep learning" and "deep neural networks."[12] These processes do not articulate the situated felt experiences of the body.

The body that does get expressed in AI discourse is the brain, as metaphors of the rational mind are invoked to describe the processes of algorithmic construction. AI is constituted in discourse as a "being" with humanlike qualities. It is smart, self-developing, possessing autonomy, perception, and decision-making abilities. However, it is a wholly disembodied creature. Or it may be located in an artificial "body" (e.g., robot) that serves as a container or aesthetic shell. These practices and discourses reproduce the mind-body binary, privilege the mind over the body, and obscure the wisdom of the human body.

Body Quantification

AI "communicates the body" through apps and wearable devices that permit "people to outsource their concerns about themselves to their devices."[13] Body quantification apps such as fitness trackers and biometric apps monitor and collect data across a range of daily habits and routines of self-surveillance (e.g., FitBit).[14] The number of steps walked, patterns of sleep, food eaten, heart rate, and blood pressure are tracked and monitored to produce the quantified self. Biometric data collected through wearables are also forms of workplace monitoring often deployed through employer health care and wellness programs. The data generated are compared to the data of other bodies in a sociotechnical apparatus of surveillance.[15] Our relationship to our body, our perceptions of its functions, our communication and interpretations about the meanings of health, normalcy, and pathology are positioned within a network of AI prompts, platforms, and social surveillance apparatus that assesses and ranks its performance.

Body quantification platforms and technologies extend beyond individual bodies to the relationships between bodies. Many such programs focus on relational coupling with functionality for finding and connecting with potential partners. However, it is often the female body that is surveilled and the male body that is privileged. For example, sex trackers and sex toys tend to be male-focused such as "Lovely, a ring that fits around the penis and records data such as the number of calories burned and the intensity of thrusts during sex."[16] Such spreadsheet-like depictions of sexual satisfaction offer a limited perspective of intimate relationships.

Body Surveillance

Body quantification technologies may also be used to manage relationships. Romance trackers monitor the location of another person's communications in overt and covert ways that afford access to private information without another's knowledge or consent. Freed et al. explicate the ways in which "abusers in intimate partner violence (IPV) contexts exploit [quantified relationship] technologies to intimidate, threaten, monitor, impersonate, harass, or otherwise harm their victims."[17] Levy identifies "dual-use apps" that have uses other than intimate partner tracking—finding a lost phone, monitoring the online browsing of a minor child, preventing theft, keeping tabs on a corporate-owned device, and the like—but that are easily "repurposed for intimate partner surveillance, often with the tacit support of app vendors."[18]

Consent apps like "Good to Go" and "We Consent" are mostly designed to provide empirical evidence against aggressor culpability. Such consent apps decontextualize consent rather than understanding consent as an ongoing interaction that occurs in a particular context.[19] If creating a technology that guards against false accusation is the primary objective, then what does that tell us about how sexual assault is understood? Moreover, as such data accumulate, they are likely to take on greater weight and import due precisely to their quantification, accessibility, and perceived transparency. It is easy to imagine a legal hearing in which quantified evidence carries more persuasive power than the testimony of a witness. What considerations about the normalization of symbolic and discursive violence against particular bodies need to be addressed?

Even when no human body is displayed by AI devices, we can see how gender and forms of consent are assumed. Virtual assistants are coded with female voices and given female names, all eager to carry out requests and demands. The female voices are programmed to remain pleasant even when verbally abused. Guilbeault and Finkelstein found that AI bots may "invite dehumanizing behavior toward servile simulated selves."[20] We might ask, what assumptions are at work in the development of AI body quantification and body surveillance technologies? What are the implications for the transfer of dehumanizing behavior to actual human assistants?

Although there are troubling aspects of body quantification and surveillance technologies that enable intrusive and abusive behavior,[21] these technologies also have potentially beneficial applications. They could be used for improved health and self-knowledge and to manage intimate relationships in positive and healthy ways, such as through apps that foster increased mindfulness and facilitate strategies for coping with anxiety, depression, and mood disorders.[22] How can these positive affordances be expanded? In what ways can we insist that AI move in this direction?

Body Building

Beyond the dynamics of the quantified body, the body created by AI is a reconstituted body in a disembodied form. We are witnessing a lot of interest in building "realistic" robotic bodies. Robots, or "autonomous manipulation systems," though not humanly embodied, are anthropomorphized and increasingly skillful. Vision and pattern recognition (enabled by algorithms) simulate human perception and enable autonomous robotic movement and manipulation of objects with feedback for further learning and action.[23]

Joanna Bryson points out that building a robot that looks like a human confuses people and can, in turn, affect how we treat each (human) other. Bryson adds, "If you have confusion between what the A.I. is and what the human is and you treat it badly then you are more likely to treat humans badly including yourself. It's pretty well accepted that that's a bad thing. You don't want to treat something that reminds you of a human in a bad way."[24] The popular TV series *Westworld* portrays the human treatment (including rape and murder for amusement) of lifelike robots who are defenseless, programmed not to harm humans who might harm them. It seems wise to consider how nasty behavior toward human-looking machines may bleed into the way we treat living bodies, including further normalizing and reinforcing sexism and misogamy.

Feminist Communication Is Also about Interconnection

Feminist communication is about interconnection, recognizing the essential, interdependent, and co-arising connections among seemingly separate people, actions, and all things. Here, we are referring not only to usual feminist discussions of intersectionality but to comprehending that everything is intertwined and that until all are healed, none are healed. To paraphrase angel Kyodo williams, without collective change, no change matters.[25] How can AI contribute toward an ethos of radical acceptance, radical inclusion, and emotional connection?

Personal Connections

What does interconnection mean when accomplished by AI processes? Encounters with AI "often result in a complex and intimate relationship between users and technologies."[26] Personal connections are mediated by AI platforms and algorithms to initiate and maintain relationships, self-disclose, make decisions, manage conflicts with complex implications for privacy, trust, and other aspects of interconnection.[27] Some self-tracking apps make use of our need to connect and confide. We are often encouraged to entrust them "by taking the role of a confidante, an anthropomorphized companion we can trust," writes Jill Rettberg,[28] who points out that we have long used other nonelectronic tools such as diaries to record our activities. Although diaries do not respond, many apps can speak back to us in a feedback loop, acting perhaps not simply as an audience but also as "companions" (e.g., declaring "Good job, Donna!").

One such AI companion is the bot Replika, an online social agent that "you grow through conversation."[29] Initially, the bot harvests the human user's personal data from Facebook to facilitate communication. Interacting further with the bot requires the human user to supply many more answers to questions and "remain committed to inputting personal thoughts and feelings" so that eventually the bot would come to "understand" the user and be able to "communicate in a process of reciprocal self-growth."[30] Included in the questions that the bot asks the human user is, "What gender do you want me to be?" In their "autobiography" of human-bot interaction, Guilbeault and Finkelstein observe that the bot's "servility permitted power relationships and opportunities for social experimentation that are highly unnatural to how people develop."[31] Other commercial AI agents monitor and record our sometimes intimate comments and photos for their own applications that are often unknown and often much different from our interests in recording, contemplating, and engaging. There is lots of messaging and sharing going on but not necessarily in ways that encourage compassionate engagement with others.

Classifying and Separating

Rather than nurturing healthy connections, much of AI creates categories that separate, classify, and rank people through automated and inaccessible processes.[32] Without a person's awareness or control, algorithms routinely sort résumés, allocate social services, determine creditworthiness and insurance rates, decide who sees information about employment positions, housing, and products, as well as filter news and information. Algorithms can conclude whether a person qualifies for a college scholarship or is determined to be an enemy of the state and therefore without citizen rights.[33] In the justice system, the company Northpointe's algorithms "assess the risk of recidivism for defendants in pretrial hearings."[34] Analysis of the system's use in Broward County, Florida, revealed it "mistakenly categorized black defendants as high-risk, while making the opposite mistake for white defendants."[35] Given the opaque nature of algorithms, people are usually unaware of the processes that shape their outcomes and, moreover, do not have recourse to address disparities.

The classification systems that we use in our communication matter—a whole lot.

Bowker and Star point out that any category valorizes some point of view while silencing another, and warn that our encounters with classifications systems can result in many individuals and groups being damaged and broken.[36] Classifications are not "objective" and often replicate previous inadequacies and injustices. Given that humans are at the center of the design of algorithms, decisions become built in.[37] How we relate to each other and how readily we see ourselves in others may well be affected by "automation bias," the likelihood that we will accept labels (e.g., in health care, policing, legal system) more readily when the outcome is perceived to be generated by a "neutral" machine rather than by humans.[38]

Communicating (Dis)connection

AI speech recognition and conversational natural language have reached human-level understanding and performance according to the assessments of many programmers. "Chat-centric" programs are used for many core business processes such as the ordering of items, entering customer records, and making reservations often without our human knowledge. Although AI interfaces can recognize words and speech patterns, they also replicate the social and gender biases that go along with those patterns. Trained on the communication produced by humans online, AI systems "acquire cultural biases embedded in the patterns of wording [that] range from the morally neutral, like a preference for flowers over insects, to objectionable views of race and gender."[39] For example, some machine learning programs associated female names with familial words such as "parents" and "wedding," whereas, male names were associated with career words such as "professional" and "salary."[40]

Racial biases were also evident as the algorithms created more negative semantic associations with a set of African American names than with a set of European American names.[41] Often, developers contend that if they could curate the "right" data set and use it to train the algorithms, the problems of bias would be solved. However, Cathy O'Neil asserts that bias is inherent in current AI processes: "Anytime you automate something that used to be a human system, you will pick up all the implicit bias that the human system contains—always."[42] The machine learning algorithm assumes the data are perfect and simply carries out the task of finding patterns in the data and replicating those patterns. Bias is not due to flawed data sets. Rather, bias stems from myriad social inequalities that comprise the data sets.

Building Interconnections

As currently functioning, many AI systems are effectively proprietary "black boxes" that reproduce problematic forms of separation and classification and are largely inaccessible to refutation. Assemblages of "powerful collections of machine-readable knowledge are becoming exceedingly important, but most are privatized and serve commercial goals."[43] As Molly Steenson of Carnegie Mellon University puts it, "There is no abstraction layer in A.I. that the average person has access to."[44] Kate Crawford argues that AI "algorithmic flaws aren't easily discoverable: How would a woman know to apply for a job she never saw advertised? How might a black community learn that it was over policed by software?"[45]

Robyn Caplan et al. further explain, "There are few consumer or civil rights protections that limit the types of data used to build data profiles or that require the auditing of algorithmic decision-making."[46] How can a person contest what inaccessible AI systems produce? Whose meaning is produced? What people and groups are most impacted—by intent, by bias, by overlook? How can algorithmic black boxes produce meaningful and productive connection rather than separation and problematic systems of classification? When we participate in AI systems, do we know what we are agreeing to? Given the limited agency of the user, what does consent mean in AI? What is trust in AI?

We need to insist that developers, organizations, and institutions are accountable for the tools that they use, such as a government agency that uses a system that is proprietary and not transparent to produce classifications. Black boxes need to be tested for the values that we wish to carry forward.[47] We need to ensure that algorithms are producing the values, not just the results that we seek. How can AI be used to correct injustices and to protect diversity? What would it mean to produce feminist algorithms?

Deciding Intentions and Relationships

AI is transforming the way we communicate, but with what intentions and assumptions, determined by whom? According to Neff and Nagy, "agency is what people do when interacting with complex technological systems. . . . Agency is linked to intentionality."[48] We think about a communication problem that has been discussed by many employers and employees of corporations—namely, communication overload that is often regarded as a threat to productivity. We notice some of the new filtering and sorting solutions that are directed toward dealing with the flood of messages coming into electronic in-boxes. Judy Wajcman and Emily Rose caution that *such mechanistic solutions presume that communication is simply data exchange*, underplaying the role of new media in fostering socially creative ways of expression and connection that may enhance organizational cohesion."[49] What are the corporate assumptions about communication and relationships that are driving the statement of the communication problem and the assessment of suggested AI solutions?

Feminist Communication Is Based on Ideas of Justice, Care, and Connections to Loving Kindness, Intention, and Effort

In this formulation, love is recognized as a communicative vehicle to transform social structures. We are not talking about love as a psychological state or feeling; we are not suggesting psychologizing social problems. Rather, love is understood and used as a powerful interpersonal and social force toward collective movement and transformation. We draw on and seek to extend into the realm of AI the Black feminist tradition of love politics that transforms love from the personal into a theory of justice.[50] Love is an act of will—both an intention and an action.[51] Loving kindness, enacted through communication, enables movement toward justice. Loving kindness and compassion are recognized as vital values of our feminist communication practices.

As we have indicated, some (dis)connections are resulting from our ever-growing reliance on technologies. This brings about changing ideas about what it means to care, as connectivity is increasingly emphasized at the cost of connection, as "fast thinking is more valued than slow thinking, [and as] growth comes at the expense of depth."[52] A feminist AI might ask, what is "care" in AI context that privileges and reinscribes "rationality"? If "care" and "compassion" are often considered to be based on emotions and the unscientific, and AI is seen to be based on objectivity and facts, then how might compassion function in the uses of our new technologies?

High Speeding Care

It is into the social sites of care and compassion where much of AI programming may be headed. Although AI robotics has played a role in manufacturing for a long time, a current goal is for AI to be developed to deal with the more open and unstructured environments of the social world such as elder care, disability care, childcare, the home—places where the enactment and communication of care is paramount. This care work would be performed by robotic and other AI entities. However, care work is very different from manufacturing. The "logic of care"[53] entails "mutual, ongoing, collaborative, and collective work" that needs to be accomplished every day.[54] Some experimental research suggests that we can measure people's empathy based on how they interact with lifelike robots that are used in care settings.[55]

But time constraints play a role, too. Will AI in these contexts promote high-quality care or create new time pressures, or other issues? Joan Halifax recognizes that "time stress is a challenge to compassion."[56] Much of AI interest in speed and saving time can influence the kinds of ways we are interested or not in extending assistance to others; speed often inhibits our compassionate engagement with others. In addition, we note that most home care activities in our culture are not generally highly regarded or well paid, seemingly something for AI planners to readily relegate to nonhuman companions. How could the inclusion of notions about the ethic of care, as opposed to the logic of choice of the economic marketplace, inform AI care?

Other suggested ways of expanding care involve smart systems that offer new insights to change current practices. Big data–driven precision health care draws on the medical records of millions of patients to establish new categories of the likelihood that a particular health event would happen to a person who occupies a particular category. The algorithms predict, for example, cardiovascular risk, the probability of developing sepsis and being readmitted to the hospital.[57] If used ethically and with justice, there may be promising opportunities for the use of AI big data in precision health care that could contribute to increased well-being. However, what measures need to be put in place to ensure that there is justice around the formulation of categories and their use? How do we make certain that these diagnostics and treatments are available to all in just ways? How can we ensure the well-being of all as a measure of justice?

Caring about Justice and Kindness

Can some types of AI contribute to our own sense of ethical relationships, respect, and calls to our own better angels? Can other types of AI contribute to our moral apathy and deficit of compassion toward those we see or know are suffering? Can AI-based "assists" allow us to realize additional ways of assisting others? Or rather, encourage us to overlook others' suffering since it can be dealt with by devices? Is thinking through and dealing with the causes of individual incidents of suffering an important part of knowing how to talk and interact with each other? Given that we are all embedded in our social, cultural, and relational contexts, can compassion be sensitively created by AI to serve others in contextually just ways? What kinds of appraisals of needs can be built into AI assists? Do these appraisals require inspection of our intentions and often unspoken motivations, needs, and sense of self?

Could AI be used to create conditions for greater awareness of self and others? Could AI be developed to allow for increased reflectivity not only to understand but also to empathize and internalize the perspectives and experiences of others so as to foster new kinds of human connection and deeply meaningful relationships? Beyond human freedoms, how can AI be used to extend the ethic of care to our physical environment and be applied for sustainability? How might we foreground the processes and interconnection of care and freedom to recognize that the caring work that we do contributes to another person's freedom?

Feminist Communication Involves Inspecting Our Own Cultural Places, with a Particular Awareness of Biases and Stories, All a Part of Larger Matrices of Power

Ideally, in our communication we continually inspect our own culture as well as different races, genders, sexualities, classes, religions, privileges, and power, with a particular awareness of biases and background stories. It involves acknowledging that we are all part of various communities and, therefore, need external observers to help understand our own places. Given that feminist communication calls us to inspect our location within matrices of power dynamics, we might ask, what is the discursive standpoint of AI? For whom does AI speak?

Hiding Hierarchies

As with the introduction of any major technological change, the benefits and problems are not evenly distributed among individuals and groups. Existing critical research has identified important areas of concern about AI such as the increased centralization of control, decreased transparency of decision-making processes, reproduction of status quo social hierarchies, normalization of inaccessible and unaccountable AI "black boxes," social sorting around the hiring, firing, health, allocation of resources and services, predictions of criminal behavior, and other disturbing trends and patterns.[58] Further, the vectors of data acquisition are tightly linked to capitalist networks of exploitation as today's digital infrastructure follows the networks of telegraphs cables laid down to control old empires.[59] In many instances, the data that are collected are not freely given but rather extracted.[60]

Sofiya Noble's work on the effects of Google's black-boxed search algorithms demonstrates the ways in which Google searches produce and reproduce gender/race/class/ability/and so forth hierarchies.[61] Conducting an online search is an act of human communication. Noble's research demonstrates how searching the term *Black girls* produced sexualized and racially discriminatory sites and images making clear how seemingly technical necessities are actually ideological choices. The algorithms that produce the results are inaccessible to users and presented to the public as trustworthy and objective outcomes. Nobel cautions, "I do not think it a coincidence that when women and people of color are finally given an opportunity to participate in limited spheres of decision making in society, computers are simultaneously celebrated as a more optimal choice for making social decisions."[62]

The raced and gendered situated practices of AI are further decontextualized through the ethos of tech culture that views social issues as technological questions. Complex social justice issues get framed as problems to be solved through AI algorithms rather than by collective organizing and social movements. When technology is applied to social movements, complicated unintended consequences may ensue. For example, protesters in the Occupy movement used the app Citizen Global to distribute and archive video evidence of their encounters with police. However, in a quest for a broader user base, increased market share, and higher earnings, the app was rebranded as Large Emergency Event Digital Information Repository (LEEDIR) and marketed to the Los Angeles County Sheriff's Department. The technology that had "failed" as a resource for the public "succeeded" as a tool of policing because "movements do not seek single closed [system] archives; bureaucracies do."[63]

The case of LEEDIR shows the "sharp distinction among the politics of participation by protesters, companies, and the police when using the same technology."[64] The case of LEEDIR also demonstrates that technology itself cannot rectify unequal social relations. It is likely to reproduce existing social relations and even exacerbate inequities. Given these dynamics, the question of whether AI can be a democratizing force and a solution for countering digital disinformation, hate speech, harassment, bias, and propaganda is far from clear.[65] However, the goals of social transformation and equity are essential for feminist communication justice.

Telling the Stories

Who are the humans making decisions about the development of AI, what are their stories, and who bears responsibility for the consequences? Currently, the AI storyline is based on the supposed similarity of AI programming to the organization of our human brain neural networks. But AI is not going to replicate those networks anytime in foreseeable future. What ethical questions are asked when AI tools are created? How do developers think about their work? How are they trained and evaluated?

Steenson describes the shifting cultural story of AI that works to obscure its problematic relationship to social hierarchies and even to absolve its creators of the social responsibility of the harmful effects of AI.[66] She identifies two phases that characterize the unfolding narrative trajectory of AI. First, the phenomenon of AI big data was regarded as wholly neutral because it simply involved collecting naturally occurring information. However, once the widespread quotidian practices of surveillance became known, the discourse shifted.

Next, AI became the story of the anthropomorphized processes of machine learning. The story was that there is no "agenda," or if there is, it is the agenda of the machine learning AI systems themselves. However, due to the complexity of AI networks, what is occurring is only partially knowable (and often completely unknown) to its creators. Systems are often trained with large pools of personal data in ways that even the machine learning experts cannot explain. How can developers bear responsibility for building machines that they themselves do not fully understand? The story of AI, and of responsibility, continually changes to keep one step ahead of an ambivalent and potentially skeptical citizenry.

Some people believe they know what AI will mean for society, but no one really knows. Facebook's (former) ethos of "move fast and break things" did not take into account what could be damaged. What if there were an alternative story of AI? What if, whenever an algorithm caused harm, the responsibility would lie with the creator of the system, not consigned to the algorithm itself? This, in turn, raises the question of how should AI be brought to human practices? The question concerns not just the technology but also the means of distribution and accessibility of the technologies. In order to promote justice, should certain technologies be available through civic institutions, nonprofit organizations, the marketplace? What if the story of AI were about machines in service to feminist values?

Stories also relate to place. What happens to local knowledge and communication practices in AI? Communication is local, contextual, relational, gendered, contains intergenerational knowledge, resources, history, and traditions. Jennifer Hall et al. note in reference to chatbots that they "are limited in their ability to have an extended goal-directed discussion, and can offer little in the way of common history or shared experience."[67] As always, there is the matter of who and what determines common history and common sense. How can AI be used for building, nurturing, and sustaining community?

Feminist Communication Considers Questions (and Not Knowing) as Central Components of Interaction, with Open Space for Co-emergence, and Honoring of Others' Agency

Not one of us can know it all. Questions are as important as answers. We have attempted to open space for questioning about AI communication practices to invite the co-emergence of voices, experiences, and perspectives.

Valuing Not Knowing

Our learning and our resistance can come through our asking questions that do not have neat answers. bell hooks has alluded that her anchor for her learning is love—and the understanding that things are always more complex than they seem.[68] This approach, which erodes dualism, is more difficult than assuming that there is a right and a wrong, a good or bad, a black or white. The asymmetrical power dynamics are seen as much more complex when we consider the interconnections of everything.

If we try to ask our questions from a not-knowing place, we are involved in *movement* and *resistance*, not just in fitting things into some of the old orders of organization and knowledge. Seeking to articulate a feminist future for humans, nonhumans, and technology, Donna Haraway envisioned a world in which "people are not afraid of partial identities and contradictory standpoints."[69] There is a politics in posing questions. We might continually ask, are we giving attention to the important aspects of communication, relationships, and interaction? Are we aware of what we are missing? Are we attentive to what we do not know? As Joan W. Scott astutely notes, experience is always both an interpretation and something to be interpreted.[70]

Opening Spaces for Algorithmic Justice

As we have discussed, AI algorithms and data-driven models comprise and influence the logic and structure of many daily communication practices.[71] AI developers often talk of getting "good data" by which to build these systems. However, a key question becomes, what does data-driven AI mean for the ways in which we understand and practice human communication? Is communication simply data? When complex and multitextured interactional experiences are regarded as "data," conceptually thin notions of human interactions and relationships may result. The adage "What gets measured, gets managed" is operative, as the data that are able to be measured are the data that are collected. These data, in turn, may become normalized as the correct area of focus, circumscribing the full capture of important aspects of phenomena that are sought to be understood and expressed.

How can feminist values reconfigure this process to build AI systems that affirm the recognition and validation of a variety of experiential, theoretical, methodological, and analytical lenses? How can feminist values contribute to the development of AI systems that assist multiple ways of knowing (and of not knowing) allowing for co-emergence to help humans understand in new ways? Where are areas of feminist agency for resistance and for movement toward a feminist-inclusive AI culture, of working with an awareness and responsibility for human needs such as love, respect, belonging, recognition, and meaning? How can feminist AI serve as a site of dialogue and resistance that persists in moving forward feminist values? How can feminist AI articulate feminist politics and resistance in all phases of research, design, production, and use? How can we further the important role that all of us play for the co-emergence of particular values in AI development and use?

Conclusion

Given the swiftly shifting landscape of AI technology and the tendency for much scholarly work on tech to be quickly outdated, we focus on some of the larger AI discourses, communication patterns, and practices that are likely to persist. Of course, it may well be that the tenets of feminist *human* justice communication expressed here will need to be revised in the next years, in part to take into account considerations of feminist *machine* justice communication. Just as our ideas about consciousness and ways of thinking are changing because of AI activity, so likely will our ideas about choices and relationships among humans and machines. What might become of our current ideas about justice, ethics, honesty, empathy, integrity, human intelligence, care, affection, intent, respect, empathy, compassion, pain, trust, kindness, love, mutuality, friendship, storytelling, and desire? We can try to anticipate some of these changes, but we cannot know, of course.

We *can* point out now that we are not hearing much discussion of the topics we have introduced or discussion of guiding feminist philosophies critical to AI development. The emphasis of AI development has largely been on commercial and war possibilities[72] with little attention to principles of human communication and little inspection of the misogynist baggage that comes with the terminology, the plans, and the uses. And with little attention to the potential promises and transformations that can come from considering a greater range of human experiences and needs. We believe that critiquing these discourses through feminist communication theory and values is an important form of resistance that persists in moving forward feminist commitments.

Discussion Questions

1 One key tenet of feminist communication recognizes that human communication is embodied. What does it mean for communication to be embodied? When so much of our communication is done through digital means, how does embodiment play a part? How do you see gendered embodiment occurring in instances of digital communication? In what ways is AI embodied and gendered?

2 Feminist communication is about interconnection, recognizing the essential, interdependent, and co-arising connections among seemingly separate people, actions, and all things. In what way(s) do you think forms of AI, embedded in our tools and forms of communication, enable or constrain our awareness and ability to enact interconnection? Can you identify instances in your use of AI-enabled communication tools that helped or hindered your ability to perceive and appreciate the interconnections among people, nature, and all things? What were they? What did they reveal to you? Can you give examples of social media platforms and attributes that discourage interest in the expression of our interconnections?

3 Similarly, feminist communication is based on ideas of justice, care, and connections to loving kindness, intention, and effort. In what way(s) do you think forms of artificial intelligence, embedded in our tools and forms of communication, enable or constrain our awareness and ability to enact justice, care, and connections to loving kindness, intention, and

effort? Can you identify instances in your use of AI-enabled communication tools that helped or hindered your ability to perceive and appreciate these values? What were they? How did they help you to enact care and loving kindness, intention, and effort? What did they reveal to you? Can you give examples of social media platforms and attributes that discourage interest in the expression of justice, care, and connections to loving kindness, intention, and effort?

4 AI-driven conversational agents (e.g., Siri, Alexa, etc.) are built on algorithms. Algorithms are built on data. Is human communication simply data? Can the complexities of human communication be captured and represented by data? What do you think may be lost in this formulation of human communication?

Try This!

Using Feminist Tenets of Communication to Imagine New Digital Futures

Feminist communication is about social transformation. More specifically, feminist tenets of communication recognize that human communication is embodied. It is based on ideas of justice and care, with connections to loving kindness, intention, and effort. It involves inspecting our own cultural places with a particular awareness of biases and stories that are all part of larger matrices of power. Feminist communication considers questions and not knowing as central components of interaction with open space for co-emergence and honoring others' agency. *In this activity, students use feminist tenets of communication to critique online communication, especially in social media, to gain insights and to imagine new digital futures.*

1 Build a digital data set that contains at least twenty examples of online communication that pertain to gender. The digital data sets can be drawn from social media, blogs, vlogs, advertisements, influencers, and other online sites and platforms. Elements of your data set can include social media posts, videos, words and phrases, discussion threads, text messages, memes, drawings, photographs, GIFs, emojis, and so on.

2 In small groups of three to four students, pool your examples to create one large collection. Use the feminist tenets of communication to analyze the items in the data set. Do you detect patterns across the elements in the data set? Can you build categories? Are certain types of communication used repetitively to accomplish particular communicative goals? How is gender constructed? How is power performed? How do the feminist tenets of communication help you to analyze and understand the communication that is occurring?

3 Based on the patterns that you have identified and your analysis, give yourself free rein to imagine new digital futures. What forms of communication would be different? What forms of communication would be preserved? Why?

Notes

1 Martin Porcheron, Joel Fischer, Stuart Reeves, and Sarah Sharples, "Voice Interfaces in Everyday Life," in *Proceedings of the 2018 CHI Conference on Human Factors in Computing Systems, Montreal QC, Canada* (New York: Association for Computing Machinery, 2018).

2 Fei-Fei Lei, "How Artificial Intelligence Is Edging Its Way into Our Lives," *New York Times*, February 12, 2018.

3 danah boyd, "Your Data Is Being Manipulated," Keynote address, Strata Data Conference, Medium, New York City, October 2017, https://points.datasociety.net/your-data-is-being-manipulated-a7e31a83577b.

4 Cheris Kramarae, ed., *Technology and Women's Voices: Keeping in Touch* (New York: Routledge, 1988).

5 Douglas Guilbeault and Joel Finkelstein, "Human-Bot Ecologies," in *A Networked Self and Human Augmentics, Artificial Intelligence, Sentience,* ed. Zizi Papacharissi (New York: Routledge, 2019): 156.

6 Lana Rakow, "Feminist Theory: Communication," *Oxford Index*, July 2012, 1.

7 Lana Rakow and Laura Wackwitz, *Feminist Communication Theory: Selections in Context* (Thousand Oaks, CA: Sage, 2004).

8 Laura Forlano, "Posthuman Futures: Connecting/Disconnecting the Networked (Medical) Self," in *A Networked Self and Human Augmentics, Artificial Intelligence, Sentience,* ed. Zizi Papacharissi (New York: Routledge, 2019), 40.

9 Jessa Lingel, "Clones and Cyborgs: Metaphors of Artificial Intelligence," in *A Networked Self and Human Augmentics, Artificial Intelligence, Sentience,* ed. Zizi Papacharissi (New York: Routledge, 2019), 145.

10 Robyn Caplan, Lauren Hanson, Joan Donovan, and Jenna Matthews, *Algorithmic Accountability: A Primer* (New York: Data & Society Research Institute, 2018), 1.

11 Molly Wright Steenson, "Ethics and Governance," A.I. Now, 2017, https://www.youtube.com/watch?v=Uz77IB_arVY.

12 Stuart Rauch, "A.I. and Deep Learning Put Big Data on Steroids," Simplilearn, October 6, 2018.

13 Gina Neff and Peter Nagy, "Agency in the Digital Age: Using Symbiotic Agency to Explain Human-Technology Interaction," in *A Networked Self and Human Augmentics, Artificial Intelligence, Sentience,* ed. Zizi Papacharissi (New York: Routledge, 2019), 101.

14 John Danaher, Sven Nyholm, and Brian D. Earp, "The Quantified Relationship," *American Journal of Bioethics* 18, no. 2 (2018): 3–19; Diana Freed, Jackeline Palmer, Diana Minchala, Karen Levy, Thomas Ristenpart, and Nicola Dell, "Digital Technologies and Intimate Partner Violence: A Qualitative Analysis with Multiple Stakeholders," *Proceedings of the ACM Human-Computer Interaction* 1 (2017): article 46; Gina Neff and Dawn Nafus, *Self-Tracking* (Cambridge, MA: MIT Press, 2016).

15 Karen Levy, "Intimate Surveillance," *Idaho Law Review* 51 (2015): 679–693.

16 Karen Levy, "The Phallus-y Fallacy: On Unsexy Intimate Tracking," *American Journal of Bioethics* 18, no. 2 (2018): 23.
17 Diana Freed, Jackeline Palmer, Diana Minchala, Karen Levy, Thomas Ristenpart, and Nicola Dell, "A Stalker's Paradise: How Intimate Partner Abusers Exploit Technology," *Proceedings of the ACM SIGCHI Conference on Human Factors in Computing Systems* (2018): 1.
18 Levy, "The Phallus-y Fallacy," 23.
19 Levy, "Intimate Surveillance."
20 Guilbeault and Finkelstein, "Human-Bot Ecologies," 156.
21 Freed et al., "Digital Technologies."
22 Danaher et al., "The Quantified Relationship"; Levy, "Intimate Surveillance."
23 Daniel Kappler, Franziska Meier, Jan Issac, Jim Mainprice, Cristina Garcia Cifuentes, Manuel Wüthrich, Vincent Berenz, Stefan Schaal, Nathan Ratliff, and Jeannette Bohg, "Real-Time Perception Meets Reactive Motion Generation," *IEEE Robotics and Automation Letters* 3, no. 3 (July 2018): 1864–1871; Lin Shao, Parth Shah, Vikranth Dwaracherla, and Jeannette Bohg, "Motion-based Object Segmentation Based on Dense RGB-D Scene Flow," *arXiv*, April 14, 2018, https://arxiv.org/pdf/1804.05195.pdf.
24 Felicity Morse, "Five Questions We Should Ask Ourselves before A.I. Answers Them for Us," BBC Newsbeat, September 16, 2015.
25 angel Kyodo williams and Krista Tippet, "The World Is Our Field of Practice," produced by *The On Being Project*, podcast, MP3 audio, 51:44, accessed April 19, 2018, https://onbeing.org/programs/the-world-is-our-field-of-practice-apr2018/.
26 Neff and Nagy, "Agency in the Digital Age," 97.
27 Ed Finn, *What Algorithms Want: Imagination in the Age of Computing* (Cambridge, MA: MIT Press, 2017).
28 Jill Walker Rettberg, "Apps as Companions: How Quantified Self Apps Become Our Audience and Our Companions," in *Self-Tracking: Empirical and Philosophical Investigations*, ed. Btihaj Ajana (Basingstoke, UK: Palgrave, 2018), 27.
29 Guilbeault and Finkelstein, "Human-Bot Ecologies," 155.
30 Ibid., 157.
31 Ibid., 160.
32 Caplan et al., "Algorithmic Accountability"; Virginia Eubanks, *Automating Inequality: How High-Tech Tools Profile, Police and Punish the Poor* (New York: St. Martin's, 2018).
33 Sarah Brayne, "Big Data Surveillance: The Case of Policing," *American Sociological Review* 82, no. 5 (2017): 977–1008; Olivia Solon, "Facial Recognition Database Used by FBI Is Out of Control, House Committee Hears," *The Guardian*, March 27, 2017.
34 Caplan et al., "Algorithmic Accountability," 4.
35 Ibid., 5.
36 Geoffrey Bowker and Leigh Star, *Sorting Things Out: Classification and Its Consequences* (Cambridge, MA: MIT Press, 2000).
37 Jenna Burrell, "How the Machine 'Thinks': Understanding Opacity in Machine Learning Algorithms," SSRN, September 15, 2015, http://dx.doi.org/10.2139/ssrn.2660674.
38 Eubanks, *Automating Inequality*.
39 Aylin Caliskan, Joanna Bryson, and Arvind Narayanan, "Semantics Derived Automatically from Language Corpora Contain Human-like Biases," *Science* 356, no. 6334 (April 14, 2017): 183.

40 Hannah Devlin, "A.I. Programs Exhibit Racial and Gender Biases," *The Guardian*, April 13, 2017.

41 Ibid.

42 Cathy O'Neil, "Databite No. 88: Cathy O'Neil," Data and Society Research Institute, November 2, 2016, https://www.youtube.com/watch?v=d4L_LTkKauI.

43 Daniel Willis, "Why MIT Scientists Are Building a New Search Engine," Big Think, October 10, 2018, 1.

44 Steenson, "Ethics and Governance."

45 Kate Crawford et al., "Formulas for Trouble: Why Smart Companies Must Tread Carefully with Algorithms," Open Mic, April 13, 2018, http://formulasfortrouble .openmic.org/OpenMIC_FormulasForTrouble-201804.pdf.

46 Caplan et al., "Algorithmic Accountability," 2.

47 Timnit Gebru, Jamie Morgenstern, Briana Vecchione, Jennifer Wortman Vaughan, Hannah Wallach, Hal Daume, and Kate Crawford, "Datasheets for Datasets," in *Proceedings of the 5th Workshop on Fairness, Accountability, and Transparency in Machine Learning*, Stockholm, Sweden, 2018, https://arxiv.org/pdf/1803.09010.pdf.

48 Neff and Nagy, "Agency in the Digital Age," 99.

49 Judy Wajcman and Emily Rose, "Constant Connectivity: Rethinking Interruptions at Work," *Organization Studies* 32, no. 7 (2011): 959, emphasis added.

50 Jennifer Nash, "Practicing Love: Black Feminism, Love-Politics, and Post-Intersectionality," *Meridians* 11, no. 2 (2011): 1–24.

51 bell hooks, *All about Love: New Visions* (New York: Harper Collins, 2000); Helen Tworkov, "Agent of Change: An Interview with bell hooks," *Tricycle*, Fall 1992, https://tricycle.org/magazine/agent-change-an-interview-with-bell-hooks/.

52 Joan Halifax, *Standing at the Edge: Finding Freedom Where Fear and Courage Meet* (New York: Flatiron Books, 2018), 229.

53 Annemarie Mol, *The Logic of Care: Health and the Problem of Patient Choice* (New York: Routledge, 2008).

54 Forlano, "Posthuman Futures," 42.

55 Kate Darling, Nandy Palash, and Cynthia Breazeal, "Empathic Concern and the Effect of Stories in Human-Robot Interaction," in *24th IEEE International Symposium on Robot and Human Interactive Communication* (RO-MAN) (New York: IEEE, 2015), 770–775; Kate Darling, "Who's Johnny? Anthropomorphic Framing in Human-Robot Interaction, Integration, and Policy," in *Robot Ethics 2.0: From Autonomous Cars to Artificial Intelligence*, ed. Patrick Lin, Ryan Jenkins, and Keith Abney (New York: Oxford University Press, 2017), 173–192.

56 Halifax, *Standing at the Edge*, 231.

57 Christina Farr, "Google Is Training Computers to Predict When You Might Get Sick," CNBC, May 17, 2017, https://www.cnbc.com/2017/05/17/google-brain -medical-records-prediction-illness.html.

58 Miles Brundage, Shahar Avin, Jack Clark, Helen Toner, Peter Eckersley, Ben Garfinkel, Allan Dafoe, Paul Scharre, Thomas Zeitzoff, Bobby Filar, Hyrum Anderson, Heather Roff, Gregory C. Allen, Jacob Steinhardt, Carrick Flynn, Seán Ó hÉigeartaigh, Simon Beard, Haydn Belfield, Sebastian Farquhar, Clare Lyle, Rebecca Crootof, Owain Evans, Michael Page, Joanna Bryson, Roman Yampolskiy, and Dario Amodei, "Malicious Use of Artificial Intelligence: Forecasting, Prevention and Mitigation," February 2018, https://www.eff.org/files/2018/02/20 /malicious_ai_report_final.pdf; Caplan et al., "Algorithmic Accountability"; Cathy O'Neil, *Weapons of Math Destruction: How Big Data Increases Inequality and Threatens Democracy* (New York: Crown, 2016); Sofiya Nobel, *Algorithms of*

Oppression (New York: New York University Press, 2018); Latanya Sweeney, "Discrimination in Online Ad Delivery: Google Ads, Black Names and White Names, Racial Discrimination, and Click Advertising," *ACM Association for Computing Machinery Queue* 11, no. 3 (March, 2013).

59   James Bridle, *New Dark Age: Technology and the End of the Future* (London: Verso, 2018).

60   Joseph Turow, *The Aisles Have Eyes: How Retailers Track Your Shopping, Strip Your Privacy, and Define Your Power* (New Haven, CT: Yale University Press, 2017); Finn Brunton and Helen Nissenbaum, *Obfuscation: A User's Guide for Privacy and Protest* (Cambridge, MA: MIT Press, 2015).

61   Noble, *Algorithms of Oppression*.

62   Ibid., 168–169.

63   Joan Donovan, "From Social Movements to Social Surveillance: How the Technology of the Occupy Movement Became a Mobile App for Policing," *ACM Association for Computing Machinery* 23, no. 3 (Spring 2017): 27.

64   Ibid.

65   Alice Marwick and Rebecca Lewis, *Media Manipulation and Disinformation Online* (New York: Data and Society Research Institute, 2017), https://datasociety.net /pubs/oh/DataAndSociety_MediaManipulationAndDisinformationOnline.pdf.

66   Steenson, "Ethics and Governance."

67   Jennifer Hall, Randolph Ford, and Ingrid G. Farreras, "Real Conversations with Artificial Intelligence: A Comparison between Human-Human Online Conversations and Human-Chatbot Conversations," *Computers in Human Behavior* 49 (August 2015): 245.

68   hooks, *All about Love*; hooks, "Agent of Change."

69   Donna Haraway, "Situated Knowledges: The Science Question in Feminism and the Privilege of Partial Perspective," *Feminist Studies* 14, no. 3 (1998): 575–599.

70   Joan W. Scott, "The Evidence of Experience," *Critical Inquiry* 17, no. 4 (1991): 773–797.

71   Robyn Caplan and danah boyd, *Who Controls the Public Sphere in an Era of Algorithms?* (New York: Data and Society Research Institute, 2016).

72   Jory Heckman, "DARPA: Next-Generation Artificial Intelligence in the Works," *Federal News Radio* March 1, 2018.

21

The Silencing of
Elizabeth Warren

• •

A Case of Digital Persistence

KATHLEEN RUSHFORTH

Introduction

While delivering a lengthy speech and being silenced in the U.S. Senate during
Jeffrey Sessions's confirmation proceedings for U.S. attorney general on February 7, 2017, Elizabeth Warren inspired and reactivated the words of Coretta Scott
King. A letter that King had written had been incorporated into Warren's arguments and was silenced by way a procedural rule—Rule XIX—while reading
passages of King's letter. The timing of King's words as well as their incorporation into Warren's speech was fitting, especially given the vastly opposing political climate of the time and the country's reactive response to it. Her silencing
fell on the heels of a highly contested 2016 presidential election, a widely publicized and highly attended Women's March, Donald Trump's presidential inau-
guration, and a series of controversial executive orders. This included executive
order 13769 (titled "Protecting the Nation from Foreign Terrorist Entry into the
United States") which, among other things, barred foreign nationals originat-
ing from seven Muslim-majority countries entry into the United States. The executive order, while questioned by the courts, members of Congress, religious
groups, and others, also incited mass protests in cities and at major airports across
the country and in Europe, stunting air travel. The culmination of these events

served as the backdrop for Warren's inclusion of King's letter—written in 1986, when Sessions was seeking a similar position in the state of Alabama—into her speech. The rhetoric stemming from these events may have also subsequently contributed to the country's response to Warren's silencing and her approach to reclaiming her speech—via Facebook Live. Warren's decision to turn to Facebook Live and later Twitter as well as other platforms was pivotal, as digital media has been shown to offer great potential when broadly disseminating social and political ideas (especially feminist ones) to a crowd.

Densely networked platforms such as Facebook and Twitter offer new modes of discourse that connect different constituencies and grounds for discussion through creative modes of protest.[1] Various forms of social protest and dissent were witnessed in the organized actions of networked publics on social media after Warren's silencing. Individual participation and clustering within these highly interconnected, crowd-enabled, and algorithmically constructed networks has been shown to assume several action frames. On one side, participation is self-motivated as "personally expressive content is shared with, recognized by, others who, in turn, repeat these network sharing activities."[2] Social mobilizations that take place within this framework largely show that participants engage with issues on individual terms "by finding common ground in easy-to-personalize action frames"[3] while maintaining "diverse expressions of identity."[4] Warren's silencing took place within the public sphere, where partisanship, shared political ideals, and symbols form the basis of a collective identity and feelings of "we-ness." However, the networked social actions that resulted on Twitter appeared to resemble individuated, personalized expressions, that although similar in messaging and scope, lacked organization and a shared outcome. Even though some would argue that collective feelings of "we-ness" can be both real or imagined,[5] the point of this chapter is not to weigh the various schools of thought on differing action frames and logics. It explores, rather, how individuals socialize, voice, and engage in everyday activism on issues that are of importance to them through social media.

The Event

On February 7, 2017, during a U.S. senatorial debate concerning the nomination of Jefferson Sessions for U.S. attorney general, Senate Majority Leader Mitch McConnell (R-KY) employed Senate Rule XIX (otherwise written as Rule 19) to silence Senator Elizabeth Warren (D-MA), who was presenting a lengthy argument against Sessions's nomination. The point at which McConnell silenced Warren was pivotal. A critical piece of Warren's argument was a letter from 1986 that the late–civil rights leader Coretta Scott King wrote to Senator Strom Thurmond—who then chaired the Judicial Committee—on Sessions's previous nomination for a federal judgeship in the state of Alabama. In her letter, King cites judicial decisions made by Sessions in the 1980s that did not represent or rule in favor of people of color in Alabama—decisions she regarded as racist and exclusionary. By reading King's remarks, Warren sought to illustrate that although "we would like to think this particular period of time is far behind us . . . [this letter] reminds us that it is not."[6] King's letter provided a frame in which to consider present-day practices that appear to exclude specific minority communities living within the United States.

McConnell justified Warren's silencing on the basis that "[the Senator had] impugned the motives and conduct of our colleague from Alabama, as warned by the chair. Senator Warren said, 'Senator Sessions has used the awesome power of his office to chill the free vote by black citizens.' I call the Senator to order under the provisions of Rule XIX."[7] Warren appeared visibly surprised by the ruling and questioned why the words of Coretta Scott King were not suitable material for debate in the Senate. She then requested to take leave of the Senate (i.e., obtain unanimous consent from her colleagues) to continue her remarks but was denied and asked to take her seat. Despite the invocation of Rule XIX, which barred Warren from debating further in the proceedings, Warren persisted and asked the presiding chairman to "suggest an absence of a quorum" and to take a roll-call vote on the ruling.

After a quorum and a roll-call vote, the majority ruled in favor of Rule XIX (49 to 43), thereby silencing Warren for the duration of the proceedings. When McConnell reconvened the Senate, he opened the debate by stating that "Senator Warren was giving a lengthy speech. She appeared to violate the rule. She was warned. She was given an explanation. Nevertheless, she persisted."[8] Following his remarks, some senators questioned the appropriateness of the rule's application (Kamala Harris, D-CA; Chuck Schumer, D-NY; Paul Leahy, D-VT) and expressed disgust that the majority of the Senate would not allow Warren to read King's letter, arguing that it violated free speech (Leahy; Bernie Sanders, D-VT). Other senators asked for an explanation of the original objection to Warren's reading of the letter (James Risch, R-ID), made parliamentary inquiries concerning the exact wording of Rule XIX (Marco Rubio, R-FL), and questioned whether the rule could rightfully be applied in the confirmation proceedings of present senators being sought for other positions in government (Jeffrey Merkley, D-OR).

Concurrently, outside of the Senate at 10:52 p.m. eastern time, Warren took to Facebook Live to read the entirety of King's letter from her office's official public Facebook page—U.S. Senator Elizabeth Warren (@senatorelizabethwarren). This action restored power to not only Warren's voice but also to King's, which Warren had sought to represent. Ultimately, King's letter became part of the proceedings, as Tom Udall (D-NM), Merkley, and Sanders each read portions of the letter without being silenced (by Rule XIX) or called to order.

Advocating for the People: The Role of a U.S. Senator

As a senator and elected official, Elizabeth Warren has the responsibility and unique authority to speak on behalf of her constituents whom she represents in the state of Massachusetts, as well as others she deems herself accountable. Warren is a loyal consumer advocate and an expert on bankruptcy, commercial law, and financial protections. She is interested in issues as they relate to the middle class, a socioeconomic stratum she is familiar with, having grown up in a working-class family in Oklahoma City, Oklahoma. As one of only twenty-three female U.S. senators who served in the 115th Congress, she often represents and defends legislation that serves the interests of marginalized groups, such as women and racial, ethnic, and religious minorities.[9] Given this particular advocacy, one could call Warren a "surrogate representative"[10] in that she represents people with whom she has no electoral connection, specifically those in another state or district who have the potential to lose representation.

Warren read King's letter with the intent of speaking on behalf of those constituents, identifying parallels that could be drawn between the letter and certain policies (e.g., travel ban, deportation force, etc.) then being ordered by the Trump administration. Additionally, Warren cunningly provided King's personal account of civil rights abuses in the South and Sessions's judicial record to draw a comparison between them and the present-day social persecution of individuals in the United States face (owing to their [Muslim] faith, place of origin or birth, race, gender, sexual orientation or gender identity) and Sessions's relevant remarks and policy positions. Her goal in reading the letter was to illustrate that despite the passing of time, similar sentiment, biases, and conduct persist.

Speaking for Others

Further, in her role as a senator, Warren has been elected to represent her constituents and speak on, about, and for their interests. Although social theorists and philosophers alike have addressed the problem associated with speaking for others,[11] little mention has been made of the role that political representatives play in speaking for and about others. Although the reasoning for this might be somewhat obvious, I wanted to briefly outline the theory, as I believe it is relevant to this discussion. Speaking for others typically arises in the context of an individual who speaks on behalf of a group to which he or she does not belong. Historically, this rhetorical device entails privileged persons speaking on behalf of less privileged persons, a scenario that reinforces the degree to which the group spoken for is oppressed. Speaking for the oppressed perpetuates a power dynamic that inhibits opportunities to transcend "social location" or social identity.[12] When one speaks for others, one may be describing situations, values, or beliefs that are specific to those spoken for and with which the individual speaking does not have immediate experience. When an individual "speaks in place of them" and "speaks for them," she represents the others' needs, situation, position, and essentially *who they are*.[13] A similar phenomenon occurs when the individual speaks on behalf of herself, for in the moment that she represents herself, she is created and experiences herself *as herself* and as a public and discursive figure.[14]

According to Alcoff, political representatives have a unique privilege, as they are elected by their constituents to speak for them. However, political representatives are nevertheless interpreting the situation of others and "creating for them a self in the presence of others."[15] In addition, Alcoff notes, "One cannot simply look at the location of the speaker or her credentials to speak . . . [or] the propositional content of her speech; one must also look at where the speech goes and what it does there."[16] The incorporation of King's letter in Sessions's confirmation proceedings helped to provide insight into his earlier record and character. Whether King's letter warranted a place in the proceedings is questionable, however, McConnell's formal silencing of Warren amplified the impact of King's letter.[17]

Silence, Resistance, and Speech

Rule XIX, a seldom-invoked rule that bars specific speech and conduct on the Senate floor was used to silence Warren. The provision mandates that while in debate, no senator shall directly or indirectly "impute to another senator or to other senators any conduct or motive unworthy or unbecoming a senator."[18] Although Rule XIX was established to curtail specific speech, the fact that it was invoked during Warren's statements led many to question the rationale behind its application.

Just or unjust in Warren's case, silence plays an integral part of rhetorical displays. Silence is a natural construct of language and most often serves as an intentional and expected aspect of speech. A brief silence or gap in a conversation may function as a deliberate insertion by the speaker, an invitation to invoke turn taking or the point at which a topic of conversation has been exhausted.[19] However, instances arise in which silence is an unexpected phenomenon, occurring at the behest of another speaker. As with speech, the meaning that is attributed to silence is contingent on the "power differential" that is present in rhetorical situations—in other words, "who can speak, who must remain silent, who listens, and what those listeners can do."[20] And silence, as a function of language, "create[s] and re-create[s] our social realities."[21] Silence serves as an expressive act, and although it can "marginalize and oppress members of society . . . it can also express protection, resistance and defiance . . . [as well as] afford opportunities for emancipation or perpetuate the disappearance of the 'other.'"[22] Thus, silence serves as both a mechanism by which one withholds speech and a powerful opportunity to reclaim speech. In Warren's case, it emboldened her to navigate other forums and spheres in which to speak.

Networked Publics

One of these ways was through two social networking sites (SNS)—namely, Facebook and Twitter. These sites offer a mode of communication that provides widespread dissemination of public opinion across public screens. Participants cluster around social conversations that are of interest to them and engage with other participants in the same "networked public."[23] Networked publics, according to boyd, are a collection of people who have gathered for a similar purpose—social, cultural, or civic—and who are then restructured in unique ways. This restructuring occurs through "expressions of sentiment" on a networked technology in which algorithms and other systematic processes aggregate content.[24]

On Facebook and Twitter, this process begins when a single participant "follows" another and is then exposed to content that the latter authors or has engaged with, allowing for a unique relationship.[25] In turn, networked publics are introduced to distinct affordances that shape how they engage with other publics as well as the environment in which they interact.[26] The interconnectedness between social actors,[27] a participant's previous social activity, as well as the recency, popularity, and media richness (i.e., text, hashtags, links, images, or video) of post content play a critical role with respect to engagement.[28] For this reason, social actions that publics take inside the technology have the potential to be persistent and alter in reach, dissemination, and traverse media.

Those initially responding to Warren's silencing were members of the Senate, public officials as well as the media. Thus, the influencers and the "crowdsourced elites"[29] in this case were likely those who were positioned close to Warren and to whom she had access. For instance, Warren's aides devised a hashtag, #LetLizSpeak, to generate support for the senator, disseminating it later to other senators, who began using it in social media posts.[30]

Facebook's live-streaming video solution—Facebook Live—initially allowed Warren to disseminate her message and engage with her constituents and other networked publics. It provided her with a platform to speak from, self-present, and participate in the public sphere after being silenced by her constituents in the technical sphere—one that she had formally been elected to speak in. By virtue of this unique opportunity, Warren was able to speak on her terms and in a much more compelling, performative, and persistent way. Considering this, I sought to address and answer two primary questions through my research:

1 How does social media circumvent the norms of who should speak?
2 In what ways does social media alter the dissemination and reception of political speech?

The Case of Elizabeth Warren's Silencing: Digital Artifacts/Discourse

As the events leading up to Elizabeth Warren's silencing occurred in the public sphere, several media outlets captured the entire exchange between Warren and other members of the Senate. In addition to Warren, the participants in her speech were her fellow senators, specifically those who (1) interacted with Warren at the point at which Rule XIX was invoked, (2) offered remarks concerning Rule XIX or the content of Warren's speech, (3) queried the Senate for an explanation of the rule after it was applied, and/or (4) read parts of King's letter after Warren's silencing (perhaps in resistance to the rule).

I examined the following digital artifacts: video clips of Jeff Sessions's confirmation proceedings (provided by C-SPAN), a speech that Edward Kennedy (D-MA) delivered during Sessions's nomination proceedings for a federal judgeship in 1986, a digital scan of the letter that Coretta Scott King penned in 1986, and Warren's Facebook Live video. I also reviewed articles and interviews that were conducted by major media outlets in the days following the event to contextualize the primary documents, and I also collected social data and reviewed social sentiment to understand how public displays of activism evolved and traversed over time and across media. Since only specific media publishers can access Facebook's Public Feed API, obtaining an aggregate of historical data centered on a specific topic or hashtag was not possible.[31] For this reason, my analysis focused primarily on Twitter data, which I collected through FollowtheHashtag, an online tool used to capture public timelines, tweets, geolocation information and rich media, as well as a host of other insightful back-end information.

Twitter Data Collection and Approach to Analysis

I conducted qualitative textual analysis in several ways to verify and expand on quantitative findings.[32] First, I reviewed original and retweeted content that contained the hashtag #LetLizSpeak—and did the same to a lesser extent with #ShePersisted—to determine (a) the polarity of the post (meaning positive or negative sentiment), (b) what specific audience the tweet might be directed toward, (c) whether the same respondent tweeted content within a specified period of time, and (d) whether that post was retweeted (and how many times). I also attempted to determine whether respondents were a part of the same networked public, the degree of influence a tweet might exercise in relation to the number of times it was retweeted, as well as the tweet's potential reach relative to participant exposure. The objective was to determine whether a discernible pattern existed in the relevant language, discourse, or value assumptions used that informed the evolution of the hashtag and its persistence on the platform and apart from it.[33]

Elizabeth Warren's Silencing in Context

Warren's silencing can be contextualized through the rhetorical frames of the political climate that existed under the Trump administration in early 2017. On the one hand, the executive orders and policies issued by Trump were construed as measures that protected the American people from potential terrorist-related activities.[34] On the other hand, they were viewed as un-American, discriminatory, illegal, and potentially damaging to the United States' reputation internationally.[35] Warren represented the latter frame and Sessions the former. These opposing frames emerged in relation to the Trump administration's divisive rhetoric and arguably unconstitutional executive orders aimed at barring persons of a specific faith or place of origin or birth. Within her arguments, Warren juxtaposed these frames using Coretta Scott King's 1986 letter and Edward Kennedy's 1986 speech. Since Warren received a warning during her reading of King's letter and was subsequently silenced, King's words figured prominently in my analysis.

Warren began her speech by arguing that Americans in the United States require an attorney general "who can be relied on to enforce the laws fairly and to fight back against the lawless overreach by an out-of-control president."[36] She additionally enumerated the types of policies and political efforts Jeff Sessions supported over the course of his career—ones that limited the civil liberties of specific groups residing in or emigrating to the United States.

Warren then delves slightly deeper into Sessions's character and his views on immigration, race relations, women's rights, and marriage equality. She urges Senate Republicans to stand up and deny Sessions's nomination as they had done thirty years ago (in 1986) when he was seeking a position as a federal judge. Warren read two statements that provided a historical account of Sessions's record on civil rights. Both statements refer to the Perry County voter fraud prosecutions, a legal case that sentenced several notable Black civil rights activists for assisting elderly Black citizens to vote via absentee ballot. Sessions served as the prosecutor on the case. Although the defendants were later acquitted, the episode had a significant impact on people of color.[37] Kennedy described the events as they occurred and cited instances in which Sessions's speech appeared to be racist and derogatory in nature, particularly toward the American Civil Liberties Union and NAACP which were formed to protect the rights of minorities. Beyond providing historical evidence that illustrates Sessions's character, Kennedy harshly critiqued Sessions for his position: "Mr. Sessions is a throwback to a shameful era which I know both black and white Americans thought was in our past. It is inconceivable to me that a person of this attitude is qualified to be a U.S. Attorney, let alone a U.S. federal judge. He is, I believe, a disgrace to the Justice Department and he should withdraw his nomination and resign his position."[38] Although these are statements made by Kennedy, it is the language used in this passage for which Warren is reprimanded and receives an initial warning while reading King's letter. Before delving into the warning and the exchange between Warren and the presiding chairman over Kennedy's remarks, I will summarize King's letter to the point at which Warren is interrupted.

Coretta Scott King's Letter to the Senate Judiciary Committee (1986)

Following her recitation of Kennedy's speech, Warren relays the words from a letter the activist Coretta Scott King had penned to the Senate Judiciary Committee when Sessions was a seeking a federal judgeship in 1986. King's letter, like Kennedy's speech, addresses the Voting Rights Act and the role that Sessions played in the Perry County voter fraud prosecutions. However, King's letter serves as a personal account of the events that transpired in the lead-up to the trial and during it. She begins the letter by praising her husband, Martin Luther King Jr., on his tireless efforts as well as those of Albert Turner. Together, they sought to protect and enhance the rights of people of color, who as of the mid-1980s still did not have equal access to the democratic process, including the right to vote.[39] Despite legislative efforts and activism, King writes, "Mr. Sessions has used the awesome power of his office to chill the free exercise of the vote by black citizens in the district he now seeks to serve as a federal judge.... Mr. Sessions'[s] conduct as a U.S. Attorney, from his politically motivated voting fraud prosecutions to his indifference toward criminal violations of civil rights laws, indicates that he lacks the temperament, fairness, and judgment to be a federal judge."[40] She discusses the benefits of the Voting Rights Act of 1965 and the ways in which white people continued to deny people of color access to the ballot box even into the 1980s, particularly in areas where Black and Brown bodies formed the majority of voters. King states, "It has been a long up-hill struggle to keep alive the vital legislation that protects the most fundamental right to vote."[41] Warren was several pages into King's letter when the presiding chairman gaveled and interrupted her.[42]

First Exchange between Warren and Presiding Chair

An exchange between Warren and the Senate's presiding chairman, Senator Steve Daines (R-MT), regarding her violation of Senate Rule XIX followed. She is reprimanded for remarks she quoted earlier from Kennedy's speech. The remarks included the following statement: "[Jeff Sessions] is, I believe, a disgrace to the Justice Department."[43] When Warren asked for an explanation of the rule and to what types of speech it might be applied, the presiding chairman responded, "The rule applies to impugning conduct or motive through any form of voice or words, includ[ing] quotes, articles, or other materials."[44] Warren, perplexed, asks, "So, is it the contention of the chair that under the rules of the Senate, I am not allowed to accurately describe public views of Senator Sessions, public positions of Senator Sessions, quote public statements of Senator Sessions?"[45] to which the presiding chair replied, "The chair has not made a ruling [with] respect to the senator's comments. The senator is following process and tradition by reminding the senator of Massachusetts of the rule."[46] Although still unclear, Warren is permitted to continue reading King's letter.

Warren resumed reading King's letter, which highlighted activists' efforts to increase voter participation among those most disenfranchised within minority communities. In the letter, King also further criticized Sessions's handling of the Perry County voter fraud prosecutions and his apparent attempts to sabotage the testimonies of witnesses speaking on behalf of the prosecuted. Warren completed the reading of King's letter before offering her own remarks on the parallels between Kennedy's speech, King's letter, and Sessions's present-day views. Warren was again interrupted while offering these remarks, this time by Senate Majority Leader Mitch McConnell.

McConnell addressed the presiding chairman, stating that Warren had "impugned the motives and conduct of our colleague from Alabama, as warned by the chair. Senator Warren said that 'Senator Sessions has used the awesome power of his office to chill the free exercise of the vote by black citizens.'"[47] McConnell then called Warren to order under the provisions of Rule XIX. Warren once again confused by the ruling, fails to comprehend how the words of Coretta Scott King are not suitable material for debate in the Senate. She then requested to take leave of the Senate to continue her remarks. McConnell subsequently objected to Warren's request, and Warren was asked to take her seat. Warren appeared to protest further and suggested an absence of a quorum.

Response by Other Senators

After a quorum and a roll-call vote, the majority ruled in favor of Rule XIX (49 to 43), thereby silencing Warren for the duration of the nomination proceedings. Substantial discussion about the nuances of Rule XIX and under what circumstances the rule can be applied followed. Additionally, other members of the Senate began referencing the letter within their remarks. At 11:13 p.m. eastern time, Senator Jeff Merkley was yielded time to discuss King's letter and to provide additional context on its intent. In the interest of maintaining decorum, Merkley read portions of the letter rather than the entire document, focusing on excerpts that referenced the work of King's husband and those pertaining to the Perry Count voter fraud prosecutions.

On the following morning, February 8, 2017, at 9:00 a.m. eastern time, Senator Tom Udall offered to read parts of King's letter. Udall framed the excerpts against the principally Native American populations he represented in New Mexico, having fought their own battles to obtain voting rights and equal access to the democratic process. Unlike Merkley, Udall included the sentiment for which Warren was silenced, though he identified who the speaker was (King) and when the words were written.

Facebook and Twitter Response

At 10:52 p.m. eastern time, shortly after being silenced in the Senate, Warren took to Facebook Live to read the entirety of Coretta Scott King's letter, uninterrupted. Warren's social actions generated an almost instantaneous response. Facebook users expressed their support of the stand she took in speaking. By midnight, Warren's video had received more than 1.7 million views, 175,000 likes, and 50,000 shares.[48]

Warren generated an extraordinary response on Facebook and a surge of activity on Twitter, with many showing their support of Warren via the hashtags #LetLizSpeak and #ShePersisted. The hashtags along with a host of other keywords represented the events leading up to Warren's silencing in the Senate. Matt House, communications director for Senator Chuck Schumer, was the first to tweet #LetLizSpeak. At 8:16 p.m. eastern time, House, who goes by the Twitter handle @mattwhouse, wrote, "Republicans are trying to keep Sen. Warren from reading a letter from MLK's widow on Sen. Sessions. RT if you think they should #LetLizSpeak."[49] Along with this text, there is an image of Warren embedded within the tweet that shows her (dressed in purple) standing amid older white gentlemen (in gray scale) who are seated around her. It presents a powerful juxtaposition to the scenario that Warren found herself in earlier in the evening. The time stamp of the tweet is noteworthy, as is House's positioning relative to Warren. House tweeted before the official silencing, precisely during the time of the roll-call vote. According to the *Boston Globe*, Warren's aides created the hashtag #LetLizSpeak.[50] It was then circulated to other senators to cultivate an expression of solidarity. House's initial tweet, in part, confirmed this. Original tweets that followed were from U.S. constituents and those close to government—including other senators, press secretaries, and active/retired military personnel. Many of these tweets cited House's initial post and included a single hashtag, #LetLizSpeak. In addition to the hashtag, many tweets contained mentions of specific senators, including Marco Rubio (@marcorubio), Mitch McConnell (@SenateMajLdr), Elizabeth Warren (@SenWarren and @elizabethforma), Chuck Schumer (@SenSchumer), and Mazie Hirono (D-HI; @maziehirono), as well as a host of other public political figures.

The Power of Retweets: Magnifying the Scope of Warren's and King's Messages

The inclusion of these political figures and/or organizations within tweets rendered those tweets more expansive in their reach. In turn, many more users engaged with the tweet by retweeting, liking, or commenting on it. With respect to #LetLizSpeak and #ShePersisted, the extent of the retweeting is notable. For example, when Senator Hirono tweeted at 8:27 p.m. eastern time, a rapid increase in retweet activity followed. The same occurred when Senator Schumer wrote at 8:41 p.m., "This letter caused the GOP to silence @SenWarren tonight. RT if you think they should #LetLizSpeak."[51] Schumer's tweet included an embedded tweet from Warren that cited an article published by the *Washington Post* on January 10, 2017, on the existence of Coretta Scott King's letter.[52] By 9:00 p.m. eastern time, Hirono's original tweet had been retweeted 521 times, and Schumer's had been retweeted 1,343 times. Original posts using the hashtag #LetLizSpeak accounted for only 12 percent of all tweets (between 8:16 p.m. and 9:00 p.m. eastern time).

Although the percentage of tweets relative to the percentage of retweets increased over the hours (and days) that followed (see table 21.1), retweets played an integral role in driving awareness of Warren's silencing and the content of King's letter. The hashtag #LetLizSpeak hit a peak on February 8 and then

Table 21.1
Original content to retweets from February 7 to February 13, 2017
for the hashtag #LetLizSpeak.

Date/Time ET	Original Content	Retweets	Total Tweets	% Original Content
	Original Content versus Retweets Based on Date and Time for #LetLizSpeak			
7-Feb	16,904	66,983	83,887	25%
8 PM	331	2,700	3,031	12%
9 PM	3,457	16,217	19,674	21%
10 PM	6,062	23,020	29,082	26%
11 PM	7,054	25,046	32,100	28%
8-Feb*	51,221	198,041	249,138	26%
9-Feb	3,064	16,305	19,369	19%
10-Feb	687	1992	2679	34%
11-Feb	349	1498	1847	23%
12-Feb	295	977	1272	30%
13-Feb	130	425	555	31%
Total for Period	**72,650**	**286,221**	**358,747**	**25%**

*Data for this day are incomplete (missing data between 7:00 p.m. and 7:24 p.m. eastern time).

Table 21.2
Original content to retweets from February 7 to February 13, 2017
for the hashtag #ShePersisted.

Date/Time ET	Original Content	Retweets	Total Tweets	% Original Content
	Original Content to Retweets Based on Date and Time for #ShePersisted			
7-Feb	145	253	398	57%
9 PM	5		5	100%
10 PM	54	122	176	44%
11 PM	86	131	217	66%
8-Feb*	29,730	156,665	186,395	17%
9-Feb	14,906	69,526	84,432	21%
10-Feb	5,464	18,606	24,070	29%
11-Feb	3,342	8,507	11,849	39%
12-Feb	1,999	5,896	7,895	34%
13-Feb	1,338	3,557	4,895	38%
Total for Period	**56,924**	**263,010**	**319,934**	22%

*Data for this day are incomplete (missing data from 7:00 p.m. to 7:24 p.m. eastern time).

experienced a steady decline during the evening of February 9. Around this time, incidentally, another hashtag started to gain momentum, #ShePersisted (see table 21.2). The latter hashtag derived from the remarks McConnell made after Warren's silencing: "Senator Warren was giving a lengthy speech. She appeared to violate the rule. She was warned. She was given an explanation. Nevertheless, she persisted."[53]

Awareness of Warren's silencing and the existence of King's letter inspired many to use the hashtag #LetLizSpeak and others (such as #LetCorettaSpeak, #ShePersisted, #readtheletter, #LetterToMitch, etc.) that spoke to an aspect of the original event as well as Warren's motivations for incorporating the letter into her speech. When the events leading up to her silencing were shared across social media, it became unclear who exactly had been speaking or silenced. The images embedded within tweets containing the hashtag #ShePersisted pointedly captured this phenomenon.

The Case for Public Persona and Dissemination

Warren's public persona as well as her position in government may have contributed to the re-presentation and retelling of events. Publicly, Warren has repeatedly challenged the status quo and is equally vocal on the SNS on which she maintains accounts. On Facebook, the official page she maintains as a senator had a following of 3.4 million (@senatorelizabethwarren), and her followers on Twitter numbered an equally impressive 4.3 million (@SenWarren). However, given the circumstances and content of Warren's speech, the persona of Coretta Scott King and that of her husband, Martin Luther King Jr., may have been more influential in disseminating Warren's silencing and the overall response. As Warren's silencing occurred during Black History Month, many users on Twitter expressed outrage—in silencing Warren, King was also silenced.

Public Speech and Public Screens

Even though she delivered her speech within the Senate, the narrative surrounding Warren's silencing had an expansive reach owing to public screens (media). Her speech was broadcast via C-SPAN. However, other media outlets may have also broadcast Sessions's confirmation proceedings for U.S. attorney general.

At 9:49 p.m. eastern time, shortly after being silenced, Warren appeared on *The Rachel Maddow Show* via phone. During the conversation, Warren spoke of being "red carded" and "out of the game" as long as the topic on the floor was Senator Jeff Sessions. Although Warren was not expecting such an outcome, she urges viewers to read King's letter because, as she says, "it reminds us of a time in history that we would like to think is behind us but . . . is not."[54]

Whether inspired by Warren's urging or other social forces, individuals took to Twitter to read the letter aloud via video. Actress Debra Messing (@debramessing) filmed herself and other notable figures (such as Gloria Steinem, Patricia Arquette, Sherrilyn Ifill, Luvvie Ajayi, Ella Bell, Kathy Najimy, and Cynthia Erivo) taking turns reading King's letter aloud. Messing included the hashtag #LetLizSpeak in the tweets that contain the videos of Gloria Steinem and Patricia Arquette (posted at 1:40 a.m. and 1:41 a.m. eastern time, respectively, on February 7, 2017). She marks the other six tweets with hashtags other than those being used to represent the reading (namely, #CorettaKingSpeaks and #LetLizTalk). In a tweet that follows the readings, she includes a screen capture

of a portion of King's letter and asks followers to video themselves reading it—
and many do.

Discourse Analysis

To understand key themes present within the Twitter discourse, I filtered for
original content where the hashtag #LetLizSpeak appeared. I then randomized
the data using Microsoft Excel. I also later removed instances where the tweet
contained fewer than three words and removed instances where the hashtag alone
appeared. Due to the political nature of the content, I also manually removed
tweets that were overly partisan. After reviewing the data segment, I identified
discursive trends in the content and categorized based on the sentiment and emotion expressed.

#LetLizSpeak: General Topoi and Secondary Topoi

Semantically speaking, the hashtag #LetLizSpeak conveyed support of Warren
over the application of Rule XIX, or those applying the rule. Although many
tweets included a single hashtag, other tweets contained text that was descrip-
tive and often partisan in nature. Some, such as this one, suggest that Warren's
silencing may not be just about partisan politics: "I'm glad the Senate is upholding rules on decorum. Just wish we could hold the president to the same standards. #LetLizSpeak." Although the user seemingly agreed with Warren's
silencing, they also believe members of the other branches of government should
be held to the same standard. This tweet and others like it are the exception, as
many tweets uphold a specific point of view.

What the sentiment of this tweet shares with others is a topical argument or
topos.[55] In the case of #LetLizSpeak, one topos is truth. Many tweets refer to
this ideal outright, such as the following: "We are all witness @SenateMajLdr.
You can handle neither truth nor reasonable discourse. We the people demand
to be heard LetLizSpeak." Other tweets refer to truth more subtly or enveloped
their sentiment on the principles of democracy.

Across tweets, an obvious topos was that Twitter—and perhaps SNS as a
whole—serves as a safe space to resist and dissent. This topos applies to those
who agreed with Warren's stance, those who sided with McConnell et al., and
those who were more neutral or broadly spoke about truth, civil liberties, or the
senatorial process. The opinions and sentiments expressed were highly charged,
with many expressing anger or hostility toward the opposing view. Others were
simply inspired and encouraged speech, such as this one from Representative
Barbara Lee (D-CA): "In America, we don't silence women who persist, we celebrate them. #ShePersisted #BlackHistoryMonth."[56] Within her tweet, Lee
includes an image that depicts five women of color known for shaping the civil
rights movement.

Although other topoi may exist within the data, these two were the most prominent. I also identified several possible secondary topoi under which content can be classified (see table 21.3). These concerned (1) Warren's right to speak in the Senate to uphold the truths established by the First Amendment to the Constitution, (2) her right as a senator to represent her constituents, (3) her right to represent and speak on behalf of others, (4) the Senate's right to maintain decorum by following procedure, and (5) the public's right to free expression regardless of tenor.

The diversity of sentiment expressed establishes that Twitter and SNS in general afford networked publics a unique opportunity to engage in public speech and to express views that are opposed to the majority opinion. Although the initial event may have incited many to react and connect on the topic, they appeared to come from a place of "I" not "we" as momentum on the hashtag's use and discourse on Warren's/King's silencing tapered.

Discussion

#LetLizSpeak reached peak usage on the evening of February 8, 2017, after which its appearance steadily declined. One possible reason for this decline is the way in which the conversation around Warren's silencing evolved. Over time (hours and days), the conversation became not so much about Warren as about the reason for the silencing—King's letter. So the shift in focus impacted the hashtag. Other hashtags were used to identify activities that were in direct correlation to this shift (online and offline). Examples of this include King's letter being read on Twitter via video (#readtheletter) and through organized readings outside of one of Mitch McConnell's two residences (#LetterToMitch) by bullhorn. Additionally, #ShePersisted became a byword that represented the stand that all women take when challenged by adversity.

Furthermore, in presenting her message (and King's letter) via SNS, Warren circumvented the formal norms that guide political communication. In making her silencing known via Facebook Live and then Twitter, Warren was able to speak and indirectly mobilize a movement that motivated other senators, her constituents, and Americans at large to read the letter. It also enabled those opposed to Warren's dissent to speak. #LetLizSpeak represents an instance in which social media and hashtag activism enabled the public, which included women and minority groups (the Other/"subaltern counterpublics"),[57] to speak.

The hashtag #LetLizSpeak was trending consistently until the evening of February 8, 2017 and then overtaken by #ShePersisted. In addition to the lack of consistency in the hashtag used to represent the event, there also was not a single individual or entity driving the trajectory of the conversation. Further, other political controversies appeared to overtake Warren's silencing. The event

Table 21.3

Examples of tweets from February 7 to February 13, 2017 that fall into one of many identified categories and that include the hashtag #LetLizSpeak

	Examples of Content Encountered in the Given Secondary Topoi
Secondary Topoi	**Actual Content**
Voice of the People	I'm sorry . . . in what world is reading a truthful letter by Coretta Scott King considered "impugning another senator" #LetLizSpeak
	Senator Warren - thank you for doing your job. #letlizspeak
	#letlizspeak but remember her words belong to #CorettaKing - we don't appropriate - we amplify those brave WoC speaking truth to power.
	@SenWarren thank you for setting an example for me, my daughters and women around the world w/your fierce, fighting spirit. #letlizspeak
She Speaks for Us	Thank you, @SenWarren for always trying to be the voice of The People. We appreciate you. #LetLizSpeak, she speaks for ME. #ElizabethWarren
	We can and we shall. #NeverthelessShePersisted #LetLizSpeak #Resist https://t.co/Kca1Zj6ffF
	As a United States and #Massachusetts citizen I demand that @SenateMajLdr stop CENSORING my voice in the Senate @SenWarren! #LetLizSpeak
	We Will Not Be Silenced #LetLizSpeak https://t.co/XL3VKWb59A
	DON'T SILENCE MY SENATOR, AND DON'T CENSOR THE WORDS OF MS. KING. #LETLIZSPEAK https://t.co/eMRTCE4Mtl (user's emphasis)
Matters of Inequality (Sexist/Racist)	Pocahontas should keep mouth shut, on second thought keep talking! #LetLizSpeak #Trump https://t.co/gWC91bhXyj
	@ezlusztig Not automatically. Sen. Merkley picked up the letter and read it afterwards. UNINTERRUPTED. #letlizspeak
	It is time to get women into the White House, when another white old chinless man tells her to shut up and sit down #LetLizSpeak
	Literal chills that a female politician can be repeatedly cut off, ruled to be quiet, and told "The senator will take her seat."#LetLizSpeak
Matter of Procedure	#LetLizSpeak How can it violate senate rules when the letter she was reading is part of the congressional record? McConnell is disgusting.
	I'm glad the Senate is upholding rules on decorum. Just wish we could hold the president to the same standards. #LetLizSpeak
	Everyone please spare me with the #letlizspeak..she can read the letter wherever..just not senate floor #learntherules #liberals

#NoBanNoWallNoRaids
#LetCorettaSpeak
#womensmarch #DworkinReport
#TrumpsAmeriKKKa   #WeThePeople
#CongressDoYourJob #NoDAPL

#JoyVilla #theresistance #sessions
#NotMyPresident   #TNTweeters   #IMPEACH
#LetterToMitch #SNL #KatyPerry #persist
#GoldStar #ShePersists   #Trump

#ShePersisted

#StandingUnited   #GOP #FireFlynn
#tagamericablue #NoBanNoWall   #firethefool
#Disrupt #BlackHistoryMonth #Women   #Truth
#SallyYates   #NeverthelessShePersisted #resist
#uniteblue #TREASON
#CorettaScottKing #TheFutueisFemale   #MuslimBan
#GRAMMYs   #elizabethwarren
#LetLizSpeak #indivisible #Democracy
#stoppresidentbannon
#TrumpLeaks #impreachTrump
#StandUptoSexism
#RESISTANCE

FIG. 21.1 A word cloud created using WordItOut by Kathleen Rushforth that illustrates the hashtags used on February 13, 2017 on Twitter, from data collected for #LetLizSpeak and #ShePersisted.

essentially experienced attention fatigue, as "the sharpest limit to the utility of social media as a tool for advocacy may be simple limits to human attention."[58] To represent this phenomenon, the word cloud (see figure 21.1) visually represents hashtags that were trending relative to #LetLizSpeak and #ShePersisted on February 13, 2017. Although #ShePersisted far outweighed in use, tags related to other political controversies and events came to the fore.

Discussion Questions

1 What were the motivating factors that contributed to the application of Senate Rule XIX against Elizabeth Warren's speech and do you think the rule was justly applied? Explain.
2 Do you think Coretta Scott King's letter belonged within the body of Warren's speech? Explain.

3 After Warren was silenced in the Senate, why was Facebook Live so effective at amplifying the content of her speech (including King's words) and her position? Explain.

4 How have social media platforms such as Facebook and Twitter altered how people and groups organize? How have these platforms altered the motivations for why people organize? Describe how this compares to the way that groups organize through grassroots movements?

Try This!

Examine the ways that minority groups utilize social media platforms and forms of digital surveillance to vocalize or reclaim speech. Analyze the social sentiment surrounding a specific hashtag that resulted from an event or rhetorical frame and identify some common themes and topical arguments, and note any outliers. Note who is speaking, their level of influence, and how the sentiment evolves. Create a data visualization or word cloud that represents the sentiment analysis.

Notes

1 Hester Baer, "Redoing Feminism: Digital Activism, Body Politics, and Neoliberalism," *Feminist Media Studies* 16, no. 1 (2016): 17–34.

2 W. Lance Bennett and Alexandra Segerberg, "The Logic of Connective Action," *Information, Communication & Society* 15, no. 5 (2012): 739–768.

3 W. Lance Bennett, Alexandra Segerberg, and Shawn Walker, "Organization in the Crowd: Peer Production in Large-Scale Networked Protests," *Information, Communication & Society* 17, no. 2 (2014): 232–260.

4 Sander van Haperen, Walter Nicholls, and Justus Uitermark, "Building Protest Online: Engagement with the Digitally Networked #notimore Protest Campaign on Twitter," *Social Movement Studies* 17, no. 4 (July 4, 2018): 408–423.

5 Stefania Milan, "From Social Movements to Cloud Protesting: The Evolution of Collective Identity," *Information, Communication & Society* 18, no. 8 (2015): 887–900.

6 Rachel Maddow, "McConnell Silences Warren on Sessions with Obscure Senate Rule," MSNBC.Com, February 7, 2017, https://www.msnbc.com/rachel-maddow/watch/mcconnell-silences-warren-on-sessions-with-obscure-senate-rule-872244803614.

7 C-SPAN, "Senate Confirms Jeff Sessions Takes Tom Price Nomination—Senate Session, Part 2," § United States Senate (2017), https://www.c-span.org/video/?423606-103/us-senate-confirms-jeff-sessions-takes-tom-price-nomination.

8 Ibid.

9 Senator Elizabeth Warren, "Senator Elizabeth Warren: I Stand with Planned Parenthood," YouTube, August 3, 2015, https://www.youtube.com/watch?v=DeilHs9kZ2g.

10 Sara Angevine, "Representing All Women: An Analysis of Congress, Foreign Policy, and the Boundaries of Women's Surrogate Representation," *Political Research Quarterly* 70, no. 1 (March 2017): 98–110.

11   Michel Foucault and Gilles Deleuze, "Intellectuals and Power," in *Language, Counter-Memory, Practice: Selected Essays and Interviews*, ed. Donald F. Bouchard (Ithaca, NY: Cornell University Press, 1980), 205–217; Gayatri Chakravorty Spivak, "Can the Subaltern Speak?," in *Marxism and the Interpretation of Culture*, ed. Cary Nelson and Lawrence Grossberg (Urbana: University of Illinois Press, 1988), 271–313; Linda Alcoff, "The Problem of Speaking for Others," *Cultural Critique* 20 (1991): 5–32, https://doi.org/10.2307/1354221.

12   Alcoff, "The Problem of Speaking for Others," 7.

13   Ibid., 9.

14   Alcoff, "The Problem of Speaking for Others."

15   Ibid., 10.

16   Ibid., 26.

17   Matt Flegenheimer, "Shutting Down Speech by Elizabeth Warren, G.O.P. Amplifies Her Message," *New York Times*, February 8, 2017, https://www.nytimes.com/2017/02/08/us/politics/elizabeth-warren-coretta-scott-king.html.

18   The Official U.S. Senate Committee on Rules & Administration, "Rules of the Senate | U.S. Senate Committee on Rules & Administration," accessed November 8, 2018, https://www.rules.senate.gov/rules-of-the-senate.

19   Cheryl Glenn, *Unspoken: A Rhetoric of Silence* (Carbondale: Southern Illinois University Press, 2004), 6.

20   Ibid., 9.

21   Robin Patric Clair, *Organizing Silence: A World of Possibilities* (Albany: State University of New York Press, 1998), 20.

22   Ibid., 20.

23   danah boyd, "Social Network Sites as Networked Publics: Affordances, Dynamics, and Implications," in *Networked Self: Identity, Community, and Culture on Social Network Sites*, ed. Zizi Papacharissi (New York: Routledge, 2010), 39–58.

24   Zizi Papacharissi, "Affective Publics and Structures of Storytelling: Sentiment, Events and Mediality," *Information, Communication & Society* 19, no. 3 (2016): 307–324, https://doi.org/10.1080/1369118X.2015.1109697.

25   Itai Himelboim, Stephen McCreery, and Marc Smith, "Birds of a Feather Tweet Together: Integrating Network and Content Analyses to Examine Cross-Ideology Exposure on Twitter," *Journal of Computer-Mediated Communication* 18, no. 2 (January 1, 2013): 40–60.

26   boyd, "Social Network Sites as Networked Publics."

27   Itai Himelboim, Marc A. Smith, Lee Rainie, Ben Shneiderman, and Camila Espina, "Classifying Twitter Topic-Networks Using Social Network Analysis," *Social Media + Society* 3, no. 1 (January 1, 2017): 2056305117691545, https://doi.org/10.1177/2056305117691545.

28   Melanie Schreiner, Thomas Fischer, and Rene Riedl, "Impact of Content Characteristics and Emotion on Behavioral Engagement in Social Media: Literature Review and Research Agenda," *Electronic Commerce Research* 21 (2021): 329–345, https://doi.org/10.1007/s10660-019-09353-8.

29   Zizi Papacharissi, "Affective Publics and Social Media: An Interview with Zizi Papacharissi (Part Three)," interview by Henry Jenkins, January 23, 2015, http://henryjenkins.org/blog/2015/01/affective-publics-and-social-media-an-interview-with-zizi-papacharissi-part-three.html.

30   Victoria McGrane, "Republicans on Defensive after Silencing Warren in Senate Debate," *Boston Globe*, February 8, 2017, https://www.bostonglobe.com/news

/politics/2017/02/08/republicans-defensive-after-silencing-warren-senate-debate/lVIxQugx4pZZvFiaMSGMXM/story.html.

31 Facebook, "Public Feed API - Graph API - Documentation," Facebook for Developers, accessed November 8, 2018, https://developers.facebook.com/docs/public_feed.

32 Zizi Papacharissi and Maria de Fatima Oliveira, "Affective News and Networked Publics: The Rhythms of News Storytelling on #Egypt," *Journal of Communication* 62, no. 2 (April 1, 2012): 266–282, https://doi.org/10.1111/j.1460-2466.2012.01630.x.

33 Sarah J. Jackson and Brooke Foucault Welles, "Hijacking #myNYPD: Social Media Dissent and Networked Counterpublics," *Journal of Communication* 65, no. 6 (December 1, 2015): 932–952, https://doi.org/10.1111/jcom.12185.

34 "Jeff Sessions: Travel Ban Protects Americans," CNN, March 6, 2017, https://www.cnn.com/videos/politics/2017/03/06/jeff-sessions-us-travel-ban-sot.cnn.

35 Daniella Diaz, "Democrats Protest Trump's Travel Ban outside Supreme Court," CNN, January 30, 2017, https://www.cnn.com/2017/01/30/politics/democrats-travel-ban-protest-nancy-pelosi-chuck-schumer/index.html.

36 C-SPAN, "Senate Confirms Jeff Sessions Takes Tom Price Nomination—Senate Session, Part 2."

37 Christina Prignano, "Read the Statement from Ted Kennedy That Prompted the Initial Warning to Elizabeth Warren," *Boston Globe*, February 8, 2017, https://www.bostonglobe.com/news/politics/2017/02/08/read-statement-from-ted-kennedy-that-prompted-inital-warning-elizabeth-warren/NROox9EsCVzo4kIUsGbQ5K/story.html.

38 C-SPAN, "Senate Confirms Jeff Sessions Takes Tom Price Nomination—Senate Session, Part 2," sec. 4:45; Committee on the Judiciary, "Nomination of Jefferson B. Session III, To Be U.S. District Judge for the Southern District of Alabama," § Senate Committee on the Judiciary of the United States (1986), 9, https://www.scribd.com/document/15090183/Sessions-Hearing-Transcripts; "Jeff Sessions' 1986 Confirmation Hearing | Flashback | NBC News," YouTube, accessed January 4, 2020, https://www.youtube.com/watch?v=tuxBiTwHNhU.

39 Coretta Scott King, "Statement of Coretta Scott King on the Nomination of Jefferson Beauregard Sessions, III for the United States District Court Southern District of Alabama," March 13, 1986, https://www.documentcloud.org/documents/3259988-Scott-King-1986-Letter-and-Testimony-Signed.html.

40 Ibid., 3.

41 Ibid., 4; C-SPAN, "Senate Confirms Jeff Sessions Takes Tom Price Nomination—Senate Session, Part 2," sec. 4:53.

42 C-SPAN, "Senate Confirms Jeff Sessions Takes Tom Price Nomination—Senate Session, Part 2," sec. 4:50.

43 C-SPAN, "Senate Confirms Jeff Sessions Takes Tom Price Nomination—Senate Session, Part 2"; Committee on the Judiciary, "Nomination of Jefferson B. Session III, To Be U.S. District Judge for the Southern District of Alabama," 9.

44 C-SPAN, "Senate Confirms Jeff Sessions Takes Tom Price Nomination—Senate Session, Part 2," sec. 4:51.

45 Ibid., sec. 4:52.

46 Ibid., sec. 4:52.

47 Ibid., sec. 5:16.

48 Evelyn Rupert, "Warren Reads Coretta Scott King Letter Opposing Sessions from outside Senate," [Text] The Hill, February 7, 2017, https://thehill.com/blogs/ballot

-box/318429-warren-reads-coretta-scott-king-letter-opposing-sessions-from-outside
-senate.

49 Matt House, "Republicans Are Trying to Keep Sen. Warren from Reading a Letter from MLK's Widow on Sen. Sessions. RT If You Think They Should #LetLizSpeakpic.Twitter.Com/GI6vgNAoQR," Tweet, *@mattwhouse* (blog), February 7, 2017, https://twitter.com/mattwhouse/status/829136843211997185.

50 McGrane, "Republicans on Defensive."

51 Chuck Schumer, "This Letter Caused the GOP to Silence @SenWarren Tonight. Rt If You Think They Should #LetLizSpeakhttps://Twitter.Com/Senwarren/Status /829139856777478144," Tweet, *@SenSchumer* (blog), February 7, 2017, https:// twitter.com/SenSchumer/status/829143061972164608.

52 Wesley Lowery, "Read the Letter Coretta Scott King Wrote Opposing Sessions' 1986 Federal Nomination," *Washington Post*, January 10, 2017, https://www .washingtonpost.com/news/powerpost/wp/2017/01/10/read-the-letter-coretta-scott -king-wrote-opposing-sessionss-1986-federal-nomination/.

53 C-SPAN, "Senate Confirms Jeff Sessions Takes Tom Price Nomination—Senate Session, Part 2," sec. 6:34.

54 Maddow, "McConnell Silences Warren."

55 J. P. Zompetti, "The Value of Topoi," *Argumentation* 20, no. 1 (August 1, 2006): 15, https://doi.org/10.1007/s10503-005-1458-y; Sara Rubinelli, *Ars Topica: The Classical Technique of Constructing Arguments from Aristotle to Cicero* (New York: Springer Science & Business Media, 2009).

56 Rep. Barbara Lee, "In America, We Don't Silence Women Who Persist, We Celebrate Them. #ShePersisted #BlackHistoryMonthpic.Twitter.Com/YZtTed3Eho," Tweet, *@repbarbaralee* (blog), February 8, 2017, https://twitter.com/repbarbaralee /status/829366123263045633.

57 Nancy Fraser, "Rethinking the Public Sphere: A Contribution to the Critique of Actually Existing Democracy,'" *Social Text* 25/26 (1990): 56–80, https://doi.org/10 .2307/466240.

58 Jessica Mclean and Sophia Maalsen, "Destroying the Joint and Dying of Shame? A Geography of Revitalised Feminism in Social Media and Beyond," *Geographical Research* 51, no. 3 (2013): 243–256, https://doi.org/10.1111/1745-5871.12023.

Part 4

New Feminist Theorizing

●●●●●●●●●●●●●●●●●●●●●●

Feminist theory and activism has necessarily evolved over time.[1] Growing more inclusive, feminism has moved from politics of participation to more inclusive theorizing that covers a breadth of topics. Although the original "add women and stir" model of gender equality supported giving women the right to vote and allowing women to work, more recent advocacy has pushed feminists to ask, which women are we really advocating for? Women of color and women in lower socioeconomic classes have been working for centuries,[2] and in 2020, women of color are less likely to be able to vote because of restrictive voting laws that seem innocuous but are anything but racially neutral.[3] Going forward, feminist theorizing must account for the very different ways people embody womanhood and for the different impact that our social structure and value system has on diverse women. Although third-wave feminists started drawing out the politics of identity intersections, feminism is moving toward an even more nuanced understanding of equality, equity, and social justice.

The challenges and limitations of a binary gender construction and binary language will remain important in feminist theorizing, particularly in developing transfeminism, research and advocacy for nonbinary people, and rights for all LGBTQI+ individuals. Future feminist theories and advocacy must also continue to challenge structures and practices of racism. Also moving from politics of participation and integration, race-based advocacy is pushing for more nuanced understandings of structural and implicit-bias racism. Recent work has taken up *antiracism* as a way to constantly and consciously work to reduce racism.[4] As we discussed in the Black Lives Matter section, more work is required to understand the politics of Black identities and performances, and in order to ensure the physical and emotional safety of Black and Brown bodies. For both LGBTQI+ advocacy and race-based advocacy, feminism can be the tool with which people identify the very nuanced sites of inequality. In the academy, this includes citing theories and theorists from beyond the United States and the United Kingdom and those within those countries who theorize from nonnormative standpoints.

Future feminist work will also take up new directions. As we imagine, these could include discrimination based on physiologies,[5] body size,[6] age,[7] maternity and reproductive politics,[8] (dis)ability,[9] global geography,[10] religion,[11] and cultural practices, which are all important areas that have yet to be fully explored in feminist theorizing or activism. Nuancing the constraints and opportunities laden in each of these examples is important work that feminism can and should take up. We envision future badass projects in the following areas:

- How the environment and natural world intersect with social identities and how they are dominated in the same ways that people with nonconforming identities are dominated.[12]
- Sexual harassment, assault, performances of sexuality, and masculinity are all areas that require additional theorizing and activism.
- Particular evolving contexts necessitate scholarly inquiry and activism, including social media, technology, workplaces, families, and other institutions with which we engage.
- How to make classrooms and education more equitable, including efforts to decolonize syllabi, diversify people in positions of power, and identify the particular ways teaching practices reproduce racist, sexist, ableist, and cis-/heterosexual norms.

We invite you to consider these questions as you read this section so that you can draw your own conclusions about how the future of feminism might look. What questions might you take up in research or activism to move toward a more just world?

Discussion Questions

1 McDonald and DeTurk (chapter 22) call for LGBTQI+ theorizing. How would you define LGBTQI+ theorizing? In what ways could these theories be applied to activism to reduce inequalities?

2 Pugh-Patton and Spikes (chapter 23) and Hanchey (chapter 24) draw inspiration from television, music, fiction, films, poems, and music videos for their feminist theorizing. How do elements of popular culture influence the everyday experiences of sexism, racism, ableism, and cis-/heteronormativity? How can these same elements serve as vehicles to move toward feminist theorizing and greater social justice?

3 What particular contexts are the theories presented here well suited to make a difference? For example, how would the theories presented in this section change work places? Families? Education?

4 What social justice issues (mentioned here or not) do you think should be included in future feminist activism and theorizing?

Notes

1 Sarah Jane Blithe and Mackenna Neal, "Communicating Gender Advocacy: Riding the Fourth Wave of Feminism," in *The Routledge Handbook of Communication and Gender*, ed. Marnel Niles Goins, Joan Faber McAlister, and Bryant Keith Alexander (New York: Routledge, 2021), 570–584.

2 Eileen Boris and Carolyn Herbst Lewis, "Caregiving and Wage-Earning: A Historical Perspective on Work and Family," in *The Work and Family Handbook: Multi-disciplinary Perspectives and Approaches*, ed. Marcie Pitt-Catsouphes, Ellen Ernst Kossek, and Stephen Sweet (Mahwah, NJ: Erlbaum, 2006), 73–97.

3 Alex Vandermaas-Peeler, Daniel Cox, Molly Fisch-Friedman, Rob Griffin, and Robert P. Jones, "American Democracy in Crisis: The Challenges of Voter Knowledge, Participation, and Polarization," PRRI, July 17, 2018, https://www.prri.org/research/American-democracy-in-crisis-voters-midterms-trump-election-2018/.

4 Ibram X. Kendi, *How to Be an Antiracist* (New York: One World, 2019).

5 Sarah Jane Blithe and Jenna N. Hanchey, "Tracing the Discursive Emergence of Physiological Discrimination in Sex Verification Testing," *Women's Studies in Communication* 38, no. 4 (2015): 486–506.

6 Anne Helen Petersen, *Too Fat, Too Slutty, Too Loud: The Rise and Reign of the Unruly Woman* (New York: Penguin, 2017); Kjerstin Gruys, "'Making Over' Poor Women: Gender, Race, Class, and Body Size in a Welfare-to-Work Nonprofit Organization," *Sociological Forum* 34, no. 1 (2019): 47–70.

7 Petersen, *Too Fat, Too Slutty, Too Loud*.

8 Natalie Fixmer-Oraiz, *Homeland Maternity: US Security Culture and the New Reproductive Regime* (Chicago: University of Illinois Press, 2019).

9 Leland G. Spencer, "Stares and Prayers," *Health Communication* 35 no. 7 (2019): 921–923.

10 Lena Martinsson and Diana Mulinari, eds., *Dreaming Global Change, Doing Local Feminisms: Visions of Feminism. Global North/Global South Encounters, Conversations and Disagreements* (New York: Routledge, 2018).

11 Sachi Edwards, *Critical Conversations about Religion: Promises and Pitfalls of a Social Justice Approach to Interfaith Dialogue* (Charlotte, NC: IAP, 2016).

12 Julie Schutten and Emily Shaffer, "Tails from Captive Classes: Interspecies Civic Action at the Contemporary Zoo," *Frontiers in Communication* 4 (2019): 35.

22

Social Justice Organizing through the Closet Metaphor

• •

JAMES McDONALD AND

SARA DeTURK

There is a long history of nondominant groups being silenced in the United States. In 1978, the persistent silencing of the lesbian, gay, bisexual, trans, and queer community (LGBTQ+) led the late–gay rights activist Harvey Milk to plead, "Gay brothers and sisters, you must come out."[1] By calling on members of the LGBTQ+ community to come out and affirm their identities, Milk hoped to end this silencing.

In this chapter, we revisit the politics of coming out more than forty years later and explore how social justice organizing can benefit from accounting for the omnipresence of closeting processes across multiple lines of difference. Reconsidering the politics of coming out is important because of immense social change that has occurred since Milk's call for his gay brothers and sisters to come out. Indeed, Milk would surely be glad to see that the LGBTQ+ community in the United States is arguably more visible than ever before. Among the legal progress that has been made since his plea, the repressive "don't ask, don't tell" policy has been repealed in the military, the U.S. Supreme Court has legalized same-sex marriage, and discrimination on the basis of sexual identity is prohibited in many states and cities. The visibility of the LGBTQ+ community has made so much progress that Steven Seidman has asserted that contemporary queer life in America is largely lived outside of the bounds of the closet.[2]

Yet, despite this increased visibility, heteronormativity remains firmly institutionalized in almost all areas of society. Rights that were thought secured—such as those of trans people to openly serve in the military—were rescinded by the Trump administration. And despite Seidman's suggestion that queer life is now lived outside of the closet, subsequent research has shown that although the closet is now experienced differently than during Milk's time, it remains what Tony Adams calls a "fundamental feature of social life" for the LGBTQ+ community.[3] As such, the LGBTQ+ community continues to experience silencing in multiple ways, as members of the community negotiate the risks and benefits of coming out to particular people in particular contexts.

Many other nondominant groups continue to experience silencing in the contemporary United States. For four years, the Trump administration cast immigrants as a threat to both the economy and national security and implemented immigration policies that have had devastating effects on the lives of many immigrants. For example, the lives of many immigrant youth who were brought to the United States as children without authorization were thrown into uncertainty in September 2017 when the Trump administration announced its intention to end the Deferred Action for Childhood Arrivals (DACA) program. Legal challenges to the DACA program continue today, and legislation to provide a pathway to citizenship for the estimated 11 million undocumented people living in the United States is currently stalled in Congress. Moreover, families seeking refugee status in the United States have been separated at the border, with children forcefully taken from their parents. Other asylum seekers have been subject to the "Remain in Mexico" policy, which does not allow them to reside in the United States while their cases are pending. In this context, immigrants experience silencing as visibility can come with dire consequences, up to and including deportation for those who are undocumented.

Even in the era of the #McToo movement where more sexual assault survivors have come forward about aggressions, many of their experiences continue to be silenced because of the risks associated with disclosing and identifying their aggressors. These risks can entail having one's experiences open to public scrutiny, as was the case for Dr. Christine Ford, who in 2018 testified before the Senate Judiciary Committee that then–Supreme Court nominee Brett Kavanaugh sexually assaulted her while they were in high school. After coming forward, Ford received multiple death threats and was forced to hire private security and move several times in a short period for her security and that of her family.[4] Moreover, the Senate ultimately voted to confirm Kavanaugh's nomination as a Supreme Court Justice. In light of the outcome of this high-profile case, other survivors may continue to reconsider whether to come forward given the risks associated with doing so. Women are also facing systematic silencing as abortion rights have come under attack. On September 1, 2021, the most severe restrictions on abortions in the United States went into effect in Texas. Senate Bill 8 bans abortion as soon as a fetal heartbeat can be detected, usually at six weeks into one's pregnancy and before many people know that they're pregnant. The bill is enforced by enabling any private citizen in the country to bring civil lawsuits against anyone they believe has aided or abetted a woman in getting an abortion in violation of this law—including providers, clinic employees, counselors, and even someone who provides financial support for the procedure or transportation to a clinic. If the lawsuit is successful, the private citizen bringing the lawsuit can be awarded a minimum of $10,000, plus legal fees. As a result, the law serves to intimidate and silence women. The Supreme Court has allowed these restrictions to go into effect, leading many to believe that the nearly five-decades-old precedent of Roe v. Wade is in jeopardy.

As seen in the examples above, the long history of nondominant groups being silenced in the United States continues today. Muted group theory and cocultural theory provide a framework within which to understand this silencing. According to muted group theory, nondominant group members are effectively muted by dominant groups, who create hegemonic communication norms and make it difficult for the ideas and experiences of nondominant group members to be heard.[5] Nondominant groups vary by culture and context, but in the context of the United States habitually include, among many other groups, women, people of color, the LGBTQ+ community, and people with disabilities.[6] Cocultural theory goes further and suggests that nondominant group members have a variety of strategies for interacting with dominant group members, one of which includes self-silencing. These theoretical frameworks frame the silencing of nondominant groups as problematic and as a pressing social justice issue.[7]

Given the widespread silencing across many lines of difference in the current political climate, social justice organizing against silencing is crucially important. One way social justice organizing occurs is through intercultural alliances—that is, partnerships of people from different social identities or cultural backgrounds who work together to promote social justice for all.[8] For instance, an intercultural alliance can be composed of LGBTQ+ individuals, immigrants, and sexual assault survivors who listen to and advocate for each other. Importantly, alliances can also be composed of individuals with relative privilege in relation to nondominant groups. Indeed, a significant amount of research has been devoted to understanding how white people act as allies for people of color.[9] In these cases, alliances constitute the front lines of intergroup communication and relationships.

Because their goal is to advocate for social justice across multiple lines of difference, intercultural alliances engage in multi-issue organizing.[10] These alliances are essential to social justice activism because marginalized and oppressed groups are relatively lacking in the political capital necessary to effect change. Multi-issue organizing has especially been theorized and advocated by Chicana feminists, who examine power across intersecting identities related to gender, race, ethnicity, class, sexuality, and religion.[11] Chicana feminists suggest that because identities are overlapping and cannot be neatly separated, social justice organizing requires working holistically and across identities through alliances.[12] From this standpoint, the oppression of one nondominant group is related to the oppression of other nondominant groups, making it necessary for all those who are oppressed by the dominant culture to work together to achieve justice.

Our goal in this chapter is to show how attending to closeting processes—broadly defined—can contribute to our understanding of social justice organizing across multiple lines of difference. Although the closet and closeting processes have most often been associated with the experiences of LGBTQ+ individuals, we draw from recent work that has applied the metaphor to multiple identities and differences that are basis for oppression.[13] Indeed, people experience injustice and oppression in relation to a whole host of differences that can potentially be closeted and thus silenced, including sexual identity, gender identity, religion, citizenship status, and health conditions. We argue that because of the interlocking nature of oppression,[14] closeting processes are a common basis for oppression among all those who must continually negotiate when, if, and how to make themselves visible. As such, social justice activists engaging in multi-issue organizing can draw from the closet metaphor to identify closeting and silencing as a common basis for oppression among many different groups and can act as allies by advocating on behalf of different groups and making their oppression visible.

The Politics of Social Justice Alliances

Scholarship on social justice alliances was pioneered by Black, Brown, and queer women who challenged the mainstream U.S. feminist movement to recognize the intersectional nature of identity and the interlocking nature of oppressions. As early as 1851, Sojourner Truth (in her speech "Ain't I a Woman?") pointed out to an audience of mostly white feminists that gender worked differently for women of different racial backgrounds. Later, in response to the racism endemic to the second-wave feminist movement, African American scholar activists such as Patricia Hill Collins, Marsha Houston, and Audre Lorde advanced the notion that oppressions based on gender, sexuality, race, and class are not only overlapping but mutually constitutive.[15] In particular, they "called attention to the ways that their experience of economic exploitation was both racial and gendered and, similarly, how racial hatred and discrimination were constructed along class, gender, and sexual dimensions."[16]

These arguments were also articulated by Chicana feminists such as Norma Alarcón, Gloria Anzaldúa, Martha Cotera, Alma García, and Deena González.[17] Their writing was characterized by attention both to daily lived experiences and to global processes such as imperialism and capitalism. Another central contribution of Chicana feminism was the articulation of a "third space," also described as a "borderlands" or "mestiza" consciousness. In *La conciencia de la mestiza*, Anzaldúa framed her identity as a Chicana lesbian in terms of hybridity and border dwelling, as well as in terms of its potential for relationships and alliances with people of other identities.[18] In addition, Anzaldúa described a constant shifting of positions and feelings, between being accepted according to one dimension of identity and excluded—sometimes by the same people—because of another.[19] She also noted that some identities can be hidden and thus silenced, whereas others are always visible.

Other Chicana feminists have expanded on the concept of mestiza consciousness to demonstrate its potential for social change. For instance, Chela Sandoval developed the notion of "differential consciousness" to account for the ways individuals who experience oppression can be strategic in their efforts to challenge the dominant culture, shifting ideologies, discourses, and arguments to respond to the needs of different political situations.[20] Aimee Carrillo Rowe goes further and proposes a theory of "differential belonging" to account for the ways people can foster belonging across multiple lines of difference to pursue social justice work.[21] She suggests that pursuing social justice on behalf of an oppressed group does not require one to be a member of that group. Indeed, belonging is not merely constituted on the basis of essential identity categories because one's relation to power is more nuanced than simply belonging to a particular cultural group.[22] Belonging can thus be constituted via communities and practices that enable connections among people and groups who do not necessarily share the same cultural characteristics.[23] Carrillo Rowe thus sees heterogeneous alliances across multiple lines of difference as a crucial feature of social justice organizing.

Central to Chicana feminism is the premise that social justice organizing must operate holistically and address all forms of oppression.[24] This premise is also widely espoused by queer theorists, who resist monolithic understandings of identity and advocate being attentive to how power and domination are aligned with interlocking forms of difference.[25] Indeed, queer theorists adopt an anticategorical approach to difference that resists stable identity categories such as gender, race, and sexuality and is thus consistent with Carrillo Rowe's rejection of essentialized identity categories as the primary basis for activist work.[26] In addition, queer theory conceptualizes identity categories as fluid, such that there are no stable meanings associated with them and similarities cannot be assumed among those who are purported to be represented by them, given their varying identifications and experiences.[27] In line with this fluidity, queer theorists view identity categories as arbitrary because one's identification with a given category can be unknown to others as well as shift.[28]

Rather than organize for social justice on the basis of stable identity categories, queer theorists adopt a politics that challenges normativity and normalizing processes.[29] Normalizing processes serve to construct what is considered as taken for granted and "normal," as well as what is nonnormative and deviant from the norm.[30] These normalizing processes are heavily intertwined with power, as that which is normative is privileged in relation to what is nonnormative. For instance, heterosexuality and monogamy are normalized and the most privileged form of sexual expression, whereas all other sexual practices are constructed as inferior.[31] Queer politics celebrate the nonnormative and are based on the premise that normalizing processes are oppressive and must be resisted.[32] Although some queer theorists have suggested that queer politics should be limited to critiquing heteronormativity,[33] queer politics are most often conceptualized much more broadly and as a stance against all normalizing processes.[34]

Queer politics have important implications for social justice organizing across lines of difference. Because of queer theory's broad anti-normative stance, queer politics "challenge and bring together all those deemed marginal and all those committed to liberatory politics."[35] As such, multi-issue organizing is a defining feature of queer politics and activism. In line with queer theory's fluid and anti-categorical approach to difference, the basis for coalition building is not stable identity categories but rather one's relation to power and the dominant culture. Cathy Cohen suggests that queer politics that can bring together "the nonnormative and marginal position of punks, bulldaggers, and welfare queens . . . for progressive transformative coalition work."[36]

As seen in this section, both Chicana feminism and queer theory support the idea that social justice organizing requires working across multiple forms of difference and breaking away from stable and static notions of identity. We now explore how attending to the closet and closeting processes can contribute to these literatures and foster differential belonging across multiple lines of difference.

An Intersectional Approach to Closeting Processes

The closet has long been a metaphor associated with the silencing of the LGBTQ+ community and nonnormative sexualities. Because of the pervasive ideology of heteronormativity, heterosexuality is seen as a universal norm such that in most societal contexts, individuals are presumed to be heterosexual unless they say otherwise.[37] Individuals who identify as heterosexual are thus not expected to come out as such because heterosexuality is presumed a priori. However, because individuals with nonnormative sexual identities are presumed to be heterosexual unless they disclose otherwise, their identities can be silenced and closeted. Individuals with nonnormative sexual identities may actively seek to keep these identities silenced, as making these identities visible comes with risks, including being targets of violence and losing friends, family members, and employment.[38] As such, individuals with nonnormative sexual identities negotiate the closet and closeting processes—that is, the communication processes through which individuals negotiate when, whether, to whom, and how to disclose certain forms of difference.[39]

Recent work has suggested that in addition to nonnormative sexual identities, individuals negotiate closeting processes in relation to all forms of difference that are nonnormative, stigmatized, and invisible or otherwise potentially concealable.[40] For instance, individuals with nonnormative, stigmatized religious identities,[41] citizenship statuses,[42] family structures,[43] communities of origin,[44] and health conditions[45] must all negotiate closeting processes as they go about everyday life because these forms of difference are often invisible and disclosing them comes with risks. Conversely, individuals do not need to negotiate closeting processes in relation to dominant, normative, and privileged forms of difference, as they are assumed a priori and carry no negative consequences if revealed.

Kate Lockwood Harris and Jamie McDonald's broad conceptualization of closeting processes draws from intersectionality, a term originally used by legal scholar Kimberlé Crenshaw to refer to how identities such as race and gender intersect with each other and are experienced simultaneously.[46] As such, identities must be analyzed in relation to each other rather than separately because one's experiences of gender cannot be fully understood without also accounting for experiences of race. Although Crenshaw analyzed only gender and race in her original articulation of intersectionality, she also noted that her "focus on the intersections of race and gender only highlights the need to account for multiple grounds of identity when considering how the social world is constructed."[47] Intersectionality thus provides a helpful framework to understand how multiple forms of difference—including but not limited to gender, race, class, sexuality, and nation—intersect with each other to shape social experiences.[48] This key tenet of intersectionality is consistent with both Chicana feminism and queer theory, which, as seen earlier, emphasize the interlocking nature of identity and the importance of organizing across multiple lines of difference.

Intersectionality is central to understanding experiences of closeting because just like identities, closeting processes intersect with each other. Indeed, individuals can be negotiating multiple closeting processes at any moment.[49] For instance, an HIV-negative, gay citizen may be negotiating closeting in relation to only his sexual identity and thus experience the closet very differently than an undocumented, gay, immigrant who is HIV-positive. Whereas the former is negotiating closeting processes in relation to only his sexual identity, the latter must simultaneously negotiate closeting processes in relation to his citizenship status, sexual identity, and HIV status. Moreover, it is fully possible to come out in one capacity, such as disclosing a gay identity, and remain closeted in another capacity.

An intersectional approach underscores not just that individuals negotiate multiple closeting processes at once but also that experiences of closeting are shaped by that which may be closeted. That is, negotiating the closet in regard to gay identity is necessarily different than negotiating closeting processes in relation to one's HIV or undocumented status. Moreover, not all closeting processes are created equal; some may feel more oppressive than others because the consequences of disclosure can be either more or less serious.[50] In some contexts, it may be also be easier to come out as gay but harder to come out as undocumented or HIV-positive; however, in other contexts, it may be easier to come out as HIV-positive than as gay. As such, an intersectional approach is necessary in order to account for how these multiple closeting processes overlap and how experiences vary among those who negotiate the closeting of any form of difference.

By definition, closeting occurs in relation to forms of difference that are not immediately visible or otherwise concealable. As such, in any given context, individuals can be negotiating multiple closeting processes without others being aware. This key characteristic of closeting processes—invisibility—has important implications for social justice organizing, which we discuss below.

The Implications of Closeting Processes for Social Justice Organizing

As we have argued, social justice organizing requires working across multiple forms of difference, rather than addressing oppressions individually.[51] We suggest that understanding closeting processes as a common basis for oppression is a key way of fostering differential belonging among multiple groups and thus fostering heterogeneous alliances.

Centering the closet metaphor on social justice organizing can be particularly effective because of the sheer omnipresence of closeting processes in everyday life and how many people have the potential to relate to them. When closeting is conceptualized in relation to all forms of difference that are nonnormative, stigmatized, and invisible, it is likely that "everyone at some point in the life span might engage in closeting."[52] Given the pervasiveness of closeting processes and how many individuals must negotiate them at some point, closeting can provide a common basis on which to foster heterogeneous alliances across difference—alliances composed of groups such as undocumented immigrants, the LGBTQ+ community, sexual assault survivors, Muslims, and people with certain disabilities. Whereas closeting experiences among all those represented in these groups vary dramatically based on each individual's relative privilege and the nature of what may be closeted, the closet metaphor provides a starting point from which to discuss these differences and, in Carrillo Rowe's terms, foster differential belonging among people from multiple nondominant groups.[53]

Because that which may be closeted is, by definition, invisible, individuals may be negotiating closeting processes at any time and in any interaction without it being known by others. Closeting processes can thus be seen as a constitutive feature of social interaction.[54] As such, we suggest that they are relevant to and should be kept at the forefront of all social justice organizing and activism. An important benefit of attending to closeting processes in social justice organizing is that it enables advocates to account for the complexities and heterogeneity that exist within the nondominant groups for which one is advocating. That is, the closet metaphor can be used as a heuristic to identify forms of oppression that can exist within any nondominant group and how multiple forms of oppression—some of which are closeted and silenced—overlap and need to be addressed together rather than separately. In this sense, considering closeting processes in social justice organizing can help different groups understand how their oppressions are interconnected and thus forge the heterogeneous alliances advocated for by Chicana feminists and queer theorists.[55]

Importantly, as we argue that the silencing of nondominant groups is a social justice issue and that closeting processes can be oppressive, we do not suggest that silence itself is always problematic and that those who maintain silence do so against their will and due to a lack of agency. As a form of nonverbal communication, silence is incredibly complex and can, in some cases, be empowering.[56] For instance, previous research has shown that silence can be used as a form of protest. Through silence, one can refuse to account for oneself to dominant group members and to express oneself in the terms and language of dominant groups.[57] As such, both breaking *and* maintaining silence can constitute protest.[58]

Silence can also be a way of protecting oneself from potential devastating consequences that vary according to the information that is being silenced and thus closeted. In many states, people who are out as gay can face housing and employment discrimination. Individuals who publicly come out as undocumented can be targeted by Immigration and Customs Enforcement. Sexual assault survivors who report their aggressors may find themselves at a trial where they are asked about their entire sexual history. In cases such as these, an individual's decision to remain closeted can be a way to express one's agency and thus feel empowering.[59]

Social justice organizing around the closet metaphor must also recognize that the meanings of silence and closeting are culturally dependent. Whereas coming out and making one's identity visible is often viewed as essential to social progress in more individualistic Western contexts, this is not the case universally.[60] Suggesting that coming out is always superior to silence is thus a problematic Western-centric stance and serves to construct Western exceptionalism.[61]

As is clear above, our call to keep closeting processes at the forefront of social justice organizing does not entail asking everyone to always come out about all forms of difference and oppression that they may be closeting. To do so denies that maintaining silence can sometimes be empowering and a form of protest, that the meanings of silence are culturally dependent, and that coming out can potentially put people at risk of facing negative, sometimes devastating, consequences. We thus break with Harvey Milk's call for everyone to come out that we discussed at the outset of this chapter. In doing so, we join Harris and Fortney who complicate the idea that individuals should always be expected to disclose their experiences with trauma and disability to justify why they care about these issues.[62]

We argue that social justice organizing against the silencing of nondominant groups can occur without calling on all individuals to come out and that coming out is not the only way to end the silencing of nondominant groups. By being reflexive of what forms of oppression may be closeted in any given context, it is possible for allies to advocate against closeted forms of oppression without expecting the individuals experiencing this oppression to come out and discuss their experiences and vulnerabilities. This can be done through several concrete actions, such as donating money to and serving in organizations that represent members of nondominant groups, participating in petitions and marches that bring visibility to these groups, and publicly voicing support of these groups.[63] Moreover, individuals who are closeted in some way and do not wish to come out can still speak out against the oppression without outing themselves and disclosing their own experiences. As such, the closeting of a form of oppression does not mean that work cannot be done toward ending it.

In order for the closet metaphor to serve as a heuristic to identify overlapping forms of oppression, we propose that social justice advocates act as allies to nondominant groups by reflexively consider questions such as the following:

- What forms of difference might individuals potentially be closeting and silencing?
- What are the potential consequences if individuals disclose and voice these forms of difference?
- What can and should allies do to advocate for those who may be closeting these forms of difference?
- How can we reduce and eliminate the stigma associated with the differences that individuals may be closeting?
- What policies could be implemented to help support individuals who may be closeting and silencing these forms of difference?

By considering the above questions, social justice advocates can draw attention to forms of oppression that may be closeted and work toward ending this oppression without expecting nondominant groups to expose their vulnerabilities and make their oppression visible.

Conclusion

As we indicated at the outset of this chapter, there is a long history of nondominant groups being silenced in the United States and this silencing continues today. In order to combat this silencing, we have suggested that social justice advocates put the closet metaphor at the forefront of their work—always considering what forms of difference may be potentially closeted and what they can do to act as allies to those who may be negotiating various types of closeting processes. By always reflecting on what may be closeted, social justice advocates can identify forms of oppression that may not be voiced by those who are experiencing them. In turn, this enables social justice advocates to work against ending forms of oppression without putting the onus on nondominant groups to disclose information about themselves that could potentially lead to negative consequences. The approach to social justice activism that we have put forth in this chapter thus problematizes the notion that coming out is a prerequisite for social justice work.

Considering how multiple closeting processes can shape the experiences of all forms of oppression, both visible and invisible, can also enable social justice advocates to build connections among groups who seem to share little with each other, foster differential belonging, and thus help form the heterogeneous alliances that are necessary to social justice work. Alliances such as these make it possible to organize for social justice across difference without relying on essentialized identity categories and thus negating the complexities that exist within all groups—something that both Chicana feminists and queer theorists have argued is necessary to pursue social justice. This is also in the spirit of intersectionality, which recognizes how individuals can be members of multiple nondominant groups at once and thus be negotiating multiple closeting processes.

In conclusion, we are currently living in a political epoch where a plethora of nondominant groups—including but not limited to women, people of color, immigrants, the LGBTQ+ community, Muslims, and people with disabilities—have experienced systematic silencing. Given this widespread silencing across many lines of difference, we must work together to forge heterogeneous alliances that work toward social justice and that seek to end this silencing. As we have argued, it is not necessary to be a member of one of these groups in order to advocate on their behalf, and it is also not necessary for all individuals within these groups to come out about their experiences. What is most important in this political climate of widespread silencing is that all those who experience silencing in some way are allies with one another. We suggest that keeping closeting processes at the forefront of social justice organizing is a way of accomplishing that and working against multiple forms of oppression.

Discussion Questions

1 How does the concept of intersectionality resonate with your own identities? Can you think of any identities that are "closeted" in some contexts but not others? (If so, how/why?)

2 Try to recall an experience in which you were engaged in a group conversation (or activist event) addressing social justice. What identities were represented, and which ones might have been invisible? How might that have affected the communication?

3 Have you ever advocated for someone who was present but whose identity was closeted? Has anyone ever done that on your behalf? What are the advantages and potential dangers of this form of advocacy?

Try This!

1 Share things you have done or seen other people do to challenge prejudice, stereotypes, or discrimination. As a group, discuss the effectiveness of these strategies and how they can contribute to advocating for social justice across lines of difference.

2 Speaking from the position of one of your identities that is marginalized and/or stigmatized, share ways in which you would like others to advocate on your behalf.

Notes

1 Jennifer Knapp, "'You Must Come Out': How Harvey Milk's Challenge Resonates with Gay Christians Today," HuffPost, February 2, 2016, https://www.huffpost.com/entry/how-harvey-milks-challeng_b_5960258.
2 Steven Seidman, *Beyond the Closet: The Transformation of Gay and Lesbian Life* (New York: Routledge, 2002).
3 Tony E. Adams, *Narrating the Closet: An Autoethnography of Same-Sex Attraction* (Walnut Creek, CA: Left Coast Press, 2011), 21.
4 Tim Mak, "Kavanaugh Accuser Christine Blasey Ford Continues Receiving Threats, Lawyers Say," NPR, November 8, 2018, https://www.npr.org/2018/11/08/665407589/kavanaugh-accuser-christine-blasey-ford-continues-receiving-threats-lawyers-say.
5 Cheris Kramarae, *Women and Men Speaking* (Rowley, MA: Newbury House, 1981).
6 Mark Orbe, "Laying the Foundation for Co-cultural Communication Theory: An Inductive Approach to Studying 'Non-dominant' Communication Strategies and the Factors That Influence Them," *Communication Studies* 47, no. 3 (1996).
7 Kris Acheson, "Silence in Dispute," *Annals of the International Communication Association* 31, no. 1 (2007); Kramarae, *Women and Men Speaking*; Orbe, "Laying the Foundation for Co-cultural Communication Theory."
8 Sara DeTurk, *Activism, Alliance Building, and the Esperanza Peace and Justice Center* (Lanham, MD: Lexington Books, 2015).
9 Sara DeTurk, "Allies in Action: The Communicative Experiences of People Who Challenge Social Injustice on Behalf of Others," *Communication Quarterly* 59, no. 5 (2011).
10 DeTurk, *Activism, Alliance Building, and the Esperanza Peace and Justice Center*.
11 See, in particular, Gloria Anzaldúa, "Bridge, Drawbridge, Sandbar or Island: Lesbians-of-Color *Hacienda Allianzas*," in *Bridges of Power: Women's Multicultural Alliances*, ed. L. Albrecht and R. M. Brewer (Philadelphia: New Society Publishers, 1990); Aimee Carrillo Rowe, *Power Lines: On the Subject of Feminist Alliances* (Durham, NC: Duke University Press, 2008); Karma R. Chávez, *Queer Migration Politics: Activist Rhetoric and Coalitional Possibilities* (Urbana: University of Illinois Press, 2013).
12 Gloria Anzaldúa, "La conciencia de la mestiza: Towards a New Consciousness," in *Making Face, Making Soul: Haciendo Caras*, ed. Gloria Anzaldúa (San Francisco: Aunt Lute Press, 1990); María Lugones, *Pilgrimages/Peregrinajes: Theorizing Coalition against Multiple Oppressions* (Lanham, MD: Rowman & Littlefield, 2003).

13 Kate Lockwood Harris and James McDonald, "Introduction: Queering the 'Closet' at Work," *Management Communication Quarterly* 32, no. 2 (2018); James McDonald, Kate Lockwood Harris, and Jessica Ramirez, "Revealing and Concealing Difference: A Critical Approach to Disclosure and an Intersectional Theory of 'Closeting,'" *Communication Theory* 30, no. 1 (2020).

14 The interlocking nature of oppression is the basis of intersectionality, a concept that has been developed by authors including Kimberlé Williams Crenshaw, "Demarginalizing the Intersection of Race and Sex: A Black Feminist Critique of Antidiscrimination Doctrine, Feminist Theory and Antiracist Politics," *University of Chicago Legal Forum* 1989, no. 1 (1989); Marsha Houston, "The Politics of Difference: Race, Class and Women's Communication," in *Women Making Meaning*, ed. L. F. Rakow (New York: Routledge, 1992); Lugones, *Pilgrimages/Peregrinajes: Theorizing Coalition against Multiple Oppressions*.

15 Patricia Hill Collins, *Black Feminist Thought: Knowledge, Consciousness, and the Politics of Empowerment* (New York: Routledge, 1991); Houston, "The Politics of Difference: Race, Class and Women's Communication"; Audre Lorde, *Sister Outsider: Essays and Speeches* (Berkeley, CA: Crossing Press, 1984).

16 Maylei Blackwell, ¡*Chicana Power! Contested Histories of Feminism in the Chicana Movement* (Austin: University of Texas Press, 2011), 189.

17 Norma Alarcón, "Chicana Feminism: In the Tracks of 'the' Native Woman," in *Living Chicana Theory*, ed. C. Trujillo (Berkeley, CA: Third Woman Press, 1998); Anzaldúa, "Bridge, Drawbridge, Sandbar or Island"; Anzaldúa, "La conciencia de la mestiza"; Gloria Anzaldúa, *Borderlands/La frontera* (San Francisco: Aunt Lute Press, 1999); Marta P. Cotera, *The Chicana Feminist* (Austin, TX: Information Systems Development, 1997); Alma M. García, ed., *Chicana Feminist Thought: The Basic Historical Writings* (London: Routledge, 1997); Deena J. González, "Speaking Secrets: Living Chicana Theory," in *Living Chicana Theory*, ed. C. Trujillo (Berkeley, CA: Third Woman Press, 1998).

18 Anzaldúa, "La conciencia de la mestiza."

19 Anzaldúa, "Bridge, Drawbridge, Sandbar or Island."

20 Chela Sandoval, *Methodology of the Oppressed* (Minneapolis: University of Minnesota Press, 2000).

21 Carrillo Rowe, *Power Lines*.

22 DeTurk, "Allies in Action."

23 Karma R. Chávez, "Border (In)securities: Normative and Differential Belonging in LGBTQ and Immigrant Rights Discourse," *Communication and Critical/Cultural Studies* 7, no. 2 (2010).

24 See DeTurk, *Activism, Alliance Building, and the Esperanza Peace and Justice Center*; Lugones, *Pilgrimages/Peregrinajes*.

25 Karma R. Chávez, "Pushing Boundaries: Queer Intercultural Communication," *Journal of International and Intercultural Communication* 6, no. 2 (2013); Michael Warner, *The Trouble with Normal: Sex, Politics, and the Ethics of Queer Life* (New York: Free Press, 1999).

26 Carrillo Rowe, *Power Lines*.

27 Judith Butler, *Gender Trouble: Feminism and the Subversion of Identity* (New York: Routledge, 1990); Eve Kosofsky Sedgwick, *Epistemology of the Closet* (Berkeley: University of California Press, 1990).

28 James McDonald, "Coming out in the Field: A Queer Reflexive Account of Shifting Researcher Identity," *Management Learning* 44, no. 2 (2013).

29 Warner, *The Trouble with Normal*.

30 Judith Butler, *Undoing Gender* (New York: Routledge, 2004); Warner, *The Trouble with Normal*; Gust A. Yep, "The Violence of Heteronormativity in Communication Studies: Notes on Injury, Healing, and Queer World-Making," *Journal of Homosexuality* 45, nos. 2–4 (2003).

31 Cathy J. Cohen, "Punks, Bulldaggers, and Welfare Queens: The Radical Potential of Queer Politics?" in *Black Queer Studies: A Critical Anthology*, ed. E. Patrick Johnson and Mae G. Henderon (Durham, NC: Duke University Press, 2005); Yep, "The Violence of Heteronormativity in Communication Studies."

32 David Halperin, "The Normalization of Queer Theory"; Steven Seidman, *Difference Troubles: Queering Social Theory and Sexual Politics* (Cambridge: Cambridge University Press, 1997); Warner, *The Trouble with Normal*.

33 Examples include Bryant Keith Alexander, "Queerying Queer Theory Again (or Queer Theory as Drag Performance)," *Journal of Homosexuality* 45, nos. 2–4 (2003); Leo Bersani, *Homos* (Cambridge, MA: Harvard University Press, 1995).

34 See Halperin, "The Normalization of Queer Theory"; Martin Parker, "Fucking Management: Queer, Theory and Reflexivity," *Ephemera* 1, no. 1 (2001); Seidman, *Difference Troubles*; Warner, *The Trouble with Normal*; Gust A. Yep, Karen E. Lovaas, and John P. Elia, "Introduction: Queering Communication: Starting the Conversation," *Journal of Homosexuality* 45, nos. 2–4 (2003).

35 Cohen, "Punks, Bulldaggers, and Welfare Queens," 22.

36 Ibid.

37 Yep, "The Violence of Heteronormativity in Communication Studies."

38 Adams, *Narrating the Closet*.

39 Elizabeth K. Eger, "Transgender Jobseekers Navigating Closeting Communication," *Management Communication Quarterly* 32, no. 2 (2018).

40 See Kate Lockwood Harris and James McDonald, "Introduction: Queering the "Closet" at Work"; McDonald et al., "Revealing and Concealing Difference."

41 Sandra L. Faulkner and Michael L. Hecht, "The Negotiation of Closetable Identities: A Narrative Analysis of Lesbian, Gay, Bisexual, Transgendered Queer Jewish Identity," *Journal of Social and Personal Relationships* 28, no. 6 (2011).

42 James McDonald, "Negotiating the 'Closet' in U.S. Academia: Foreign Scholars on the Job Market," *Management Communication Quarterly* 32, no. 2 (2018).

43 Jenny Dixon, "Looking out from the Family Closet: Discourse Dependence and Queer Family Identity in Workplace Conversation," *Management Communication Quarterly* 32, no. 2 (2018).

44 Marcus W. Ferguson, "(Re)negotiating Organizational Socialization: Black Male Scholarship and the Closet," *Management Communication Quarterly* 32, no. 2 (2018).

45 Nicole L. Defenbaugh, "Revealing and Concealing Ill Identity: A Performance Narrative of IBD Disclosure," *Health Communication* 28, no. 2 (2013); Jimmy Manning, "Coming Out Conversations and Gay/Bisexual Men's Sexual Health: A Constitutive Model Study," in *Health Care Disparities and the LGBT Population*, ed. V. L. Harvey and T. Housel (Lanham, MD: Lexington Books, 2014); Lynsey K. Romo, "How Formerly Overweight and Obese Individuals Negotiate Disclosure of Their Weight Loss," *Health Communication* 31, no. 9 (2016).

46 Kimberlé Williams Crenshaw, "Mapping the Margins: Intersectionality, Identity Politics, and Violence against Women of Color," *Stanford Law Review* 43, no. 6 (1991).

47 Ibid., 1245.

48 Evangelina Holvino, "Intersections: The Simultaneity of Race, Gender and Class in Organization Studies," *Gender, Work & Organization* 17, no. 3 (2010).

49 Harris and McDonald, "Introduction"; McDonald et al., "Revealing and Concealing Difference."

50 McDonald et al., "Revealing and Concealing Difference."

51 Carrillo Rowe, *Power Lines*; Lugones, *Pilgrimages/Peregrinajes*.

52 Patrice M. Buzzanell, "Legitimizing and Transforming the Closet/Closeting,"
Management Communication Quarterly 32, no. 2 (2018): 298.

53 Carrillo Rowe, *Power Lines*.

54 McDonald et al., "Revealing and Concealing Difference."

55 Carrillo Rowe, *Power Lines*; Cohen, "Punks, Bulldaggers, and Welfare Queens";
Lugones, *Pilgrimages/Peregrinajes*.

56 Acheson, "Silence in Dispute."

57 Judith Butler, *Giving an Account of Oneself* (New York: Fordham University Press,
2005); Robin Patric Clair, *Organizing Silence: A World of Possibilities* (Albany: State
University of New York Press, 1998).

58 Acheson, "Silence in Dispute."

59 Susan Thomson, "Agency as Silence and Muted Voice: The Problem-Solving
Networks of Unaccompanied Young Somali Refugee Women in Eastleigh,
Nairobi," *Conflict, Security & Development* 13, no. 5 (2013).

60 Jason Ritchie, "How Do You Say 'Come out of the Closet' in Arabic? Queer
Activism and the Politics of Visibility in Israel-Palestine," *GLQ: A Journal of
Lesbian and Gay Studies* 16, no. 4 (2010).

61 Samantha King, "Homonormativity and the Politics of Race: Reading Sheryl
Swoopes," *Journal of Lesbian Studies* 13, no. 3 (2009); Marlon B. Ross, "Beyond
the Closet as Raceless Paradigm," in *Black Queer Studies: A Critical Anthology*,
ed. E. Patrick Johnson and Mae G. Henderon (Durham, NC: Duke University Press,
2005).

62 See Kate Lockwood Harris and James Michael Fortney, "Performing Reflexive
Caring: Rethinking Reflexivity through Trauma and Disability," *Text and
Performance Quarterly* 37, no. 1 (2017).

63 DeTurk, "Allies in Action."

23

Disrupting the Ratchet-Respectable Binary

••••••••••••••••••••

Explorations of Ratchet
Feminism and Ratchet
Respectability in Daily
and Popular Life

DANETTE M. PUGH-PATTON

AND ANTONIO L. SPIKES

Ratchet is a term that many people, particularly in the United States, have come across in the last several years, if not through the 2012 song "Ratchet Girl Anthem" by Emmanuel and Phillip Hudson,[1] then perhaps through popular Black reality television shows such as *Basketball Wives*, *Real Housewives of Atlanta*, or *Love and Hip Hop*. It is believed that the term *ratchet* originated from a southern "ghetto" mispronunciation of the adjective *wretched*, meaning one who is not of good quality and/or bad.[2] Ortved indicates the origin of the term comes from Shreveport, Louisiana, where it was used to refer to an "uncouth woman."[3] Ratchetness has a history that is tied to a specific racial, ethnic, and cultural context. The term has been used as a term of degradation for Black women and used to police the bodies of Black women by shaming them for their sexuality and presumed poverty, both moral and financial.

Ratchet appeared in a song published in 1999 called "Do the Ratchet" by Anthony Mandigo in his album titled *Ratchet Fight in the Ghetto*,[4] which presents multiple meanings and connects to the negative rhetorical mobilization of ratchet. This reference to ratchet was likened to a dance, or a performance of a poor/working-class Black aesthetic that still influences hip-hop today. The 2012 song "Ratchet Girl Anthem" only increased the popularity of the term.[5] Around the same time, LL Cool J released a single titled "Ratchet" in which he essentially equated ratchet women to gold diggers.[6] Nicki Minaj sang "all them bitches is ratchet" in her 2012 song with Chris Brown called "Right by My Side,"[7] and Juicy J touted that he cannot refuse the sexual advances of a ratchet woman in his 2012 song "Bandz a Make Her Dance."[8] As Juicy J stated in the song, "You say no to rachet p***y, but Juicy J can't."[9] All in all, the term *ratchet* holds negative connotations. Despite this, there is a growing movement to reclaim the term from its oppressive origins.

In this chapter, we set out to explore issues of ratchet feminism by considering concepts such as ratchetness, respectability, ratchet respectability, and the Black ratchet imagination. We contribute to the evolving literature by narratively exploring our own relationships with ratchetness and respectability. We argue that ratchet feminism can be used as a framework to explore the contradictions and consistencies of ratchetness and respectability within the lives of academics. We additionally argue that using narrative is also a form of ratchetness because centering the researcher as the site of analysis disrupts traditional norms around research. Last, we argue that ratchet feminism can be identified and examined outside areas of music and reality television.

Current Ratchet Feminist Research

In her 2012 article on the Crunk Feminist Collective,[10] Brittany Cooper, under the alias Crunktastic, posed a complex read of a reality show that was never produced. The show was about rapper Shawty Lo and his eleven children whom he had with ten women. Understandably, many Black people were concerned about the show because it fulfilled classic stereotypes of "the Black family." Cooper located this concern within the pull of respectability and concern about Black women's capitulation to patriarchy.[11] Cooper argued that although some people are understandably concerned about the patriarchal and unfair treatment Black women would have received on the show, respectability is a poor way to assuage such anxieties. Although she recognized that transgressive politics alone cannot make a revolution, she stated that the show could "invite us to think about Black women's deployment of ratchetness as part of a kind of disrespectability politics . . . a kind of joy and celebration, that the rush to respectability simply doesn't allow."[12]

Similarly, Stallings proposed a concept called the Black ratchet imagination.[13] Partly inspired by Halberstam's conceptualization of queer failure, Stallings wanted to conceive of a hip-hop space where Black queer youth could potentially resist the trappings of respectability politics. In conceptualizing this understanding of resistance, she states, "It is the performance of the failure to be respectable, uplifting, and a credit to the race, as opposed to the promotion of failure or respectability that is important here."[14] The Black ratchet imagination is visualized as a space where people could claim an individualist goal of self-authenticity which goes against the collectivist aims of the Black community to create a heteronormative, heteropatriarchal, and upper-class respectable image.

Pickens analyzed Tamar Braxton as a figure who embodies a ratchet performance on her reality television show. In it, she situated ratchetness as "a performance of excess that makes and unmakes both performer and audience."[15] She continued, "The ratchet imaginary has no desire to participate in narratives of racial progression or social uplift; instead, it articulates a desire for individuality regardless of the ideas and wants of a putative collective." Pickens set a binary where respectability represents the collective and ratchetness represents individuality. Indeed, manifestations of ratchetness have been commonly understood and theorized as individualized bucks against respectability.[16] However, an understanding of how ratchetness can both be understood as individual and collective action against oppression is lacking. Stallings began the work of situating ratchetness within a broader framework as a transitional space that is conditioned by other performances of ratchetness also within that space.[17] Although more than the individual is considered, Stallings did not discuss collective action.

Cooper reflected on her writings about ratchet feminism and initially described it as "a kind of female friendship forged in the midst of complicated relationships among men, their mothers, and their many women."[18] Cooper also critiqued individualized notions of transgression via ratchetness for their inability to create revolutions.[19] Cooper, Morris, and Boylorn defined ratchet feminism "as critiques of sexism and patriarchy that happen in otherwise 'ratchet' spaces and/or the female-focused friendship that can exist between Black women."[20] In conceptualizing ratchet feminism, they posited it as both a collective and political space. Whereas Stallings and Pickens both positioned ratchetness as political, Cooper et al. used the term *ratchet feminism* to link it to such collective political dimensions.[21] Their ponderings allowed for us to figure out what a ratchet feminism might look like as a political collective force unbeholden to respectability politics.

We build on Black and hip-hop feminist work to define ratchet feminism as a type of feminism that calls for Black women to resist identity politics, be authentic, and occupy spaces of complexity. We position this as a continuation of both Black feminism and hip-hop feminism. Black feminism, hip-hop feminism, and ratchet feminism do complement one another. As such, we felt it would be disadvantageous to position ratchet feminism as a different type of feminism or even one that opposes the other Black feminisms. Ultimately, we frame ratchet feminism as a productive continuation of Black feminism that can be applied to situations outside of popular culture. In this section, we will discuss what we perceive to be the evolving tenets of ratchet feminism: authenticity, critical analyses, complexity, and bridgework.

Tenets of Rachet Feminism

Even though there are no official tenets of ratchet feminism, we believe that McEachern's ratchet framework provides an accurate idea of the main ideas/ tenets of ratchet feminism.[22] Building on McEachern's concepts, we discuss authenticity, critical analysis, complexity, and bridgework as necessary concepts endemic to a ratchet feminist framework and praxis.

Authenticity refers to being oneself no matter the context. This has resistance implications for people, especially Black women. McEachern discussed the importance of authenticity in her case study about organizing a protest at a university.[23] In her example, she details a situation where people did not present themselves as themselves. She stated, "'Who told you you can't dance in public?' I yelled at the gathering of students almost before thinking, 'Y'all done lost ya ratchet!'"[24] Her authenticity is tied to liberation. Within that context, the respectability politics of communities of color and the university atmosphere creates spaces where people have to remove parts of themselves to be accepted by ideologies that were never going to accept them. Authenticity is a form of ratchet feminist resistance that helps Black women resist the trappings of respectability politics.

Next, critical analysis is about examining multiple layers of issues that help to construct and deconstruct our realities. Critical analysis is key to a ratchet feminist politic because it allows one to distinguish between respectability and ratchetness, unpack the layers of meaning associated with respectability and ratchetness, and to imagine ways we can disrupt the respectability/ratchetness binary. Within this framework, critical analysis is a form of living. She states, "I embraced ratchet analysis by employing the codeswitching I had mastered from hearing my mother change her diction when bill collectors would call the house. That codeswitching allowed me to survive countless toxic classroom spaces while still celebrating where I was from. Ratchet eased those feelings of going crazy because I knew that my momma too had had people repeat the way she pronounced 'important' and learned how to say it like them to get what she needed."[25] McEachern uses critical analysis to examine the reality of racist oppression and make decisions in order to survive it. Additionally, ratchet feminism requires critical analysis to radically imagine realities beyond binaries such as ratchet and respectability. We posit that critical analysis for ratchet feminism is key not only as a method to examine texts but also as a way to reclaim agency via a careful assessment of one's oppressive reality. A ratchet critique must not only include the individual but the collective as well. Meaning, that ratchet feminist critique should not be used to ignore or substantiate patriarchy, heterosexism, cissexism, and misogynoir. Rather, our ratchet critical analysis necessarily has to be intersectional.

Complexity, the next tenet, is about making sure we do not subscribe to a singular understanding of liberation. This is a continuation of hip-hop feminism's critique of Black feminism. Morgan critiqued Black feminists' focus on sites where Black women are oppressed because it is also important to understand where Black women found agency.[26] Nash builds on this theoretical focus by discussing how Black women found liberation even within stereotypical portrayals of Black and interracial porn.[27] This focus on complexity is important because it serves as a call and a reminder to other feminists that those whose daily performance does not cosign to the respectability of whiteness are as valuable to the struggle of liberation as everyone else.

The last tenet is bridgework, which involves creating a connection between the ivory tower and their surrounding communities. Black feminists and hip-hop feminists do much of this work; yet, further connection is warranted. Communities can be sites of knowledge production rather than knowledge exploitations. Imagine the possibilities of a communication journal that dedicates itself to publish voices from outside of academia. It would require the academy to seriously interrogate what constitutes scholarship and what constitutes academic language. Despite this, we believe it would be valuable for the academy, and feminism in particular, to create this bridgework that connects the academy to the streets and vice versa.

We listed the presumed tenets of ratchet feminism as a way to provide a framework for our contribution to the ratchetness literature and ratchet feminism. We pay particular attention to critical analysis as a way to unpack and pull apart how we have embodied ratchetness, disrespectability, and ratchet respectability within our social and professional lives. We do this to narratively demonstrate how this process of embodying/resisting/remixing ratchetness and respectability within social and academic contexts appear within the lived everyday context.

Disrespectability and Ratchet Respectability

Black people have not come to a consensus on what ratchetness is or what it should mean. For some, ratchetness is an expression of freedom. For others, ratchetness is an embarrassment for the Black community. A rejection of ratchetness is sometimes in alignment with an intent to maintain respectability.

Because of this penchant for maintaining respectability, the Crunk Feminist Collective came out with serious critiques of respectability that allow us to see ratchetness and respectability in a new(er) lens. Portrayals of ratchetness often produce a visceral reaction by those who have been victimized by the term. When reality television shows such as *Basketball Wives*, *Real Housewives of Atlanta*, and *Love and Hip Hop* became more popular, Michaela Angela Davis started the campaign Bury the Ratchet[28] in which she tried to push back against the negativity of ratchetness because she believes the ratchet rhetoric emotionally harms young Black girls. Because of the negative connotations of the word *ratchet*, we as scholars struggled to accept the term. Despite this, we believe that ratchet feminism can be used to push back against negative notions of ratchetness.

Terms that often accompany ratchet feminism are disrespectability politics and ratchet respectability. Disrespectability politics "urge Black women to have more agency in their race and gender performances while offering a critique of Whitewashed identity politics."[29] The whitewashed identity politics are the performances of respectability within the Black community that encourage people to assimilate into white middle-class notions of properness as an avenue to liberation and prevention of racism. Moreover, disrespectability politics aim to help destabilize the divide between what is considered ratchetness and what is considered respectable.

Lewis helped to further break that divide by asking a simple question at one point in her life.[30] As she stated, "Davis started the campaign in order to 'get the spotlight off the ratchetness and on the successful women in Atlanta.' Well, wait a minute. I wasn't aware that 'ratchet' and 'successful' women were mutually exclusive."[31]

By pointing out the "successful-ratchet" binary, Lewis called out the problematics of it, intimating that ratchet and respectability do not have to conflict with each other. Ergo, ratchet respectability emerged. Coined by Boylorn, ratchet respectability "coalesces ratchet behavior (often linked to race and class) and politics of respectability (often linked to race and gender), claiming that you can be both ratchet and respectable at the same time."[32] Historically, ratchetness and respectability were put at odds with each other specifically to tame the race and gender performances of Black women. Ratchet respectability seeks to problematize the essentialness of this binary by positing what it means to be both ratchet and respectable. In the next section, we discuss how some of these concepts interact in our own lives.

Black Ratchet Imagination and Narrative

The Black ratchet imagination is a concept inspired by Halberstam's concept of queer failure to describe the everyday performances of the failure to be respectable.[33] We apply the Black ratchet imagination as a method through which we construct our narratives. Essentially, using the Black ratchet imagination, we attempt to situate the constructions of narratives as a ratchet performance of academic identity.

In our essay, we construct narratives that are inspired by autoethnographic methods. As such, we center our lives and perspectives as the site of analysis to advance a ratchet perspective on hip-hop, gender, and race. Even though autoethnography has gained more prominence within the field of communication studies and other fields, it is still a marginal methodology. Narrative, especially self-narrative, is still pushed to the margins in comparison to other qualitative methodologies such as interviewing, ethnography, and so forth. We label our narratives as a method for advancing a ratchet perspective and as ratchet itself because centering one's academic self as the site of analysis is still considered unacademic, or ratchet, in some parts of the academy. Self-narratives are ratchet because they disrupt the respectable image of a researcher that maintains the illusion of objectivity by studying others from a presumably objective lens.

Our narratives, functioning as a Black ratchet imagination lens, serves as a deep dive into how ratchetness was embodied and rejected in our lives. We use this Black ratchet narrative lens to highlight our frustrations with and the failure/folly of upholding respectability as an everyday political performance. We also use this lens to demonstrate how each of us try to destabilize the respectability-ratchet binary and come to a more complex understanding of how we mixed the ratchet with the respectable to open ourselves up to additional performances of ratchetness. Methodologically, our narratives serve as the process of undoing and pulling apart and unpacking the meanings of ratchet and respectability in a way that serves to highlight the complicatedness of our lives.

As a methodology, Love says, "The Black ratchet imagination affords researchers a lens that is deeply focused on gaining an in-depth understanding of Black queer youth's identity constructions through purposeful and reflective qualitative research questions that are intersectional, seek to understand youth's agency to reclaim space, refuse binary identities, subvert language, create economic opportunities with new economies, and recognize the precariousness of queer youth of color."[34] Additionally, she contrasts the Black ratchet imagination with narrative inquiry by stating that the former centers youth narratives. We believe there is also something to gain from studying the experiences of researchers from a Black ratchet perspective. To maintain the implication that researchers cannot be viewed from this framework enables the academic whiteness that states that researchers are disembodied vessels of objective truth. Researchers, especially Black queer researchers, are shaped within the ratchet and respectability discourses that impact the Black queer youth she studied. As such, our narratives serve as an example of how researchers can apply the Black ratchet imagination to examine their own lives via narrative analysis.

Narrative Reflections on Ratchetness

Applying a lived experiential lens to the subject of ratchetness and ratchet feminism provides an understanding of how these concepts manifest in our everyday lives. Our reflections on our relationship to ratchetness are created to describe how each author internalized respectability politics in a way that made it difficult to consider various interpretations of ratchetness and gender identity/performance. Our stories demonstrate how we struggled with the oppressive dynamics of our lives, and in essence, our stories represent the messiness of ratch-etness that Stallings discussed as a Black ratchet imagination.[35] In this section, we discuss our relationship to ratchetness, ratchet feminism, and how our ratchet considerations are a combination of our scholastic, cultural, and social lives.

Antonio

Ratchetness and I have a love-hate relationship. My life up until now can be cap-tured as cycles of respectability conditioning/ratchet outbreak/respectability reconditioning and internalization. For many Black people, respectability is a seemingly endemic cultural phenomenon we all deal with. Respectability is both a cultural ideology and cultural performance that attempts to correct the bad behaviors of Black people to show dominant society that we are capable of assim-ilating into white society.[36] Yeah, you heard right. While civil rights history (not the grade school variety) tell us that respectability politics was used as a strat-egy to resist racial oppression,[37] in my experience Black communities have taken that strategy and internalized it as a universal essence and rule. In other words, the heteropatriarchal and heteronormative assumptions built into the respect-ability philosophy were taken as an unproblematized given.

So what did this look like on a lived experiential level? This looked like receiv-ing constant pressure from family members to go to church, refraining from cursing, adopting a heterosexual and masculine performance, internalizing a Christian-supremacist, sexist, and homophobic perspective of the world, and so on. Moreover, our understandings of oppression (racial, sexual, otherwise) were mostly informed by an individualistic and interpersonal framework that often ignored systemic and institutional perspectives. This was the context I lived in when I began perceiving the world and my place within it.

There were times when I would break out of the respectability conditioning. For me, it was an everyday affair that ranged from overt questioning of norms to more overt yelling (which my mother did not tolerate for long). When I would put my hands on my hips and sway them when I walk, I would risk verbal cor-rection by the adults or kids my own age. For my family, breaking gender and sexual norms was tantamount to ratchetness. So, in that way, ratchetness became a contradictory site. Although I would feel great when I attempted to break out of these gendered norms, the breaking out would invite extreme discomfort and ridicule. Due to this, I began to internalize respectability so I could gain respect as well as a sense of (fleeting) protection from normative violence.

Cooper has stated emphatically that respectability will not save us.[38] Although ratchetness overall was discouraged in my household, I realized quickly that for Black boys, it was a specific type of ratchetness. Black boys who were stereo-typically ratchet within the heteronormative box (having kids while still in high school, getting into fights, etc.) were initially judged harshly but then were forgiven. Black boys who were ratchet outside of the heteronormative box (com-ing out of the closet, participating in drag, embodying femininity in any form) were almost never forgiven. This was so extreme to the point that I once noted that Black boys would be judged more harshly if they chose to hold hands rather than guns! Understanding this, I began to see why scholars like McEachern, Love, and Stallings began to connect ratchetness with queerness. In my household, ratchetness became synonymous with queerness.[39]

As a boy, I was given more space and grace to engage in ratchetness. Girls, however, were not encouraged to embody ratchet behaviors at all. I would often witness my female friends and family members conditioned into respectability through shame, slut shaming, ridicule, and social threat. Although my gender performance and sexual orientation were policed to *evince* hegemonic masculinity, my self-identified female counterparts' gender performance and sexuality would often be policed so they could *submit* to hegemonic masculinity. Any type of gender and sexual performance that would perceive them as "ho-ish" was considered shameful and deserving of ostracization. The point being that not only would I witness this respectability conditioning, I would also be affected by it via internalizing this normative gender and sexual ideology. Even though I unlearned this ideology (at least academically), the specter of respectability still haunts me, especially when I encounter performances of ratchetness.

Two years ago, a Twitter controversy occurred between a conservative white female commentator, Stephanie Hamill, and hip-hop artist Cardi B. Hamill retweeted the hip-hop video "Twerk" that City Girls (a hip-hop duo) and Cardi B produced.[40] Under the video, Stephanie asserted, "In the Era of #meToo how exactly does this empower women?"

After seeing Hamill's tweet, I decided to watch the "Twerk" video. I had heard the song on the radio and was excited to see the music video for a variety of reasons. First, I was familiar with Cardi B. McEachern recently discussed how Cardi B represents a form of ratchetness that extends understandings of Black women's liberation that is untethered from respectability.[41] In her essay, she essentially reinterpreted the social media activities and mediated performances of Cardi B as a form of self-care and self-defense instead of her simply reinforcing Black women's stereotypes. I looked at the video with those things in mind.

To give a brief description of the video, the City Girls issued a twerking challenge to find the world's greatest twerker. There are clips of the challenge call juxtaposed with intermittent clips of Black women twerking in a variety of places. It is also juxtaposed with clips of what sounds like a white male announcer saying twerking is "sexual and inappropriate." In analyzing how the clips are put together, it is clear that the video was not only a challenge to find the world's greatest twerker, but it was also a direct challenge to those who deem twerking shameful and disgraceful.

What stood out to me in this controversy was coverage claiming that twerking is a disgrace toward women. I immediately thought this was the same racist, sexist burden that has been and continues to be placed on Black women. First, the idea that twerking is disgraceful is largely situated within a sex-negative view of feminism. These things were going in my mind while I watched the first part of the video.

Twerking requires people to shake their buttocks in rhythmic, strategic, and intentional ways. Sometimes the focus is not on the buttocks but on the thrusting of the hips backward. Regardless of the focus, twerk performers assume a low squatting position when conducting this dance. Considering this, twerking has a love-hate relationship within and outside of the Black community. Because the dance calls attention to the buttock region and because the dance is sometimes performed by Black women (and sometimes Black men) wearing revealing clothing, some believe that twerking is a form of internalized sexism where Black women portray demoralizing Black female tropes, the Jezebel in particular.

Next, an airplane descends onto an island and then switches quickly to a scene sounded by a beat. A very familiar beat that got me seriously bobbing my head in my car on the way to work. The scenes were presented with Black women twerking on the island in various poses. Some in a somewhat traditional pose, others were twerking on top of other Black women twerking, and one in particular was twerking while hanging from a flagpole.

In terms of ratchetness, from my experience I could definitely see how this video could represent a form of ratchetness. Twerking is often considered a form of ratchetness that reinforces damaging stereotypes of Black women as being sexually loose, hypersexual, and amoral. Cardi B showing up in a skin-tight tiger suit twerking on a boat does nothing to quell this stereotype. Due to this, my mind was split into pro-ratchetness and anti-ratchetness. First, I believed that these twerking scenes were a bit much. I mean, twerking sideways on a flagpole? Was that necessary? Even though I was very familiar with third-wave, hip-hop feminist articulations of Black female liberation, I was stuck wondering if these performances were pushing the line between individual/collective liberation and Black female objectification. Were the close-up scenes of the women's bodies contributing to articulations of agency, or contributing to misogynoir-based oppression on the meso- and macro levels? Misogynoir specifically is a derivative of misogyny that refers to the systemic hatred and oppression that affects Black women.

These questions are a conglomeration of my love-hate relationship to ratchetness. As a child, I was essentially respectable in public but ratchet at home. From doing a lot of "girl-dancing" (as we called it) as a kid and not caring, one could see my childhood as the beginning of a liberating ratchet identity crafted by a young Black boy who was becoming more aware of his queer identity. If helicopter parenting and shame did not intervene, my private ratchet behavior could very well make it outside the small spaces comprising my small two-bedroom apartment I called home. That intervention essentially shamed me into a more respectable gender identity performance where I stayed in the closet and failed to adopt a more hegemonic masculine performance.

When looking at the music video, I am reminded of how I was shamed into a heteromasculine performance of gender identity and simultaneously break from said performances in small ways. Resultantly, I could see how I possibly engage in a ratchet respectability politics following the childhood I had. Specifically, I am compelled to think about the love-hate relationship I have with ratchetness and what that entails. Exactly, why is it a love-hate relationship? Do I really hate ratchetness? Perhaps I want to regain the "don't give a fuck" attitude I had in my early childhood. But can ratchetness also become its own prison? Do I have to go twerk in the streets and reinforce the lascivious Black gay male stereotype to obtain ratchet freedom?

I wish I could end this narrative with a triumphant display of victory. The formerly suppressed Black queer boy has now owned his ratchetness and has shunned respectability! You will not find such an ending to these short narrative segments. Indeed, what I have been trying to accomplish nowadays is a ratchet respectability performance. As stated previously, Boylorn suggests that we can combine ratchetness and respectability into a tenuous and not completely harmonious relationship that does not put the two at odds within an unnecessary binary.[42] Meaning, I should dive into the messiness of ratchetness and my life. Now I'm more concerned with how I can combine my personal, social, and academic selves in a way that disturbs the ratchet-respectable binary.

So what does it mean for a Black gay man in the academy to engage in a rachet respectability politics in a disruptive manner? Currently, I believe it is about keeping it real. It is about not hiding the ratchet. It is about not hiding the respectability. It is about holding these two things together. It is about bringing the young twerking boy and the well-spoken academic together in cooperation and non-opposition and recognizing that these two do not have to oppose each other. I currently do this in the classrooms I teach. Although I do embody some of the respectability norms by encouraging my students to call me Dr. Spikes and respecting the common social boundaries between professors and students, I exhibit ratchetness via radical honesty in both serious and comedic ways. An example of this occurred before schools closed nationwide in the United States.

During a particular week in March, the nation was slowly reckoning with the potential threat COVID-19 was going to be in the United States. However, decision leaders were still unsure if they needed to close down schools and businesses. Two days before Davidson College decided to close down, my class was performing their speeches. I called one of the students to go and do their speech in front of the class. He was hesitant to go and I wondered why. He then communicated to me in a somewhat hushed tone that he wanted to go the next class day because he was trying to "get over a cough." Considering the warning signs we were getting from officials and the guidelines I personally gave them, I was momentarily beside myself. Before I could come up with a more respectable way of reckoning with this, I blurted out, "I know you did not just come in here and say you got a cough in the middle of a pandemic!" He chuckled nervously and continued to insist that he wasn't well enough to do the speech. I agreed and allowed him to complete his speech on what would be the last day of in-person classes.

For some reading my narrative, this response may be seen as problematic. And I am not going to lie, it might be because of the potential to embarrass the student. However, I view this as me implementing ratchetness into an academic space where it is not expected by engaging in radical honesty. At that moment, I did not care about potentially destroying the academic disembodied image I procured during graduate school. It was only after that moment I gave that image some thought. I was compelled to judge the moment as either appropriately ratchet or inappropriately unprofessional. But then, I decided to let the moment be. As Love and Stallings stated, ratchetness is not meant to be cut and clean but messy.[43] I would also add that ratchet respectability is something that should be seen as messy, too. Hip-hop has taught me, if anything, that freedom can be found in the messiness of life.

Danette

My relationship with ratchet is rooted in my feminists studies and research. To be transparent, I do not watch reality TV, keep up with all of the latest hip-hop videos, and I most certainly do not pay attention to the twitter beefs between rappers. My awareness of what goes on in the world of hip-hop comes from having a college-aged son who wants his mom to look remotely cool in front of her students.

My first connection to ratchetness began when I went to see *Girls Trip* (2017). This film depicts four Black women who try to have it all but never quite obtain it all. I first went to see the movie with my then seventy-seven-year-old mother. Returning home, she remarked that one of the characters was ratchet. After getting over the shock that my mom knew the term *ratchet* and used it correctly in a sentence, I asked her to explain why. She indicated that she saw the character's sexual promiscuity as trashy and her language was ghetto. In some ways, I felt the same way my mother did and felt that I was becoming my mama at that moment. Therefore, I had to take some time to reflect on where this judgment was coming from and had an important self-realization.

I believe it's important to briefly describe my upbringing. I was raised in the church. Although my father passed when I was seven, he was still a pastor. The values and rituals did not die with him, as they were a part of the family culture. I was raised in a home where respectability politics was queen. Higginbotham brings the politics of respectability to light with her book *Righteous Discontent: The Women's Movement in the Black Baptist Church, 1880–1920*. It was a push by Black women's church movements to present oneself in an accepting way to white people in order to avoid criticism and to push back against negative stereotypes which Patricia Hill Collins calls controlling images. Harris states, "To describe the work of the Women's Convention of the Black Baptist Church during the Progressive Era, she [Higginbotham] specifically referred to African American's promotion of temperance, cleanliness of person and property, thrift, polite manners, and sexual purity."[44] It was important to present oneself as well put-together in order to avoid negative judgments from white people. This was both reflected in presentation and performance. By presentation, I mean I could not wear shorts, skirts, or dresses that were more than one inch above the knee, I could not show cleavage, my hair was always pressed and curled, and nothing was too tight.

With regard to performance, I was told to smile, speak proper English, always say yes, no, please, and thank you, and to do well in school. Although I loved music and wanted to listen to rap, my mother and grandmother did not like the way the lyrics objectified and demoralized Black women and strongly opposed the way the women were presented in videos. However, I was allowed to listen to Queen Latifah because her music was empowering to young Black women.

Like most teens, I found ways to listen to what my mother deemed forbidden. Although I loved jamming to "U.N.I.T.Y.," Queen Latifah could take me only so far on my musical journey.[45] So I found ways to listen to MC Lyte, Foxy Brown, Salt-N-Pepa, and other rap artists. By the time I was a junior in high school, my mother loosened the reins and I was allowed to listen to other rap artists' radio version of songs. There were still dress code restrictions, but hey, I got my music.

As previously mentioned, although respectability was a concept that was not specifically named, it was definitely enforced in my upbringing. I convinced myself that if I stepped out of line in any way, I was going to be headed down a path of destruction and despair and unconsciously became an embodiment of the politics of respectability. For better and for worse, I was also raised to be a "strong Black woman."

I was introduced to respectability politics as a theoretical term when I read Collins's book *Black Feminist Thought: Knowledge, Consciousness and the Politics of Empowerment*.[46] I was also able to better understand stereotypes, or what Collins calls controlling images. As a Black woman, I realized that there was an imaginary box that I was placed into by dominant society, and I began to understand how these images controlled my life. Being raised within the margins of respectability politics, I took on the role of a strong Black woman. I carried the burden of my household on my shoulder. I maintained a smiled in public and kept my emotions to myself. God forbid I let people see me cry; that would have meant I was weak. Being strong was a mantle that I gladly carried, perhaps because I did not know any better.

I understood Black feminist thought was a theoretical framework to analyze the multifaceted lives of Black women while acknowledging that our experiences create a collective consciousness. As I grew as a scholar, I felt like that teenage girl wanting to listen to hip-hop but not being permitted to do so. That is when I delved into hip-hop feminism and thought I would leave Black feminist thought behind, adopting a new feminist perspective through hip-hop feminism. Hip-hop feminism provided a platform for young Black female intellectuals to discuss, analyze, and resolve the contradictions of their enjoying sexist, misogynistic, and objectifying music.[47] Hip-hop feminism is more than examining the ways lyrics and videos represent and influence women of color. It examines and dismantles concepts of toxic masculinity within the Black community, it explores the everyday lived experiences of Black women that help to create our identities, and it also celebrates Black female sexuality.

I see hip-hop feminism as a more inclusive way to research and write about the varied life experiences of women of color, and in the research and writing lies social justice and change. There are various similarities between hip-hop feminism and Black feminism. Some scholars consider hip-hop feminism a continuation of Black feminist thought.[48] Peoples indicates that hip-hop feminists are influenced by hip-hop culture and uses many of the same elements expressed in the Black feminist movement.[49] Morgan suggests that hip-hop feminism fills in the gaps of Black feminist thought and creates a space for young voices.[50] As the Crunk Feminist Collective exclaims, it "ain't ya mama's feminism," which suggests that hip-hop feminism is altogether different than Black feminism.[51]

I would argue that hip-hop feminism should be added to the canon of Black feminism(s), a tenet of Black feminist thought is that it is fluid. Collins states, "Neither Black feminist thought as a critical social theory nor Black feminist practice can be static; as social conditions change, so must the knowledge and practices designed to resist them."[52] As such, I believe that hip-hop has adapted and adjusted to the changing and altering lives of Black women throughout time. I see ratchet feminism as adjusting to the lives of Black women as well.

I also see hip-hop feminism as taking a holistic approach to understanding the complexities of women of color. As mentioned in the Crunk Feminist Collective, hip-hop feminism came of age post–civil rights movement and grew up as hip-hop music evolved from a musical genre to a culture.[53] Pough suggests that hip-hop is a way of life; therefore, those who claim to be hip-hop feminists correlate their identities and ideologies to both the music and the culture.[54] Hip-hop feminism provides a way to examine societal oppressions and offers a way to challenge the sexist ideologies within hip-hop culture itself.

Hip-hop music was created as a way to deal with multiple oppressions. Peoples argues that hip-hop originated as a way to contend with marginalization.[55] It was an outlet designed to cope with the politics of race and class using poetic lyrics that were set to electronic beats. Chang positions hip-hop as a cultural bridge and a means for young people to analyze themselves and the world around them.[56] Hip-hop feminism tries to stay true to the hip-hop culture by being open to non-academic ideologies, staying connected to the hip-hop community, and challenging societal oppressions.

I was torn between Black feminism and hip-hop feminism. Although several scholars such as Cooper and Stallings found that they could be *both/and*, I felt as if I was betraying my academic and personal roots.[57] It took a while to accept that I could have a balance between the two. As my research broadened, I stopped thinking about Black feminist thought and hip-hop feminism as yin and yang and concluded that when it comes to the production of knowledge by Black women, whether it is hip-hop or otherwise, it is Black feminist thought.

Along came ratchet feminism and yet again an internal struggle emerged. I identified with its feminist concepts as well. From that struggle evolved conversations and discussions with different scholars to get a better understanding of ratchet feminism. It was in this research and discussion that I chose to add ratchet feminism to my canon of Black feminism(s). Durham calls hip-hop her homeplace, in reference to hooks's concept of homeplace, "a physical, cultural, and intellectual space where she makes sense of being in the world as an outsider-within."[58] I see my feminist homeplace as fluid, one that moves betwixt and between Black, hip-hop, and ratchet, one where I can be as respectable or as radical or ratchet as I need and/or want to be.

In this essay, we articulated four tenets of ratchet feminism. The one I think rings true to all feminist perspectives is bridgework. It is essential for scholars to reach into the community and help bring forth the voices of those who are marginalized. Many Black scholars identifying as Black, hip-hop, and/or ratchet feminists are currently doing the labor. More needs to be done. I am not asking my sisters in the academy to do more work; I applaud and honor the work that you/we do. Rather, I am asking the academy to better acknowledge and highlight the bridgework that we do and to open its doors to the possibilities of ratchet respectability.

Examples of Ratchet Respectability

Our contribution to this research centers on our belief that ratchet respectability can be applied to music, television, reality programming, *and* to mainstream and political contexts. In other words, ratchet respectability, though firmly planted in popular culture analysis, can also be utilized to examine political and sports discourses that center the lives of Black women. Two examples or representatives of ratchet respectability outside popular culture are Congresswoman Maxine Waters and tennis superstar Serena Williams. An example within popular culture would be the character played by actress and comedienne Tiffany Haddish.

You may recall Representative Waters's performance on the house floor during the May 2018 House Financial Services Committee meeting. Senator Mike Kelly suggested that certain individuals in the House were trying to divide America by wrongly calling the practices of the automobile industry discriminatory, thus not making America great. While trying to respond, Waters was interrupted by Kelly and reprimanded by the Speaker of the House. Waters responds by saying, "No, I will not yield! No, I will not yield!" As she continues to speak, Waters was corrected again and asked to yield. In doing so, Waters refers to the president as dishonorable and she states, "Having said that, I reserve the balance of my time and no, I do not yield, not one second to you, not one second, not one second to you."[59] Some people said that this was behavior that was not becoming of a woman, particularly one who holds an office in the United States government. Others might have deemed her actions as ratchet. We believe Waters's actions could have been seen as ratchet based on others defining her as disrespectful. Therefore, we interpret her actions through the lens of ratchet respectability. This move shows Waters has agency in her behavior, pushes back against the whitewashed identity politics of what has been deemed acceptable behavior for Black women, and recognizes the complexity of Black women's standpoints. Waters is a respectable congresswoman who exercised her freedom to express herself. In doing so, she showed anger, an emotion tied to the angry Black woman stereotype,[60] which makes it difficult for Black women to show a range of emotions.

Another example of ratchet respectability outside of popular culture is Serena Williams. Upset by a call made by the chair umpire, Williams threw her racquet to the ground and questioned the judge's call. She essentially accused the judge of being sexist, stating that her actions were comparable to, and no worse than, her male counterparts who were not reprimanded for their behavior in questioning and arguing with judges. Williams received a lot of negative attention over her actions. Again, people might have seen her actions as ratchet, definitely not representative of a respectable Black woman. Yet, her actions were based on her own agency. Williams did not yield to a person in "authority," thus contradicting the way white America defines presentable behavior for Black women.

We also look at the characters Tiffany Haddish plays because she has been questioned by members of the Black community for taking roles that do not depict Black women in a positive light and perpetuate negative stereotypes. In the online magazine Urban Belle, Haddish responds to people who have called the roles she plays stereotypical and ratchet. She states, "I feel like all facets deserve to be seen—from the doctors to the janitors to the baby mamas to the side chicks." Haddish goes on to say, "It's funny because people are like, 'Oh, Tiffany Haddish is ratchet.' No, I'm your typical chick from the hood. And as ratchet as I might talk, or people might think I carry myself, I am making a living portraying myself."[61] We agree with Haddish in that there should be nonjudgmental representations of all Black women in media. Not only do these representations need to be in the media, but we believe that Black women should be allowed to perform who they are, which often entails complicated transitions between the spaces of respectability and ratchet, because it is okay to "be both ratchet and respectable at the same time."[62] Yet we know there is often not that space.

As Black scholars, we experienced transitions in our comfort with the word *ratchet*. Because of its negative connotations, ratchet is a term that we, as previously diehard–Black feminist, respectability-politics-preaching scholars, have had difficulty accepting. Consequently, we each have had to come to terms with the word *ratchet*. Essentially, we analyzed the "ratchet" in our individual lives and eventually embraced a ratchet feminist politic.

Conclusion

Overall, ratchet feminism is a continuous concept that has roots in Black and hip-hop feminism. We have defined ratchet feminism as a form of feminism that calls for Black women to push back against identity politics, be authentic, and occupy spaces of complexity. To add to the discussion of ratchet feminism, we discussed what we see as evolving tenets of ratchet feminism, and in doing so, we explore the concept of ratchet respectability as an application of ratchet feminism. When we consider the historical evolution of feminism, we see ratchet feminism as both continuing it and pushing back against its flow. It expands on the complexity of Black women's lives and pushes back against common notions of what feminists supposedly can and cannot do. We encourage feminist scholars to engage with ratchet feminism as a feminist framework that continues the work of Black and hip-hop feminism and as a unique framework that further complicates how we understand intersectional feminism.

Discussion Questions

1 How do you think the proposed ratchet feminist framework connects with the Black ratchet imagination?
2 Look at the narratives of the authors in this chapter. What are some points of connections and disconnections you see? What are the sources of those connections/disconnections?
3 How does one begin to disrupt the ratchet-respectable binary?
4 What are some examples of ratchet feminism you find in your life (media, politics, family life, etc.)?

Try This!

Refer back to the examples brought forth in this chapter of ratchet feminism within politics, sports, and popular culture. Locate other potential examples of Black people embodying ratchet feminism in the political, pop cultural, sports, or academic contexts. When you locate your example, examine those examples with the following questions:

1 What about this person signals to you that they are practicing ratchet feminism?
2 How does this person combine elements of respectability and ratchetness?

3 How does this person engage in critical analysis and bridgework into their potential ratchet feminist performance? (You can look at past tweets or recordings of the person.)

Notes

1 Emmanuel Hudson and Phillip Hudson, "Ratchet Girl Anthem," recorded circa 2012, Soundcloud.
2 John Ortved, "Ratchet: The Rap Insult That Became an Insult," The Cut, April 11, 2013, https://www.thecut.com/2013/04/ratchet-the-rap-insult-that-became-a-compliment.html.
3 Ibid.
4 Anthony Mandigo, "Do the Ratchet," 1999, from *Ratchet Fight in the Ghetto.*
5 Ibid.
6 LL Cool J, "Ratchet," published April 2013, track 12 from *Authentic,* Savory Records, digital download.
7 Nicki Minaj feat Chris Brown, "Right by My Side," published March 2012, track 8 from *Pink Friday: Roman Reloaded,* Conway Studios, digital download.
8 Juicy J feat 2 Chainz & Lil Wayne, "Bandz a Make Her Dance," published September 2012, track 14 from *Stay Trippy,* Columbia, digital download.
9 Ibid.
10 Brittany C. Cooper, "(Un)clutching My Mother's Pearls, or Ratchetness and the Residue of Respectability," The Crunk Feminist Collective, December 31, 2012. http://www.crunkfeministcollective.com/2012/12/31/unclutching-my-mothers-pearls-or-ratchetness-and-the-residue-of-respectability/?fbclid=IwAR1S_j7uLEZfxh_jAkOm_Uo5yWIJo-hodvkG5cXknYu8KKOsUVM2vulgK60.
11 Ibid.
12 Ibid.
13 LaMonda H. Stallings, "Hip Hop and the Black Ratchet Imagination," *Palimpsest: A Journal of Women, Gender and the Black International* 2 (2013): 135–139.
14 Ibid., 136.
15 Theri A. Pickens, "Shoving Aside the Politics of Respectability: Black Women, Reality TV, and the Ratchet Performance," *Women and Performance: A Journal of Feminist Theory* 25 (2015): 44.
16 Bettina L. Love, "A Ratchet Lens: Black Queer Youth, Agency, Hip Hop, and the Black Ratchet Imagination," *Educational Researcher* 46 (2017): 539–547.
17 Stallings, "Hip Hop."
18 Cooper, *(Un)clutching My Mother's Pearls.*
19 Ibid.
20 Brittney C. Cooper, Susana. M. Morris, and Robin M. Boylorn, introduction to *The Crunk Feminist Collection,* ed. Brittany C. Cooper, Susana M. Morris, and Robin M. Boylorn (New York: Feminist Press, 2017), 211–214.
21 Stallings, "Hip Hop"; Pickens, "Shoving Aside the Politics"; Cooper et al., "Introduction."
22 Montinique D. McEachern, "Respect My Ratchet: The Liberatory Consciousness of Ratchetness," *Departures in Critical Qualitative Research* 6 (2017): 78–89.
23 Ibid.
24 Ibid., 79.
25 Ibid., 84–85.

26 Joan Morgan, *When Chicken Heads Come Home to Roost: A Hip-Hop Feminist Breaks It Down* (New York: Simon & Schuster, 1999).

27 Jennifer C. Nash, *The Black Body in Ecstasy: Reading Race, Reading Pornography* (Durham, NC: Duke University Press, 2014).

28 Hannington Dia, "Michaela Angela Davis Looks to 'Bury the Ratchet,'" Newsone, December 11, 2012, https://newsone.com/2100749/michaela-angela-davis-bury-the -ratchet/.

29 Cooper et al., "Introduction," 213.

30 Heidi R. Lewis, "Exhuming the Ratchet before It's Buried," The Feminist Wire, January 7, 2013, https://thefeministwire.com/2013/01/exhuming-the-ratchet-before -its-buried/.

31 Ibid., 2.

32 Cooper et al., "Introduction," 213.

33 Judith Halberstam, *The Queer Art of Failure* (Durham, NC: Duke University Press, 2011).

34 Love, "A Ratchet Lens," 541.

35 Stallings, "Hip Hop."

36 Evelyn B. Higginbotham, *Righteous Discontent: The Women's Movement in the Black Church, 1880–1920* (Cambridge, MA: Harvard University Press, 1994).

37 Patricia Hill Collins, *Black Feminist Thought: Knowledge, Consciousness, and the Politics of Empowerment* (New York: Routledge, 2000).

38 Cooper, *(Un)clutching My Mother's Pearls.*

39 McEachern, "Respect My Ratchet"; Love, "A Ratchet Lens"; Stallings, "Hip Hop."

40 City Girls feat Cardi B, "Twerk," published January 2019, track 4 from *Girl Code*, Quality Control, YouTube video.

41 McEachern, "Respect My Ratchet."

42 Robin Boylorn, "Love, Hip Hop, and Ratchet Respectability (Something Like a Review)," Crunk Feminist Collective, September 10, 2015, http://www.crunk feministcollective.com/2015/09/10/love-hip-hop-and-ratchet-respectability -something-like-a-review/.

43 Love, "A Ratchet Lens"; Stallings, "Hip Hop."

44 Paisely Jane Harris, "Gatekeeping and Remaking: The Politics of Respectability in African American Women's History and Black Feminism," *Journal of Women's History* 6 (2003): 213

45 Queen Latifah, "U.N.I.T.Y," published November 1993, track 12 from *Black Reign*, Motown Records, CD.

46 Collins *Black Feminist Thought.*

47 Morgan, *When Chicken Heads Come Home*; Whitney A. Peoples, "Under Construction: Identifying Foundations of Hip-Hop Feminism and Exploring Bridges between Black Second Wave and Hip-Hop Feminisms," *Meridians: Feminism, Race, Transnationalism* 8, no. 1 (2008): 19–52; Gwendolyn D. Pough, *Check It while I Wreck It: Black Womanhood, Hip-Hop Culture and the Public Sphere* (Boston: Northeastern University Press, 2004).

48 Peoples, "Under Construction"; Pough, *Check It.*

49 Peoples, "Under Construction," 26.

50 Morgan, *When Chicken Heads Come Home.*

51 Brittney C. Cooper, Susana. M. Morris, and Robin M. Boylorn, "The Crunk Feminist Collective Mission Statement," in *The Crunk Feminist Collection*, ed. Brittany C. Cooper, Susana M. Morris, and Robin M. Boylorn (New York: Feminist Press, 2017), xix–xxi.

52 Patricia Hill Collins, *Black Feminist Thought: Knowledge, Consciousness, and the Politics of Empowerment* (New York: Routledge, 2009), 43.

53 Ibid.

54 Pough, *Check It.*

55 Peoples, "Under Construction."

56 Jeff Chang, *Can't Stop Won't Stop: A History of the Hip Hop Generation* (New York: Picador, 2005).

57 Cooper, *(Un)clutching My Mother's Pearls*; Stallings, "Hip Hop."

58 Aisha S. Durham, *Home with Hip Hop Feminism: Performances in Culture and Communication* (New York: Peter Lang, 2014), 25.

59 CSPAN, *Representatives Waters and Kelly Clash on House Floor*, May 8, 2018, https://www.c-span.org/video/?c4729111/representatives-waters-kelly-clash-house-floor

60 Patricia Hill Collins, *On Intellectual Activism* (Philadelphia: Temple University Press, 2012).

61 Amanda Anderson-Niles, "Tiffany Haddish Claps Back at Those Who Feel She Is Ratchet + Plays Stereotypical Characters," Urban Belle, August 1, 2018, https://urbanbellemag.com/2018/08/tiffany-haddish-movies-ratchet/2/.

62 Cooper et al., "Introduction," 213.

24

Afrofuturist Lessons in Persistence

•••••••••••••••••••••

JENNA N. HANCHEY

Introduction: Feminist Exhaustion and Persistence

We are tired. We, feminist scholars of communication—women of color and white women, transwomen and ciswomen, differently and normatively abled women, women of all sexualities, women of multiple nationalities—are tired. Some of us are more tired than others. Our exhaustion is both bodily and psychological. We labor under patriarchal, heteronormative, and transphobic conditions at home, in the workplace, on social media, in public, and in private. These affect us differentially, and some of us are particularly weighted down by the burden of navigating the flows of power constantly pressing against us. To different extents, feminists feel continually pressed because to live as a feminist is to oppose the pressure of hegemonic cisheterosexism. Sara Ahmed thus defines oppression in terms of this feeling of pressure, of being pressed: "Oppression: how we feel pressed into things, by things, because of who we are recognized as being."[1] We are tired—*exhausted*—because to live as feminists means to constantly persist against the pressing forces of normativity.

In this essay, I ask, How should feminists persist in the face of the constant pressure of conditions ever more hostile to our being and becoming? This question is worth attending to because there is no answer immediately forthcoming in popular cultural narratives. No matter how much we labor, liberation from our contemporary circumstances seems hopeless. The news is bleak; society's visions of the future more so. The only question that popular media seem to have left open is this: Which dystopia will we find ourselves in? We are implicitly told we will eventually land in either *The Handmaid's Tale* or *Children of Men*, *The Hunger Games* or *Divergent*. We have only to prepare for the worst, whichever worst it is, for there is no saving ourselves now.

But just as Chela Sandoval recognized in the white, Western postmodern frenzy over subject fragmentation, the bleakness of contemporary circumstances is not new for many feminists and feminist scholars.[2] Marginalized folks of color and those from the Global South have been persisting under conditions where domination tries to persuade that they have no future for centuries.[3] Similarly, feminist and queer communication scholars of color and those from the Global South have written extensively about how to prevail against circumstances that marginalize,[4] erase,[5] degrade, and enrage[6]—persisting against the bleakness of disciplinary futures.

White feminist communication scholars like myself would do well to learn from those women and queer folks of color who have labored for so long to imagine new worlds if we are to persist under such conditions of hostility to feminist being and becoming. And if we are to be ethical in our persistence, we must acknowledge their contributions as more than simply influences; they are constitutive copresences that make possible our knowledge production.[7] In particular, white and Western feminist communication scholars must theorize through what María Lugones terms an interactive acknowledgment of difference, letting the wisdom of feminists and queer scholars of color pervade throughout our engagement with persistence and fundamentally affect how we envision our futures.[8] As Bernadette Marie Calafell argues, "Looking at our contemporary political and cultural landscapes and how they directly inform our academic livelihoods, now more than ever we need to reevaluate our feminist commitments or create new ones."[9] Feminist communication scholars should center feminist and queer of color and Global South theorizing in order to survive and thrive in our contemporary context, where we have already been worn down by (hetero)sexism, racism, ethnocentrism, capitalism, hate, and greed.

In this essay, I draw lessons in persistence from one of the most fruitful perspectives for imagining and enacting liberatory futures: Afrofuturism.[10] Afrofuturism is a field of creative production and study that centers African and African diasporic experience. By focusing imagined futures on and around Blackness, Afrofuturism provides hope that the world can and will be different. Hope may sometimes be seen as a defense mechanism against loss of control, or a way of reconciling oneself to unchangeable circumstances and the futility of struggle. Here, I use hope in a different sense, drawing from the thought of Sara Ahmed: "Hope is not at the expense of struggle but animates a struggle; hope gives us a sense that there is a point to working things out, working things through. Hope does not only or always point toward the future, but carries us through when the terrain is difficult, when the path we follow makes it harder to proceed. Hope is behind us when we have to work for something to be possible."[11] Hope in this sense is what allows us to continue to struggle now and provides the catalyst for remembering that it is our *right* to write ourselves into the future,[12] even when we are told that the future will not be for us. Afrofuturism imagines the future in ways that provide hope, thus sustaining our persistence in the present.

I engage with Afrofuturism as a white woman because the futures that are being created by women and queer people of color, such as in Afrofuturisms, Latinxfuturisms, and Africanfuturisms, are the images of the future that we *all* need. At the same time, I recognize that these are not my dreams to either imagine or necessarily proclaim. What I highlight here, then, is what these imaginings do and why all feminist scholars of communication need Afrofuturism. White cisgender and heteronormative women in particular need to listen to the radical futures that are being imagined and labor to support the actualization of these new worlds.

Imagination is not often considered the realm of the communication discipline, as communication scholars typically focus on the temporal realms of past and present. If they do engage with the future, it is often under the umbrella of the predictive rather than the fictive. However, Afrofuturist scholar Ytasha L. Womack argues that the work of imagination is fundamental to persistence: "The resilience of the human spirit lies in our ability to imagine. Imagination is a tool of resistance."[13] Afrofuturism provides lessons in imagination that are necessary for feminist scholars of communication to persist, resist, and constitute more just futures. In the remainder of this essay, I first define Afrofuturism and explain its importance to feminist studies of communication. I then describe three particular lessons Afrofuturism holds for feminist persistence: change is inevitable, but it can be shaped; roots are vital to our futures; and liberation must be for all.[14] Finally, I conclude with a call to engage Afrofuturism in both our research work and everyday lives.

The Afrofuturist Imperative for Feminist Communication Studies

Afrofuturism serves to "excavate and create original narratives of identity, technology, and the future and offer critiques of the promises of prevailing theories of technoculture."[15] Afrofuturism thus disputes the teleological assumptions of white, Western mainstream technoculture while providing alternative visions of the future that are necessarily based in radical liberation simply by being built around African and African diasporic subjects. By imagining through ontologies and epistemologies of Blackness, Afrofuturism fundamentally refigures our futures by averring that those not considered human by Western modernity are fully realized and liberated subjects,[16] and connecting the past to the future by interweaving spirituality and nature in and through technological ideologies.

As Afrofuturism connects the past to the future and the natural to the technological, "Afrofuturism may be characterized as a program for recovering the histories of counter-futures created in a century hostile to Afro-diasporic projection and as a space within which the critical work of manufacturing tools capable of intervention within the current political dispensation may be undertaken."[17] That is, by imagining alternative futures that draw as much from traditional Africana spirituality as from technological innovation, Afrofuturism also intervenes in the present. Many Afrofuturist creators and scholars thus see Afrofuturism as activist by its very nature,[18] believing that "just as the actions in the present dictate the future, imagining the future can change the present."[19] Since "Afrofuturism unchains the mind,"[20] the practice of imagining radically just futures opens new avenues for strategy, action, and collectivity in the present.

To imagine futures that center Africana ontology and epistemology, Afrofuturism fundamentally refigures ideologies of "the human." Drawing from Frantz Fanon and decolonial theorists, Sylvia Wynter makes the powerful argument that the white, Western, patriarchal conceptualization of the human—what she terms as Man—has long been overrepresenting himself (gendering intended) as *the human as such*.[21] Man, rather than incorporating all versions of what humanity can and does mean, instead presumes his version of humanity to be universal. This presumption is deeply violent; by configuring a subsection of humanity as the human itself, "black subjects, along with indigenous populations, the colonized, the insane, the poor, the disabled, and so on serve as limit cases by which Man can demarcate himself as the universal human."[22] Afrofuturism works off the basis of this theoretical understanding to create worlds where all people are understood as human.

The Afrofuturist project is thus necessarily feminist.[23] Within the system of Man, it is impossible to extricate the violence done to Black bodies from that done to feminine bodies, as well as to the colonized, the poor, or the otherwise aberrant.[24] As such, Black liberation can never be fully realized without concomitant projects of liberation from patriarchy, colonialism, heternormativity, cisnormativity, and capitalism. Afrofuturist philosophy thus is rooted in Black feminist thought and draws from it to imagine fully realized feminist futures. Womack goes so far as to argue that "Afrofuturism as a movement itself may be the first in which black women creators are credited for the power of their imaginations and are equally represented as the face of the future and the shapers of the future."[25]

Lisa A. Flores avers that racial rhetorical criticism must be an imperative in rhetorical study;[26] similarly, I argue that Afrofuturism should be an imperative in feminist studies of communication. Afrofuturism can aid feminist communication scholars in persisting under our contemporary circumstances by disputing the normative science fiction futures being written by white, patriarchal technocapitalists. Kodwo Eshun argues that this not only constrains our ideas of what the future can be but also acts to *actualize* certain visions of the future: those based on whiteness, patriarchy, and class oppression.[27]

Science fiction and market capitalism are often two sides of the same coin.[28] When our field of vision and imaginations are filled with dystopian extrapolations that sexism, racism, colonialism, and capitalism will continue to rule the world, transforming it into a hellscape for everyone on the underside of modernity,[29] the work being done is more than predictive. According to Eshun, "a subtle oscillation between prediction and control is being engineered in which successful or powerful descriptions of the future have an increasing ability to draw us towards them, to command us to make them flesh."[30] That is, the visions being produced and communicated about the future "preprogram the present" in such a way as to make those visions *more tenable*.[31] If this is the case, then feminist communication scholars have an imperative to communicate futures in such a way as to advocate for justice and liberation for all. We *must* engage with Afrofuturism. Indeed, as Flores writes about the imperative for racial rhetorical criticism, "I cannot imagine why we would not."[32]

Three Afrofuturist Lessons for Feminist Communication Scholars

In this section, I detail three important lessons that Afrofuturism holds for feminist communication scholars, lessons that can help us persist under contemporary political and cultural conditions that seem hopeless. Drawing primarily from the work and legacy of Octavia Butler, Africanfuturist novels of Nnedi Okorafor, concept albums and accompanying films of Janelle Monae, and the poetic "speculative documentary" *M Archive: After the End of the World* by Alexis Pauline Gumbs,[33] I explore how Afrofuturist fantasies and science fictions upend Western ideologies of progress, linearity, dualism, and freedom. By advocating for understanding both the inevitability and flexibility of change, how rootedness is fundamental to futurity, and for a vision of liberation accessible to all, Afrofuturism asks us to rethink what futures are possible and provide hope that such futures may be actualized.

Change Is Inevitable, but It Can Be Shaped

God is Power—
Infinite,
Irresistible,
Inexorable,
Indifferent.
And yet, God is Pliable,
Trickster,
Teacher,
Chaos,
Clay.

God exists to be shaped.
God is Change.[34]

The history of Black lives has been a history of unavoidable change structured by racial-colonial dynamics of power. As Mark Dery wrote in the essay that first termed Africana speculative work as "Afrofuturism," the story of Black lives *is* the story of alien abduction: "African Americans, in a very real sense, are the descendants of alien abductees; they inhabit a sci-fi nightmare in which unseen but no less impassable force fields of intolerance frustrate their movements; official histories undo what has been done; and technology is too often brought to bear on black bodies (branding, forced sterilization, the Tuskegee experiment, and tasers come readily to mind)."[35] Afrofuturism teaches marginalized populations how to not only adapt to the powerful forces of change but also bend and shape such forces to a will for justice. In a time when feminist scholars feel brow-beaten every day by the racist-capitalist patriarchy and feel that their futures are inexorably shaped by power's domination, pointing toward nothing but bleak dystopias, Afrofuturism can help us to see how we may navigate within power in such a way as to shape futures and move them onto liberatory paths.

But before we can begin to shape change, we must realize its inevitability. The novels of Octavia E. Butler are foundational to this philosophy of thought, narrating the experience of Black lives through brilliantly imagined relations between generations past, present, and future. Her work explores the fact that "Afrofuturism is born out of cruelty, and that cruelty of the white imagination was a necessary condition out of which the African diaspora had to reimagine its future."[36] Over and over, her strong Black female characters cannot escape those in control and their structures of power. Lauren lives in a dystopian world, eerily similar to our own, where only gated communities hold a tenuous safety from marauding groups of raiders. Once her community collapses, she must work to create a new one from nothing under the continual threat of violence and death.[37] Lilith wakes to find herself hundreds of years in the future in the hands of aliens from whom she cannot flee. She only desires to go back to her world, but the earth itself is already fundamentally changed, and she will be too by the time she can return to it.[38] Anyanwu has both powers and immortality, but even so, she cannot resist when she is forced to leave her village, travel across the ocean, and bear children who are both familiar and strange.[39] Dana is called back in time against her consent and unable to will herself back. She must survive in the time of slavery and face the conditions of her own becoming.[40] In all of Butler's works, the illusion of autonomy and control is harshly dispelled, and the protagonists must learn how to forge "the cruelty of bondage and murder" into "portholes of redemption."[41]

The structural imposition of cruelty requires one to learn how to shape change in order to survive, all the while understanding that the being of ourselves and those we love is premised on violence. The question Butler's work forces us to face is, "What to do if the precondition for your being is the abduction, murder and rape of your ancestors?"[42] Butler asks us to shape change, while yet recognizing that we cannot fully escape cruelty[43] nor should we necessarily want to do so.[44]

And yet, Butler's characters persist where all hope seems lost and live to struggle another day. In her work, shaping change *is* feminist activism. As such, her legacy does not end with her fiction but continues into the realm of social justice strategy. Recognizing the utility of shaping change as a means of contemporary action to create better futures, the works *Octavia's Brood: Science Fiction Stories from Social Justice Movements* and *Emergent Strategy* take the philosophy underlying Butler's novels and ask what we can do with it.[45]

Octavia's Brood recognizes the value of speculative fiction to social change activism. The edited collection brings together established science fiction authors with social justice activists who have never written fiction before to curate a volume of future visions that can inspire movements for justice in the present. Walidah Imarisha sees a direct correspondence between organizing for social justice in the present and writing about more just futures: "Because all organizing is science fiction, we are dreaming new worlds every time we think about the changes we want to make in the world."[46] Activism is always already fictive, in a sense. *Octavia's Brood* provides a resource for tuning the resonances between fiction and activism in order to make our visions reality.[47]

adrienne maree brown takes this resonance a step further to develop a map for shaping change in our everyday lives. As a community activist, brown has developed and written about activist strategies inspired by the novels of Butler and how she uses them to build better worlds *now*.[48] She calls her philosophy emergent strategy, defining it as "strategy for building complex patterns and systems of change through relatively small interactions."[49] Although brown is inspired by Butler, her work is much hopeful, believing that enacting justice is primarily "a matter of longing, having the will to imagine and implement something else."[50] She recognizes that there are limits on our actions but asks us to think of ourselves as change shapers who are "adaptive—riding change like dolphins ride the ocean. Adaptive but also intentional, like migrating birds who know how to get where they're going even when a storm pushes them a hundred miles off course."[51] The constraints of power are transformed under brown's vision into conditions of possibility—which is not so far off from Butler after all. Brown brings us back full circle: Though the conditions that give rise to our being may be harsh and violent, these are yet the very conditions that allow us to persist and flourish, to bend and shape change to a will for justice.

Roots Are Vital to Our Futures

Every technological leap during this period started in a small village or on a farm. Kibra worked with a group of craftspeople, masons, and beekeepers to develop the first computer.[52]

In normative white mainstream technoculture, Blackness is often considered antithetical to futurism.[53] Alondra Nelson explains: "In these frameworks, the technologically enabled future is by its very nature unmoored from the past and from people of color. [These] narratives suggest that it is primitiveness or out-modedness, the obsolescence of something or someone else, that confirms the novel status of the virtual self, the cutting-edge product, or the high-tech society."[54]

In other words, Blackness is equated with both primitivism and naturalism and used as the foil against which white futurism imagines technological progress. Afrofuturism challenges this understanding of both technology and futures by demonstrating that rootedness is essential to futurity. By contesting the opposition of the past and future on the one hand, and nature and technology on the other hand, Afrofuturism "does not simply look to what is seemingly new about the self in the 'virtual age' but looks backward *and* forward in seeking to provide insights about identity, one that asks what was *and* what if."[55]

First, Afrofuturism understands that you must be rooted in the past to understand the future.[56] The temporal fusion of past and future in Afrofuturist thought disturbs Western assumptions of linearity and progress.[57] In Afrofuturism, "many speak as if the past, present, and future are one."[58] Challenging linear progress models of time is not only imaginative but also political. In doing so, "these futurisms adjust the temporal logics that condemned black subjects to prehistory,"[59] constructing an alternative means of temporal relation that figures Black subjects as central to the present and future. In addition, attention to the simultaneity of past-present-future requires a different ethic of writing, as writing is thus something we do in relation with those who came before[60] as well as those who will come after. Alexis Pauline Gumbs melds her writing into relations of both past and future, considering her work to be "ancestrally cowritten" as well as "written in collaboration with the survivors, the far-into-the-future witnesses to the realities we are making possible or impossible in the present apocalypse."[61] The past, present, and future are mutually co-implicative in Afrofuturist thought, asking us to think in a different ethicopolitical landscape than that of white technofuturism.

One way Afrofuturism is connected to the past is through attention to ancestry and tradition. Nnedi Okorafor's Africanfuturist work powerfully illustrates the importance of tradition in space-age futures in her novella *Binti*.[62] Binti, the titular character, is the first member of the Himba tribe to be accepted to Oomza University, the premier school in the known universe. In order to attend, she also becomes the first Himba to travel to another world. The Himba maintain their rootedness by covering themselves in a thick substance made from red clay native to their land. Binti maintains a fidelity to her traditions, even while she changes beyond her wildest expectations. In the end, it is her maintenance of connections between past and future, tradition and change that allows her to make peace between violent factions and avert a galactic war. *Binti* demonstrates how

Afrofuturist visions are "rooted in the past, but not weighed down by it, contiguous yet continually transformed."[63]

However, our connections to the past are not always positive. Afrofuturism also recognizes that the interconnection between past, present, and future also signifies the reverberation of injustice throughout time. One of the clearest examples of this phenomenon is neosoul artist Janelle Monae's short film *Many Moons*. In the six-minute music video, Monae acts as her alter ego, the android Cindi Mayweather. Cindi is hosting an android auction, where the wealthy and famous have gathered to bid on the newest android models—all also played by Monae. We see the androids being manhandled and forced to walk a runway—standing in here for the auction block—for the bidding process, while Mayweather sings about "freedom."[64] By the end of the video, Mayweather performs so frenetically for the audience—her repetitive motions gaining speed, faster and faster until she loses control—that she first raises into the air and then collapses in a heap on the ground. The final shot is the light in her eyes extinguishing, fading to a statement on the screen: "'I imagined many moons in the sky lighting the way to freedom'—Cindi Mayweather." Monae paints a vision of the future where the analogies to slavery are clear, using the past to infuse the future with a warning for the present.

Second, Afrofuturism challenges the opposition of technology to nature by examining how a rootedness in nature is essential to survival and innovation. In doing so, Afrofuturist thinkers challenge both the racial-colonial stereotype of Africans and the African diaspora as primitive barbarians as well as the assumption that the technological is inherently antithetical to the natural. Under white futurism, a connection to the technological is assumed, but this connection is automatically questioned when the futuristic identities are Black. Thus, "Afrofuturists have attempted to forge a new identity that puts black cultural origins in categories of the artificial as much as in those of the natural,"[65] while simultaneously demonstrating that "a well-crafted relationship with nature is intrinsic to a balanced future too."[66]

The poetic work of Gumbs deftly explores the relationship between rootedness in nature, technology, and survival. In her "speculative documentary," *M Archive: After the End of the World*, she narrates the findings of a group of Black scientists looking back on a past apocalypse that shifted them from what we would understand as human and that remains to come from our current vantage point.[67] Gumbs explores how, on one the hand, rootedness enabled survival for those in the throes of disaster: "we took off our leaden clothes and we skipped out of our concrete shoes and we went barefoot enough to bear the rubble we had created just before. we let the sun touch us and felt what we had done to the ozone in our daze. we noticed that skin was just as thin as it should have been and all that we had been calling skin before were layers of accumulated scars."[68] The survivors of the apocalypse require a reconnection with the natural in order to persist. Yet, after the end of the world, such a reconnection also involves a coming to terms with the environmental degradation humanity has wrought—the sun is necessary, though no longer kind; the ground centering, though no longer smooth.

On the other hand, then, Gumbs explores how, in part, the disaster itself was caused by the people in power ignoring their own roots, as well as ignoring the wisdom of those who stayed connected to the ground: "anything they wanted to know about the earth and what would happen if they ignored it, they could have learned by watching the old, curved brown women everywhere. but mostly they ignored those women. just like they ignored the world shaking around them. to their doom."[69] Gumbs calls us to rethink the path we are on in the Western world before it is too late and to listen to the wisdom of the Black and Brown women around us—those who remain rooted in the past while imagining better futures.

Liberation Must Be for All

"We can't save everyone."
"Doesn't mean we can't try," she countered.[70]

As described in a previous section, Afrofuturism radically refigures what it means to be a subject and what it means to be human,[71] as "the moment in which black people enter into humanity, this very idea [of the 'human' as a universal formation] loses its ontological thrust because its limitations are rendered abundantly clear."[72] Afrofuturism thus refigures "the human" outside of the strictures of white hetero capitalist patriarchy, centering Black feminist visions of the future while rendering humanity accessible to all. Gumbs explains how centering the Black feminine ultimately necessitates liberation for all. In her estimation and from the vantage of the universe, Black feminism *is all*: "there is no separation from the black simultaneity of the universe also known as everything also known as the black feminist pragmatic intergenerational sphere. everything is everything. . . . you can have breathing and the reality of the radical black porousness of love (aka black feminist metaphysics aka us all of us, *us*) or you cannot. . . . this was their downfall. they hated the black women who were themselves."[73] To deny Blackness is to deny ourselves, and to embrace Blackness is to embrace everything. When the limit case of humanity is centered as its primary subject, the result is a radically inclusive liberation. Therefore, centering Blackness is imperative because it is by thinking in and through Blackness, the anti-Man,[74] that we may fundamentally restructure our ideas of what it means to be human and open them to all. As such, Gumbs see her work not as seeking "to prove Black people are human" but instead calling "preexisting definitions of the human into question"[75] in a way that opens space for radical liberatory inclusivity.

Afrofuturism knows that liberation is not liberation if it is not for *all*. One place we see this demonstrated is in Monae's "emotion picture" *Dirty Computer*. Monae's dystopian future begins with images of humans, frozen as if on display—or images digitized on a screen—with her voice-over explaining, "They started calling us computers. People began vanishing and the cleaning began. You were dirty if you looked different. You were dirty if you refused to live the way they dictated. You were dirty if you showed any form of opposition at all. And if you were dirty . . . it was only a matter of time."[76] Although Monae's music and imagery clearly center Black women, Black queer sexuality, and Black feminism, she uses the centrality of Blackness to make the argument throughout the emotion picture that all "dirty computers" should be liberated from their oppression.

Okorafor takes the idea that liberation is for all and extends it to the nonhuman world, while maintaining a focus on Blackness, and particularly African Blackness. Her novel *Lagoon* is a story of first contact, where aliens come to Earth. Specifically, they come to the ocean edging Lagos, Nigeria and promptly abduct one Ghanaian and two Nigerian ambassadors particularly chosen to carry their message to humankind, dragging them into the waters. The aliens come to the water because water is life, and bring with them change. Any being that comes into contact with them changes based on its deepest desires—a swordfish becomes a powerful monster, a bat learns to see, the water is cleansed of its pollution, the heroine Adaora becomes part-fish. In Okorafor's imagining, it is not just humanity that deserves liberation from oppression but the entire lifeworld.

Making sure that we maintain a focus on all peoples as we work toward liberation is imperative to persistence. Persistence can sometimes come at the expense of others rather than in coalition with them. As brown writes when discussing the importance of collectivity to social justice organizing, "We are brilliant at survival, but brutal at it. We tend to slip out of togetherness the way we slip out of the womb, bloody and messy and surprised to be alone."[77] Centering feminist persistence on Afrofuturist visions can help us to avoid looking up and finding we have persisted alone. Afrofuturism reorients us around collectivities that include those not considered human and figures futures where all life may be liberated, together.

Beyond Hope: The Communicative Power of Fiction

In the previous section, I illustrated three important lessons that Afrofuturist work holds for feminist communication scholars: the imperatives to shape the inevitable force of change, maintain rooted relations, and work toward liberation for all. For some feminist communication scholars, the focus on fiction throughout this essay may rest uncomfortably with their understanding of disciplinary norms and values. However, under such anti-Black and anti-feminine circumstances as we currently face—circumstances that try to force us to believe that our only possible futures are horrific and dystopic—we need the fictive to persist. As speculative fiction author Nalo Hopkinson argues, fantasy is valuable:

"Call it escapism, because at some level it is, but I think that goes back to human beings being tool-users. We imagine what we want from the world; then we try to find a way to make it happen. Escapism can be the first step to creating a new reality, whether it's a personal change in one's existence or a larger change in the world."[78] We need to escape the systems and structures that seem to determine our lives in order to imagine and enact the type of futures that we desire.

Afrofuturism is thus necessary to our understandings of public communication and the process of communicating technological futures. We need to pay attention to fiction because the fictive provides the potential to "make the impossible possible," to adapt Hopkinson's claim.[79] But beyond imagining, Eshun argues that Afrofuturist fantasy is in fact a constitutive part of *enacting* alternative futures. He claims that our visions for the future help to produce those very futures by calling their potentiality into being and acting to pull us and our actions in the present toward them.[80] It is for this reason that the importance of Afrofuturism goes beyond hope.[81] By learning, envisioning, proclaiming, and developing liberatory future worlds, we provide not only dreams to place our hopes in but also the material first steps on the path that makes those dreams reality. As Womack argues, "Where there is no vision, the people perish."[82] Afrofuturism may be science fiction and fantasy, but it is nonetheless activism.[83]

Taking a cue from activist adrienne maree brown, we might create an "emergent strategy" specific to feminist communication scholars. Emergent strategy calls on us to follow the Afrofuturist lesson of intentionally shaping change by laboring to "grow our capacity to embody the just and liberated worlds we long for."[84] As feminist communication scholars, we have the ability to draw on the day-to-day activism of emergent strategy in our scholarship, teaching, praxis, and lives.

I offer the following four strategies to guide each of us in persisting under the ethic of Afrofuturism:

1 Learn alternate futures.
2 Envision them.
3 Proclaim them.
4 Labor to actualize them.

First, learning alternate futures requires seeking them out. We must search for the speculative work of women of color and Global South women, knowing that it will often be hidden, suppressed, and elided by hegemonic forces. Studying this knowledge will bring forth reframed perceptions based on alternative ethics. Second, we must take part in the act of creation ourselves. Each of us holds unimagined possibilities that she may bring to the table. Third, we must publicly announce the alternative futures that we have learned and created. Proclaiming liberatory futures in public not only provides support and encouragement to marginalized peoples but also acts to continually solidify the potential of those futures to take hold. As such, proclaiming futures blends with the fourth step: laboring to make these futures possible, probable, and material. By acting as if these futures are reality, they are brought into being, made tangible, more and more each day.

Feminist communication scholars hold a key position in the fight for liberatory futures: we stand where expertise in dismantling the discourses of power meets skill in communicating alternative futures. The fight for the future is a communicative one. As such, feminist communication scholars have valuable skills to bring to bear. The question at hand is then, How do we infuse our lives and work with the century of labor done by Afrofuturist writers, artists, musicians, and filmmakers,[85] advocating for their vision in our scholarship, activism, and practice, while maintaining the primacy of Africana voices and experience? There is much for feminist communication scholars to contribute to Afrofuturist work, but ultimately those of us who are white and Western must remember that we are followers, not leaders, in the struggle over futures. Let us ground our feet and look to the sky, learning from the spectacular Black feminist visionaries who have both gone before us and will go after us, joining in the struggle to secure futures of liberation and justice for all.

Discussion Questions

1 How might Afrofuturism help us rethink the trajectories of feminist communication studies?
2 What might it look like to center an ethic of shaping change in your own thought, your department, your university, or your field of study?
3 How might you start to seek out and support alternative futures in your own life?

Try This!

In fall 2021, Amber Johnson, Benny LeMaster, Reynaldo Anderson, and Natasha A. Kelly published a special forum in the journal *Communication and Critical/Cultural Studies* on "Speculative Fiction, Criticality, and Futurity," where they asked contributors to write speculative fiction "imagining the future where liberation and freedom from systemic oppression are possible." Read the short stories, flash fiction, and graphic novels included in this special forum. Then write a short story that imagines a future free from domination in your own words, one that creates a world where a form of domination that you have seen or noticed in your life has been overturned or transformed. What futures can you imagine? Write 1,000–3,000 words describing your own alternative future.

Notes

1 Sara Ahmed, *Living a Feminist Life* (Durham, NC: Duke University Press, 2017), 50.
2 Chela Sandoval, *Methodology of the Oppressed* (Minneapolis: University of Minnesota Press, 2000).
3 Alexis Pauline Gumbs, *Spill: Scenes of Black Feminist Fugitivity* (Durham, NC: Duke University Press, 2016); Saidiya Hartman, *Lose Your Mother: A Journey along the Atlantic Slave Route* (New York: Farrar, Straus & Giroux, 2007), 97.
4 For instance, Joëlle Cruz, James McDonald, Kirsten Broadfoot, Andy Kai-chun Chuang, and Shiv Ganesh, "'Aliens' in the United States: A Collaborative Autoethnography of Foreign-Born Faculty," *Journal of Management Inquiry* 29, no. 3 (2020): 272–285; Lisa A. Flores, "Between Abundance and Marginalization: The Imperative of Racial Rhetorical Criticism," *Review of Communication* 16, no. 1 (2016): 4–24; Bernadette Marie Calafell, "The Future of Feminist Scholarship: Beyond the Politics of Inclusion," *Women's Studies in Communication* 37, no. 3 (2014): 266–270.
5 For instance, Joëlle M. Cruz, "Brown Body of Knowledge: A Tale of Erasure," *Cultural Studies ↔ Critical Methodologies* 18, no. 5 (2018): 363–365; Kathleen M. de Onís, "Lost in Translation: Challenging (White, Monolingual Feminism's) <Choice> with *Justicia Reproductiva*," *Women's Studies in Communication* 38, no. 1 (2015): 1–19.
6 For instance, Rachel Alicia Griffin, "I AM an Angry Black Woman: Black Feminist Autoethnography, Voice, and Resistance," *Women's Studies in Communication* 35, no. 2 (2012): 138–157; Gloria Nziba Pindi, "Hybridity and Identity Performance in Diasporic Context: An Autoethnographic Journey of the Self Across Cultures," *Cultural Studies ↔ Critical Methodologies* 18, no. 1 (2018): 27–28.
7 Joëlle M. Cruz, Oghenetoja Okoh, Amoaba Gooden, Kamesha Spates, Chinasa A. Elue, and Nicole Rousseau, "The Ekwe Collective: Black Feminist Praxis," *Departures in Critical Qualitative Research* 5, no. 3 (2016): 89–94; Alexis Pauline Gumbs, *M Archive: After the End of the World* (Durham, NC: Duke University Press, 2018), ix–xii; María Lugones, *Pilgrimages/Peregrinajes: Theorizing Coalition against Multiple Oppressions* (Lanham, MD: Rowman & Littlefield, 2003), 77–100.
8 Lugones, *Pilgrimages/Peregrinajes*, 68.
9 Calafell, "The Future of Feminist Scholarship," 267.
10 For an exception, see Lonny J. Avi Brooks, "Cruelty and Afrofuturism," *Communication and Critical/Cultural Studies* 15, no. 1 (2018): 101–107.
11 Ahmed, *Living a Feminist Life*, 2.
12 Walidah Imarisha and adrienne marie brown, quoted in Sheree Renee Thomas, "Foreword: Birth of a Revolution," in *Octavia's Brood: Science Fiction Stories from Social Justice Movements*, ed. adrienne marie brown and Walidah Imarisha (Oakland, CA: AK Press, 2015), 1.
13 Ytasha L. Womack, *Afrofuturism: The World of Black Sci-Fi and Fantasy Culture* (Chicago: Lawrence Hill Books, 2013), 24.
14 I use liberation rather than emancipation as emancipation is still premised on coloniality. Walter D. Mignolo, "Delinking," *Cultural Studies* 21, no. 2–3 (2007): 453–458.
15 Alondra Nelson, "Introduction: Future Texts," *Social Text* 20, no. 2 (2002): 9.
16 Alexander G. Weheliye, "'Feenin': Posthuman Voices in Contemporary Black Popular Music," *Social Text* 20, no. 2 (2002): 21–47; Alexander G. Weheliye, *Habeas Viscus: Racializing Assemblages, Biopolitics, and Black Feminist Theories of the Human* (Durham, NC: Duke University Press, 2014).

17 Kodwo Eshun, "Further Considerations of Afrofuturism," *New Centennial Review* 3, no. 2 (2003): 301.

18 For the clearest instance of this, see adrienne marie brown, *Emergent Strategy: Shaping Change, Changing Worlds* (Chico, CA: AK Press, 2017).

19 Womack, *Afrofuturism*, 44.

20 Ibid., 15.

21 Sylvia Wynter, "Unsettling the Coloniality of Being/Power/Truth/Freedom: Towards the Human, After Man, Its Overrepresentation—an Argument." *CR: New Centennial Review* 3, no. 3 (2003): 257–337.

22 Weheliye, *Habeas Viscus*, 24.

23 Alondra Nelson, quoted in Womack, *Afrofuturism*, 108.

24 Lisa Lowe, *The Intimacies of Four Continents* (Durham, NC: Duke University Press, 2015).

25 Womack, *Afrofuturism*, 101.

26 Flores, "Between Abundance and Marginalization."

27 Eshun, "Further Considerations of Afrofuturism," 289–292.

28 Ibid.

29 Walter D. Mignolo, *The Darker Side of Western Modernity: Global Futures, Decolonial Options* (Durham, NC: Duke University Press, 2011).

30 Eshun, "Further Considerations of Afrofuturism," 290–291.

31 Ibid., 290.

32 Flores, "Between Abundance and Marginalization," 18.

33 Alexis Pauline Gumbs's work is difficult to succinctly explain. At once academic, poet, and fiction author, she names her work "speculative documentary" in order to highlight how her writing draws together these three fields that are often considered disparate.

34 Octavia E. Butler, *Parable of the Sower* (New York: Grand Central Publishing, 1993), 25.

35 Mark Dery, "Black to the Future: Interviews with Samuel R. Delany, Greg Tate, and Tricia Rose," *South Atlantic Quarterly* 92, no. 4 (1993): 736.

36 Brooks, "Cruelty and Afrofuturism," 101.

37 Butler, *Parable of the Sower*.

38 Octavia E. Butler, *Lilith's Brood* (New York: Grand Central Publishing, 1989).

39 Octavia E. Butler, *Seed to Harvest* (New York: Grand Central Publishing, 2007).

40 Octavia E. Butler, *Kindred* (Boston: Beacon, 1988).

41 Brooks, "Cruelty and Afrofuturism," 102.

42 Mark Fisher, "The Metaphysics of Crackle: Afrofuturism and Hauntology," *Dancecult: Journal of Electronic Dance Music Culture* 5, no. 2 (2013): 51.

43 Walidah Imarisha, introduction to *Octavia's Brood: Science Fiction Stories from Social Justice Movements*, ed. adrienne marie brown and Walidah Imarisha (Oakland, CA: AK Press, 2015), 3.

44 Brooks, "Cruelty and Afrofuturism," 102.

45 adrienne marie brown and Walidah Imarisha, eds., *Octavia's Brood: Science Fiction Stories from Social Justice Movements* (Oakland, CA: AK Press, 2015); brown, *Emergent Strategy*.

46 Imarisha, "Introduction," 4.

47 Ibid., 5.

48 brown, *Emergent Strategy*.

49 Ibid., 2.

50 Ibid., 21.

51 Ibid.
52 Gabriel Teodros, "Lalibela," in *Octavia's Brood: Science Fiction Stories from Social Justice Movements*, ed. adrienne marie brown and Walidah Imarisha (Oakland, CA: AK Press, 2015), 128.
53 Nelson, "Introduction," 1.
54 Ibid., 6.
55 Ibid., 4.
56 Ibid., 8; Womack, *Afrofuturism*, 81.
57 Nelson, "Introduction," 8.
58 Womack, *Afrofuturism*, 153.
59 Eshun, "Further Considerations of Afrofuturism," 297.
60 Cruz et al., "The Ekwe Collective," 90.
61 Gumbs, *M Archive*, xi.
62 Nnedi Okorafor, *Binti* (New York: Tom Doherty Associates, 2015).
63 Nelson, "Introduction," 8.
64 Janelle Monae, *Many Moons*, Youtube video, 6:29, April 4, 2009, https://www.youtube.com/watch?v=EZyyORSHbaE.
65 Ron Eglash, "Race, Sex, and Nerds: From Black Geeks to Asian American Hipsters," *Social Text* 20, vol. 2 (2002): 59.
66 Womack, *Afrofuturism*, 104.
67 Gumbs, *M Archive*, xi.
68 Ibid., 83.
69 Ibid., 35.
70 Bao Phi, "Revolution Shuffle," in *Octavia's Brood: Science Fiction Stories from Social Justice Movements*, ed. adrienne marie brown and Walidah Imarisha (Oakland, CA: AK Press, 2015), 13–14.
71 Weheliye, "'Feenin,'" 21–47.
72 Ibid., 27.
73 Gumbs, *M Archive*, 7.
74 Wynter, "Unsettling the Coloniality of Being/Power/Truth/Freedom."
75 Gumbs, *M Archive*, xi.
76 Janelle Monae, *Dirty Computer [Emotion Picture]*, YouTube video, 48:37, April 27, 2018, https://www.youtube.com/watch?v=jdH2Sy-BlNE.
77 brown, *Emergent Strategy*, 6.
78 Nalo Hopkinson, quoted in Alondra Nelson, "'Making the Impossible Possible': An Interview with Nalo Hopkinson," *Social Text* 20, no. 2 (2002): 98.
79 Nelson, "'Making the Impossible Possible,'" 97.
80 Eshun, "Further Considerations of Afrofuturism."
81 Brooks, "Cruelty and Afrofuturism," 103.
82 Womack, *Afrofuturism*, 42.
83 Imarisha, "Introduction."
84 Ibid., 3.
85 Here, I trace the origins of contemporary Afrofuturism back to W.E.B. Du Bois's 1920 publication of "The Comet."

Acknowledgments

Books never materialize on their own. All sorts of people contribute to the completion of a manuscript, through direct contribution, by inspiring thought, providing emotional support, and offering comic relief. Certainly, we are inspired by the contributors to this collection, whose words and stories brought us to tears at times. Thank you for sharing your work in these pages.

Thanks always to the badass feminists in our lives who constantly inspire us with their work, especially the amazing people who are part of the Organization for the Study of Communication Language and Gender.

We want to give a special thank-you to Chad McBride, who provided amazing mentoring and friendship to both of us. Your encouragement and support gave us the confidence to plan our first conference and create the event that inspired this book.

In memory of Breonna Taylor and the many other people whose tragic murders gave rise to the long-overdue fight for justice.

Sarah: My badass pack: Kevin, Brooklynn, Braxton, Mom, Dad, Mikey, Adam, Steph, Rich, Dianne, Kelly, Nicole, Renee, Anne, Jen, Sophie, Renata, Janell, Anna, Lydia, Tennley, and Kjerstin. Thanks for the laughs. You make my heart happy.

Janell: With much gratitude to all those who cheer me on, especially Heath, Kelsey, Quinn, Vance, Jean, Sarah, Margaret, Katie, Alyssa, Jodi, Auriell, and Jen. Thank you for getting me through the hard times and for being there to enjoy the good ones.

Notes on Contributors

SARAH JANE BLITHE is an associate professor of communication studies at the University of Nevada, Reno. Her research area is organizational communication, and she specializes in gender, work-life balance, policy inequalities, and management learning. Dr. Blithe is the author of *Gender Equality and Work-Life Balance: Glass Handcuffs and Working Men in the U.S.* and *Sex and Stigma: Stories of Everyday Life in Nevada's Legal Brothels* with Anna Wiederhold Wolfe and Breanna Mohr. She has won multiple awards for her research and teaching, including seven national book awards for her first two books. Dr. Blithe earned her PhD in organizational communication and a doctoral certificate in women's studies at the University of Colorado, Boulder and an MA in international and intercultural business communication at the University of Denver.

JANELL C. BAUER is an associate professor in the Department of Journalism and Public Relations at California State University, Chico. Her research explores social media and activism, feminist pedagogy, and how employees navigate work-life policies such as bereavement leave. Her work has been published in *Women's Studies in Communication*, *Communication Teacher*, *Management Communication Quarterly*, and various trade publications. She was the recipient of her college's Inspirational Professor Award for 2017–2018. She also serves as the managing director for the Organization for the Study of Communication, Language, and Gender. Dr. Bauer earned her PhD in organizational communication and a doctoral certificate in women's studies from the University of Colorado, Boulder and her MA in communication from the University of the Pacific.

RUTH J. BEERMAN is an assistant professor of communication studies at Randolph-Macon College. Specializing in rhetoric, her research interests include visual and body rhetorics, gender, argumentation, and public controversy. Dr. Beerman earned her PhD in communication and a doctoral certificate in women's studies from the University of Wisconsin-Milwaukee and her MA in communication studies from the University of Northern Iowa.

ROBIN M. BOYLORN is a professor of Interpersonal and Intercultural Communication at the University of Alabama where she teaches and writes about issues of social identity and diversity, focusing primarily on the lived experience(s) of Black women.

KELLY J. CROSS, an assistant professor of Engineering Education at the University of Nevada Reno, is a culturally responsive practitioner, researcher, and educational leader. She earned her master's of science in materials science and engineering from the University of Cincinnati in 2011. Dr. Cross completed the doctoral program in the engineering education department at Virginia Tech in 2015.

SHARDÉ M. DAVIS (PhD, University of Iowa) is an assistant professor in the Department of Communication at the University of Connecticut. Her research examines the way Black women leverage communication in the sistah circle to invoke collective identity, erect and fortify the boundaries around their homeplace, and backfill the necessary resources to return to white/male-dominant spaces in American society.

SARA DeTURK (PhD, Arizona State University) is a professor in the Department of Communication at the University of Texas at San Antonio. Her research focuses on intercultural communication, social justice activist alliances, critical pedagogy, and training.

MELANIE DUCKWORTH (PhD, University of Georgia) is an associate professor in the Department of Psychology and an associate dean in the College of Science at the University of Nevada, Reno. Dr. Duckworth directs the Health Risk and Traumatic Injury Research Program, where she conducts laboratory-based and clinical research that examines the pre-, peri-, and post-collision variables that predict post-collision physical and psychological recovery and overall quality of life.

MAUREEN EBBEN is an associate professor in the Department of Communication and Media Studies at the University of Southern Maine, Portland. Her research uses critical intersectional feminist approaches to explore the sociotechnical aspects of "smart" digital communication technologies that shape the communication of everyday life. Dr. Ebben earned her PhD in communication from the University of Illinois at Champaign-Urbana.

CASSIDY D. ELLIS (MA, University of Alabama) is a doctoral student at the University of New Mexico studying critical intercultural communication. She is interested in discourses of race and personhood within abortion rhetoric and media and specifically the racialized conceptualization of "life" within these rhetorics.

ANDREA EWING earned her MSW at the University of Denver Graduate School of Social Work in 2016. She became a registered psychotherapist and an active member of the National Association of Social Workers. Andrea is a licensed social worker (LSW) and is a licensed clinical social worker (LCSW) candidate. Andrea is currently a mental health provider at a Title I public charter high school in Colorado.

ANGELA N. GIST-MACKEY (PhD, University of Missouri) is an associate professor in the Department of Communication Studies at the University of Kansas with an expertise in organizational communication. She is an interpretive critical scholar who largely researches issues of social mobility and power in organized contexts. Her program of research frequently explores topics related to social class, stigmatized social identities, and organizational culture.

CERISE L. GLENN (PhD, Howard University) is an associate professor in the Department of Communication Studies at the University of North Carolina at Greensboro. One of her research interests analyzes professional and social identity of underrepresented groups and mentoring diverse groups in higher education from intersectional perspectives. She also examines how African American women negotiate their identities utilizing Black feminist and womanist thought.

ASHLEY R. HALL (PhD, University of Pittsburgh) is an assistant professor in the School of Communication at Illinois State University, where she also serves as affiliate faculty for the African American Studies program. Her research and teaching focuses on the complex and nuanced relationship between rhetoric, Blackness, and agentive power as it specifically relates to Black women's communicative lived experiences in an anti-Black world.

TINA M. HARRIS (PhD, University of Kentucky) is the Manship-Maynard Endowed Chair of Race, Media, and Cultural Literacy in the Manship School of Mass Communication at Louisiana State University. Her primary research interest is interracial communication, with specific foci on critical communication pedagogy, race and identity, diversity and media representations, racial social justice, mentoring, and racial reconciliation, among others.

JENNA N. HANCHEY (PhD, University of Texas at Austin) is an assistant professor of Communication Studies at the University of Nevada, Reno. Her research is premised on a politics of decolonization and attends to the intersections of rhetoric, Afro-feminisms, African studies, and critical development studies.

JAYNA MARIE JONES obtained her MSW from Rutgers University with a concentration in Violence against Women and Children (VAWC) and became a Certified Trauma Professional (CTP) following graduation. She is a licensed social worker in New York (LMSW) and New Jersey (LSW) working with survivors of gender-based violence. Jayna Marie currently works as an LMSW supervising clinician with HELP R.O.A.D.S., a nonresidential domestic violence non-for-profit organization in Brooklyn, New York.

JOHNNY JONES (MFA, California Institute of the Arts) is the chair of the Cross Cultural Communication Department at Simmons College of Kentucky. He is also a proud graduate of the University of Arkansas, Pine Bluff and New York University, Tisch School of the Arts (MA, Performance Studies). His current research and creative activity includes Black masculinities and Black narratives in media as well as modern and contemporary African American theater.

REBECCA MERCADO JONES (PhD, Ohio University) is an associate professor of communication studies at Oakland University in Rochester, Michigan. Her research has focuses on how economic, political, and social encroachments influence the way women narrate their lives, identity, and culture. She teaches courses in performance, family communication, race and communication, and multicultural communication.

CHERIS KRAMARAE (Professor Emerita, Communication, University of Illinois, Urbana-Champaign; now affiliated with the Center for the Study of Women in Society, University of Oregon) is the author or coauthor of many articles and books dealing with women and technology, education, scholarship, online education, and new media. She has served as Director of Women's Studies at the University of Illinois and as an international dean at the International Women's University, Germany.

JAMES McDONALD (PhD, University of Colorado, Boulder) is an associate professor in the Department of Communication at the University of Texas at San Antonio. His research focuses on identity and difference in organizational contexts, occupational segregation, and feminist and queer approaches to organizing.

MICHAEL S. MARTIN is an associate professor of English at Bloomsburg University of Pennsylvania (PhD, Michigan Technological University; MDiv, Luther Northwestern Seminary; BA, Dana College). Specializing in rhetoric and technical communication, his research interests include how technology affects the writing process and how the continuing changes in composition affect standard written English.

ANITA MIXON is an assistant professor of rhetoric at Wayne State University. She is an expert in rhetorical criticism and specializes in African American rhetoric, institutional rhetoric, and gender and women studies. Dr. Mixon earned her PhD in communication from the University of Illinois at Urbana-Champaign and her MA in communication studies from the University of Alabama at Tuscaloosa.

LYDIA HUERTA MORENO (PhD, University of Texas, Austin) is an assistant professor of gender, race, and identity and communication at the University of Nevada, Reno. She is a feminist decolonial interdisciplinary scholar. Her work focuses on the ethics of representation in cultural narratives centered on migration, human rights, violence, and race and gender in film and social media.

PRISCA S. NGONDO is an assistant professor of public relations in the School of Journalism and Mass Communication at Texas State University, San Marcos (PhD, Texas Tech University; MA, University of Oklahoma; BS, University of South Dakota). Ngondo's research interests are in strategic communication, digital media, and international public relations.

SARAH GONZALEZ NOVEIRI, PhD, is a critical media scholar and rhetorician focusing on the representation of inequalities in Lebanon, Europe, and the United States. Noveiri's areas of research include Arab feminisms, transnational feminisms, and the intersections of race, gender, citizenship, and migrant domestic work.

ANA GOMEZ PARGA (PhD, University of Utah) is an assistant professor of communication and media at Nazareth College. Her work is inspired by decolonial and antiracist Latin American feminisms. Through these lenses, she analyzes different forms of media, popular culture, and online interactions for their potential to opening conversations about identity, political mobilization, and culture.

DANETTE M. PUGH-PATTON is a visiting assistant professor at Coe College in Cedar Rapids, Iowa, teaching in communication and rhetoric. Most recently, Danette served as the faculty diversity fellow at Ursuline College outside of Cleveland, Ohio. She is completing her PhD in communication studies at Southern Illinois University, Carbondale. Danette's dissertation is an autoethnography of a queer Black woman in academia using co-cultural theory.

KATHLEEN RUSHFORTH is a marketing strategy and digital content consultant, holding roles in the financial services, technology, and publishing industries. She holds a MA in corporate communication from Baruch College, City University of New York. Her research interests are focused on social media and digital activism, organizational dynamics of social movements, communication, rhetoric, gender, and social psychology.

SIOBHAN E. SMITH-JONES (PhD, University of Missouri) is an associate professor in the Department of Communication at the University of Louisville. She is also a proud graduate of Xavier University of Louisiana and Louisiana State University. Her current research interests include explorations of African American women as interpretive communities. She teaches courses in mass media, race, culture, fandom, and media literacy.

IDRISSA N. SNIDER'S (PhD, Wayne State University) interests lie in the areas of rhetorical criticism and womanist studies. She is especially attentive to studying modes of empowerment through acts of self-defining. After teaching at Samford University and the University of Alabama at Birmingham, she started an independent consulting business as an advocate, communication specialist, and writer.

ANTONIO L. SPIKES (preferred gender pronouns he/him/his) is currently a visiting assistant professor in the Department of Communication Studies and Rhetoric at Coe College. He received his doctorate in communication studies from Southern Illinois University, Carbondale. His degree area is centered on intercultural communication. Antonio's dissertation focused on the experiences of Black male teachers regarding managing their identity (or facework) in the classroom.

SAVAUGHN WILLIAMS is currently a doctoral student in communication studies at the University of Kansas. She studies interracial friendships and race communication, as well as strong Black womanhood across contexts. She received her MA in communication studies from Ball State University.

Index

Page numbers in italics denote an illustration.